STUDIES IN MATERIAL CULTURE RESEARCH

Edited by Karlis Karklins

Published by
THE SOCIETY FOR HISTORICAL ARCHAEOLOGY

Ronald L. Michael, editor

Anthropology Section
California University of Pennsylvania
California, Pennsylvania 15419

2000

ISBN 1-886818-06-1

Composition by
TransVisions
Uniontown, Pennsylvania

CONTENTS

Contributors

CHARLES S. BRADLEY, Material Culture Research, Ontario Service Centre, Parks Canada, 1600 Liverpool Court, Ottawa, Ontario K1A 0M5, Canada

PHIL DUNNING, Material Culture Research, Ontario Service Centre, Parks Canada, 1600 Liverpool Court, Ottawa, Ontario K1A 0M5, Canada

GÉRARD GUSSET, Material Culture Research, Ontario Service Centre, Parks Canada, 1600 Liverpool Court, Ottawa, Ontario K1A 0M5, Canada

JANE E. HARRIS, Milltown Cross, RR 1, Montague, P.E.I. C0A 1R0, Canada

OLIVE R. JONES, Material Culture Research, Ontario Service Centre, Parks Canada, 1600 Liverpool Court, Ottawa, Ontario K1A 0M5, Canada

KARLIS KARKLINS, Material Culture Research, Ontario Service Centre, Parks Canada, 1600 Liverpool Court, Ottawa, Ontario K1A 0M5, Canada

JOHN D. LIGHT, Material Culture Research, Ontario Service Centre, Parks Canada, 1600 Liverpool Court, Ottawa, Ontario K1A 0M5, Canada

PETER J. PRIESS, 234 Carroll Road, Winnipeg, Manitoba R3K 1H6, Canada

LESTER A. ROSS, 2667 Garfield Street, Eugene, Oregon 97405, U.S.A.

LYNNE SUSSMAN, Low, Québec J0X 2C0, Canada

Introduction

Several years ago, the Material Culture Research Section of Parks Canada deliberated how best to disseminate its collective knowledge in light of federal government downsizing which was directly impacting on the Parks publication program. While many worthwhile projects were proposed, the one that finally won out was the preparation of one or more volumes of Studies in Material Culture Research. Fiscal restraint prescribed that the articles be based on existing knowledge and not require any new research. To find out what the historical archaeological community really needed along this line, given that the list of potential articles was quite extensive, questionnaires were sent to a diverse group of individuals active in North American historical archaeology, land and marine. The feedback was used to prepare the present volume which is intended for use by archaeologists, material culture researchers, and others who deal with materials recovered from historical sites. The topics of the papers are quite varied and bring together information from a wide array of sources.

Metal artifacts are among the most frequently encountered, but because they corrode and disintegrate so rapidly once covered by moist earth, few are ever found intact and, thus, have received relatively little attention, especially as compared to ceramics and glassware. To rectify this situation, this volume contains four articles which deal with metal artifacts.

The first of these, **A Field Guide to the Identification of Metal** by John D. Light, provides a basis for identifying the different metals and alloys that are commonly encountered in archaeological contexts. All the major metals are discussed in alphabetical order, and a brief historical background for each group is provided, along with suggested terminology and a glossary of metal-working terms.

The second article, by Lester A. Ross and John D. Light, presents **A Guide to the Description and Interpretation of Metal Files**. This not only provides much useful information regarding the identification and cataloguing of this commonly encountered tool, but also provides insight into object reuse. Files were a ready source of steel in frontier situations and a close inspection of ferrous-metal tools from isolated sites may reveal that they began life as files.

Metal components of cutlery are relatively easy to identify but are often difficult to date because some attributes continued in use for a long time. **Composite Table Cutlery from 1700 to 1930** by Phil Dunning points out what is characteristic of the seven periods into which the study period has been divided. Certain attributes were long lived thus combinations of them need to be considered when analyzing cutlery, not just single characteristics.

Much has been written about door hardware over the years, but the information is spread over hundreds of books, articles, catalogues, and other sources. Furthermore, some of the material is contradictory. To synthesize as much information on this extensive subject as possible, as well as to point out the contradictory material, and to try and establish a standardized terminology, Peter J. Priess prepared the final metal-related article on **Historic Door Hardware**. This heavily illustrated article provides an in-depth look at this vast topic from simple strap hinges and door hooks to complex box locks.

A massive body of knowledge already exists on ceramics so this volume is slim on this artifact class. Both historical and prehistoric archaeologists alike, however, still have not resolved how best to deal with the quantification and statistical manipulation of ceramic remains in site collections. In **Objects vs. Sherds: A Statistical Evaluation**, Lynne Sussman describes the results of treating sherd counts as statistical equivalents to object counts. Standard statistical tests are applied to the same artifacts–once as sherd counts and once as object counts. The differences between the results are striking and will, it is hoped, influence how researchers deal with ceramics in the future.

Smoking Pipes for the Archaeologist by Charles S. Bradley presents a concise overview of pipes of all materials, though the emphasis is on white clay specimens. As the article is based primarily on material in the collections of Parks Canada, emphasis is on Canadian and British material. The basic information concerning classification, recording, and interpretation, however, is applicable to material from just about any historical site worldwide.

Electrical artifacts comprise a group that is being encountered in ever-increasing numbers as historical archaeologists probe more and more sites of the late 19th and 20th centuries. Unfortunately, the researcher faced with these artifacts has no experts to turn to for guidance nor are there any comprehensive studies. To help alleviate this situation and point the researcher in the right direction, Gérard Gusset has compiled **A Preliminary Annotated Bibliography on Electrical Artifacts**. It is divided into several sections for ease of reference and the annotations further narrow the scope of each entry.

A wealth of information exists on glass tableware, one of the most commonly encountered artifact groups. In **A Guide to Dating Glass Tableware: 1800 to 1940**, Olive R. Jones does not duplicate these details but summarizes the datable attributes, introduces the primary and secondary sources, and acquaints the reader with additional references which provide in-depth information concerning specific decoration or manufacturing processes. Emphasis is placed on the less expensive tablewares as these are the ones most commonly encountered by archaeolo-gists, and on the products of the United States, Britain, and Canada.

The final article also deals with glass, this time in the form of **Eighteenth-Century French Blue-Green Bottles from the Fortress of Louisbourg, Nova Scotia**. This site-specific report has been included as Louisbourg has produced the largest and most varied collection of blue-green bottles in North America. Prepared by Jane E. Harris, it was initially published in 1979 in Parks Canada's *History and Archaeology* series. As this is still the principal report on the subject and the 1979 publication has long been out of print, it was decided to update the article and include it in this volume. The inventory includes four different bottle forms in use at the fortress between 1713 and 1758.

It is hoped that the nine articles presented in this volume will enable researchers to better understand, classify, and interpret their collections. It is a further hope that those who are helped by the material presented in these pages will, in turn, prepare other such volumes so that our fund of knowledge continues to grow and our discipline prospers.

KARLIS KARKLINS
MATERIAL CULTURE RESEARCH
ONTARIO SERVICE CENTRE
PARKS CANADA
1600 LIVERPOOL COURT
OTTAWA, ONTARIO K1A 0M5
CANADA

JOHN D. LIGHT

A Field Guide to the Identification of Metal

Introduction

Despite the fact that the excavation of an historical site normally yields an abundance of metal, this material is not extensively understood by archaeologists. Difficulties often begin in the field lab, and erroneous descriptions applied there can remain attached to an object for a long time. Usually problems relate to identification and description; the person in the lab is constantly asking: what is the stuff made of and what do I call it? For example, is it possible to call iron everything made from the element iron, and what is brass and how can it be differentiated from any other yellow metal? This field guide has been written to help solve these problems.

It should be emphasized that this is neither a laboratory guide to metals, nor a discourse on the artistic nuances between the metal of one era and that of another. Neither does it deal with every known metal as some, such as cobalt and platinum, are uncommon or of minimal importance or both. For these and other metals not discussed herein, consult general works like Tomlinson (1851) and Tylecote (1992). The only purpose of this guide is to suggest terminology and explain the cogent features for which one should look when attempting to provide the rudimentary, but accurate, descriptions which are required of field lab staff. Accordingly, there are only brief descriptions of alloy percentages such as may be necessary to give a minimal description of something, and the technology of manufacture is usually avoided. For example, rolled gold is mentioned, but the means used to make dissimilar metals roll together evenly is left unsaid. Antimony and bismuth are mentioned, not because they are found archaeologically, but because they are important as alloys in some common metals.

So, too, although processes of production and manufacture of metals often need to be expounded for the greatest clarity, space constraints in this article permit only rudimentary mention of production methods or manufacturing techniques. Further reading is, therefore, required for a clear understanding of the subject. Some good general works include Van Nostrand (1947), Mullins and Shaw (1968), Doyle (1969), Knauth (1974), Dick (1975), and Brady et al. (1997).

The principal metals are discussed in alphabetical order. A brief glossary of unfamiliar terms is provided at the end of the guide.

Aluminum

Aluminum is a lightweight, soft white metal, tending to blue. It is very malleable and ductile, and can be polished; indeed, one of its early uses was to serve as a replacement for silver on reflectors. This was not because it was less costly–in fact, it was a rare and expensive metal originally–but because its long-term performance was better than silver. Aluminum and most of its alloys resist corrosion very well in air because a film of protective oxide forms on the bare metal surface. If subjected to prolonged exposure, the oxide becomes a dull bluish-gray.

The fairly recent discovery of metallic aluminum (1825) and its even more recent application to the production of objects (the first aluminum item was a royal baby rattle, ca. 1855), make it useful for dating. Meager commercial production of aluminum began in England in the 1860s and 1870s, but it was World War I that provided the real growth for the aluminum industry. During the war, 90% of all the aluminum produced was consumed by the military, but after the war it became increasingly available to consumers. Between the wars, numerous alloys were developed and innovative production techniques were generated so that after the shortages of World War II, aluminum became universally available to the consumer.

During the 19th century, aluminum was used for jewelery, ornaments, reflectors, novelty items, and wire for embroidery, including military banners and epaulets. Aluminum leaf sometimes replaced silver leaf. Napoleon III saw the

Studies in Material Culture Research, 2000:3—19.

possibilities it offered for lightweight military equipment and stimulated research into aluminum metallurgy.

Pure and industrial research into the metallurgy of aluminum has produced a bewildering array of alloys and production techniques. Commercially viable aluminum alloys have been made with the following metallic and non-metallic elements: silver, copper, lead, bismuth, manganese, magnesium, silicon, zinc, lithium, chromium, platinum, nickel, and tin. Although they were the first ones developed, only iron-aluminum alloys lack a commercial use. For this reason, only the designation aluminum or aluminum alloy should be given to an object in the field lab.

Aluminum is not normally difficult to identify. The best indications are weight and color. Although the oxide can resemble tin oxide in color, the lack of weight will betray aluminum.

Antimony

Antimony is a bluish-white, extremely brittle metal which is not found commercially in its pure form. Its only commercial use is as an alloy with other metals, particularly copper and tin, with which it forms Babbitt's metal for bearings, and copper, zinc, and tin with which it forms Britannia metal. Another alloy, called tutania after its English inventor William Tutin who produced it in 1770, is 32 parts antimony, 8 parts brass, and 7 parts tin. It was used for such things as buckles, buttons, and spoons. In most alloys, however, antimony is undesirable because it imparts its inherent brittleness to the alloy.

Arsenic

Arsenic was once regarded as a metal (Partington 1835:118; Ure 1848:82) because its physical properties resembled those of metals, but it is now classified as a semimetal because it does not resemble metals in its chemical properties (Brady et al. 1997:68). It is a common constituent of the ores of many metals but, although it appears as an ingredient in various alloys and compounds, arsenic is never found archaeologically in pure form. It is volatile,

steel-gray in color, brittle, about as hard as copper, and extremely poisonous. It is now chiefly used industrially in pigments, bearing metal, lead shot, and glass production as well as in poisons, insecticides, and herbicides. Historically, it was used in glass production and is found in alloys, especially copper alloys such as "white tombac." It is generally undesirable as an alloy because it imparts its inherent brittleness.

Bismuth

Bismuth is a reddish-white, extremely brittle metal which is not found commercially in its pure form. Its only commercial use is as an alloy with other metals. The addition of bismuth to an alloy lowers the melting point, which makes it particularly useful for such things as solders and printers type metal.

Copper

Copper is a soft, orangey-red metal which is both very malleable and very ductile. It has been used continuously since antiquity, and is very possibly the earliest known metal. It may readily be remelted, alloyed, and cast, or reused in some other way; so, despite the fact that it is the second most common metal after iron, it is never found as scrap in the same quantities. Copper does not cast well because it flows poorly into a mold and sets badly on its surface in the mold. However, because of its ductility and malleability, it rolls and hammers easily; so most copper objects are hammered, drawn, rolled, or stamped.

Pure copper is commonly found. For example, because it is an excellent conductor, and because impurities lower its conductivity, electrical apparatus–like wire and bus bars–are ordinarily pure copper. Water tubes and pipes are also made from pure copper because of its easy solderability and general resistance to corrosion, and in the days of black powder, barrel straps, scoops, etc., were copper because it will not spark. Copper's conductivity led to its service in cookware, a usage which continues today. Copper-clad wooden hulls, sheathed as protection against borers which avoid copper, are well known as are the distinctive sheet roofs, green from a protective film of carbonate, on many famous buildings.

Despite the very common nature of these objects, the most frequent use of copper is in alloys, both as the principal metal and as an additive. There are three principal alloys of copper: bronze, brass, and nickel-silver. The subject of copper alloys is vast, and numerous books, many very current, have been written on the topic, among them Hughes and Rowe (1986); Fennimore (1996); Brady et al. (1997). Earlier sources like Ure (1848) and Tomlinson (1851) also have good articles on many metals including such copper alloys as bronze and brass. What follows here is only meant to cover the salient points.

Copper Alloy

Copper can be alloyed with many metals and, through the centuries, almost every conceivable alloy has been attempted. In this work, copper is discussed as an additive under the principal metal. As the primary metal, copper is alloyed in a wide variety of ways. Although some authorities, especially more modern ones, maintain that there are two broad categories for all copper alloys–bronzes and brasses (Van Nostrand 1947:198)–it is generally conceded that there are three common alloys: bronze, brass, and nickel-silver (Ure 1848:338 ff.; Child and Townsend 1988:11; Gentle and Feild 1994:447-448). In the simplest terms, bronzes are copper-tin alloys, brasses are copper-zinc alloys, and nickel-silvers are brass with nickel added. It is not uncommon, however, to find an alloy of copper, zinc, and tin in various ratios.

As with all alloys until around the late 19th century, the proportions of each metal in the mixture were but indistinctly known by the founder. Copper alloys were mixed by eye for particular characteristics, such as color and hardness, and they were mixed with metals which were never perfectly refined. Copper alloys, like pewter, were also often remelted and reused. Furthermore, the crucibles were small (Singer et al. 1958:609) and it was not unusual to cast a single object from two or more crucibles containing imprecisely mixed alloys. For example, a late 18th-century candlestick belonging to a colleague (P. Dunning collection), has a mottled bronze-brass appearance, although it was likely intended to be bronze. What appears to have happened is that two crucibles, each containing slightly different mixtures, have been poured together into the neck of the mold. This object is far from unique.

Despite the fact that the colors of copper, brass, bronze, and nickel-silver are different and easily differentiated, the difficulty of knowing exactly what alloy is involved it makes advisable in most field lab situations to use the term "copper alloy" rather than a specific term. Even for someone who is familiar with the problems of identification, terms such as "probable brass" or "probable bronze" are often more useful for an initial catalogue than a precise designation. Nickel-silver, on the other hand, is frequently marked as such (EPNS: electro-plated nickel-silver), and it is probably just as easy to identify it uniquely as it is to identify it as a copper alloy.

All copper alloys can be easily plated, and many varieties were. They can also be used as a plating, one example being brass over ferrous metal.

Copper alloys are also commonly joined together by a form of soldering called brazing. Brazing refers to a group of soldering processes in which the filler metal is a non-ferrous alloy with a melting temperature higher than approximately 1000°F, but less than the melting temperature of the metal(s) to be joined. In practice this often means an alloy of copper and zinc, so the process of soldering with brass is called brazing. Sometimes tin or silver are part of the filler metal.

BRONZE

Bronze is a copper-tin alloy. It was the first deliberate alloy known in antiquity (Meier 1970:4), a development so significant that an "age" was named after the metal. The bronze statuary, weapons, and axes of classical antiquity are well known, as are the famous Chinese bronzes. Bronze, being hard and brittle, is very difficult to work, so the normal method of manufacture is by casting. In this regard, it is a superior metal. Even so, lead, which increases the fluidity of molten bronze, was frequently added, especially to artistically important pieces or pieces which had to set up finely. The color of bronze varies with the alloy, but it can be anywhere from brown through coppery-orange and red-gold to pale gold. It is always darker and redder than brass.

Unlike pewter, bronze is extremely resonant, and it is often used for bells. Bronze alloys are noted for toughness and strength, as well as the ability to wear well and resist corrosion. For this reason cannon, bushings, pressure castings, gears, and the like were frequently made of a bronze, and the metal was often named for its purpose, such as gunmetal and bell metal. One kind of bronze which has a specific name is speculum. A very brittle metal which is one-third tin and two-thirds copper, speculum was used for the mirrors of telescopes because it has a brilliant blue-white color and can take a very high polish.

BRASS

The uses to which brass were put are legion. Tableware, kitchen utensils, personal items of adornment, lighting devices, scientific implements, tools, writing implements, building hardware, locks, weapon furniture, and marine fixtures are just some of the manifold uses of brass.

Brass is a copper-zinc alloy. Though not nearly as old as bronze, it has, nevertheless, been known for many centuries, but it is a more difficult alloy to achieve because at the melting temperature of copper, zinc is volatile. The whiteness of the zinc modifies the redness of the copper when it is alloyed, so that at 95% copper, the mixture is quite coppery-red. As more zinc is added, it becomes more pale, until at about 75% copper and 25% zinc, the alloy is a very sallow yellow. Then, as more zinc is added, the mixture becomes a deeper yellow until at about 30% copper it suddenly turns white. Together with the color changes come changes in ductility, fusibility, hardness, and malleability. These traits also change with the addition of aluminum, antimony, arsenic, iron, lead, nickel, and/or tin, all of which have at one time or another been alloyed with brass in various proportions.

Most brass was cast because it is an excellent casting metal. It will take fine, detailed designs in the mold, and can be decorated and highly polished afterwards. Decoration is commonly found on brass objects because it is easy to engrave, etch, paint, plate, punch, or raise. Brass can be drawn, rolled, spun, stamped, or wrought as well, though some alloys were better suited for one or another of these processes. Brass, for example, was difficult to spin, and a practical means of using this known process was only developed for brass in 1851 (Kauffmann 1979:78-79). Special alloys were devised for one or more of these manufacturing methods, as well as for specific usages. Names were often developed, especially during the 19th century, for specific alloys, not only to denote special characteristics, but also for marketing. Some of the more common names (besides just plain brass) were bath metal, Dutch gold, gilding metal, latten, Manheim gold, Muntz metal, pinchbeck, Prince's or Prince Rupert's metal, red brass, similor, standard English brass, tombac, and yellow metal (Fennimore 1996:18).

Brass is ductile and malleable, takes plating (tin or zinc) very well, and itself serves as a plate for ferrous metal. It can be easily remelted and cast and reused in other ways, so it is not found in large quantities as scrap. Blacksmiths formerly scavenged brass objects and them into pieces small enough to serve as raw material for brazing. The corrosion products of brass are green, though it is characteristically resistant.

NICKEL-SILVER

Nickel-silver is an alloy of copper, zinc, and nickel. The Chinese produced it for centuries, and it was imported into Europe under the name paktong. Europeans had been both searching for its secret and making objects using the imported metal since the 18th century, but it did not go into production in Europe until the late 1820s (Gentle and Feild 1994:448). It is brass with nickel added, thus some authorities wish to classify it as a kind of brass, but it was not historically understood, probably because of its color, in that manner. It is a distinctive, hard, tough, very versatile metal which can be cast, drawn, hammered, rolled, spun, and stamped.

As with other copper alloys, its composition can vary considerably and, not infrequently, a different name goes with a different composition.

For example, Ure (1848:341) gives the following percentages for nickel-silver according to the purpose for which it is intended: as a silver substitute - 50% copper, 25% zinc, 25% nickel; as an alloy for rolling - 60% copper, 20% zinc, 25% nickel [sic]; as an alloy for candlesticks, bells, etc. - 60% copper, 20% zinc, 20% nickel, 3% [sic] lead ; and "genuine" German silver - 40.4% copper, 31.6% nickel, 25.4% zinc, 2.6% iron. Aside from German silver, names which have been used for nickel-silver include, among others, white copper, Argentine (argentan), electrum, Nevada silver, paktong (also pakfong, packfong, and petong), tutenag (also toothenague, and tooth and egg—an old name for zinc mistakenly applied to paktong), and Silveroid.

The alloys vary widely, thus so does the color which can range from white to several shades of pale yellow. It resists tarnishing and corrosion very well. Fortunately, nickel-silver is frequently marked. Unfortunately, despite the nickel content, it is not magnetic.

When it was first produced, nickel-silver was used as a base for fused silver plate (Sheffield plate), but when electro-plating superseded the old plating methods in the 1850s, nickel-silver became the preferred base metal because any wearing away of the silver was not immediately obvious. Cutlery was produced in both plain nickel-silver and EPNS. The former, of course, was the cheaper of the two.

Ferrous Metal

Ferrous metal is the term for any metal, whether pure or an alloy, whose principal ingredient is the element iron (Fe). Iron is the most abundant metal on the planet, but it is not found in nature (except for a few meteorites) in a usable form. To obtain iron, its ore must be processed in some manner.

Unlike most other metals, iron is magnetic, and the vast majority of ferrous metals are magnetic, so this is a good test if one is unsure about the identity of a metallic object. Unfortunately, a few modern ferrous alloys are non-magnetic, as are some of the products of the decomposition of iron. All iron made before the last quarter of the 19th century is magnetic.

Cast Iron

Cast iron, as its name implies, was once molten. In its molten state, it was poured into some form of mold or channel either to produce a finished product, like a stove or cannon, or to produce an object of manageable size for further processing, like pig iron. Cast iron is high in carbon content (approximately 3% to 4.5%), making it brittle and subject to fracture under a sufficient impact load. It cannot be forged by a smith and apart from remelting in a blast furnace, it can only be reused with great difficulty.

There are three basic types of cast iron: "gray," "mottled," and "white." Gray cast iron contains a relatively high proportion of carbon present in the form of flake graphite, whereas in white cast iron the carbon is combined chemically with other elements and is therefore not "free" as it is in graphitic carbon. Mottled cast iron is a mixture of gray and white in varying degrees and, therefore, falls between the two in any descriptive categories. Although white cast iron is finer, has a higher carbon content, is harder, more resistant to wear and compression, and is more brittle than the more-coarse gray cast iron, it is unwise to attempt the classification of iron without sufficient experience and proper expertise. All three types of cast iron are subject to brittle fracture; they break in such a way as to show little or no evidence of plastic deformation. In other words, like ceramic, cast iron does not bend. Like ceramic, too, cast iron may be mended.

If the break in the cast iron is fresh, the surface of the fracture will betray the variety of cast iron by its appearance. The surface of a fresh fracture of gray cast iron will appear gray because of the graphitic carbon, the mottled iron will appear uniformly speckled; and the white cast iron will likely show columns of crystals, like ice crystals on a window, pointing to the surface of the mold, along with sporadic black spots. Should casting defects be present, they are liable to be more obvious in white cast iron than in other irons.

Despite these distinctions, it is appropriate to stress that any attempt to classify cast irons (indeed any metals) without sufficient experience and training is fraught with difficulties. It is best in a field lab simply to class the material as "cast iron" and defer further analysis.

Wrought Iron

From the discovery of the production of iron until this century, the common ferrous material has been wrought iron, also known just as iron. Wrought iron was *the* common smith's stock until the early part of this century. Its current rarity is a major obstacle for those engaged in historic craft enactment who give more than lip service to historical accuracy because both the techniques and the processes of manufacture vary, sometimes considerably, between wrought iron and its modern equivalent, mild steel. Aston and Story (1942) present a good introduction to wrought iron.

Iron was made either by the direct process in bloomeries or by the indirect process in blast furnaces. In either case, it was forged (wrought) by hammers and, in later periods, rolled in mills before it reached market. Wrought iron contains slag which, through hammering or rolling, becomes aligned in stringers throughout the body of the piece. These stringers are called either grain (because of the obvious similarity to wood grain) or fiber by a smith. Metallurgists prefer tighter usage, referring to stringers as fiber, reserving the term grain for crystalline structures within metals. It is these stringers, however, which give iron its unique properties. Its heterogeneity makes it easy to recognize if the surface has corroded enough to make this characteristic visible. If not, it looks much like any other ferrous metal.

Steel

Before the modern steel-making processes, steel was any mixture of iron and carbon containing up to 1.7% carbon and minor amounts of other elements (such as manganese, silicon, and phosphorous) depending on the ore. Carbon steel is harder and more durable than iron. It, like most steels, has a critical transformation temperature range during which it undergoes changes in properties. This characteristic allows for heat treating (annealing and tempering) in order to achieve maximum softness or hardness or the right balance of the two.

Although steel could be made directly in a bloomery, the common method of making iron and steel from about the 16th century on was in the blast furnace where steel could not be made directly. Pig iron from the blast furnace was used to make wrought iron. All the carbon was burned off the pig and the resulting "bloom" was forged or rolled into sheets or bars of wrought iron. The carbon-free iron, however, did not wear well and carbon had to be reintroduced (the commercial process was called cementation) to give it hardness and durability. This resulted in added cost, and steel was both costlier and in shorter supply than iron. The first reintroduction of carbon into iron was called blister steel. If blister steel were run through the process a second time it was called shear steel. A third time produced double-shear steel. Each step made the steel more expensive, so blister steel tended to be used for coarse applications and shear steels for more refined purposes. The important thing to stress here, however, is that wrought iron and carbon steel made from wrought iron are visibly indistinguishable.

It should be noted, too, that iron and steel can also be, and often were, welded together to make a single object, such as an iron pick with steel points. A good weld will leave little trace on an uncorroded object, so it may appear that there is only one material present.

Although they look the same, iron and steel were used differently. They can often be differentiated by this means. For example, files were always steel, as were the business ends of tools (the faces of hammers and the bits of axes), while the central portions of tools and bolts were almost invariably iron. It is impossible (and also not the place here) to list all the potential variations. It needs to be pointed out, however, that the distinction between iron and carbon steel can be made by one who is familiar with ferrous artifacts. Without this familiarity (as in a normal field lab situation), it is best to refer to the material as ferrous metal, *not* iron or steel, and defer closer identification. Barraclough (1976) provides more information on steel.

Cast Steel

In 1740, a new steel–crucible steel, also known as cast steel–was introduced to the commercial market. The inventor of the commercial process, Benjamin Huntsman, took blister steel, melted it in a glass-furnace crucible, skimmed off the slag which rose to the top (the material which produced the wrought iron fiber) and cast the material in an ingot. The ingot could be forged like any other steel, but having been molten and cast, it was a homogeneous carbon steel which no longer had a fibrous structure. It was, therefore, sought after for fine or delicate applications in which the fiber could be considered an inconvenience, such as watch springs, table knives, and fine files. Cast steel was extremely scarce and correspondingly expensive; however, by about 1800, it became fairly common to see knife blades marked "cast steel." This became a quality mark and, like other quality marks, it was sometimes abused.

Although cast steel is a homogeneous ferrous metal which is easy to differentiate from wrought iron or steel made from wrought iron, it is impossible to distinguish cast steel visually from most modern steels; indeed, in the late 19th century, objects made of Bessemer steel (Gale 1967:95) were often marked "cast steel" (which was true in the very literal sense) in order to gain market share.

Mild Steel

Mild steel is the modern equivalent of wrought iron but without the slag stringers which give iron its fibrous structure. After the invention of the Bessemer process in 1856, mild steel gradually replaced wrought iron as the everyday stock of the blacksmith, who used it to make all of the objects normally made of iron. Today, wrought iron is unavailable commercially in the western world, having been replaced by mild steel. Without training and experience, it is not possible to identify it visually.

Mild steel is highly ductile and malleable, though less so than wrought iron, but it has greater tensile strength. Mild in this context means soft (as in mild weather), and though mild steel may contain as much as 0.25% carbon, it cannot be tempered. With no, or virtually no, carbon, it is known as very mild steel. It may be case hardened; turned into steel on its surface by being packed in carbon and "baked." Historic craft enactments by smiths are usually hampered by having to use mild steel in place of wrought iron because it changes the work patterns of traditional blacksmithing.

Alloy Steels

Alloy steels, of which there are now many, began to appear in the last quarter of the 19th century. After the Bessemer process for making steel was discovered in 1856, it was realized that other elements than carbon could be mixed with iron on a commercial basis. In 1868, R. F. Mushet produced the first of the true alloy steels by producing a tungsten alloy called self-hardening steel. This steel made machine tools more effective. Other alloys using chromium, nickel, and manganese followed quickly. Some of these alloys could not be worked by hand blacksmiths, but appeared only in machine-made forms.

Trying to distinguish most alloy steels from mild steel or cast steel is a task best left to an analytical lab, so "ferrous metal" is the best designation for field lab purposes.

STAINLESS STEEL

One easily recognizable form of alloy steel which has been commercially available only since the 1920s is stainless steel. All stainless steels, of which there are dozens, contain chromium in the alloy. There are three types of stainless alloys: austenitic, ferritic, and martensitic. They are impossible to differentiate visually.

Austenitic stainless steels are the most common. They contain nickel and small amounts of carbon, but sometimes manganese and nitrogen are used as nickel substitutes. If these steels are improperly heat treated, they can be prone to a kind of decomposition called intergranular corrosion, and if small specks of corrosion are present on a stainless steel object, it is likely austenitic stainless. Ferritic stainless steels contain high chromium and no nickel, while martensitic stainless steels contain balanced amounts of nickel, carbon, and chromium.

Austenitic stainless, which is the most expensive, is used where oxidation resistance and strength at high temperature are needed in addition to corrosion resistance. Food preparation equipment and machinery are typical applications. The cheapest, ferritic stainless steels, tend to be used where less strength, and even less corrosion resistance, can be tolerated, such as in automobile body trim. Finally, martensitic stainless is the hardest and is used for things like cutlery and razor blades where wear resistance is at a premium.

The best quick way to distinguish between the various varieties of stainless steel is magnetism. Austenitic stainless steels are non-magnetic, while the other two types are magnetic.

Plated Ferrous Metal

There are five metals commonly used to plate ferrous metal: tin, zinc, brass, nickel, and chromium. The plate is always thin enough to allow the magnetism of the ferrous metal to be evident.

BRASS PLATE

Iron objects can be plated with brass either by dipping or electroplating. It was common in the last 150 years to plate such things as bedsteads, lamps, and architectural fittings with brass. Magnetism will reveal if a "brass bed" is solid or plated.

CHROMIUM PLATE

Chrome is a blue-white, very hard metal which is extremely resistant to corrosion and can be polished to a mirror finish. It has been around for most of the 20th century, but only after World War II did it become common to use it for commercial electro-platings on such things as automobile trim. The bright color and high shine are the best keys for quick identification purposes.

Another thing to look for is the fact that when chrome is plated over base metals, it tends to flake or peel. For this reason it is usually plated over a thin coating of nickel or, occasionally, copper. All three of these metals can produce greenish corrosion products, so the color is not a reliable guide.

NICKEL PLATE

Nickel is only occasionally found in its pure state on such things as scalpel handles, but its normal use is as either a plating or an alloy. As a plating on ferrous metal, it was used on a multitude of things such as car parts, the tops of salt and pepper shakers, and bicycle fittings. Nickel is a hard metal and resists scratching and abrasion well.

Nickel plate is shiny and white. It does not corrode easily, but when it does, the oxide is a faint yellowish-green which remains very hard, though not as hard or shiny as chrome.

TIN PLATE

Tin is very seldom found in its pure form. It takes a high polish and is also non-toxic, thus it was used at one time as a foil wrap for candies and cigarettes but, after World War II, it was replaced by aluminum foil. Tin is a soft, silvery-white metal which sometimes has a yellow tinge from the oxide. When it corrodes it is dull gray. Its lack of toxicity, coupled with its stability and resistance to corrosion, led to its widespread use as a coating for a wide variety of food containers including copper cookware, early Sheffield plate, and tin cans.

The most common use for tin is in making tin-plate, or plated ferrous metal, from which tin(ned) cans are made. Although iron has been tinned since the middle ages, tin-plate has only become commonplace since the early 19th century. John and Simcox (1966) give more information on tin-plate.

ZINC PLATE

Zinc plating on ferrous metal is known as galvanizing. Originally, and still frequently, steel plate was dipped in molten zinc, but today the zinc is often deposited electrolytically. Freshly applied zinc is bright, but it becomes drab quickly. Dipped zinc is easily identified by its blue-gray color and dull, camouflage-suit-like pattern, or mottled finish.

Galvanizing is used on metal exposed to the elements, such as corrugated iron, roofing, and garbage cans. Although the first patent for "zincing" iron was granted in 1837 (Hunt 1863:559), it only became common in the 1860s.

One 19th-century process, of Morewood and Rogers, used galvanizing on tin-plate for even greater protection.

The value of zinc plating lies in the fact that zinc itself is corrosion resistant and that it is above iron and steel on the galvanic scale. This means that it will corrode preferentially to the iron substrate, thus protecting it. The ferrous metal will not begin to corrode until most of the zinc has disappeared. The difficulty is that acids and alkalis both readily attack zinc, so it cannot be used in most places where tin plate is common.

Modern electrolytic platings are more evenly applied and dried so it is harder to identify them. They also retain the original bright blue-silver color of zinc better, which can sometimes be confused with chrome. It is usually smaller exposed objects which are electrolytically galvanized, such as nuts, bolts, screws, and bicycle parts.

Gold

Pure gold is yellow, soft, malleable, and very heavy. It is known as a "noble" metal because it does not tarnish or corrode. It is seldom found pure, but is usually alloyed with some metal like silver or copper in order to harden it. An ancient silver-gold alloy was known as electrum. Alloys with a gold content below 75% (18 carat) can tarnish.

There are numerous gold alloys which are designated by the term carat, or the measure of concentration by weight based upon 24 units. Carat is used to describe the purity of an alloy; so if 22 of the 24 parts of the ounce (gram) are gold, it is called 22 carat. If 10 of the 24 parts are gold, it is 10 carat, and so on. The other parts of the alloy are not specified, but silver, copper, and platinum are common additions. The addition of copper produces "red gold," while the addition of silver or platinum produces "white gold."

Substantial pieces of gold are required by law to be hallmarked, except for coins which are produced according to a legal standard which may vary slightly from place to place. Coins, which are made from very high carat alloys known as fine gold, can vary from 19 to 22 carats according to the jurisdiction.

Although gold is legally supposed to be hall-marked, the fact is that much gold is not. This is because it is easy to remelt and cast gold, and a jeweler often cannot guarantee the gold content of the new alloy. For example, a client may request that a jeweler manufacture a new piece from several bits of "old gold." Even if the jeweler knows the number of carats in each piece of old gold, it is still difficult, if not impossible, to know exactly the number of carats in the new piece, though this may be roughly estimated. The "other metal or metals" are almost always unknown.

For this reason, jurisdictions set standards for alloys. In Britain, for example, the standard alloys are 22, 18, 15, 12, and 9 carats. Only pieces of like carats are supposed to be melted together to make new pieces, but this is impossible to control. If, as in the example above, the "old gold" were a mixture of 12 and 9 carat pieces, the new piece of jewelery cannot be stamped by the jeweler according to the legal standards. It was, accordingly, safer and easier for the jeweler to ignore the hallmark. The lack of a hallmark on what is obviously gold, therefore, should not cause concern.

Gold is usually easy to identify because of its color and nobility, despite the fact that different alloys give various tints. The alloys, on the other hand, are impossible to classify visually unless a mark is present. Marks can be obtained from a number of standard reference works such as Jackson (1964).

Gold also appears in the form of a number of coatings including the following.

Gold Leaf

Gold leaf is very thin gold foil applied with glue over some molded or carved substrate.

Gilding

Gilding is the application of a surface layer of gold over some base metal, the varieties of which are legion. Sometimes a particular gilded metal has a name, as has gilded copper or copper alloy which is known as ormolu. From the last half of the 19th century to the present, gilding has almost always been done by electroplating. The operator can produce a very thin layer, and this, coupled with the fact that the pure gold of the electroplated layer does not wear well, means that objects gilded during this period now often show little evidence of gilding.

The other sort of gilding common before electroplating was mercury gilding. Mercury and gold were heated together to form a paste which was then applied to the base metal. The mercury disappeared as vapor upon heating, and the gold was left upon the object. This could be buffed or left matte but, in either case, mercury gilding invariably produced a thicker layer.

Rolled Gold

Rolled gold is a sandwich of metals, with two outside layers of gold or gold alloy enclosing a core metal like silver or nickel-silver. This is then rolled into a sheet of the desired thickness which is subsequently used in the manufacture of jewelery. Gold wire or braid can also be made this way.

Lead

Lead, which has been known for several millennia, is a very heavy, soft, malleable, and slightly ductile metal. When the surface is freshly exposed, it is a silvery-blue color, but the oxide which forms fairly quickly is dull gray. When oxidized, it is very resistant to corrosion. It is not uncommon to find "pure" lead archaeologically because of its softness, malleability, and corrosion resistance. It was often used for channeling water in pipes, drains, and gutters or pump wells in ships, and masons used it to anchor building hardware. Its heft made it useful for weights, and sailors used it for sounding leads to gauge depth. As shot or bullets, it was sometimes pure, sometimes alloyed, and always ubiquitous. Lead is most typical encountered as an alloy.

The earliest lead alloys were with tin, which is also an ancient metal. Tin and lead are soluble in each other, so virtually any proportion of each is possible. When lead predominates in these alloys, the metal is colored a dull metallic

blue, but when tin is the major element, the color is yellowish-white. In broad general terms, and roughly speaking, when the two metals are mixed in equal parts they yield solders. When the tin is high, pewter is produced, and when lead predominates, the mixture creates bearing metals, battery grids, and toy soldiers. Of course, lead need not be alloyed with tin alone. The addition of silver to lead (95%-97% lead and 3%-5% silver) produces a high-temperature solder, and antimony, bismuth, and copper are often found singularly or in combination with either lead and/or tin.

The addition of antimony and/or bismuth to lead or lead-tin alloys greatly increases their hardness, ductility, and casting abilities. For this reason, printing type is almost always made of lead-antimony-tin alloys. The addition of bismuth to lead-tin lowers the melting point and gives a fusible alloy. Copper increases the hardness, and lead-based bearing metals usually have copper in them to make them wear better.

Lead is easy to recognize from its color, weight, and malleability, but it should be borne in mind that it alloys easily and that lead alloys are extremely common. There are numerous clues, some of which have been suggested here, which can be followed. For example, if something which is very clearly lead is also hard, that is a transparent indication of an alloy. Nevertheless, no alloy can be determined with precision outside of an analytical lab, so in an archaeological field lab, the best designation is probably "lead or lead alloy."

Solder

Soldering involves the joining of two pieces of metal, either of the same or different composition, by another metal compound or alloy which melts and fuses at a lower temperature than those being joined. The joining is thus effected by surface adhesion without melting the base metals, as in welding.

While a number of metals and alloys were used as iron solders, lead-based alloys, often with the addition of zinc or tin, were common because of the low melting temperature of lead. A zinc compound called spelter was used to solder brass, but was also sometimes used on iron. Brazing, a specialized form of soldering, is described in the section on "Copper Alloy."

Magnesium

Magnesium is a light, malleable, silver-white metal which is ductile when heated. It is not likely to be found in its pure form archaeologically, but it might not be unusual to discover it in one of its alloys, almost always an aluminum alloy, as a surface find on some sites.

Although it was discovered in 1808, and isolated in 1828, the metal was not used industrially until the 1910s, when it was employed in photographic flash powder and as a deoxydant in nickel alloys. World War II gave a great impetus to its production. During the war, it was used for lightweight castings, as well as for incendiary bombs and flares because it burns with an intense white light. Today there are many commercial uses for magnesium, but it is most familiar as a lightweight alloy with aluminum and zinc in engine castings and as airframes, etc. It is still used in flares.

Mercury

Mercury, which has been known since antiquity, is the only metal which is liquid at room temperature. It will not stick to glass as do other liquids and, at room temperature, it is slightly volatile. Its liquid nature and its silver-white color give rise to its other name, quicksilver. If inhaled or ingested, it has a poisonous effect on the body.

Mercury forms alloys, always known as amalgams, with most metals, but not with iron and platinum. Almost every child who declines to brush regularly becomes acquainted with an amalgam. Mercury is or has been used in scientific apparatus, electrical switches, pigments (vermilion), the manufacture of explosives, the recovery of gold and silver by the amalgamation process, and various medical treatments.

Mercury is very easy to identify. If it is found during excavation, it should be kept in a sealed container.

Nickel

Nickel is a hard, silver-white, scratch- and abrasion-resistant, ductile, malleable, magnetic metal which is resistant to tarnishing and corrosion and is capable of taking a high polish. It has been used by the Chinese in argentic and cupric alloys for nearly two millennia, but it was not isolated until the Swede Cronstedt did so in 1751, partly because of its very high melting point (1455°C). It was subsequently occasionally used in its pure state, especially in the late 19th century, for such things as fancy livery and scalpel handles, but is now normally used almost exclusively either as a plating or as an alloy. As an electroplating on ferrous metal, it was used on such things as car parts and bicycle fittings. Nickel plate is shiny and white. When it corrodes, the oxide is a faint yellow-green which remains very hard; indeed, nickel is harder than iron.

As an alloy, nickel is used with many metals, including aluminum, chromium, copper, steel, tin, and zinc. Most goes into the production of austenitic stainless steels. Nickel is usually alloyed with another metal as the base, but high-nickel alloys such as the monels, which are essentially nickel-copper alloys used for such things as marine applications and household appliances, are usually identified by their magnetism. The identification of nickel alloys is only possible in an analytical laboratory with the proper equipment, thus hard white magnetic metals should be classified in the field lab only as nickel alloys.

Silver

Pure silver is a very bright, white noble metal capable of taking a high polish. It is soft (though not as soft as gold or lead) and, as a consequence, it is almost never found pure. Silver is most frequently alloyed with copper. Though there are numerous silver-copper alloys—like hard silver (83.33%), coin silver (90%), and Britannia silver (95.8%)—the most common and famous alloy is sterling silver which contains 92.5% silver. Unlike gold, British sterling (and

Britannia) silver are consistently hallmarked because the alloy standards do not present an insoluble problem to the jeweler. Silver of other countries may have more complex hallmarking or may not be hallmarked at all. Marks can be obtained from a number of standard reference works like Currier (1970).

Although silver is a noble metal which resists corrosion, it is highly prone to tarnishing from sulfur. Any sulfur-containing material or atmosphere such as wool, eggs, or coal smoke will thus stain silver rapidly. The initial tarnish is blue/purple, but this deepens to a brown/black color.

Silver, being a costly metal, was often applied over cheaper base metals so that it could be made available to a wider public and, indeed, silver plate is more common than sterling. The chief plating methods are reviewed below. Numerous reference works (Blair 1987) document other, more unusual, methods.

Silver Leaf

Silver leaf, like gold leaf, is thin foil applied with glue over some molded or carved substrate.

Close Plating

Before the invention of electroplating, close plating was the only effective way to plate ferrous metal. It has been used since about the 14th century, but it became widely used in the 19th century for objects which required both beauty and durability. Close plating is common on such things as fancy horse livery, clothing accessories, candle snuffers, and so on. It is not unusual to find it stamped with maker's marks.

The process was as follows: cleaned iron or steel was dipped in molten tin. The object was then wrapped with silver foil and heated with a smoothing iron until the silver was soldered to the ferrous metal beneath. This produces a hard surface which can be polished.

Close plating can be identified by magnetism and by the presence of typical iron corrosion wherever the surface layer has been breached. It is also common for the silver to flake wherever the soldering is imperfect.

French Plating

Known in England as French plating, this was a method of covering brass and copper with silver. The object to be plated was polished, heated, and then bathed in nitric acid in order to prepare the surface to accept the silver. Pure silver leaf was then burnished onto the base, pressure and heat causing the silver to adhere. Though it remained in use after the advent of electroplating in the 1840s, French plating was incapable of standing heavy use, and did not provide a really permanent plate (Hughes 1970:9-10).

Electroplating

Electroplating began to be used commercially on many different metals in the 1840s. Silver was usually electroplated over some alloy of copper like Britannia metal or nickel-silver.

Aside from the fact that these pieces were usually marked with the familiar EP (this always means "electro-plated with silver") stamps–EPBM (Electro-Plated Britannia Metal) or EPNS (Electro-Plated Nickel-Silver)–the easiest way to identify plate is to look for worn patches. Usually a yellow or red tinge beneath the silver will betray the copper alloy.

Old Sheffield Plate (Fused Silver Plate)

Sheffield plate is similar to rolled gold. Essentially, it is a sandwich with silver as the bread on either side and a copper alloy as the filling, although on rare occasions the sandwich was "open-faced." When heated, fused, and rolled into sheets, it was used to make all manner of items. The process was developed in the 1740s, and superseded by electro-plating 100 years later (Wyler 1949:5, 8).

The silver layer of old Sheffield plate is thicker than EP silver, and it was frequently stamped with a maker's mark. Despite these differences, the distinction between different kinds of plating should probably not be attempted in a field lab.

Although old Sheffield plate was developed in Sheffield and most of the production came from there, it was not the only place where it was produced. The wider and broader term, "fused silver plate," is preferred by most authorities today.

Imitation Silver

Most silver imitations were unsuccessful. Pewter, for example, served often as a silver substitute (Child 1988:12) and sometimes as an imitation (Massé, Michaelis, and Kauffman 1971:36), but it fooled few because of the dominant tin content of pewter. Occasionally, an alloy appeared which became a successful imitator of silver. One such, called melchior, which was popular in the early 20th century, was a mixture of copper (55 parts), nickel (23 parts), zinc (17 parts), iron (3 parts), and tin (2 parts) (Massé, Michaelis, and Kauffman 1971:36). It is usually copper-nickel alloys like melchior and nickel-silver which are the most effective silver imitators.

Tin

Tin is very seldom found in its pure form. It takes a high polish and is also non-toxic, thus it was used at one time as a foil wrap for candies and cigarettes, a task which aluminum foil took over after World War II. Tin is a malleable silvery-white metal with a bluish tinge, which sometimes has a yellow tint from the oxide. It corrodes dull gray. It is softer than zinc but harder than lead and is ductile at 100°C.

The two most important uses for tin are as a protective plating for copper and, especially, for ferrous metal (see Ferrous Metal and Tin Plate), and as an alloy, often with copper and zinc, in several important metals like bronze, bell metal, and bearing metal. Most often tin is an additive, but there is one very common alloy in which it is the principal metal: pewter.

Pewter and Britannia Metal

What follows is not meant to be a treatise on pewter, but rather to show how complex the subject is. Books have been written on pewter (Michaelis 1971; Cotterell et al. 1972), and much of what has been written is contradictory. Despite this, pewter is a recognizable metal, although it reminds one of what Mr. Justice Potter of the U.S. Supreme Court once said about pornography: "I can't define it, but I know it when I see it." Cotterell says the same (Cotterell et al. 1972:39-40)!

Pewter, which has been known since antiquity, is a tin alloy. Aside from its lack of resonance (it "clunks" when tapped), the fact that it is an alloy with a high tin content is about the only universally true statement which can be made about pewter. The various other metal additions have usually been added to the tin merely for the purpose of strengthening it, although sometimes economics (usually greed or lack of capital) have made strange alloys. Though there are standards regarding pewter's formulation today, these either did not always exist or were not followed, and there have been an astonishing variety of compositions through the years (Cotterell et al. 1972:39, 50-51). This has been exacerbated by the fact that it is very easy to remelt and recast pewter, and this was frequently done (Peal 1971:15). Pewter objects may occasionally have different parts of them (such as the handle and the body of a tankard) cast from different crucibles or spoons containing different alloys, or even have the same body cast from two different spoons of slightly different alloys, the one spoon not holding enough for the complete object. This appears to have been the case with a 16th-century pewter object from the Basque shipwreck site at Red Bay, Labrador (Dunning 1990).

The variety of deliberate formations has been further complicated by the fact that accidental and conscious additions, sometimes in considerable quantities, as well as trace elements, often show up in pewter alloys. Antimony, lead, copper, bismuth, zinc, silver, mercury, iron, nickel, and arsenic, either as deliberate or accidental additions, have all appeared in pewter (Unglik 1984:22). Romano-British pewter, a tin-lead alloy, varied from 47% to 99.2% tin, although the norm was between 62% and 80% tin. This carried through the Middle Ages (Peal 1971:79). Though most knew the dangers of lead and tried to regulate it, the regulations were seldom, if ever, effective. In the late Middle Ages, a tin-copper alloy began to appear (Peal 1971:26, 87). This alloy, in about a 4:1 ratio, is what is often referred to as "fine pewter" (Massé, Michaelis, and Kauffman 1971:51). Antimony was then added to the mix in varying proportions from 100:17 to 9:1 (Pemberton's alloy) (Massé, Michaelis, and Kauffman 1971:51). The systematic, deliberate addition of antimony appears to have begun in the 18th century, and as the use of antimony increased, the use of lead declined. Modern pewter, by definition, contains no lead, though, in fact, trace amounts are often found.

Late in the 18th century, James Vickers developed a new, improved pewter called Britannia metal which is more durable and has better molding qualities than pewter. Britannia metal is an alloy of tin, antimony, and copper. There are several varieties of Britannia metal, a typical one being Queen's Metal: 88.5% tin, 7.1% antimony, 3.5% copper, and 0.9% zinc (Child and Townsend 1988:12). Some collectors will refuse to accept Britannia metal as a type of pewter, not for scientific reasons, but because it is both "late" and defined. Nevertheless, it is accepted by most as a variety of pewter simply because it is a tin alloy (Peal 1971:171), and this should be the classification used by archaeologists. Britannia metal is often stamped "BM" and frequently plated (see Silver).

Pewter objects can be cast in molds, hammered from plate or both, lathe turned after molding, stamped, or formed by spinning. Stamping and spinning are invariably confined to Britannia metal among the pewters (Massé, Michaelis, and Kauffman 1971:54; Cotterell et al. 1972:40) because these are industrial processes which require not only a consistent alloy but also the harder, more ductile, nature of Britannia metal. A case may be made that Britannia metal largely displaced pewter because of industrial exigencies (Montgomery 1973:17-19), especially as the ability of Britannia metal to take electroplating became known (Massé, Michaelis, and Kauffman 1971:54).

Britannia metal is the hardest, thinnest, and lightest of the pewters, but all have the unmistakable look and feel of tin. The colors vary depending on the alloy, and everything from a shiny silvery-blue to a dark dull gray may be found.

Lead pewters suffer from "pewter disease," an affliction mentioned by most commentators on pewter (Massé, Michaelis, and Kauffman 1971:69; Peal 1971:26-27). It is characterized by pock marks or boils which appear on the surface of the metal, and is due to an imperfect alloy–a separation of one of the constituent elements from the others. Cotterell even suggests that pewter disease is a way by which one can tell fake from real pewter (Cotterell et al. 1972:41)

Zinc

Zinc is a bluish-white metal which was not isolated as a metal until the 18th century, although it was known for centuries before. It is not found commercially in its pure form. Acids and alkalis attack zinc rapidly. Like tin, its two most important uses are for plating, especially for ferrous metal where the process is called galvanizing (see Ferrous Metal and Zinc Plate), and as an alloy, often with copper, nickel, and tin, in several important metals like brass, Britannia metal, and nickel-silver. Today it is sometimes used as a base in some die-casting alloys, but mostly as an additive in aluminum, copper, and magnesium casting alloys. It is harder than both tin and lead.

Collectors sometimes refer to any zinc-alloy castings of whatever composition as spelter (Perry 1974:186). Spelter is a commercial name for molten zinc which comes from the name (*spailter* or *speauter*) given by 17th-century Dutch traders to the zinc brought from China. The name was also applied to a yellowish zinc compound used to solder brass. Its color was imparted by the small amount of copper it contained.

Glossary

Alloy: The combination of metals by fusion. When mercury is one of the metals, the alloy is termed an amalgam. Alloys acquire new properties which are different than the original metals. They are usually designated by the chief or base ingredient; for instance, a copper alloy will be mostly copper.

Annealing: Annealing is a process which makes use of the ability of steel to "soften" when it is heated above its critical transformation temperature and then slowly cooled. The process was crucial in the days when only carbon steel existed because, to work a carbon-steel object with a carbon-steel file, the one had to be soft and the other hard. Although a smith almost always used the term to refer to the softening of steel, it has a wider meaning and can refer to the softening of other metals or to the slow, controlled cooling of materials like glass.

Block tin: Pure tin, cast into blocks.

Brazing: The process of soldering with brass is called brazing. It involves joining two pieces of metal by fusion using an alloy of copper and zinc (brass), and sometimes tin or silver, which melts and fuses at a lower temperature than the pieces being joined.

Brittle: Subject to disintegration under pressure, especially under impact loads.

Ductile: Often confused with malleability (q.v.), ductility is the ability of a metal to remain together without cracking or breaking when drawn. Metal for wire must be ductile.

Fusibility: Before metals are rendered liquid by heating, they become pasty. It is at this temperature that they will fuse. All metals are fusible, but the temperature at which this occurs varies greatly among metals: from a few hundred degrees Celsius for tin, bismuth, and lead, to thousands of degrees for nickel, manganese, and tungsten.

Malleability: A malleable metal can be beaten into thin sheets without cracking or breaking. It is often confused with ductility (q.v.). Brittle metals are not malleable; thus, wrought iron is malleable, cast iron is not.

Pig iron: The tapping of a blast furnace involved removing a ceramic dam in order to allow the molten contents of the furnace to flow out into a channel dug into the sand floor in front of the blast furnace. The fancied appearance to a suckling animal together with the weight of the metal caused the main channel to be called the sow and the side channels, pigs. This is pig iron. The only use of pig iron (besides ballast for ships) was to make wrought iron.

Soldering: Soldering involves joining two pieces of the same or different metals by another metal or alloy which melts and fuses at a lower temperature than those being joined. While a number of alloys were used as iron solders, lead-based alloys, often with the addition of zinc or tin, were common. Brazing (q.v.) is a specialized form of soldering.

Spinning: An industrial process whereby sheet metal is made into a hollow vessel by the pressure of a roller against the sheet which is being held by a spinning lathe tailstock. The sheet is pressed into a form block on a revolving headstock spindle. Many vessels made of copper alloy and Britannia metal were spun.

Welding: Welding is the process of uniting two or more heated pieces of fusible metal by compression (usually hammering). There were other means of joining metal, namely riveting, brazing, or soldering, but welding, when it could be used successfully, was the most effective of these. Forge welding was eventually replaced by gas and electric welding both of which were faster and required less skill. These processes were developed in the late 19th century, but they were not practicable until the 20th century.

Conclusion

The task of rectifying a very large blind spot in historical archaeological research begins with the ability to identify correctly metals; but it only begins here. On historical sites, objects made of metal are simultaneously both the most profuse and the least understood of artifacts. Archaeologists who are able accurately to identify unmarked Staffordshire pearlware teaware and date it to the half decade are often unable even roughly to describe how an axe was manufactured, or even from what material it was made.

There are a number of reasons for this situation, not the least of which is the enormous complexity of the subject. Metal objects are made from a great number of substances and come in a bewildering number of forms. Furthermore, most metals corrode, obscuring surface details and often reducing an object to a handful of rusty fragments. This is further complicated by the fact that relatively little has been written about archaeological metal. Add to all this the difficulty, if not impossibility, of dating most metal (which renders it archaeologically "unhelpful"), as well as the all too frustratingly real-time constraints under which archaeology operates in today's hyper society, and there is every incentive for the researcher to defer or ignore the hard task of learning about and mastering metals and metal artifacts.

Still, these are not acceptable excuses. Metal is generally part of every archaeological assemblage and it demands interpretation. It is in our collections, but not in our site reports. We are thus losing information, sometimes a great deal of crucial information. Assuming a desire to correct the deficiency, the long slow process of reversing the existing apathy towards archaeological metal must begin by each of us being able to answer the question: what is the stuff made of and what do I call it?

REFERENCES

ASTON, JAMES, AND EDWARD B. STORY
1942   Wrought Iron: Its Manufacture, Characteristics and Applications. A. M. Byers, Pittsburgh, PA.

BARRACLOUGH, K. C.
1976   Sheffield Steel. Mooreland, Buxton, Derbyshire, England.

BLAIR, CLAUDE (EDITOR)
1987   The History of Silver. Macdonald, London, England.

BRADY, GEORGE S., HENRY R. CLAUSER, AND JOHN A. VACCARI
1997   Materials Handbook, 14th edition. McGraw-Hill, New York, NY.

CHILD, ROBERT E., AND JOYCE M. TOWNSEND (EDITORS)
1988   Modern Metals in Museums. Institute of Archaeology, London, England.

COTTERELL, H. H., ADOLPHE RIFF, AND ROBERT M. VETTER
1972   National Types of Old Pewter. The Pyne Press, Princeton, NJ.

CURRIER, ERNEST M.
1970   Marks of Early American Silversmiths. Robert Allan Green, Harrison, NY.

DICK, WILLIAM B.
1975   Dick's Encyclopedia of Practical Receipts and Processes, or How They Did it in the 1870's. Funk and Wagnalls, New York, NY.

DOYLE, LAWRENCE E.
1969   Manufacturing Processes and Materials for Engineers. Prentice-Hall, Englewood Cliffs, NJ.

DUNNING, PHIL
1990   Sixteenth-Century Domestic Metals Recovered from Red Bay, Labrador (Sites 24M and 29M). Manuscript, Parks Canada, Ottawa, Ontario.

FENNIMORE, DONALD L.
1996   Metalwork in Early America: Copper and Its Alloys. Henry Francis du Pont Winterthur Museum, Winterthur, DE.

GALE, W. K. V.
1967   The British Iron and Steel Industry: A Technical History. David and Charles, Newton Abbot, Devon, England.

GENTLE, RUPERT, AND RACHAEL FEILD
1994   Domestic Metalwork: 1640-1820, revised and enlarged by Belinda Gentle. Antique Collectors Club, Woodbridge, Suffolk, England.

HUGHES, G. BERNARD
1970   Sheffield Silver Plate. Praeger, New York, NY.

HUGHES, RICHARD, AND MICHAEL ROWE
1986   The Colouring. Bronzing and Patination of Metals. Crafts Council, London, England.

HUNT, ROBERT (EDITOR)
1863   A Supplement to Ure's Dictionary of Arts, Manufactures and Mines. D. Appleton, New York, NY.

JACKSON, CHARLES JAMES
1964   English Goldsmiths and Their Marks. Dover, New York, NY.

JOHN, W. D., AND ANNE SIMCOX
1966   Pontypool and Usk Japanned Wares with the Early History of the Iron and Tinplate Industries at Pontypool. The Ceramic Book Company, Newport, England.

KAUFFMAN, HENRY J.
1979   American Copper & Brass. Bonanza, New York, NY.

KNAUTH, PERCY
1974   The Metalsmiths. Time-Life, New York, NY.

MASSÉ, H. J. L. J., RONALD F. MICHAELIS, AND HENRY J. KAUFFMAN
1971   Chats on Old Pewter. Dover, New York, NY.

MEIER, JERZY W.
1970   Non-Ferrous Metals Casting, History and Forecast. Department of Energy, Mines and Resources, Ottawa, Ontario.

MICHAELIS, RONALD F.
1971   Antique Pewter of the British Isles. Dover, New York, NY.

MONTGOMERY, CHARLES F.
1973   A History of American Pewter. Henry Francis du Pont Winterthur Museum, New York, NY.

MULLINS, WILLIAM W., AND MILTON C. SHAW (EDITORS)
1968   Metal Transformation. Gordon and Breach, New York, NY.

PARTINGTON, CHARLES F.
1835   *The British Cyclopædia of the Arts and Sciences.* Orr & Smith, London, England.

PEAL, CHRISTOPHER A.
1971   *British Pewter and Britannia Metal.* Peebles Press, London, England.

PERRY, EVAN
1974   *Collecting Antique Metalware.* Doubleday, New York, NY.

SINGER, CHARLES, E. J. HOLMYARD, A. R. HALL, AND TREVOR I. WILLIAMS (EDITORS)
1958   *A History of Technology*, Volume 5. Clarendon Press, Oxford, England.

TOMLINSON, CHARLES (EDITOR)
1851   *Cyclopædia of Useful Arts.* James S. Virtue, London, England.

TYLECOTE, R. F.
1992   *A History of Metallurgy.* The Institute of Metals, London, England.

UNGLIK, HENRY
1984   A Case of a Broken Pewter Flagon from Red Bay, Labrador: Nondestructive Analysis by X-Ray Fluorescence Spectroscopy. Manuscript, Parks Canada, Ottawa, Ontario.

URE, ANDREW
1848   *A Dictionary of Arts, Manufactures and Mines.* D. Appleton, New York, NY.

VAN NOSTRAND
1947   *Van Nostrand's Scientific Encyclopedia.* Van Nostrand, New York, NY.

WYLER, SEYMOUR B.
1949   *The Book of Sheffield Plate.* Crown, New York, NY.

JOHN D. LIGHT
MATERIAL CULTURE RESEARCH
ONTARIO SERVICE CENTRE
PARKS CANADA
1600 LIVERPOOL COURT
OTTAWA, ONTARIO K1A 0M5
CANADA

LESTER A. ROSS
JOHN D. LIGHT

A Guide to the Description and Interpretation of Metal Files

Introduction

Files can often be identified as a discrete artifact class, due in part to their composition and surviving stylistic attributes. Oxidation of the ferrous alloys will obscure many important attributes. After physical brushing or careful chipping of a limited amount of the corrosive encrustation and rust, most significant attributes can be identified. Comparisons of these attributes with historical illustrations, and the identification of historical manufacturers, provides useful information for functional, geographical, and temporal interpretations.

Files are originally constructed as tools for specific tasks and functions. These functions can be inferred from the files themselves and from the contexts in which they are found. For example, a smooth, 3-square file recovered from a fur trade site probably represents a gun-working tool (Karklins 1983:139, 155, 159). Rough, coarse, and bastard files recovered from a site may represent the tools of a stone mason or sawyer. An assemblage of smooth and second-cut files may indicate the presence of an instrument maker or cutler. Functional interpretations are often speculative, due to the lack of an adequate assemblage of tools and by-products or to limited historical evidence. To extract interpretive data and comparative information from the files recovered from historical sites requires a common lexicon for file attributes, types, sizes, and historical equivalents. The first requirement should be the adoption of a standard terminology for describing stylistic attributes.

There are nearly as many artifact cataloguing systems as there are archaeological research organizations. It is not the intention of this guide to put forward any one system as superior, but rather to provide terminology by which archaeologists can communicate their findings.

Many historical trades used files. Some file shapes (such as flat files) had universal applications, so they cannot be given a specific functional attribution. Frequently, however, files were designed to do a particular job, but because they were so task-specific, they were rare; e.g., a wood carver's rifflers or a shoemaker's channel file (a tool for cleaning out a channel cut in leather so that stitches may be recessed). These files often had unique trade names. Occasionally, however, names were given to trade-specific tools without reference to other usage, so the same word might refer to two or more quite different objects, as is the case with a farrier's, shoemaker's, and marble worker's float. This guide represents a rudimentary introduction for the description of files. It cannot replace the hard task of understanding (as opposed to knowing about) the tool itself (Nicholson File Co. 1956); but in metal research, it is unfortunately still a case of: "One foot up and one foot down, That's the way to London town."

File Description

File Definition

A file is the generic name for any metal tool with raised teeth or ridges on one or more of its surfaces which is used to reduce, smooth, or sharpen the surface of another material through abrasion (Figure 1). The word can be used as a verb, not only to describe the action of reducing the surface of something, but also as a direct synonym for the verb "sharpen," as in, to file an axe. All files have two attributes in common: one or more working faces and multiple cutting teeth. Included within this category are tools commonly identified as the burnishers, floats, rasps, rifflers, and steels used for abrading wood, metal, stone, leather, hooves and fingernails, bone, and teeth. Since files could also function as fine cutting implements when used on edge, they were occasionally utilized for scoring or incising bone, glass, shell, etc. From descriptions available in early historical accounts, files were primarily associated with metal working activities, presumably reflecting their historical

Studies in Material Culture Research, 2000:20—31.
Permission to reprint required.

development within the metal trades (Biringuccio 1540:216, 307, 363; Moxon 1703:15-17;
Appleton 1851:760ff; Ure 1864:708ff).

Historical Development

Metallic files in Europe were probably introduced during the initial years of the "metal
age." Archaeological examples of ferrous files
have been recovered from 1st- to 3rd-century
Roman camps in Britain, and based upon the
diversity of styles during that period, prior
temporal development must have been extensive.
Functionally, files appear to have been initially
developed as metal working tools (I Samuel
13:21), but by the "Age of New World Explora-
tions," functional variations included at least
wood-working tools as well. As such usages
imply, files had to be strong, relatively durable,
and manufactured from materials harder than the
material upon which they were used.

General Features and Methods of Manufacture

Since files were intended for hard usage
on relatively inflexible substances, they were
commonly manufactured from steel. Prior to
the introduction of special alloy steels in the
late 19th century, ferrous metals which were
considered suitable for files were carburized
(casehardened) wrought iron, blister steel, shear
steel, and crucible or cast steel. Methods for
manufacturing files from these carbon steels were
known by most blacksmiths, but because of the
precise skills and specialized tools required to
produce good-quality steel files with uniformly
spaced teeth, a specialized class of smiths were
soon recognized–the filesmiths. By the 18th
century in Great Britain, filesmiths had established their own society, and by the 19th century,
specialists within the profession included file
forgers, file grinders, file cutters, and file harden-

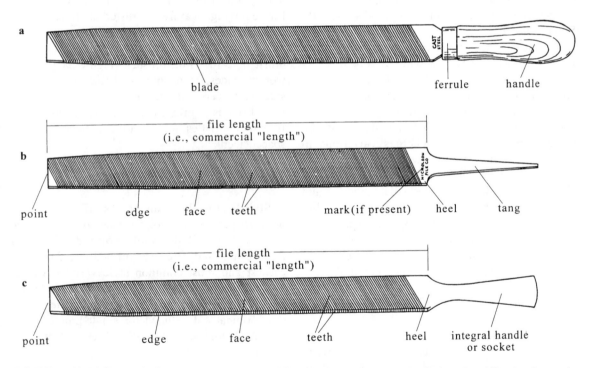

FIGURE 1. Metal file terminology and types: *a,* metal file showing major parts; *b,* single-pointed file showing major
attributes (J. H. Ashdown Hardware Company 1904:91); *c,* single-pointed file showing tang variation.

ers (Tomlinson 1854:643-645; Lloyd 1913:58-61, 317).

Prior to the late 19th century, files were generally hand made. Wrought iron or steel bars were forged into variously shaped file blanks. Steel bars were annealed to soften their surfaces for teeth cutting. These blanks were next ground to attain the proper shape and smoothness, and each tooth was individually cut with a hand chisel and hammer. Exact precision was required by the file cutter in order to stamp each tooth precisely parallel to, and only a fraction of an inch beyond, the preceding tooth. Whether the file was flat or round, a flat chisel was used to cut the teeth. For round files, as many as 22,000 individual cuts had to be made. After cutting, the maker's or factory mark was stamped into the file, usually on its heel, tang, or center. Wrought-iron files were case hardened. Next, the steel file was coated with a thick saline solution in order to prevent oxidation and cracking, heated, straightened, and quench-tempered to an exact hardness. Finally, each file was tested, cleaned, oiled, and shipped to awaiting suppliers (Tomlinson 1854:643-645; Spon 1898:76-77).

To fulfill various functional requirements, files were manufactured with a wide variety of cross sections; came in a multitude of shapes, sizes, and weights; and had many teeth configurations and spacings. Variations in shape and cross section were indicative of the shape of the surfaces being abraded, whereas variations in size and teeth attributes were related to the surface area being abraded and to the degree of abrasion desired. Most files (file blades) could be utilized without additional accessories, but handles were often desired by tradesmen who relied daily upon the use of files. The exception is the butchers' steel which always appear to have had handles, and sometimes guards.

Associated File Accessories

File blades were commonly used with attached wooden handles which could be removed when a blade became worn and placed on the tang of another blade (Figure 1a). Such handles normally required the use of brass or iron ferrules for reinforcement, but non-reinforced handles were also used, though usually these were homemade by the user. Occasionally, for convenience of working, a file holder (Nicholson File Co. 1878:66-68) was employed, but such items were rare.

The only other commonly associated articles found with file blades are their cleaning tools. All files tend to clog with the material they are abrading, and they must be kept clean for optimum use. Tapping, carding, brushing, or rubbing the file on an apron are common ways of keeping a file clean. More difficult cleaning jobs call for special techniques. Oil is removed by wiping off the excess, rubbing the file with chalk, charcoal, or any soft non-clogging substance which will absorb the oil, and carding. This was, in fact, a common procedure as new files were factory oiled before they were shipped. Soft substances like wood can be removed by immersing the file in boiling water and carding. Heating the file in order to burn off the clog runs the risk of drawing temper.

Three articles were manufactured for cleaning the spaces between the teeth: file brushes, file cards, and file picks. File picks were used for removing heavily encrusted material or for cleaning between coarse teeth, and such picks were normally stored in the handle of a file brush or card. File brushes (Figure 2) had two working sides for medium and fine cleaning; one side with coarse bristles and the other with fine wire bristles. File cards (Figure 2) had only fine wire bristles for cleaning between closely spaced teeth.

File Stylistic Types and Attributes

Stylistically, files can be classified into four basic shapes: single-pointed files, double-pointed files, self-handled double-pointed files, and double-handled files (Figures 1b-c, 3). The earliest and most common style was the single-pointed file, which served as the basic model for later stylistic variations. File attribute terminology, originally developed for single-pointed files, remained consistent for all subsequent stylistic variations.

Single-pointed Files

Single-pointed files (Figure 1b-c) came in many stylistic variations, but generally all had

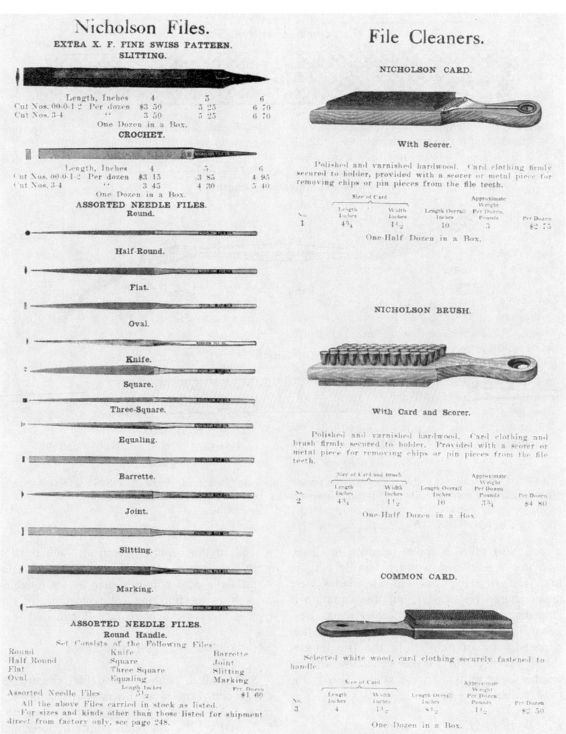

FIGURE 2. File cleaners and uncommon files advertised in The George Worthington Company catalogue (1916:250).

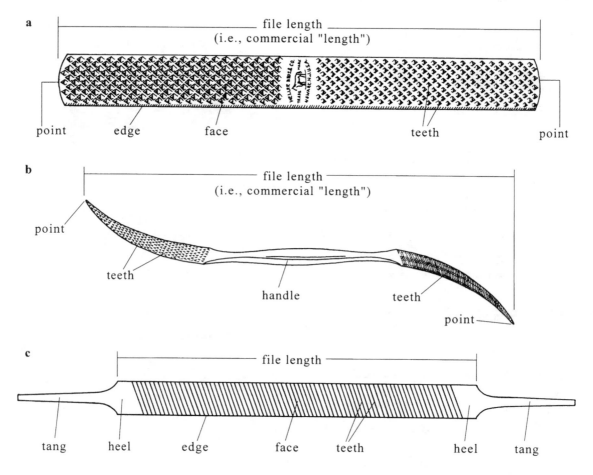

FIGURE 3. Metal file types: *a,* double-pointed rasp showing major attributes; *b,* self-handled, double-pointed file showing major attributes; *c,* double-handled file showing major attributes. (Drawing by Dorothea Larsen.)

a tang (also called a spike) intended for insertion into a socketed wooden handle (Figure 1*a*). Occasionally, socketed file blades were manufactured (Figure 1*c*), but this variation is exceedingly rare. Maker or factory marks were generally placed on or near the heel, either perpendicular or parallel to the file length. When placed parallel, marks generally occurred on the upper portion of the tang. This is the most common sort of file.

Double-pointed Files

Double-pointed files (Figure 3*a-b*) required no attached handle, thus no tang was present. Usually, such files were divided into two symmetrical portions with maker or factory marks placed in the center. Teeth on each portion were not always identical, and thus such files could serve dual purposes such as for roughing as well as for finishing. A typical file of this type is the farrier's horse rasp (Figure 3*a*).

Self-handled, Double-pointed Files

Self-handled, double-pointed files (Figure 3*b*) are generally known as rifflers or riffler files and rasps. As a rule, opposing ends of such files had totally different teeth configurations, and were thus intended as dual purpose tools. As with the double-pointed files, maker or factory marks were stamped in the center of the tool, in this case, on the handle. Files used by wood carvers were typically rifflers.

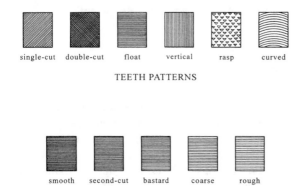

single-cut double-cut float vertical rasp curved

TEETH PATTERNS

smooth second-cut bastard coarse rough

TEETH SPACING GRADES

FIGURE 4. File teeth patterns and spacing grades. (Drawing by Dorothea Larsen.)

Double-handled Files

Double-handled files (Figure 3c) came either with two self-handles or with two tangs for socketed wooden handles. Such files were generally homemade, and were rarely stamped with a maker's mark. Designed as two-man files, they were commonly quite long, reaching a length of up to 4 ft. (1.2 m), and were "occasionally found in wheelwright's and coachsmith's workshops" where they were used to file hot metal (Salaman 1975:390).

Attributes

In addition to having one or more working faces and multiple cutting teeth, there may be additional attributes present on files. These attributes include: one or more edges with or without teeth (so that one may file into a corner or a dovetail without affecting one edge) a heel and tang (on single-pointed files only), and one or two handles or points. Functionally, the most important attributes of a file are the configuration and spacing of its teeth, together with the shape and cross section of its faces.

Teeth Configurations

Teeth configurations on file faces consist of six basic patterns: single-cut, double-cut, float, vertical, rasp, and curved (Figure 4). Such configurations are the result of variations in tooth types (continuous ridge vs. discrete barbs),

tooth angles (diagonal, horizontal, vertical, or curved) and presence or absence of overlapping teeth (single-cut vs. double-cut). Size of teeth vary according to both the spacing between individual teeth and the depth to which each tooth has been cut. The decline of hand manufacture and the advent of mechanization, though it did not cut down on the number of styles offered for sale by the industry, did cut down on the minute eccentricities which one may encounter in a close examination of spacing or depth or angle of cut. These differences should enable one to determine whether a file is machine- or hand-made, although file cutters were highly skilled and this can often be difficult to detect. Nevertheless, despite the idiosyncratic nature of hand-made tools, various grades of tooth size were historically acknowledged. There were at least five major grades recognized: smooth, second-cut or middle, bastard, coarse, and rough (Figure 4). Occasionally, a finer grade, known as dead or dead smooth, was utilized, but its use was rare because emery and tripoli or crocus took over from files as fine abrasives. Determining exact historical sizes for archaeological files is currently impossible, but relative sizes can be inferred by matching specimens with known historical illustrations. Sizes determined by this method, however, must be considered somewhat inaccurate. Blending various combinations of teeth patterns and spacing grades produced a wide variety of styles which were referred to by such descriptive terms as single-cut bastard, double-cut smooth, rasp coarse, etc. (Figure 5). When such styles were combined with file shapes and cross sections, the resulting product was a distinctive file type.

File-Blade Shapes

File-blade shapes were extremely variable, and no consistent classification system has yet been recognized. Numerous catalogues and mechanical dictionaries contain file classifications, but there are usually slight disagreements between them (Chambers 1738; Smith 1816; Ure 1848; Tomlinson 1854; Knight 1867; Orr and Lockett Hardware Company 1898; J. H. Ashdown Hardware Company 1904; Wood, Vallance 1911; George Worthington 1916; Smith 1916; Simonds Canada Saw Company 1952; Roberts 1976;

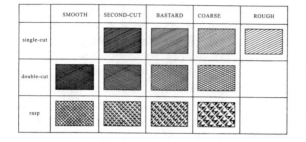

FIGURE 5. File teeth styles. (Drawing by Dorothea Larsen.)

Lee Valley Tools 1986). Shapes historically identified as pillar, tapering, knife, etc., appear to have been defined by a polythetic set of attributes including face shape, cross section, relative length, and teeth configurations. Presently, face shapes cannot be adequately defined by referencing historical terminology. Apparently, shape definitions would only be possible through exhaustive research into shape variability, and such research has not been undertaken. Presently, the only method for recording face shapes is the complete description of file attribute variations: parallel-edged faces; slightly tapering edges; face formed with one straight and one curved edge; etc. Somewhat similar in its difficulty to be classified is a file's cross section (Tomlinson 1854:640-642; Nicholson File Co. 1878).

File-Blade Cross Sections

Historical terms for file cross sections are relatively common, but they vary and no exhaustive classification system has been recognized. Styles of cross section have been defined (Figure 6), but their historical usage has been somewhat inconsistent.

In order to create a distinctive file style, the manufacturer had to combine all the attributes mentioned above into a single tool. The total possible number of styles which could have been produced is extremely high, and no extensive research has been completed on the number of styles known historically or archaeologically, although it is highly probable that before the industrial revolution, the variation in styles was more limited than after.

Historical Archaeological Interpretations

Historical Varieties

SHAPE

Stylistic variations for files were exceedingly numerous because they were often designed for very specific tasks. Among the more common names applied to files were the terms burnishers, files, floats, rasps, rifflers, and steels. Examples of a few of the terminological and stylistic variations within these groups are shown in Figures 2, 7-8.

Unusual or odd shapes can often be ascribed to a particular trade or function, whereas the more common shapes tended to be used freely for handiwork or other assorted purposes and by separate trades.

SIZES

Files were customarily sold by length. For single-pointed files, length implied the length of the working face, whereas for double-pointed

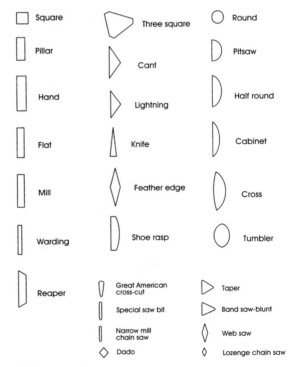

FIGURE 6. File blade cross sections. (Drawing by Dorothea Larsen.)

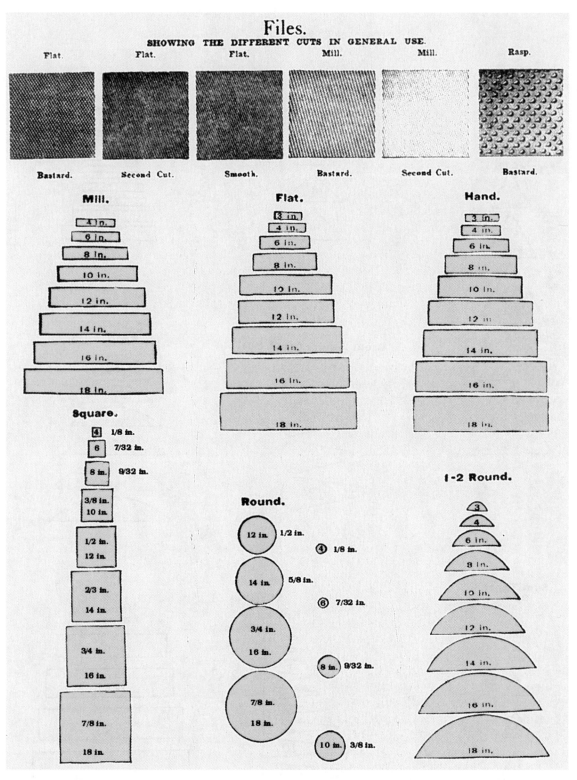

FIGURE 7. File teeth patterns, cross sections and sizes in The George Worthington Company catalogue (1916:242).

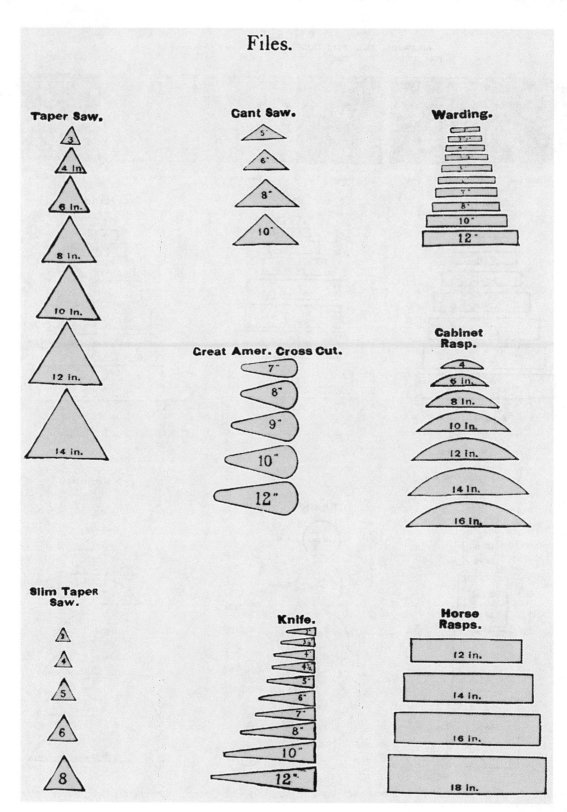

FIGURE 8. Additional file cross sections and sizes in The George Worthington Company catalogue (1916:243).

files, length implied the total file length. The more common sizes ranged between 3 and 20 in. (7.5 and 51 cm), but larger sizes were also manufactured. Occasionally, extremely large files were sold according to their weight. A large blacksmith's rubber might be denoted as an 84 lb. (2.4 kg) file. Generally, larger files are coarser, and are therefore intended for rougher jobs.

File-Blade Use

Every archaeological assemblage is unique, so it is difficult to discuss the question of file-blade use without pre-judging a particular collection, but some suggestions may be made without presupposition. Some idea of the probable specific uses of individual sizes, forms, etc., may be gained from Nicholson File Company (1956) and Salaman (1975), even though they are nearly contemporary works. This is because the nature of the tool itself, and hence the job which it is capable of performing, has not changed in many centuries.

The problem faced by archaeologists is to identify, if possible, how the files in a site assemblage were used. In many cases this may not be possible. Nevertheless, context may provide important, and even definitive, clues. The presence of a warding file in a general smithy along with a key blank and several smaller bits of lock hardware, for example, is convincing evidence that locksmithing was a normal part of the activities of the smith (Light and Unglik 1987:18-20). A broken half round bastard file in the same context, however, reveals little; not because it was a useless tool, but because it was *too* useful, for there were a multitude of applications for which it could have been used.

Even negative information may be informative. Files are so useful, and therefore so common, that not to find them in an expected situation should raise comment. Not to find warding files in a locksmith's shop, or wood rasps in a carpenter's shop, should raise eyebrows. Not to find *any* files in a smithy would be *very* bizarre.

FILE-BLADE USE-WEAR

Normal file wear generally consisted of the gradual wearing down of the teeth, with such wear resulting in the flattening of each tooth through abrasion. Excessive usage resulted in the breakage of teeth, with single teeth generally being partially broken. Usually such breakage was exhibited as a line or space across the teeth. Files were manufactured of hard, brittle steel, thus excessive pressure or abnormal usage commonly resulted in blades snapping into two parts, or portions being broken off file points. When worn or broken files were no longer considered as suitably sharp, they were either used for a different task, discarded, recut, reconditioned, or reworked into other types of objects, the latter option being extremely common.

FILE-BLADE REUSE

Worn files can be reused in many ways. Their owners may assign them to new duties, as for example when a smith used his dull horse rasp (actually the coarse file portion) as a hot rasp (a blacksmith's term used to refer to the action of smoothing the end of a forging or workpiece while it is still hot) or when a file which could no longer cut metal was used on wood. It is also possible to recondition a file by cleaning it with a file card and immersing it in an acid bath. The process was usually not worth the effort, but it was common enough for the Nicholson File Co., in one of its publications (Nicholson File Co. 1878:79), to threaten litigation against anyone who reconditioned their files and resold them leaving the mark intact. Eventually, however, the file became useless and it had either to be discarded, recut, or reworked.

To re-cut a file, it must be annealed (softened), ground to remove the old teeth, re-cut, and tempered (hardened). There were companies which specialized in recutting files. After the material revolution in the steel industry following 1860, however, it became increasingly uneconomical to recut worn files, and it is no longer practiced. Re-cut files were sometimes marked as such.

FIGURE 9. Files reworked into combination tools: *a,* chisel/saw set; *b,* half-round file/chisel; *c,* rasp/hoof knife; *d,* bastard file/saw set. (Photograph by Rock Chan.)

Most commonly, files served as the raw material for new tools (Figure 9). Since files were manufactured from high-quality steels, they were highly regarded for reuse by local blacksmiths. The practice was ubiquitous, and virtually every archaeological assemblage from excavated smithies contains reworked files. Even after tool steel became readily available, the habit continued and is still prevalent today among the few remaining smiths. A worn file could be reforged into any number of other shapes, and once properly retempered, the metal could serve a wide variety of purposes. Known examples of reworked files include such tools as chisels, gouges, knives, scrapers, and hammers (Light 1991). Normally, such reworked tools can be detected by the presence of distorted and flattened file teeth, but another sign of such reworking is a discarded hot-cut tang. Such reworking should be noted as part of artifact discussions and descriptions.

Finally, there is a special case which requires comment. It sometimes happens that a user needs a file and another tool for a particular job. Rather than deal with two tools, he may have the file reworked into a combination tool (Figure 9) (Light 1991). For example, the file/saw set illustrated in Figure 9d allows the user both to sharpen and set saw teeth without putting down one tool in order to pick up another. These combination tools are uncommon but not rare.

Conclusion

As an important, readily recognizable class of artifacts containing a multitude of shapes and functions, files are virtually ubiquitous. It is frequently possible, either through its context or the tool itself, to discern the use of a file. It is highly desirable for archaeologists to be able to properly describe and interpret files because of their intelligibility, importance, diversity, and ubiquity. This work is intended to guide the way to this end.

REFERENCES

APPLETON AND CO.
  1851   *Appleton's Dictionary of Machines, Mechanics, Engine-work, and Engineering.* D. Appleton, New York, NY.

BIRINGUCCIO, VANNOCCIO
  1540   *Pirotechnia.* Venice. Reprinted 1959, M.I.T. Press, Cambridge, MA.

CHAMBERS, EPHRAIM
  1738   *Cyclopaedia: or, An Universal Dictionary of Arts and Sciences,* 2nd edition. Midwinter, Bettesworth, et al., London, England.

GEORGE WORTHINGTON COMPANY
  1916   Catalogue. George Worthington Company, Cleveland, OH.

J. H. ASHDOWN HARDWARE COMPANY
  1904   *Wholesale Hardware Catalogue.* J. H. Ashdown Hardware Company, Winnipeg, Ontario.

KARKLINS, KARLIS
  1983   Nottingham House: The Hudson's Bay Company in Athabasca, 1802-1806. Parks Canada, *History and Archaeology* 69:3-281. Ottawa, Ontario.

KNIGHT, EDWARD H.
  1867   *Knight's American Mechanical Dictionary.* Hurd and Houghton, New York, NY.

LEE VALLEY TOOLS LTD.
  1986   *File Catalogue 1986.* Lee Valley Tools Ltd., Ottawa, Ontario.

LIGHT, JOHN D.
  1991   Recycled Files. Parks Canada, *Research Bulletin* 285. Ottawa, Ontario.

LIGHT, JOHN D., AND HENRY UNGLIK
  1987   A Frontier Fur Trade Blacksmith Shop, 1796-1812, revised edition. Parks Canada, *Studies in Archaeology, Architecture and History.* Ottawa, Ontario.

LLOYD, G. I. H.
  1913   *The Cutlery Trades: An Historical Essay in the Economics of Small-scale Production.* Frank Cass, London, England. Reprinted 1968, Augustus M. Kelley, New York, NY.

MOXON, JOSEPH
  1703   *Mechanick Exercises: or the Doctrine of Handy-works.* Midwinter, London, England.

NICHOLSON FILE COMPANY
  1878   *A Treatise on Files and Rasps.* Nicholson File Company, Providence, RI. Reprinted 1983, The Early Industries Association, South Dartmouth, MA.
  1956   *File Filosophy and How to Get the Most Out of Files.* Nicholson File Company, Providence, RI.

ORR & LOCKETT HARDWARE COMPANY
  1898   *Catalogue of Mechanics' Tools.* Orr & Lockett Hardware Company, Chicago, IL. Reprinted 1975, Robin Hood Publications, Berkeley, CA.

ROBERTS, KENNETH D.
  1976   *Tools for the Trades and Crafts: An Eighteenth Century Pattern Book. R. Timmins and Sons, Birmingham.* Kenneth D. Roberts, Fitzwilliam, NH.

SALAMAN, R. A.
  1975   *Dictionary of Tools Used in the Woodworking and Allied Trades, ca. 1700-1970.* Allen and Unwin, London, England.

SIMONDS CANADA SAW COMPANY
  1952   American Pattern Files and Rasps [Catalogue]. Simonds Canada Saw Company, Montreal, Quebec.

SMITH, JOSEPH
  1816   *Explanation or Key, to the Various Manufactories of Sheffield, With Engravings of Each Article.* Reprinted 1975. The Early American Industries Association, South Burlington, VT.

SPON, E., AND F. N. SPON
  1898   *Spons' Mechanics' Own Book.* E. and F. N. Spon, London, England.

TOMLINSON, CHARLES (EDITOR)
  1854   *Cyclopaedia of Useful Arts.* James S. Virtue, London, England.

URE, ANDREW
  1864   *Dictionary of Arts, Manufactures, and Mines.* D. Appleton, New York, NY.

WOOD, VALLANCE, LTD.
  1911   *Wholesale Catalogue of Shelf and Heavy Hardware; Bar Iron and Steel; Cutlery; Guns; Ammunition; Fishing Tackle; Factory, Mill, Miners' and Lumbermen's Supplies.* Wood, Vallance, Toronto, Ontario.

LESTER A. ROSS
2667 GARFIELD STREET
EUGENE, OREGON 97405

JOHN LIGHT
MATERIAL CULTURE RESEARCH
ONTARIO SERVICE CENTRE
PARKS CANADA
1600 LIVERPOOL COURT
OTTAWA, ONTARIO K1A 0M5
CANADA

PHIL DUNNING

Composite Table Cutlery from 1700 to 1930

Introduction

The early manufacturing technology of steel table cutlery has been documented for many years (Ure 1849:385-386; Tomlinson 1854:480-488; Lloyd 1913; Himsworth 1953; Smithurst 1987). As well, there are several publications on fine quality cutlery of the 17th and 18th centuries in museums and private collections (Bailey 1927; Hayward 1957; Victoria and Albert Museum 1979). With few exceptions (Noël Hume 1969:177-180; Kidd 1972; Wade 1982; Moore 1995; Stone 1998), however, cheaper-quality cutlery has been largely ignored. Accordingly, this work focuses on the description (Figure 1) and dating of steel table cutlery with handles of less expensive materials (commonly called "composite cutlery") from ca. 1700, to the rise of stainless steel in the 1920s.

The dating of early examples of composite cutlery depends upon comparison with similar hallmarked silver pieces, pieces with known cutlers' marks, examples from datable archaeological contexts, and iconographic evidence. By the 19th century, trade catalogues, patent records, and mail-order catalogues help to fill out the picture.

Knives and forks with matching handles and steel blades and tines are extremely rare before the third quarter of the 17th century. By the 1660s, they could be found on the tables of the affluent, and handles were of costly materials such as silver, ivory, semiprecious stone, mother-of-pearl, or tortoise shell (Davis 1976:183, No. 196; Victoria and Albert Museum 1979:13, Nos. 40, 43). Extant examples usually have a ferrule of silver between the handle and the blade or tines (Figure 2). The tang is of either the rat-tail or through form (Figure 3).

By the early 18th century, the use of matching knives and forks had become more widespread,

and the major manufacturing centers of Sheffield and London were producing cutlery similar in form to their finer wares, but of less-expensive materials. For over 200 years, such cutlery was a popular alternative to silver, silver-plate, or better-quality steel. Recognizing that the old does not give way overnight to the new, it is possible to assign date ranges (with some overlap) to these pieces based on stylistic changes, innovations in manufacturing methods, and new handle materials.

1700-1740

The typical knives and forks of this period have handles of bone or wood. By far the most common form for the handle is the "pistol-grip," so called because the down-curved handle resembles the pistol handle of the period. This shape first appears in the late 17th century. Like better-quality cutlery, knives and forks have rat-tail or through tangs. In place of a silver ferrule, the bolster is heavier and forged as an integral part with the blade and tang (Figure 4).

Steel was more expensive than iron, thus knives of all qualities were made with a steel blade and an iron bolster and tang welded to it. This lapped join often forms a visible mark called a "thumbprint" at the base of the blade (Figure 5). The table knife has a blade with a strongly concave back, a bulbous tip, and convex edge which tapers to the bolster (Figure 4).

One recognizably Continental table knife form (Figure 6) is occasionally found on French-occupation sites in North America (Tremblay 1996:101, 111, Figure 23a, Figure 30b). The blade is narrow, tapering, and turns up at the tip, which is not bulbous like on English knives. The back of the blade has a low hump, and the bolster is very small. Both rat-tail and through tangs were used with this form. Blades of this type were made in cutlery centers all over Continental Europe. The shape appears by about 1700, and is found throughout the period of the French regime, until about 1760. Similar blades do not appear on English or American

Historical Archaeology, MCR 2000:32—45.
Permission to reprint required.

knives until the 1920s (below). Interestingly, one of the names given them at that time was the "French shape."

It should be noted that knives became stained from acidic foods, and were subject to regular and vigorous polishing and occasional sharpening. These processes can drastically modify the shape of the blade (Figure 7), making dating difficult and creating confusion between Continental and very worn English blades. As mentioned above, Continental blades normally have a very small bolster.

The fork has two long, straight or slightly curved tines and a rounded shoulder. The shank usually narrows to a waist and broadens again to meet the handle. Occasionally the shank is balustroid as in Figure 2, but weaker in form.

1720-1770

By the 1720s, the flat tang began to be used regularly on table cutlery alongside rat-tail and through tangs. Flat-tanged table knives have been found *very* occasionally on late 17th-century French sites (Faulkner and Faulkner 1987:243, Figure 8.18), but do not seem to be associated with English knives and forks until the introduction of the "hump-backed" blade (below). This tang (Figure 3) has the same profile as the complete handle, with two scales riveted to either side. This construction allowed

FIGURE 2. Set of small-size dessert cutlery with mother-of-pearl handles and silver ferrules, ca. 1700-1730. The knife is 19 cm long overall. Less-expensive cutlery followed the same forms with cheaper handle materials, no ferrule, and simplified shaping of the heavier bolster and shank. (Don Carpentier Collection.)

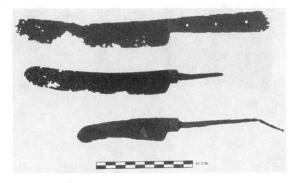

FIGURE 3. Table knives of the late 18th or 19th century. *Top*, flat, full or scale tang (scales would be pinned to either side of the tang); *center*, rat-tail tang (the tang is cemented and/or pinned into the handle); *bottom*, through tang (the tang passes through the length of the handle and is peened over a washer or butt cap).

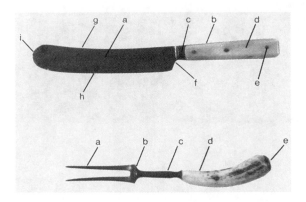

FIGURE 1. Knife terminology: *a,* blade; *b,* handle (in this case with a flat, full or scale tang); *c,* bolster (integral); *d,* scale; *e,* pin; *f,* choil or heel; *g,* blade back; *h,* blade edge; *i,* blade tip. Fork terminology: *a,* tines or prongs; *b,* shoulder; *c,* shank; *d,* handle (in this case with a rat-tail tang); *e,* butt cap.

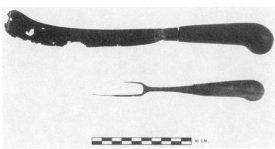

FIGURE 4. Knife and fork (non-matching) of forms and materials typical of ca. 1700-1740. The knife handle is of wood; the fork handle is of bone. Both are variations of the "pistol-grip" shape. (Fork: Colonial Williamsburg Collection.)

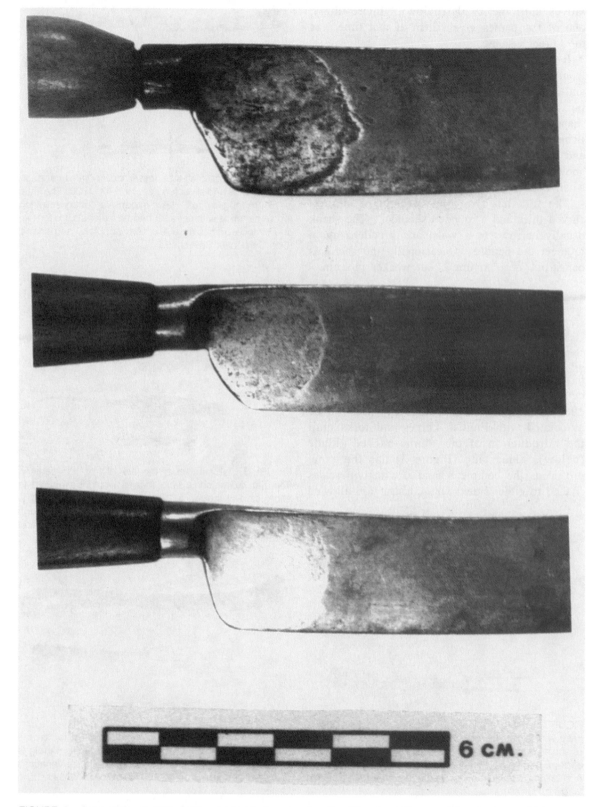

FIGURE 5. Late 18th- or 19th-century knife blades showing the "thumbprint" caused by the lap weld between the steel blade and the iron tang and bolster.

FIGURE 6. Continental European table knife blades, ca. 1700-1760. This form is found on French occupation sites in North America. *Top*, rat-tail tang; *bottom*, through tang.

smaller, thinner pieces of bone, wood or other material to be used with less wastage. Another shape of handle appeared with the new tang: it is wedge-shaped, tapering towards the blade. Bone handles of this form are frequently decorated with rather coarsely scored hatching or cross-hatching (Figure 8). The pistol-grip was also made with the flat tang (Figure 9). It, too, is sometimes heavily scored (Figure 10). Antler (called "stag" or "buck") was used both for scales on a flat tang and as the full handle with a rat-tail tang similar to the (later) fork in Figure 1 (Stone 1974:176, Figure 95*i*). Antler and bone may have the pith or marrow exposed on the end, thus handles often have an iron or, occasionally, a brass butt cap (Figure 11). These caps are attached with two pins which may be present even when the cap has been lost. Full handles of antler continued to be popular into the 20th century, and the attached cutlery must be dated by form and manufacturing methods. Bovine horn was also used. D. Gooking, for example, advertised "Maple, horn & buck haft Table Knives and Forks" in the *Boston News-*

FIGURE 8. Wedge-shaped handles of ca. 1720-1770 with coarsely scored bone scales.

Letter of 1 December 1748. Lighter-colored horn came from oxen and black horn from Indian water buffalo (Dyson 1936:12; Hardwick 1981:135-136). Wood, bone, ivory, and even bovine horn can present a similar and confusing appearance to the naked eye. Bone and ivory, for instance, may become stained brown from burial and resemble some dark, close-grained woods or horn. To add to the problem, bone was often polished to look like ivory, or carved and stained to imitate antler. The latter was called "sham buck" or "forbuck" (Dyson 1936:22). Until the introduction of new materials in the 19th century, the form of the handle is more important than the material for dating purposes.

During the 1720-1770 period, some knife blades acquired a hump on the back close to the bolster (Figure 9). This form is sometimes called "scimitar shaped" today (Noël Hume 1969:178), but the term can be confusing as historically it was used to describe a knife with

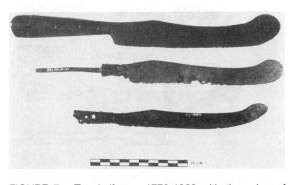

FIGURE 7. *Top*, knife ca. 1770-1820 with the edge of the blade showing minimal wear; *center,* contemporary knife with the edge heavily worn and the choil almost gone; *bottom*, knife so heavily worn that it is impossible to determine whether a choil was originally present.

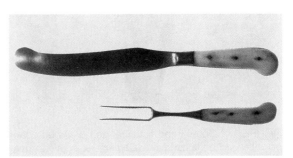

FIGURE 9. Knife and fork ca. 1720-1770 with flat tangs and bone scales in pistol-grip shape.

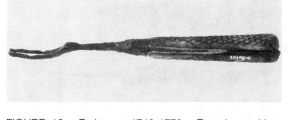

FIGURE 12.   Fork, ca. 1740-1770.   Two tines with a pronounced scoop to the rounded shoulder. The handle has a flat tang with scored bone scales.

FIGURE 10.   Heavy flat-tang pistol-grip handles ca. 1720-1770 with coarsely scored bone scales.

a simple concave back (Smith 1816; Gordon, MacKay & Co. 1913:389). The term "hump-backed" is used here as it is less prone to confusion.

The tines and shank of the fork continued in form much as they had since the beginning of the century. In the 1740s, however, some forks developed a pronounced scoop to the shoulder (Figure 12). Better-quality forks occasionally have three tines and more strongly modeled balustroid shanks.

1760-1800

Major changes in the forms of both knives and forks took place during the 1760-1800 period. Although the pistol-grip continued to be popular on silver cutlery, by the 1780s it was superseded by a variety of new shapes found on cheaper wares. The wedge-shaped handle became less broad at the butt with less of a taper towards the blade. The decorative scor-ing often found on these narrower scales was usually more complex and done with more care than previously (Figure 13). This decoration continued into the third quarter of the 19th century on English cutlery. The narrower wedge was also used on plain handles in bone, wood, ivory, and horn, all with rat-tail tangs (Figures 14, *top and center,* 20). A variation on the wedge-shape has the butt angled rather than straight across (Figure 14, *bottom*). The angled butt was popular until about 1820. Some rat-tail tangs were inserted into the hollow of partially intact metapodial bones of sheep which had been filled with resin or other composition. These were capped on the butt end, but the caps are frequently missing (Figure 15). By the late 1760s, green-stained handles became popular, both in ivory and bone (Figure 14, *bottom*).

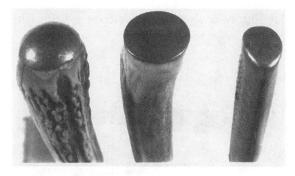

FIGURE 11.   Domed and flat steel and brass butt caps on antler and bone handles. (*Center,* Genevieve Duguay Collection).

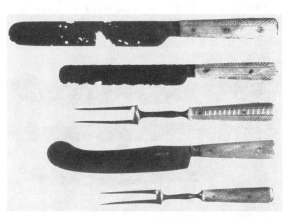

FIGURE 13. Scored decorations on bone scales typical of the late 18th and 19th centuries. The taper to the handle is not as pronounced as on earlier examples.

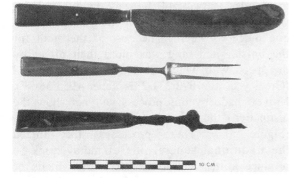

FIGURE 14. *Top and center,* late 18th- or 19th-century knife and fork with rat-tail tangs pinned to wedge-shaped wooden handles; *bottom,* fork ca. 1770-1820 with rat-tail tang and green-stained bone handle with angled butt.

FIGURE 16. Knife and fork with flat tangs and scales of pressed horn with elaborate decoration (late 18th to mid 19th century).

Bovine horn had for many years been decorated by heating and pressing pieces in molds with designs, producing small items such as snuff boxes and, occasionally, cutlery handles. By the end of the 18th century, there was a vast variety of pressed horn handles (Figure 16), and they stayed popular through to the middle of the 19th century. Better-quality knives sometimes had "balance handles." The hole drilled for the rat-tail tang was extended deep enough that a weight could be inserted to counterbalance the blade and prevent it from touching the table when set down (Figure 17). The balance handle continued to be used through the 19th century

(Russell and Erwin Manufacturing Company 1865:357).

During the 1760s, the knife blade developed a choil or heel at the bolster (Figure 18). By the 1780s, some knives had lost the hump-back so that the back and edge of the blade were parallel. By the end of the century, there was a choice of hump-backed, curved, or straight blades on table knives (Figure 19). Stamped marks (Figure 20) such as "BEST CAST STEEL" or "SHEAR STEEL" are found on blades from this period until well into the 19th century. These marks indicate the quality of steel from which the blade was made. Until the 1780s, table knives usually had fairly large blades, averaging 16-18 cm in length including the bolster (dessert knives and forks were smaller, but were

FIGURE 15. Knife and forks of the late 18th to mid 19th century with rat-tail tangs inserted into the hollow of partially intact metapodial bones of sheep which are filled with resin and the butts capped. *Top,* knife missing butt cap; *center,* fork with butt cap and pin inserted into resin to hold it; *bottom,* fork with resin exposed and tines worn short from cleaning.

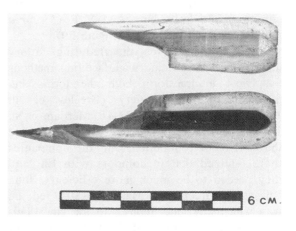

FIGURE 17. Balance handle of ivory with the counterweight still in place.

made with ferrules and lighter bolsters [Figure 2]). From the last decades of the 18th century through most of the 19th century, a much wider range of blade sizes was available, varying from about 12.5 cm up to 18 cm in length (Figures 13, 19). Of all the characteristics of knife blades, length is the least reliable for dating.

By about 1770, the shoulder of the fork became squared, retaining the scoop that had appeared a few decades earlier (Figure 12). At the same time, average-quality forks began to be made with three tines, which had previously been found only on fine cutlery (above). A choice of forks "With 2-3 or 4 Prongs" (Smith 1816) was available into the third quarter of the 19th century, when the two-tined fork finally lost favor (Figure 21).

1800-1850

With the exception of the hump-backed blade, which disappeared by about 1820, and the two-tined fork, the forms of knives and forks current at the end of the 18th century continued to be made in Sheffield late into the fourth quarter of the century (Silber and Flemming 1883:74-75; Harrod's Stores 1895:736-738). These forms were the products of a technology that had not changed in England since the 17th century (Ure 1849:385-386; Tomlinson 1854:480-488). English knife blades in the early part of this period were occasionally marked with the initials of the reigning monarch: G R for *Georgius Rex* (18th century to 1830) and W R for *William Rex* (1830-1837). By Queen Victoria's reign (1838-1901), the practice was much more common, and knives marked V R (*Victoria Regina*) are found regularly (Figure 20).

In the United States, the fledgling cutlery industry was introducing manufacturing methods that were to transform both the forms and materials of table cutlery (Greeley et al. 1872:229-238; Taber 1955:32-41; Merriam et al. 1976:8-30). Massachusetts and Connecticut were the centers of production, and the companies there realized that to compete with England they needed to be much more efficient. John Russell of Greenfield, Massachusetts, led the way with many innovations. In the late 1830s and 1840s, he introduced the trip-hammer for forging knives, steam power to augment water power, and a power press for cutting and shap-

ing blades. By 1844, he was making a knife with the blade, bolster, and tang forged from one piece of steel. The cost of the steel for the bolster and tang was more than offset by the speed with which the knives were produced (Greeley et al. 1872:231-232; Taber 1955:36-37). Knives made by this process will not show the distinctive "thumbprint" of joined steel and iron (Figure 5). These processes still utilized the traditional square rods of metal stock to produce knifes and forks. If a knife blade or fork tines and tang were stamped or rolled from sheet steel and a separate bolster attached or "applied," cutlery could be made even more cheaply. Proposals for this process were patented in the United States by 1838 (United States Patent Office 1838), and in England by 1840 (Great Britain, Patent Office 1857). The sheet steel of the period, however, was often too brittle or too weak for cutlery. It was not until the 1850s that the quality of sheet steel began to improve.

1850-1870

Experimentation with stamping and rolling processes for knives and knife blades continued through the 1850s and 1860s. During this period, many knives were still made with steel blades and iron bolsters and tangs, but the parts were formed by mechanized drop-hammers, rather than hand forged, before being welded together. Sheet steel forks were easier to make as they did not need to retain a sharp edge and were subject to less stress and wear than knives. Although table cutlery of sheet steel was being made in the 1850s, it did not account for a large share of the market. As is often the case with wars, the American Civil War (1861-1865) caused an acceleration in both technology and production methods. Much of the output of the New England cutlery makers, however, was directed to wartime needs such as bayonets and utility/butcher knives (Taber 1955:38-41). The cargo of the wrecked steamboat *Bertrand* illustrates this. This vessel sank on the Missouri River in 1865, on its way to the gold mining districts of Idaho and Montana with goods for the miners. Almost all of the butcher knives in the cargo (95 of 106) were made of sheet steel with an applied bolster patented in 1860 by Lamson and Goodnow of Massachusetts (below).

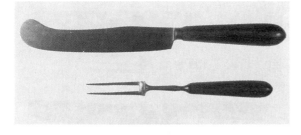

FIGURE 18. Knife and fork ca. 1770-1820. The knife blade retains the hump-back but has a choil or heel. The fork has a squared, scooped shoulder. Both have rat-tail tangs and plain wood handles.

FIGURE 20. English knife blades with stamped "W R" (1830-1837) and "V R" (1838-1901) marks.

The 69 table knives and 66 forks, however, were of English manufacture, produced using traditional methods (U.S. Department of the Interior, *Bertrand* Collection: catalogue. Nos. 156/1-57, 157/1-69, 2202/1-6, 2203/1, 2204/1, 2434/1).

Both war and post-war demands led to numerous patents for bolsters. Joseph Gardiner, an employee of the Lamson and Goodnow Company, invented a stamped bolster in 1860 that had several imitators over the next few years (Figure 22) (United States Patent Office 1860). The most successful form of applied bolster over the long term was the cast-on bolster of tin or tin alloy. A bolster of this type was patented by James Frary in 1866 (United States Patent Office 1866). The tang of the knife or fork was clamped in a mold, often with the scales

in place on the tang. The metal for the bolster was poured into the space left for it and flowed around the tang. The earlier examples with this bolster are fairly simple (Figure 23), sometimes with a butt cap made in the same way (Landers, Frary and Clark 1869:36-41). By the early 1880s, elaborate decoration was added by pressing or cutting designs into the wood scales which would be filled by the molten metal (Figure 24). This decoration was also used with bone scales. To prevent the scales from scorching, the metal used had to have a low melting point and the handles were cooled quickly.

The same principle of casting metal onto the steel tang was in use by 1869, to form the entire handle of cast-iron (Figure 25). These handles were usually japanned black to retard rusting

FIGURE 19. Table-knife blade shapes and lengths available at the end of the 18th century. *Top*, curved blade (with rat-tail-tang and wooden handle; 21 cm long overall); *center*, hump-backed blade (with flat tang and scored bone scales; 23 cm long overall); *bottom*, straight blade (with through tang and horn handle; 26 cm long overall).

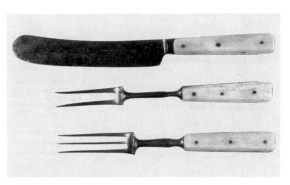

FIGURE 21. Knife with matching two- and three-tined forks with flat tangs and bone scales. Two-, three-, and four-tined forks were available with common cutlery starting in the late 18th century.

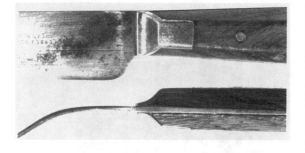

FIGURE 22. Cutlery made with Joseph Gardiner's 1860 patent (Lamson and Goodnow assignees). The bolster is of two separate pieces of stamped sheet steel, pinned onto the tang in the same way as the scales.

FIGURE 24. Knives and forks showing some of the many decorative patterns in cast-on tin alloy, ca. 1880-1920s. *Top*, with bone scales; *bottom,* with wooden scales.

(Landers, Frary and Clark 1869:33). This was some of the cheapest cutlery, and was priced in the same range as sheet-metal knives and forks with no bolsters at all (Figure 26). Cheap, bolsterless cutlery sometimes had a "half-tang" or "slot-tang." Instead of a full-sized flat tang with two scales, a half-length flat tang was inserted into a slot in a wood handle and held with two pins (Figure 26).

Another alternative to scale tangs was the hard or vulcanized rubber handle with a rat-tail tang (Figure 27). Charles Goodyear had discovered in 1839 that the addition of sulfur to natural rubber produced a strong, durable product (Hillman 1986:20). The John Russell Company tried this material in 1853, with little success (Taber 1955:38), but by the 1860s, rubber handles "warranted to stand hot water" (W. A. Currier 1862:7; Landers, Frary and Clark 1869:22) begin

to appear in catalogues.

The major rival to composite cutlery appeared in 1867. In that year, Matthew Chapman, an employee of the John Russell Company, patented table cutlery with the blade or tines and complete handle formed "from one piece of steel" (Figure 28) (United States Patent Office 1867). This solid-steel cutlery could be nickel- or silver-plated depending on the quality (Landers, Frary and Clark 1869:23). It would eventually eclipse earlier types and is the basis for most of the steel cutlery used today. It was many years, however, before it replaced all the competing technologies and forms.

Throughout the second half of the 19th century, England lagged behind the United States in the introduction of new technology. Labor in England was cheap, re-tooling and new machinery expensive, and the old system well

FIGURE 23. Sheet-steel forks. *Top*, with cast-on tin-alloy bolster; *center*, with cast-on bolster and butt plate; *bottom*, with scales missing and bolster and butt plate still attached.

FIGURE 25. Knife and fork of sheet steel with handles of cast iron, late 1860s-1910s. The knife retains the original japanning on the handle to retard rust.

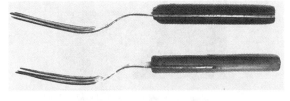

FIGURE 26. Inexpensive bolsterless sheet-steel forks. *Top,* with a flat tang and wooden scales; *bottom,* with a half-tang slotted into a wooden handle.

FIGURE 28. *Top and center,* solid-steel fork and knife made using Chapman's 1867 patent. This fork was offered as a set with the knife from the 1880s onward; *bottom,* this "non-matching" fork was sold as a set with the knife from the late 1860s and, occasionally, into the 1930s.

established (Grayson 1995:5-15, 57-58). For instance, forged knives and forks of English manufacture with handles of antler and buffalo horn (Figure 29) were still offered into the 20th century alongside newer types of cutlery (T. Eaton Co. 1901:157; Hudson's Bay Company 1910:178). It will be obvious from this work that if Sheffield had kept pace with New England in manufacturing methods, some cutlery could be much more closely dated.

1870-1890

This period saw the introduction of an important new handle material, and the increasing use of technologies developed from 1850 to 1870. Rubber handles continued to gain popularity in the 1870s, and by the 1880s, most catalogues carried them (F. A. Walker 1871:42; Francis T. Witte Hardware 1883:14; Merriam et al. 1976:83). The black-colored rubber had a precedent in the ebony and stained-black wood handles that had been made since the 18th century. Cast-on bolsters and butt caps on wood

and bone handles, mentioned above (Figure 24), developed a seemingly infinite variety of simple decorative motifs (Francis T. Witte Hardware 1883:11*a*-13*a*). Other types of applied bolsters for sheet-steel table cutlery disappeared from catalogues by the early 1880s. Bolsterless handles and handles of cast-iron continued to be used for the cheapest cutlery (Montgomery Ward Co. 1884:105).

Around 1870, separate inventors in England and the United States developed a semi-synthetic material based on cellulose (wood dust, linen, paper) and nitric and sulfuric acids. This new substance, cellulose nitrate, resembled ivory in color. It had many trade names including Celluloid, Xylonite, Zylonite, and Ivoride. Cutlery handles were one of the first products made from celluloid in 1872, and were being sold by the John Russell Company in that year (Greeley et al. 1872:235-236; Hillman 1986:21-22). Legal

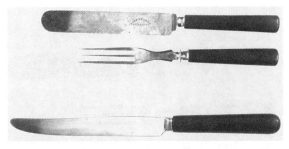

FIGURE 27. Cutlery with hard or vulcanized rubber handles. *Top and center,* knife and fork, 1860s-1910s, with handles impressed "GOODYEARS PATENT MAY 6. 1851". The knife blade is stamped "HARD RUBBER/CUTLERY Co"; *bottom,* knife with slipper-shaped stainless-steel blade, 1920s or 1930s.

FIGURE 29. Knife and forks with round, tapering horn handles and through tangs. *Top and center,* knife and fork of late-18th-century form and manufacturing methods, but possibly made in Sheffield into the 20th century; *bottom,* sheet-steel fork with cast-on bolster dating from the late 1860s through the 1910s.

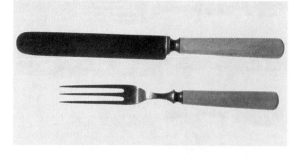

FIGURE 30. Cutlery with celluloid handles, 1880s-1930s.

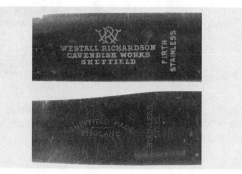

FIGURE 32. *Top*, stamped mark on a stainless-steel slipper-shaped knife blade, 1920s-1930s; *bottom*, etched mark on a blade of the same material and period.

restrictions, however, limited its use in the 1870s, and it is the 1880s before it becomes common as a handle material (Figure 30) (Francis T. Witte Hardware 1883:14; Hillman 1986:21). In 1883, a method was developed for graining celluloid so that it would better resemble ivory (Figure 31) (Hillman 1986:22).

Also in 1883, a method was patented for etching names and trademarks on knife blades (Figure 32) (Taber 1955:43). Previously names and devices were stamped into blades, and stamping continued to be used by many manufacturers into the 20th century.

The first solid-steel knives of the late 1860s and 1870s were paired with a fork which, to the modern eye, does not appear to match. These forks, often in the "fiddle" or "tipped" pattern (Figure 28), matched the spoons of the period and imitated pieces made by a silversmith rather than a cutler. By the 1880s, solid steel forks that matched the knife rather than the spoon began to appear in catalogues (Merriam et al. 1976:84). The earlier "non-matching" sets, however, continued to be offered by some suppliers well into the 20th century (Montgomery Ward 1926:550; J. H. Ashdown Hardware 1935 [insert of 1937]:C-13 to C-14).

1890-1920

With few exceptions, there is little change in cutlery during the 1890-1920 period. There was a slow increase in the number of synthetic handles being offered, and a gradual decrease in the number of curved knife blades. Even so, the same range of cutlery sold in the 1880s was still available.

From the mid-1890s to the 1910s, cast-iron handles were made with decorations in the casting (Figure 33) (Sears, Roebuck 1897:107; Gordon, MacKay 1910:381; Hudson's Bay Company 1910:178). Cast-iron handles generally disappeared from mail-order catalogues by the 1920s.

About 1900, another semi-synthetic material, made from milk extracts, appeared. This mate-

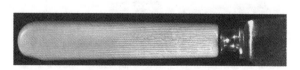

FIGURE 31. Celluloid handle showing graining patented in 1883 to more closely resemble ivory.

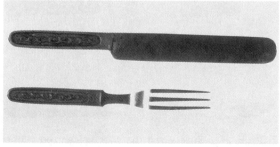

FIGURE 33. Sheet-steel knife and fork with decorated cast-iron handles of the mid-1890s to the 1910s.

FIGURE 34. Knives of stainless steel with celluloid handles, 1920s-1940s. The knife blades show variations on the "slipper" or "French" shape. The third knife from the top has a slip-on bolster.

rial, commonly called casein, was occasionally used for cutlery handles but was never as widespread as celluloid (Hillman 1986:24). Casein can be difficult to distinguish from celluloid without burning or chemical testing (Katz 1984:146-147).

1920-1930

Several steel alloys that would not rust or stain were developed from about 1910 to World War I. None of them worked well for cutlery, as they tended to be brittle and their manufacture required special equipment and new skills. During the war, the American and British governments took over the production of "stainless" steel for military purposes and, by the war's end, many of the technical problems had been overcome. Most manufacturers, however, still had to change equipment and methods to use the new alloys, and this was costly. As well, the public was suspicious of the new product. The new processes were imperfectly understood by many makers, thus the first post-war products tended to crack and split, and knives would not keep an edge (Taber 1955:47-48). As late as 1927, the same page of the Montgomery Ward (1926:550) catalogue was offering both nickel-plated steel cutlery and "bright, rust-resisting stainless steel." Through the 1920s, stainless steel gradually improved and gained favor. Trade names for the various alloys were

myriad: Norust, Nevastain, Rustproof, Unstainable, and Everclean are but a few (Grayson 1995:57-64).

Along with the new steel, a new blade shape appeared on table knives (Figures 27, 34). This tapering blade with a slightly humped back was called a "slipper" or "French" shape. It is the first of the modern shapes that we still use today. It was originally considered a steak or "meat" knife, and it is shown in catalogues with the standard straight and curved "table" or "dinner" knives (Daniel Low & Co. 1926:91; T. Eaton 1927:223). Within a few years, however, it had gained acceptance for table-knife duties as well.

Knives with stainless-steel slipper-shaped blades sometimes had a bolster that was made separately (Figure 34). These bolsters were slotted to slip over the bare tang and slide up to meet the blade. The handle would then be cemented or molded onto the tang. Such bolsters are found in various metals including tin alloy, nickel-plated brass, and steel. After World War I, aluminum alloys began to be used occasionally as handle material (Montgomery Ward 1922:525), but they were rarely advertised in the 1920s or 1930s.

By the late 1920s, composite cutlery held only a fraction of the market. Although a range of wood, bone, antler, and rubber handles could still be found, most mail-order catalogues offered several pages of inexpensive stamped nickel- and silver-plate compared to a page or less of composite knives and forks (Montgomery Ward 1926:416-419, 550; Sears, Roebuck 1927:754-761). Except for knives and forks with handles of celluloid and the first modern synthetic plastics such as Bakelite (Hillman 1986:24-26), composite table cutlery all but disappeared during the 1930s.

Conclusion

The main features for the dating of table cutlery in the 18th century are stylistic. Some knives acquired humped backs in the 1720s, and choils appeared in the 1760s. By the end of the century, several new blade forms had appeared. Forks acquired a square shoulder around 1770, and three-tined examples become more common about the same time. Little change occurred in the first half of the 19th century, but manufacturing methods being developed in the United States were to have a major impact. In the second half of the 19th century, the main changes were technological. Sheet-steel cutlery was introduced in the 1850s, and was common by the 1860s. Cast-on bolsters were introduced in the 1860s. Hard rubber handles became common at about the same time. Celluloid handles were introduced in the 1870s, and became common in the 1880s. All-steel cutlery was patented in 1867. In the 20th century, stainless steel and the slipper-shaped blade appeared after World War I.

Through all of this change, some cutlery continued to be made using older forms and manufacturing techniques. Although it is sometimes possible to put a *terminus post quem* on cutlery, it is often much more difficult to put a *terminus ante quem* on a style or technology.

REFERENCES

BAILEY, C. T. P.
 1927   *Knives and Forks: Selected and Described.* The Medici Society, London, England.

DANIEL LOW & CO.
 1926   *Year Book* [catalogue] for 1927. Boston, MA.

DAVIS, JOHN D.
 1976   *English Silver at Williamsburg.* Colonial Williamsburg Foundation, Williamsburg, VA.

DYSON, B. RONALD
 1936   *A Glossary of Words and Dialect Formerly Used in the Sheffield Trades.* Reprinted 1979, Sheffield Trades Historical Society, Sheffield, England.

F. A. WALKER & CO.
 1871   *Illustrated Supplement to Our Catalogue of 1871.* Boston, MA.

FAULKNER, ALARIC, AND GRETCHEN FEARON FAULKNER
 1987   *The French at Pentagoet, 1635-1674.* The Maine Historic Preservation Commission and The New Brunswick Museum, Augusta, ME.

FRANCIS T. WITTE HARDWARE CO.
 1883   *Hardware, Cutlery and Guns.* New York, NY.

GORDON, MACKAY & CO.
 1910   *General Catalogue.* Toronto, Ontario.
 1913   *General Catalogue.* Toronto, Ontario.

GRAYSON, RUTH, WITH KEN HAWLEY
 1995   *Knifemaking in Sheffield & The Hawley Collection.* Published for Sheffield Hallam University, PAVIC Publications, Sheffield, England.

GREAT BRITAIN, PATENT OFFICE
 1857   *Manufacture of Knives and Forks. Greaves' Specification. A.D. 1840, No. 8540.* George Eyre and William Spottiswoode, London, England.

GREELEY, HORACE, LEON CASE, EDWARD HOWLAND, JOHN B. GOUGH, PHILIP RIPLEY, F. P. PERKINS, J. B. LYMAN, ALBERT BRISBANE, AND REV. E. E. HALL
 1872   *The Great Industries of the United States.* J. B. Burr and Hyde, Hartford, CT.

HARDWICK, PAULA
 1981   *Discovering Horn.* Lutterworth Press, Guilford, Surrey, England.

HARROD'S STORES
 1895   *Price List, May, 1895.* Reprinted 1972 as *Victorian Shopping.* David and Charles, Newton Abbot, Devon, England.

HAYWARD, J. F.
 1957   *English Cutlery: Sixteenth to Eighteenth Century.* Victoria and Albert Museum, London, England.

HILLMAN, DAVID
 1986   A Short History of Early Consumer Plastics. *Journal of the International Institute for Conservation-Canadian Group* 10 and 11:20-27.

HIMSWORTH, J. B.
 1953   *The Story of Cutlery: From Flint to Stainless Steel.* Ernest Benn, London, England.

HUDSON'S BAY COMPANY
 1910   *Fall and Winter Catalogue 1910-1911.* Reprinted 1977, Watson and Dwyer, Winnipeg, Manitoba.

J. H. ASHDOWN HARDWARE CO. LIMITED
 1935   *Ashdown's General Catalog* (containing insert page dated July 1937). Winnipeg, Ontario.

KATZ, SYLVIA
 1984   *Classic Plastics.* Thames and Hudson, London, England.

KIDD, KENNETH E.
 1972   The Dating of Cutlery Objects for the Use of Archaeologists. Parks Canada, *Microfiche Report Series* 46. Ottawa, Ontario.

LANDERS, FRARY AND CLARK
 1869   *Illustrated Catalogue and Price List of Table Cutlery and Hardware.* New Britain, CT.

LLOYD, G. I. H.
 1913   *The Cutlery Trades: An Historical Essay in the Economics of Small-Scale Production.* Reprinted 1968, Augustus M. Kelley, New York, NY.

MERRIAM, ROBERT L., RICHARD A. DAVIS, JR., DAVID S. BROWN, AND MICHAEL E. BUERGER
 1976   *The History of the John Russell Cutlery Company 1833-1936.* Bete Press, Greenfield, MA.

MONTGOMERY WARD AND CO.
1884   *No. 35, Spring and Summer Catalogue 1884.* Chicago, IL.
1922   *Catalogue No. 97, Fall & Winter 1922-23.* Chicago, IL. Reprinted 1969, H. C. Publishers, New York, NY.
1926   *Catalogue No. 105, Fall and Winter 1926-27.* Baltimore, MD.

MOORE, SIMON
1995   Table Knives and Forks. *Shire Album* 320. Shire Publications, Buckinghamshire, England.

NOËL HUME, IVOR
1969   *A Guide to Artifacts of Colonial America.* Alfred A. Knopf, New York, NY.

RUSSELL AND ERWIN MANUFACTURING COMPANY
1865   *Illustrated Catalogue of American Hardware of the Russell and Erwin Manufacturing Company.* Reprinted 1980, Association for Preservation Technology, Ottawa, Ontario.

SEARS, ROEBUCK AND CO.
1897   *Consumers Guide, Catalogue No 104.* Chicago, IL. Reprinted 1968, Chelsea House, New York, NY.
1927   *1927 Fall and Winter Catalogue.* Chicago, IL. Reprinted 1970, Crown Publishers, New York, NY.

SILBER AND FLEMMING
1883   *The Illustrated Catalogue of Furniture and Household Requisites.* Reprinted 1991 as *The Victorian Catalogue of Household Goods.* Studio Editions, London, England.

SMITH, JOSEPH
1816   *Explanation or Key, to the Various Manufactures of Sheffield, with Engravings of Each Article.* Reprinted 1975, The Early American Industries Association, South Burlington, VT.

SMITHURST, PETER
1987   The Cutlery Industry. *Shire Album* 195. Shire Publications, Buckinghamshire, England.

STONE, LYLE M.
1974   Fort Michilimackinac, 1715-1781: An Archaeological Perspective on the Revolutionary Frontier. *Publications of the Museum, Michigan State University, Anthropological Series* 2. East Lansing.

STONE, ROBERT
1998   The Evolution of the Knife and Fork, 1500-1880. Paper presented at the 27th Annual Meeting of the Association for Living Historical Farms and Agricultural Museums, Waterloo, Ontario.

T. EATON CO.
1901   *Catalogue, Fall and Winter 1901-1902.* Reprinted 1970, Musson, Toronto, Ontario.
1927   *Catalogue, Spring and Summer 1927.* Reprinted 1971, Musson, Toronto, Ontario.

TABER, MARTHA VAN HOESEN
1955   *A History of the Cutlery Industry in the Connecticut Valley.* Department of History of Smith College, Northhampton, MA.

TOMLINSON, CHARLES (EDITOR)
1854   *Cyclopaedia of Useful Arts, Mechanical and Chemical, Manufactures, Mining and Engineering,* Volume 1. George Virtue, London, England.

TREMBLAY, YVES
1996   *Les Ustensiles, les objets de couture et le luminaire de Place-Royale.* Gouvernement du Québec, Québec.

UNITED STATES PATENT OFFICE
1838   *Mode of Making Table Knives and Forks, Letters Patent No. 737, George Ropes, May 10, 1838.* United States Patent Office, Washington, DC
1860   *Table Cutlery, Letters Patent No. 27,357, Joseph W. Gardner, March 6, 1860.* United States Patent Office, Washington, DC. [NB: The Lamson and Goodnow Company were the assignees of this patent.]
1866   *Improvement in Manufacture of Knives and Forks, Letters Patent No. 58,242, James D. Frary, September 25, 1866.* United States Patent Office, Washington, DC.
1867   *Improvement in Table Cutlery, Letters Patent No. 70,525, Matthew Chapman, November 5, 1867.* United States Patent Office, Washington, DC.

URE, ANDREW
1849   *A Dictionary of Arts, Manufactures and Mines.* D. Appleton, New York, NY.

VICTORIA AND ALBERT MUSEUM
1979   *Masterpieces of Cutlery and the Art of Eating.* Victoria and Albert Museum, London, England.

W. A. CURRIER
[1862] *Catalogue. W. A. Currier's Kitchen, House Furnishing and Stove Warehouse.* Haverhill, MA.

WADE, BARBARA J.
1982   Cutlery from the Fort at Coteau-du-Lac, Quebec. Parks Canada, *History and Archaeology* 61. Ottawa, Ontario

PHIL DUNNING
MATERIAL CULTURE RESEARCH
ONTARIO SERVICE CENTRE
PARKS CANADA
1600 LIVERPOOL COURT
OTTAWA, ONTARIO K1A 0M5
CANADA

PETER J. PRIESS

Historic Door Hardware

The Door

Doors come in a variety of forms, designs, and qualities but they all require two basic features: (1) a means of movement (opening and closing), and (2) a means of being secured (Figure 1a-e). Movement is achieved with some form of hinging device, while security is provided with a variety of different devices including hooks, bolts, latches, and locks.

The objective of this work is to consider the various categories of door hardware; define their basic characteristics of form, material, and manufacture; and present variations of form, design, or technology that may assist in identifying cultural affiliation or date. Attention is also given to items from an archaeological perspective where whole or undistorted objects are seldom the norm. The period covered is generally that of the European presence in North America with emphasis on the 18th and 19th centuries.

Hardware Research

Door hardware, as a component of building hardware, has attracted the interest of a small and varied group of 20th-century researchers. The results of this work have appeared in a variety of published and unpublished sources. Hence, an initial challenge is to determine what is already known about the subject through the work of others. A bibliography by Pruden (1974), followed by an annotated one by Priess (1978), were attempts to provide help for others who might venture into hardware research. The body of available literature has not grown substantially since that time.

The most extensive recent information on various categories of door hardware was provided by Donald Streeter in a series of articles published primarily by the Association for Preservation Technology (Streeter 1954, 1970, 1971, 1973a, 1973b, 1974a, 1974b, 1975a, 1975b, 1976, 1980,

1983). An earlier major effort was that of Sonn (1928), who recorded numerous examples of early building hardware and published an extensive group of illustrations. Other early investigators were Henry C. Mercer and Wallace Nutting. Mercer's area of activity was southeastern Pennsylvania where he documented early structures, collected architectural samples and hardware, and promoted the idea of hardware being a means of interpreting or dating early structures (Amsler 1989b). Nutting's (1921) interest was in the century after 1620, but his information is less detailed and we generally do not know details on provenience of an item (Schiffer et al. 1979).

One of the essential components of shared research is the consistent use of common terminology. There are several sources for building hardware to assist the endeavor. F. J. Butter has produced what is probably the most extensive documentation, beginning with a history of locks (Butter 1931), followed by a glossary (Butter 1948), and culminating in an extensive dictionary (Butter 1968). These are presented from a British perspective and thus differ on some questions such as handedness of doors (on which side do they open), but still provide the most extensive statements on building hardware. Other sources such as Towne (1904) or Eras (1957) have occasionally included more extensive glossaries. A glossary for door locks, using a variety of sources, has been published (Priess 1979) but in a series with only a limited circulation. The frequency with which building hardware is discussed in detail in archaeological reports has not yet forced the issue for consistent terminology.

Material and Manufacture

The predominant material for the manufacture of building hardware into the 19th century was wrought iron, though other materials, often brass, were occasionally used. The principal type of manufacture was hand forging, but casting was an occasional alternate manufacturing type.

Wrought iron is "a two-component metal consisting of high purity iron and iron silicate–a

Studies in Material Culture Research, 2000:46—95.
Permission to reprint required.

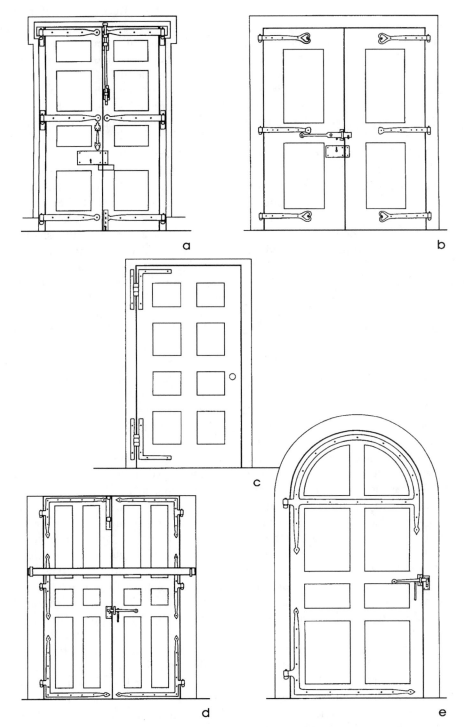

FIGURE 1. Examples of hardware on 18th-century doors: *a,* entrance doors of Independence Hall, Philadelphia, Pennsylvania; constructed 1732 (strap hinges with either driven or plate-mounted pintles, and a combination of sliding bolts, a rim lock, and a thumb latch); *b,* church in Tadoussac, Quebec (strap hinges with some reinforced pintles, and a combination of a rim lock and thumb latch); *c,* Pringle House, Charleston, South Carolina; constructed ca. 1765 (pair of HL hinges); *d,* center doors from Congregational Church, Little Haddam, Connecticut; constructed 1794 (strap and vertical strap hinges, designed to fit around door panels, and a combination of a thumb latch, sliding bolt, and a drop bar); *e,* side door of the Congregational Church (extended and supplemented strap hinges on a driven pintle, and a thumb latch). (After Sonn 1928[2]:Plates 129, 133-135.)

particular type of glass-like slag. The iron and the slag are in physical association, as contrasted to the chemical or alloy relationship that generally exists between the constituents of other metals" (Aston and Story 1939:1). Its advantages are that it resists corrosion, is easy to forge, and is readily forge welded (Aston and Story 1939:59, 65, 78; Gayle and Look 1980:42)

Hand forging involves a variety of techniques, often applied to the metal when hot, to alter the size, shape, and appearance of a piece of metal and, occasionally, to join it to other components to form an object. The end product can be as simple as a nail or as complex as a door lock. Although the techniques and products may be similar, hand forging can be done by an individual blacksmith working in a local community or by a group of smiths working in a manufacturing district producing items for export or trade. The products are basically the same.

A major characteristic of hand forging is the potential for flexibility in design and craftsmanship. Items produced locally can reflect local tastes and the ability of the local craftsman. The smith can produce anything within his capacity and anything that his customers may require. This can mean the rapid adoption of new styles or fashions as well as the perpetuation of previous styles. This can also mean the existence of poor workmanship if no other alternatives exist. Production in a factory setting will likely be less flexible, involving a larger number of smiths, producing for a larger market, probably producing more standardized forms, and possibly producing fewer variations of form. Consumer selection of hardware would be determined more by what was available (being produced) than by personal preference.

The nature of wrought iron also means that repairs or changes can be made locally. A broken or out-of-style item need not be discarded. Repairs can be made, an item can be modified to take on a new form, or it may simply serve as stock for a blacksmith to shape into an entirely different object. For archaeologists, a major consequence of this is that wrought iron objects are often relatively scarce in excavations.

Forged objects may show a variety of features which help to identify the techniques and process of production. Recognition of many of these is facilitated by corrosion which accentuates the fibrous nature of wrought iron. Forge-welded joints appear as an overlap of two layers of metal. Hammering to change the shape of the metal may be apparent as individual hammer blows, especially on the back of an object where the marks would not be visible when the object was in place. The usual objective for the exposed surfaces of an object would likely have been to make the metal relatively smooth. In an item of wrought iron which has been hammered into shape, the fibers of the metal will follow the shape of the object because they have been deformed to accomplish the shape rather than being cut. A wrought-iron object shaped by machine cutting will have its fibers parallel and running off the edge of the object where they have been cut. Holes in forged objects are often punched rather than drilled. These are recognizable by the deformation of the metal around the hole. The punching operation will drag the metal and produce a raised ridge around the hole on one side. Hand riveting is likely to produce a surface similar to a rose-head nail: a number of facets representing a number of individual hammer blows. Machine riveting, on the other hand, will be smoother and more regular; the riveted surface possibly being completely smooth or having a regular pattern repeated from one example to another.

Casting was initially an infrequent alternate method for producing door hardware. The material could be brass or iron. The use of cast iron had begun by the latter part of the 18th century. Casting involves pouring molten metal into a form to produce the required shape of an object. The cast form can be finished subsequently by drilling, filing, polishing, or other procedures to create the final product. Cast iron is too brittle to be shaped by many of the procedures of hand forging. Neither can it be heated and hammered into another shape, nor forge welded to other components. A broken item of cast iron often cannot be repaired. Items of cast brass are formed by similar processes with some greater flexibility for the final product. Casting is also a process which cannot be as readily carried out locally. Although brass can be melted in a blacksmith's forge fire and, thus, cast into usable objects at a local level, this is not possible with iron.

Cast-iron objects, unless they can be repaired by a few available techniques such as riveting, become discards once broken.

Cast brass may have been used for lock housings and occasionally for other items. Brass can be highly polished and it could have been seen as aesthetically more attractive. Brass is also a non-sparking material and its use in some contexts, such as in areas of gunpowder storage, however, may have been preferable, if not essential. An all-brass door lock or hinge is likely to indicate a special context rather than simply a wish to have a more attractive item. With the increased use of cast iron in the 19th century, brass also became a more common material for the manufacture of some components of lock mechanisms.

Hardware–which at the beginning of European settlement in North America was virtually all hand forged of wrought iron–underwent a number of changes in material and technology from that time until the end of the 19th century. Advances in metal technology in the 18th century allowed a greater use of cast iron. The introduction of rolled plate (shaped by rollers rather than by hand hammering) around the end of the 18th century resulted in changes in the appearance or style of some objects. Mechanization of manufacture during the 19th century resulted in the machine manufacture of many items, the standardization of shapes and sizes, and the reduction of peripheral finishing techniques such as thinning and beveling. Machine or mass production often seems to have emphasized speed at the expense of appearance. Techniques which had been applied in hand forging, partially to reduce the quantity of metal required to make an object, also resulted in objects with greater aesthetic appeal. Techniques to thin, taper, or bevel items were reduced or eliminated with the result that some objects took on a more-massive and less-appealing appearance. Cheaper raw materials became increasingly available as the methods of producing rolled-sheet and bar iron improved, creating a change in the cost relationship between material and labor. "Technically, smiths became less frugal in their use of iron, and work became heavier, with less labour expended to reduce sizes to earlier dimensions" (Streeter 1983:2).

As Sonn (1928[1]:9, 11) has indicated, "there is little if anything in the field of American wrought iron that one might justly claim as being distinctly indigenous or novel in design and execution . . . early American wrought iron is therefore . . . a mixture largely British in character because British colonists generally predominated, but with a dash of the French, Italian, Spanish, Dutch, and German." The hardware of any specific area would depend on the nature of its cultural background, the mixture of cultures, the level of dominance by any one of them, and the level of persistence of the non-English component. Extensive recording and analysis of regional styles has yet to be carried out.

The change in hardware styles through time in North America has also been characterized as a transition from the conspicuous to the concealed (Amsler 1989a). Surface-mounted items provided opportunity and incentive for ornamentation, as well as matching design to a specific application (Figure 1d-e). By the end of the 19th century, however, hinges had virtually disappeared from view and door locks were soon to follow. Both items were relegated to the door edge where they could only be seen when the door was open. Ornamentation continued to be included on some cast hinges, even appearing on areas which would not be visible once the hinges were attached. Although the lock itself disappeared from view, reference to early 20th-century sources will readily demonstrate the extensive effort applied to the ornamentation of such lock accessories as knobs, handles, and back plates (Towne 1904; Sargent 1910). Opportunities for the visible ornamentation of hinges became virtually nonexistent except for the persistence of surface-mounted items in special, public, or monumental circumstances.

Door Hardware Categories

According to tradition, a considerable amount of various sorts of hardware was turned out by individual craftsmen who worked at their own forges in different localities. This usage may largely account for the broad diversity of forms in which certain articles appear. Owing to their general lack of similarity, it is somewhat difficult to make coherent groups of the types of latches, hinges and other products, and the classification can be accomplished only in a broad way (Kelly 1924:197).

Any attempt to offer an overview of door hardware must first acknowledge the enormity of the task and the impossibility of providing anything more than a general overview. For much of the period in question, hand-forged items could be (and often were) produced by local craftsmen responding to a range of local conditions including their own ability or lack of it, the availability of suitable materials, local tastes and preferences, and the acceptable range of creativity. Variations of form and size are possible and likely, especially for public or other substantial buildings. Any attempt to describe or illustrate the total range of any hardware category will only last until the next collection is evaluated and new forms are found. Hence, the descriptions which follow attempt to provide general information on hardware groups based on function and general similarity of form. The assessment of specific collections will still have to rely on descriptions of items which belong to, but do not match, any other items in the same category.

Hinging

Movement of a door is accomplished through the use of hinges. Although it is possible to make a hinge from wood, leather, or other flexible materials, these are not as likely to survive in an archaeological context. They are also likely to be of a simple and basic form, providing little or no substantial information concerning their age or cultural affiliation. Their presence likely implies a makeshift application or limited economics.

A hinge is any device which allows a door to open and close. It has to consist of two basic components; one immovable and attached to the door frame, and another movable and attached to the door. There must also be a joint, a means of connecting the two components and allowing them to move relative to one another. The movement of a door is always perpendicular to the line of the joint. In most cases the joint is vertical and the door moves in a horizontal plane. At least two hinges are required for the operation of a door. Each component, with the exception of pintles, can be referred to as a leaf or flap (Butter 1968:20).

With the exception of a strap hinge, the joint of a hinge consists of two or more loops or "knuckles" (Butter 1968:154) joined by a pin or other system. A hinge can be characterized in terms of the number of knuckles in a complete joint (the knuckles are designated as "parts" and the hinge is described as a 2-part or 3-part, for example). All hinges using knuckles must also have some means of keeping the connecting pin in place. For some cast varieties, this can be accomplished by enclosing the pin completely within the metal. For others, the pin can be (1) riveted at each end, producing a "fast joint" (Russell and Erwin 1865:116), in which case the pin cannot be removed from the joint; (2) held fast in one of the knuckles; or (3) equipped with an enlarged upper end or finial to prevent it from falling out of the joint.

If the pin is riveted into place, the door cannot be removed from its frame without detaching one side of the hinge. Otherwise, the pin can be removed to divide the hinge into two separate leaves. Two-part hinges can also work like a strap hinge and pintle with one leaf being lifted off the other, thus allowing a door to be removed without detaching any part of the hinges. Hinges of this nature have the pin attached permanently in the lower knuckle and are designated as "lift off" (Butter 1968:161), "heave off" (Peabody Essex Museum, Philips Library [hereafter PEM], Volume 2), or "loose joint" (Sargent 1910:517).

Hinges are either mounted on the surface or the edge of a door and the two parts may be symmetrical or not. Surface-mounted hinges are divided into a number of categories based on form. Edge-mounted hinges are considered within the butt-hinge category.

SURFACE MOUNTED HINGES

Early hinges in North America were predominantly, if not exclusively, surface-mounted types, and appeared in a wide variety of sizes and shapes. On a relatively simplistic level, the major categories or subdivisions (based on general similarities of form and mechanism and, where possible, on historical sources) are strap hinges, double-strap hinges, T-strap hinges, and H-type hinges. These categories may differ somewhat from what others have used but represent an attempt to organize a variety of forms into a small number of groups. The analysis of actual hinges in a collection may still require descriptions or illustrations of specific items to illuminate their similarity to and divergence from the common forms.

STRAP HINGES

The hinges of monumental doors served not only to permit them to swing open and to close, but were a precious means of assembly for the woodwork which frequently consisted of parallel planks held together solely by the ironwork of the hinges. Even where doors were assembled in frames, the hinges were designed to cover the greater part of their surfaces, and their harmonious meanders were generally well studied, with the intention of reinforcing the framework of the doors. In many cases where the hinges themselves were considered insufficient, the smiths made separate pieces of iron, matching or complementing their decorations, and applied them on the doors in the places which needed added strength (Frank 1950:128-129).

A strap hinge consists of a metal strap which extends horizontally across a door and is anchored to the door frame by a pintle. Although it may be more appropriate to designate them as horizontal-strap hinges, to differentiate them from vertical-strap hinges, the more traditional designation of strap hinge is retained here. Their history in North America extends from the beginning of European settlement to the present. They were mostly forged from wrought iron for much of this period. During the 19th century, however, manufacture shifted to machine or mass-production methods, initially using wrought iron and then steel. Strap hinges can be defined in terms of their basic form, but there is considerable variety in shape and size.

A basic requirement of a strap hinge is for it to be relatively long and narrow and oriented horizontally on the door (Figures 2-3). It must have a vertical socket at one end to accommodate the pintle. They can be characterized in terms of the extent of taper from the socket to the end, the nature of the end finish (the presence and form of an ornamental finial or other termination), the presence of thinning toward the finial, the presence of beveling on the edges, the nature of socket manufacture, and

the length of the socket relative to the widest part of the strap.

Strap hinges are generally straight and often taper from the socket to a decorative finial (Figure 2a, d-f). The length of the socket is usually the same as the maximum width of the strap (Figure 2a, d-f). The strap will have a number of holes along its length, including one in the finial, to permit attachment to the door. Attachment could have been either with nails, bolts, or rivets and, when they became more readily available, screws. The major stress on a hinge is near the socket; hence fasteners may be concentrated toward this end and the hinge can be tapered and thinned toward the finial. This also results in a saving of material and produces an object of greater aesthetic appeal. The strap may infrequently have a widening near the socket to provide an area for additional fastening holes (Figure 2b). Called a nailing plate, the widening is often rounded or diamond shaped.

The finial or end is usually a widening of the strap and can have a great variety of shapes (Figure 4). Simple finials may be circular, diamond, or spear shaped. On straps with less taper, if any, the end may be splayed into a fishtail or dovetail shape (Figure 4e-f).

Hand-forged strap hinges may be differentiated to some extent on the basis of cultural affiliation. Dunton (1972:10-12) suggests that English hinges are more likely to have a continuous taper from socket to finial, whereas French hinges frequently have what he calls "compound tapers" (a taper towards the socket as well as the finial, or an extensive untapered section between the socket and finial). It also appears that French hinges are more likely to have little or no taper, ending in a relatively simple splay (Figure 2e-f) (Duhamel du Monceau 1767:Plate 13). Nailing plates are generally considered to be associated with Dutch hinges (Sonn 1928[2]:Plates 137, 139, 140), although they also appear on French examples (Sonn 1928[2]:Plates 140-141). Hinges with widened sections near the socket but with no additional fastening holes appear to be from German contexts (Sonn 1928[2]:Plate 142; Streeter 1983:Figure 16). Finials appear in a variety of shapes. The simple splayed fishtail on an untapered or slightly tapered strap may more commonly be a French feature. A bifurcated

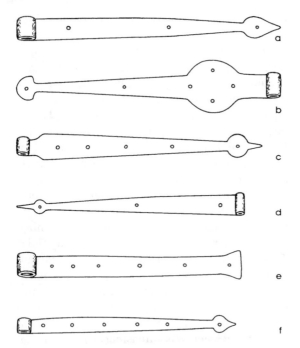

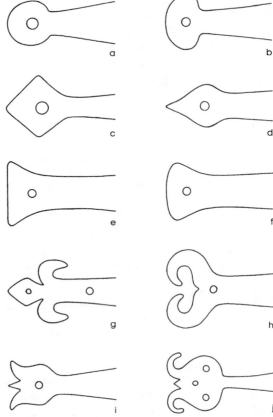

FIGURE 2. Forged strap hinges of the 17th and early 18th centuries: *a,* Bronck House, Greene County, NY, possibly late 17th century; *b,* Youmans House, Greene County, NY, possibly 17th century; *c,* Ensign John Sheldon House, Deerfield, MA, 1698; *d,* Pennsylvania hinge, early 17th century; *e-f,* Fortress of Louisbourg, Nova Scotia. (*a-d,* after Sonn 1928[2]:Plates 137-138; *e-f,* after Dunton 1972:Figures 1, 6.)

FIGURE 4. Common finials on hinge straps: *a,* round; *b,* bean; *c,* diamond; *d,* spear; *e,* splayed (squared end); *f,* splayed (rounded end); *g,* fleur-de-lis; *h,* bifurcate (the two ends can take on a variety of shapes or convolutions); *i-j,* tulip; both *e* and *f* can also be termed "fishtail" or "dovetail."

curved-scroll finial appears on a French hinge (Sonn 1928[2]:Plate 140), but is also known from 17th-century English examples (Alcock and Hall 1994:22). Circular or ovate finials are more commonly English (Sonn 1928[2]:10), while tulip finials are more frequently associated with Germanic contexts (Sonn 1928[2]:11).

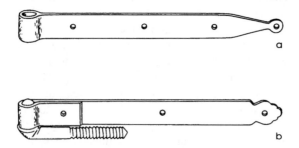

FIGURE 3. Examples of machine-made strap hinges of the 19th and early 20th centuries: *a,* "heavy welded hook hinge;"; *b,* "heavy wrought hook hinge" (*a,* after Russell and Erwin 1865:114; *b,* after Sargent 1910:877.)

Fleur-de-lis finials appear on both English and Continental European hinges (Sonn 1928[1]:74, [2]:Plates 145-146).

Changes in the 19th century–such as the introduction of mass production, the reduction of local hand forging, and a probable shift from the use of strap hinges on houses to outbuildings–resulted in a change in the form and quality of strap hinges. Hinges took on a bulkier appearance as tapering, thinning, and edge beveling received less emphasis. Rather than tapering for their full length, strap hinges tended to be untapered except for a short distance near the finial (the taper allowed for creation of the finial). Thinning and edge beveling appeared less frequently. Locally forged hinges for outbuildings might also be made from old

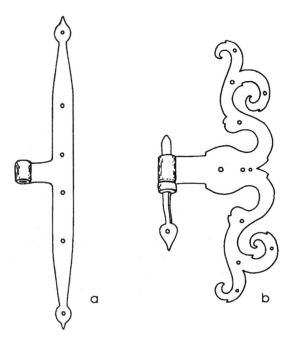

FIGURE 5. Vertical strap hinges: *a,* straight strap with spear finials; *b,* "ram's horn" form. (After Sonn 1928[2]:Plates 129, 177.)

by Sonn (1928[2]:Plates 175-184) and Streeter (1983:9), is at variance with Moxon (1703:22) and, therefore, is not considered appropriate.

A vertical strap hinge is one which pivots on a pintle and is primarily vertical, or parallel to the line of the pin (Figure 5). There is still a requirement for a short horizontal section for the socket. Some vertical strap hinges may consist of a simple straight strap, possibly with decorative finials (Figure 5*a*), but often they are in the form of two serpentine arms that diverge from a central point to form what is occasionally called a "ram's-horn" (Figure 5*b*) or "stag-horn" hinge or shape (Streeter 1983:Figure 14). This designation can be confusing since the hinge may have little resemblance to an actual ram's horn and may at times be made to look more like the cock's-head hinge discussed below or some other feature. A more generic approach would be to call such shapes "serpentine" with additional descriptive terms used, if necessary, to identify their more-specific form. Vertical strap hinges seem to be hand-forged types, and are more likely to appear in the 18th century or earlier.

COMBINATION STRAP HINGES

Some strap-hinge forms do not fit well into either the strap or vertical-strap category because they have parts oriented in several directions (Figure 6). For want of a better term, it is recommended that these be called combination strap hinges. Such hinges, most of which were probably hand forged, still functioned with a pintle. Because of the range of possible variations in shape, any description of them would have to note the general nature of the various components and their direction or relationship, as well as other information such as the nature of the taper, finial, or other ornamentation.

Combination strap hinges may have been created to provide additional support in specific contexts or to add aesthetic appeal. Sonn (1928[2]:Plates 129, 141, 187) illustrates a number of examples, including some intended for shutters (Sonn 1928[2]:Plate 187). One style is still listed in 1865, by Russell and Erwin (1865:114) as "rolled blind hinges." There are no styles listed for doors.

wagon tires, a readily available source of stock, with no attempt to eliminate the rounded edges or the fastening holes. An example of expediency in machine manufacture is a style in which flat stock is simply cut into the required length with one end shaped into a socket. The latter is not welded and the strap end simply has enough overlap with the hinge to allow the first fastening to pass through both layers of material (Figure 3*b*). The cutting may produce an ornamental end on the strap with the mirror image of this ornament appearing on the other end of the strap. There is no other ornamentation, such as a taper or beveling.

VERTICAL STRAP HINGES

Although strap hinges are primarily horizontal, some are vertical. There does not seem to be a good generic term for these hinges in the historical sources. Hence, the term "vertical strap," as suggested by Dunton (1972:13), is proposed here, but without being as all-encompassing as he would have it. The term "side hinge," as used

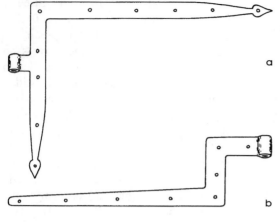

FIGURE 6. Combination strap hinges: *a,* from the center door of the Congregational Church, Little Haddam, Connecticut, 1794; *b,* from St. Paul's Chapel, New York City, 1766. (After Sonn 1928[2]:Plates 129, 141.)

MISCELLANEOUS STRAP HINGES

One occasionally encounters a hinge form that does not readily fit into any of the major strap-hinge categories or any others for that matter. One such (Figure 7), illustrated by Streeter (1983:Figure 12), cannot rightly be considered a strap hinge. It is included here, however, because it requires a pintle, one with a pointed pin. The hinge body consists of a hollow cone with a tapered shank which is driven into the door. The example is from a Spanish context in

San Juan, Puerto Rico, but Streeter (1983:Figure 12) notes that other examples also exist.

PINTLES

Strap hinges generally hang and pivot on a pintle, a pin (generally vertical) that is attached to the door frame. Pintles can be categorized by the method of manufacture or by the means of attachment.

Pintles are produced in one of two ways, and involve one or two pieces of metal. A one-piece pintle is produced from a single piece of metal; one end is forged into a circular pin and the other is formed into a device for attachment (Figure 8*a-d, i-j*). The pin and the attachment are usually at right angles to each other. A two-piece pintle has the pin as a separate piece

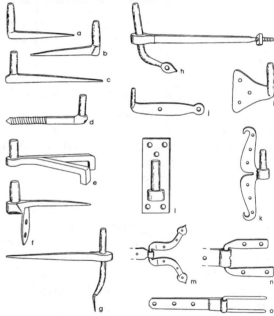

FIGURE 8. Pintle types: *a,* one-piece, driven; *b,* one-piece, driven with dent at heel; *c,* one-piece, driven with reinforced heel; *d,* one-piece, screwed, with additional support for hinge around pin, machine made; *e,* two-piece for masonry; *f,* two-piece, driven with reinforcing on shank; *g,* two-piece, driven with reinforcing on pin; *h,* two-piece, bolted; *i,* one-piece, plate (butterfly) type; *j,* one-piece strap type; *k,* two-piece, vertical strap (serpentine) type; *l,* two-piece, riveted through plate; *m-n,* surface-mounted staple type; *o,* driven-staple type. (*a-b, e-f, i, k,* after Dunton 1972:Figures 21, 24, 26, 27, 33; *c-d, g-h, j, l, n,* after Harris 1971:Figures 30, 37-40; *m,* after Sonn (1928[2]:Plate 147; *o,* after Russell and Erwin 1865:114.)

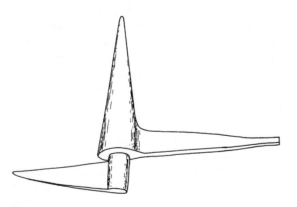

FIGURE 7. A conical hinge and pintle from a Spanish context. (After Streeter 1983:Figure 12.)

of metal set into a loop (Figure 8e-h, k-l). This type of construction provides a bearing surface for the hinge around the entire pin whereas in a one-piece pintle the bearing surface is only the relatively narrow section at the bend which connects the pin to the body.

The attachment of a pintle is either in the form of a shank or a plate. A shank is inserted into the frame; a plate is mounted on the surface. Pintles with shanks may be inserted into the frame in several different ways. In the most common, the shank tapers to a point and is driven in like a nail (Figure 8a-c, f-g).

In the 19th century, shanks were also threaded and screwed into pre-drilled holes (Figure 8d). If the back of the frame were accessible, a threaded shank could function like a bolt and be anchored with a nut (Figure 8h). A plain shank could be riveted or held in place with a tapered key.

In the case of stone and brick walls, the shanks are generally mortared into place. To help anchor them, the pintles are usually two-piece with the shank consisting of two arms with bent ends (Figure 8e).

Pintles with shanks are often reinforced, being supported by an arm below the shank. The reinforcement is usually a continuation of the pin (Figure 8g-h), but may also be forged from the shank (Figure 8f). When present, the reinforcement will likely be on a two-piece pintle with the pin continuing through the loop and ending in a finial similar to those on strap hinges (Figure 8g-h). The finial will have one or more fastening holes through it and be attached to the door frame below the pintle. The reinforcement provides additional support for large hinges or heavy doors, but may also be ornamental. Reinforced pintles seem to be more a product of hand-forging (no reinforced types are offered by Russell and Erwin [1865:113-114] in their catalogue).

Pintles attached to a surface are held in place with a mounting plate having holes for nails, screws or, possibly, bolts or rivets. The pintle may be of the one- or two-piece variety, and the plate may be rectangular, a vertical strap, dovetail shaped, or even imitate the strap shape of the hinge. Some types of surface-mounted pintles are of two-piece construction with the shank riveted through an additional mounting plate (Figure 8l).

In their 1865 catalogue, Russell and Erwin (1865:113-114) offer several pintle types. The majority are driven, but there are also plate-mounted, bolt, and screw types while the 1910 offering by Sargent & Company (1910:877, 879) includes only plate-mounted and screw types.

An alternative to a pintle exists in the form of a staple or loop. The associated hinges are still considered strap types because the joint consists of a socket and a pin rather than two or more knuckles held together by a pin. The staple may have tapered shanks and be driven into the door frame, or it may be perforated for surface attachment (Figure 8m-o). Such an arrangement is not easily disassembled since the hinge cannot be detached from the staple and, hence, the staple would have to be detached from the frame. Russell and Erwin (1865:114) offer such an item which is called a "scuttle door" hinge (Figure 8o).

The specific form of pintle used may be influenced by the amount of room available for its attachment. A driven, screwed, or bolted pintle is suited for a narrow frame, while a surface-mounted dovetail plate or strap requires more width.

One feature of pairs of pintles is that one pin may be slightly longer than the other. This allows each hinge to be aligned separately with its pin, one at a time, making it easier to rehang a door. Two pintles with pins of different lengths found together in an archaeological context could represent a pair.

DOUBLE-STRAP HINGES

A double-strap hinge is a surface-mounted hinge in which both sides are some form of strap (generally linear in nature). The term has no historical lineage and is suggested here as a means of differentiating such hinge forms from others and facilitating their description. Hinges considered within this category have generally been included in a "strap hinge" group (Russell and Erwin 1865:112; Sargent 1910:1133) or described as strap hinges with "side members" (Sonn 1928[2]:Plate 154). The hinge may be symmetrical or asymmetrical, depending on the nature of the two leaves. The joint, rather than being a socket and pin as for strap hinges, consists of two or more knuckles held together by a pin, forming a multiple-part joint.

In addition to describing a double-strap hinge as symmetrical (Figure 9*b-c*) or asymmetrical (Figure 9*a*) and describing the type of joint (2-part, 3-part, etc.), the attributes of the two leaves can be described using terms applied to strap hinges. This includes the nature and extent of tapering, thinning, and beveling, and the type of finial.

One form of double-strap hinge is the butterfly type (Figure 9*b*). Such hinges seem to have a more consistent shape, being symmetrical with each strap expanding towards a squared-off end. The ends may be slightly convex to impart a less-bulky appearance. Ornamentation may consist of beveled edges or notches filed into the end. Butterfly hinges do not seem to have persisted beyond the hand-forging era (they are not included in the Russell and Erwin [1865] catalogue).

An uncommon joint variant has a socket-and-loop arrangement; the proximal end of the moveable flap has been formed into a socket which encircles a loop on the strap or plate which is attached to the doorframe (Figure 9*d-f*). These have been designated as "wrapped" (Sonn 1928[2]:Plate 155; Streeter 1974b:Figure 5) or "loop pin" joints (Dunton 1972:37), but loop joint is the suggested terminology. The hinge socket for this type of joint is often substantially shorter than the maximum width of the hinge, the hinge having a sharply tapered section adjacent to the socket as well as a gradual taper toward the finial. Unfortunately, the attempt at categorization falls apart somewhat with loop-joint hinges. Some may consist of two symmetrical straps joined by a loop (Figure 9*d-e*), but there are others where the anchor side of the hinge is more like a plate or even a vertical strap (Figure 9*f*). The overall appearance is more like that of a T-strap or cross-garnet hinge, discussed below, but otherwise the hinge does not fit comfortably into the characterization of this hinge category. The options of including such hinges either with double-strap or cross-garnet hinges are equally awkward. It may be preferable to include hinges with a plate or vertical strap anchor and a loop joint in the double-strap category, recognizing that the multiple knuckle joint of a cross garnet would have been more difficult to produce and may have been used more for imported hinges rather than locally made ones.

As with the staple-type joint on a strap hinge, the loop joint cannot be disassembled and a door equipped with them could not be removed without detaching either the hinge or the anchor. Another feature of this joint is that it has considerable play and would likely be too loose for an entry door. It is a type more suited for a crate or trap door although large examples may have functioned on entry doors.

Hand-forged double-strap hinges are less common than strap hinges with pintles. The difference in the amount of effort required to

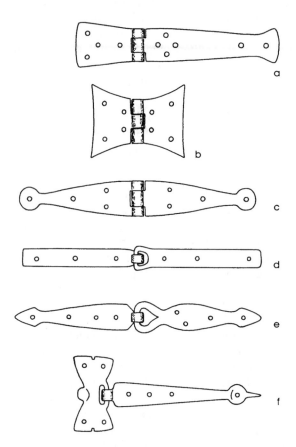

FIGURE 9. Double-strap hinges: *a*, asymmetrical strap, 3-part joint; *b*, symmetrical strap (butterfly), 3-part joint; *c*, symmetrical strap, 3-part joint; *d-e*, symmetrical strap, loop joint; *f*, asymmetrical strap (strap and plate), loop joint. (*a-b, e-f*, after Sonn 1928[2]:Plates 157, 159, 162; *c-d*, after Harris 1971:Figures 30-31.)

produce them may explain this situation. A double strap also requires a wider frame to accommodate the anchor side of the hinge, even if the anchor is the smaller flap. A symmetrical form with tapered straps and rounded ends is a common machine-made form for the post-1850 era (Russell and Erwin 1865:112).

A hinge may occasionally have more than one joint. In this case the main strap, attached to a door, is segmented, allowing the door to be folded into two or more narrower sections. This may be found on strap hinges but is more likely to appear on double-strap types, either symmetrical or asymmetrical.

T-STRAP OR CROSS GARNET HINGES

A T-strap or cross-garnet hinge has a horizontal strap attached to the door and a vertical strap attached to the doorframe, the two parts connected by a multiple-part joint. The term "cross garnet" has been used historically for a form of this hinge (Moxon 1703:18), but the origin of the designation is unclear. The vertical strap is called the "cross" (Moxon 1703:18). *The Builder's Dictionary* (1981) uses the term "garnets" for a hinge type but provides no further clarification. Butter (1968:41) provides a useful differentiation by limiting the term "cross garnet" to T-shaped hinges in which the joint is "shorter than the length of the vertical flap." Although historically such hinges have also been designated "T hinge" (PEM, Volume 16), Butter's definition will be used here to differentiate between the two major joint sizes.

A cross-garnet hinge may be seen as a combination of a strap hinge and an H-hinge although it is not the contention here that the form developed out of a combination of the two. In fact, it is more likely that the two forms existed side by side until the early 19th century. There are a number of differences which may have historical significance and indicate that the cross garnet had its own line of development. The horizontal strap leaf is similar to that of a strap hinge in that it has the potential for taper, thinning, edge bevel, and an ornamental finial. The finials are similar to what may appear on a strap hinge. The joint end of the horizontal strap is shaped into one or more knuckles which mesh with the knuckles of the vertical strap. For a

3-part joint, the horizontal strap will always have the central knuckle. For cross-garnet hinges, the central knuckle is considerably shorter than the width of the strap (Figure 10a-b). This relationship does not persist for T-strap hinge types (Figure 10c-d).

The vertical strap component is generally straight (untapered), much like one side of an H-hinge. The ends may have finials like a strap hinge or be ornamented, such as the foliate finials of an H-hinge (Streeter 1974b:Figure 2). The vertical strap usually lacks any ornamentation

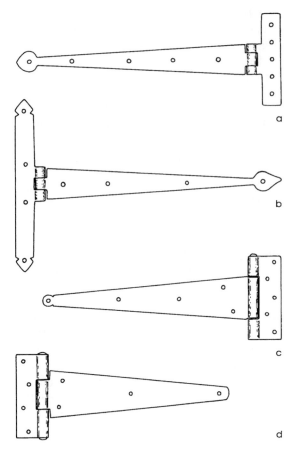

FIGURE 10. Cross-garnet and T-strap hinges: *a,* cross garnet with plain vertical strap, 3-part joint; *b,* cross garnet vertical strap with finials, 3-part joint; *c,* T-strap with plain vertical strap and minimal finial on horizontal strap; *d,* T-strap with plain strap ends. (*a,* after Sonn 1928[2]:Plate 156; *b,* after Streeter 1974b:Figure 4; *c,* after Russell and Erwin 1865:112; *d,* after Sargent 1910:1133.)

regardless of how the horizontal arm is finished, being simply squared at the ends (Figure 10*a*).

The cross-garnet hinge comes in a variety of sizes. The general indication is that smaller sizes may have been cut and shaped from sheeting or thin plate, but that the larger sizes were forged from flat stock. The joint on the horizontal arm is forged and cut from the same stock as the remainder of the arm. It has been noted, however, that the joint component on the vertical strap is often a separate piece of metal lapped with the strap and forge welded into position (Priess and Streeter 1974:24, 32-33). The knuckles would have been cut and filed to shape after the joint section had been welded, as described by Moxon (1703:20-21). This differs from H-hinges in which the joint always seems to have been formed from the same piece of metal as the remainder of the hinge.

The cross-garnet hinge has a lengthy history in North America and appears to be associated primarily with English contexts. Frank (1950:Plate 41) and d'Allemagne (1924:139) both illustrate hinges of similar form, some of which are presumed to be French, and which d'Allemagne dates to the 15th and 16th centuries. The general configuration is that of a cross garnet but the ornamentation consists of cut-out designs. Similar forms have not been recorded for North American contexts and it is questionable whether the cross garnet was used in French or other non-English contexts.

The 19th century saw the introduction of the machine-made T-strap hinge, one in which the joint extended the full length of the vertical strap. Technology for machine production of hinges was probably introduced by the 1840s. Martineau (1866:610-611) credits the invention to America but a patent was registered in Britain in 1836 (Great Britain, Office of the Commissioners of Patents for Inventions [hereafter GBO] 1873:18). The process involved cutting a blank with tabs or tongues which were then shaped into knuckles using dies. The ends of the tabs butted on the body of the hinge rather than being joined to it, as had been the case with forge welding. Machine production of a hinge is recognizable by the open joint for the knuckles. T-strap hinges, looking much as they do today, are illustrated in the 1865 catalogue of Russell and Erwin (Figure 10*c*). On these,

the horizontal strap is tapered, and they have an almost imperceptible circular finial. The vertical strap is equally unornamented and the hinge would likely have been intended more for outbuildings. Hinges made during the late 19th century should reflect the general shift from wrought iron to steel.

Both the cross-garnet and T-strap hinges are ideal where only a relatively narrow frame is available for attachment of the vertical strap. Depending on their size, these hinges could be applied to small cupboard doors, as well as to gates, larger room doors, and building doors. Plainer styles, especially those which were available toward the end of the 19th century, were probably more appropriate for outbuildings or gates.

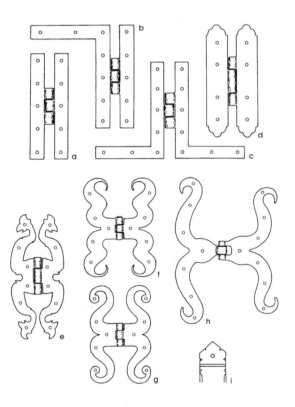

FIGURE 11. H-type hinges: *a*, H-hinge with plain ends; *b*, HL-hinge with plain ends; *c*, HLL-hinge with plain ends; *d*, H-hinge with ornamental ends; *e*, "cockshead" H-hinge; *f-g*, serpentine form of H-hinge; *h*, serpentine form of H-hinge with loop joint; *i*, common form of ornamentation. (After Sonn 1928[2]:Plates 164-165, 167, 169-170.)

H-TYPE HINGES

Shaped like the letter H when opened flat, the H-hinge consists of two vertical "straps" connected by a joint (Figure 11a). In most instances, the joint is separated from the vertical components by a short horizontal strap segment, allowing the hinge attachment to be slightly distanced from the edge of the door and frame. In terms of categories already discussed, an H-hinge could be considered a double vertical-strap hinge.

The HL variation differs only in having a horizontal extension at the end of one of the vertical straps (Figure 11b). This extension may provide an aesthetically more pleasing appearance, but probably also added strength to the door assembly. An uncommon variation is the HLL-hinge in which each flap has a horizontal extension, both at the same end of the hinge (Figure 11c). All such hinges are attached to the surface of a door.

H-type hinges appear to have been in use since the beginning of major European settlement in North America (the 16th or 17th century). Their origin is unknown, but in North America they seem to be associated primarily with the English. D'Allemagne (1924:Plate 139) illustrates several ornamented examples and attributes them to the 15th and 16th centuries. Frank (1950:129, Figure 173), in discussing early French ironwork, illustrates a similar form and considers it to have been "generally" used for room doors. Use of such hinges, however, may not have persisted in French contexts since they do not appear in either Duhamel du Monceau (1767) or the *Recueil de planches* (1764-1766).

Although the H-type hinge has a basic form which differentiates it from other hinges, there are many variations of form and size. The two leaves—except for the addition of horizontal extensions—are identical. Observations on a small number of examples also suggest that each side is made of a single T-shaped piece of metal. The end of the short horizontal strap is first rolled back to form the joint and then lapped and forge welded to the back of the hinge. It is likely that the gaps which allow the knuckles to mesh are cut out and filed to size at the end of this process. A similar process is described by Moxon (1703:19-22) for the manufacture of a cross garnet and other hinges.

Streeter (1973a:30, 33) notes the existence of examples in which the ends of the knuckles are butted on the hinge, rather than being lapped and welded. Iron H-type hinges commonly have 3-part joints; brass examples are illustrated with 5-part joints (PEM, Volume 6). There do not appear to be examples of H-hinges with loop joints.

Several sample books of the early 19th century (presumably English) illustrate brass HL-hinges from 8 to 12 in. (20 to 30 cm) in length (vertical measure), but also offer that they "may be had of any Size requir'd" (PEM, Volumes 6, 11). The horizontal extension of an HL requires a wide, flat surface for attachment, something not often available on a door frame. The double-L could be used on a folding door where a wide, flat surface would be available on both sides of the hinge joint.

H-type hinges also exhibit variation in ornamentation and shape. Ornamentation of the basic shape is often in the form of decorative ends, such as the foliate shape (Figure 11d), possibly created through forging but often likely created by filing (Figure 11i). If Moxon's (1703:18) description is typical of the production process, the hinge—complete with ornamentation—would be cut out of a sheet of metal and finished by filing. Streeter's (1973a:26) perspective is that decorative finials "did not persist much past the mid-18th century."

A more elaborate variation of the basic H-shape is the so-called "cockshead" hinge. Although it appears in a variety of shapes, the common feature is a serpentine shape to each side, often with a terminal resembling a cock's head (Figure 11e). A more generic description would be "serpentine," to indicate its sinuous nature (Figure 11f-h). The French designation, *à moustache* (Dubé 1991:Figures 31-32), provides a different perspective, but may be considered as equally generic.

Although the designation of this style as an H-hinge may not suit everyone, it is used here because of a basic similarity between the two. Both are usually symmetrical and composed of two vertical components connected by a much shorter joint section. The joint usually consists of two or more knuckles forming a continuous socket or tube for the pin which holds the two sides together. The pin is usually not attached to either side of the hinge except in the case of a 2-part lift-off joint where the pin has to be fixed in the lower knuckle.

The H-hinge and the cockshead variation appear widely among early North American building hardware. They probably continued in use until replaced by butt hinges during the late 18th and early 19th centuries. If the hinge material is identifiable, it would likely be wrought iron and show some evidence of hand manufacture (forging, filing, etc.). H-type hinges had a variety of applications, depending on their size. The smallest probably functioned on cupboards, but the larger ones may have been used for shutters or doors. A large shutter and a small door might require the same size hinges. Hence, the presence of only a hinge cannot be used as conclusive evidence for a particular type of closure (door or shutter,

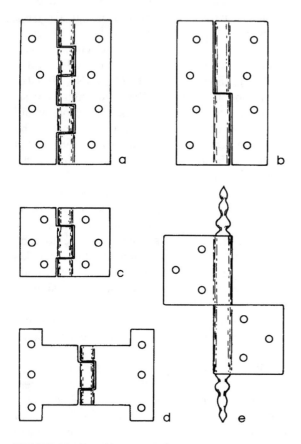

FIGURE 12. Butt hinges: *a,* "fast joint;" *b,* "loose joint" (2-part joint); *c,* "square butt;" *d,* "parliament hinge;" *e,* "French hinge." (*a-b,* after Sargent 1910:517; *c-e,* after PEM, Volumes 3, 12.)

room or cupboard door). The presence of brass examples is suggestive of quality as well as interior use.

BUTT HINGES

Hinges attached to the edge of a door and to the inside surface of the door frame are referred to as "butt" hinges. They are generally symmetrical, and relatively narrow to accommodate the thinness of the door. When opened flat, the hinge is either square or rectangular in outline (Figure 12*a-c*). The joint consists of two or more knuckles connected by a pin or some other device (a secret joint). Only the joint and possibly a small portion of the leaves are visible on a closed door. Although intended to be attached to a door edge, a butt hinge may also be used on the surface of a door and some hinge types of similar form are, in fact, intended to be used as surface hinges.

The origin of butt hinges is unclear. They are mentioned, without description, in *The Builder's Dictionary* (1734) and are illustrated in a major 18th-century French source: *Recueil de planches* (1764-1766:Plate 343, Figure 9). "Square butts" were offered for sale in Boston in 1756 and 1757 (Dow 1927:230-231). They may not have become popular, however, until a process for casting them in iron was developed during the latter part of the 18th century. The first patent for "casting hinges ready jointed, or with false knuckles or joints and pins, in cast iron" was registered in England in 1775 (Woodcroft 1854:297; GBO 1873:1). The wording of the patent suggests a process for a specific type of joint rather than a new process for producing hinges. Support for this perspective appears in an account of 1866, which explains that the patent was "for joining the two halves or flaps of the hinge in the casting, instead of casting them separately and fitting them together afterwards" (Kendrick 1866:103).

Streeter (1973a:47) discusses the advantage of casting hinges. He sees the process of producing the joint during casting as a major time and labor saver. The process would also allow the large-scale production of identical items, using a common pattern. Casting would have been the only practical method for producing butt hinges until the introduction of machinery to carry out the various cutting and shaping steps. The shift to butt hinges, however, may also have been due to a shift in taste, as suggested by Amsler (1989a:13-14), rather than simply a shift in technology.

Although it is not known when butt hinges were introduced, the appearance of cast-iron examples likely took place during the last quarter of the 18th century. Mercer (1924:178), Hommel (1944:3), and Streeter (1973a:43) all indicate that the use of cast-iron butts began in the United States shortly after the Revolutionary War. Cast-iron butt hinges appear in various English pattern books dating from around the beginning of the 19th century (PEM, Volume 3). Their use persists through the 19th century (Russell and Erwin 1865:116-117) and into the 20th century (Sargent 1910:518-520). Cast-brass examples were also available throughout the same period (Russell and Erwin 1865:117-118; Sargent 1910:524-528).

As discussed for T-strap hinges, the beginning of mechanized production of hinges, initially in wrought iron and brass and more recently in steel, seems to have begun during the second quarter of the 19th century.

Butt hinges are characterized by the number of knuckles in the joint (2-part, 3-part). Hinge dimensions, determined when the specimen is opened flat, are specified as length (parallel to the joint) and width (perpendicular to the joint). The length is often greater than the width.

Commercially produced butt hinges, those appearing in catalogues, are divided into three major categories based on width: narrow, broad (PEM, Volume 9; Russell and Erwin 1865:116), and intermediate (the latter usually has no specific designation but may be referred to as "middle width" [PEM, Volume 15]). Specimens in which the joint is half the hinge's width (each leaf is square) may be referred to as "square butts" (Figure 12c). Hinges with joints substantially shorter than the width were generally intended to be attached on the surface rather than on an edge and should not be designated as butt hinges, even though such hinges are grouped under the general category of butt hinges in some catalogues (Russell and Erwin 1865:115).

A special form of butt hinge is the "shutter" or "parliament" hinge. It is intended to be attached to an edge but is also similar to an H-hinge in its general shape (Figure 12d). Despite the H-shape, they should not be considered as H-hinges. The vertical component of each leaf is relatively narrow compared to the horizontal central section. Fastening holes are limited to the vertical components whose expanded ends provide additional space for them. This design is intended to move the joint away from the point of attachment so that a shutter or door will swing away from the frame and lie flat against the wall when completely opened. The fact that such an action is commonly required of a shutter may explain the designation "shutter hinges." The significance of the "parliament" designation is unknown.

Another special form of butt hinge, in use by the beginning of the 19th century (PEM, Volumes 3, 10, 12), is the "skew joint" or "rising" hinge. This has a 2-part joint in which the abutting surfaces of the two knuckles are at an oblique angle to the line of the joint. In turning, one side of the hinge moves up relative to the other, allowing a door to pass over a carpet or some other obstruction on the floor when opened. The door will also tend to close automatically if not held open (Butter 1968:225). The material of the hinge is thicker than that of other hinges because of the additional stress on the joint. Initially this was achieved by casting the hinges, and later by using thicker plate in mechanized production techniques. Rising hinges were also created by putting a threaded pin in the joint. This was called a "screw rising joint" (PEM, Volume 15).

Cast-iron hinges are often found with impressed marks. These may be as simple as "3 x 3" (indicating the dimensions in inches), but also include such designations as "ASKEW AND PAXSON," "N.ENG.BUTTCo," "BALDWIN PATENT," or "THOS CLARK" (Streeter 1973a:45-46). The latter marks have yet to be identified; neither Baldwin nor Clark have so far been found in patent records.

Cast-iron butt hinges may have been plain initially. Sample books of the early 19th century (PEM, Volumes 2, 3, 5, 6) and catalogues around mid-century (Russell and Erwin 1865:116-117) do not illustrate any other forms. Various forms of surface ornamentation, however, appear slightly later and into the 20th

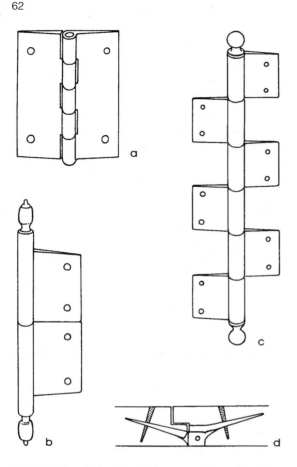

FIGURE 13. *Fiche*-type hinges: *a*, square, butt-hinge shape; *b, fiche à vase*; *c, fiche à vase*, multiple leaves per side; *d*, method of attaching a *fiche*, cross-section view. (*a-c, e*, after *Recueil de planches* 1764-1766:Plate 32; *d*, after Dunton 1972:Figure 20.)

hinge's presence on the door surface through the use of hinge plates. These are "usually ornamental, adapted for attachment to the surface of a door, fitting at one end against the knuckle of a butt, and intended to give the effect of a strap hinge" (Towne 1904:22). Hinge plates are not included by Russell and Erwin (1865) in their catalogue, possibly because such did not yet exist. By 1904, however, Yale and Towne was offering hinge plates in almost one hundred different designs (Towne 1904:847-869). They were probably used more on public or commercial buildings rather than smaller domestic/residential ones.

A hinge resembling a butt hinge, and designated *fiche*, appears in several 18th-century French references (*Recueil de planches* 1764-1766:Plate 33; Duhamel du Monceau 1767:153, Plate 14). Also referred to as mortised hinges (Dunton 1972:54), they may be found on sites occupied by the French. The hinges generally consist of two perforated, square or rectangular leaves thinned toward the outer edge (Figure 13*a-c*) and intended to be set into slots in the door edge and frame (Figure 13*d*). They may also have more than two leaves (Figure 13*c*). The hinges are held in place by fasteners which pass through the wood and one or two hole in either leaf. Once attached, only the joint (knuckles) and the nails holding the hinge in place would be visible.

There are two basic forms of *fiche*. One is rectangular, like a butt hinge, when opened flat (Figure 13*a*). Duhamel du Monceau (1767:Plate 14, Figures 9-11, 30) illustrates a method for manufacturing this form: a piece of plate is folded-over and sections are cut out to form the knuckles. The second form, more like a hinge and pintle, is composed of two square or rectangular components with one positioned above the other (Figure 13*b*) (Duhamel du Monceau 1767:Plate 14, Figure 6). The lower one holds a pin and serves as the pintle while the upper one has a socket which pivots on the pin. On a closed door, the two components would present to view a long tube or socket. This type of hinge may also have an ornamental finial on either end and is then designated a *fiche à vase* (Figure 13*b-c*) (Duhamel du Monceau 1767:116, 296). These hinges were probably intended pri-

century (Sargent 1910:518-519). The purpose of elaborate surface ornamentation that would not be visible once the hinge was attached or when the door was closed is unclear.

Butt hinges were produced in a great variety of sizes, not all of which would have been appropriate for room doors. Hinges 1 or 1 $\frac{1}{2}$ in. (1.5 to 3.8 cm) in length would have been best suited for smaller cupboard doors. In the absence of the correct size, however, even undersized hinges would have been pressed into use.

Although the introduction and proliferation of the butt hinge during the 19th century relegated door hinges to a less conspicuous role, some attempts were eventually made to maintain the marily for furniture or cabinets (Dunton 1972:54) but if large enough, they would also have been, theoretically at least, suitable for building doors. Duhamel du Monceau (1767:116) notes that they are suitable for light doors but not large gates. They appear on sites with French occupations such as Fort Michilimackinac (Stone 1974:Figure 133) and the Fortress of Louisbourg (Dunton 1972:Figures 12-20). The *Recueil de planches* (1764-1766:Plate 32, Figure 29) illustrates a skew-joint variety of the *fiche à vase* and credits its invention to the author (*de mon invention*).

English manufacturers of the late 18th and early 19th centuries were offering hinges similar to the *fiche à vase* (PEM, Volumes 2, 3, 13, 15), designating them either as "French hinges" (Figure 12e) (PEM, Volumes 3, 15) or "heave out" or "heave off" hinges (PEM, Volumes 2, 13). The illustrations suggest that such hinges were intended to be attached to a surface rather than set into mortises as were the *fiche*. It is further likely that they were intended to be attached to the door edge so that, as with the *fiche* or an ordinary butt hinge, only the joint would show when the door was closed. Specified sizes range from 5 to 7 in. (13 to 17 cm) (PEM, Volume 15), possibly excluding the ornamental finials on the pin, with a smaller size (4 $\frac{1}{2}$ in. [11 cm]) specified for shutters (PEM, Volume 3). Since none has been reported in North American contexts, it is possible that they were not common on this continent.

MISCELLANEOUS HINGES

Simmons and Turley (1980:135-137) describe a hinge which does not easily fit into any of the previous categories. It is called a "snipe," a "staple", or an "eyelet" hinge. "Known in the English seaboard colonies, but . . . used there far less frequently than in the Spanish Southwest" (Simmons and Turley 1980:136), it consists of two eyes or staples hooked together (Figure 14) with one component (leaf) driven into the door frame and the other driven into the door edge. Both may have been driven in an angle so that their ends protruded from the wood and could be clinched. Such a hinge would not be recognizable in an archaeological context if the two components become separated. These hinges are not known to have been pro-

duced by factory methods and likely date to the hand-forged period of an area.

Securing

A door can be secured or held in place, usually in the closed position, by a variety of devices. Their selection is determined by the type of securing and the level of security required. A hook, sliding bolt, or even a door spring will suffice if the intention is simply to hold the door closed. A latch is preferable, however, if operation of the securing device is required equally from both sides of a door. A lock is required if control is to be limited to a select few. Both latches and locks can be further limited to operation from one side of a door. Devices which require a key for part of their operation are dealt with in the locks section even though they may be called latches in historical terminology.

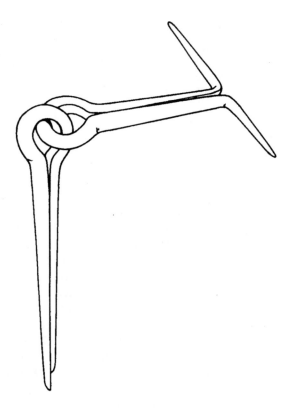

FIGURE 14. "Snipe" hinge.

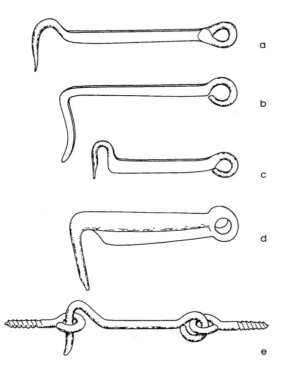

FIGURE 15. Latch hooks: *a*, hand forged with rising hook and lapped and welded eye; *b*, hand forged with non-rising hook and butted eye; *c*, hand forged with rectangular to flat shank, rising hook, and butted eye; *d*, hand forged with flat shank, rising hook, and end perforation, "Hispanic style;" *e*, machine made, wire stock. (*a-b*, after Priess 1972:Figure 3; *c*, after Dunton 1972:Figure 96; *d*, after Simmons and Turley 1980:Chapter 11, Plate 18; *e*, after Sargent 1910:893.)

LATCH HOOKS

Latch hooks, also commonly called gate hooks, have a straight shank with a pivot eye at one end and a hook at the other. The hook engages a second eye or staple, thereby retaining something in position. The most common device for holding a door open or closed (Streeter 1983:Figure 74), latch hooks are generally simple pieces of hardware and, until the ready availability of heavy wire or round bar stock in the 19th century, were forged from square or rectangular stock. The end of the rod forming the eye, which was often forged with a round cross section, either butted on the shank (Figure 15*b-c*) or was lapped and forge welded in place (Figure 15*a*). At the opposite end, the hook either bent down directly from the line of the shank (Figure 15*b*) or, more commonly, rose above the shank before descending (Figure 15*a, c*). The shanks were generally plain. Ornamentation, when present, usually consisted of twisting along part of the shank.

Latch hooks are anchored at the pivot end with an eye or staple, while the hook end engages another eye or staple (Figure 15*e*). Both are often driven or screwed into wood. Their manufacture parallels that of the latch hook, wire being used when it became available during the 19th century, but previously they were generally forged from square stock. Examples possibly cast in brass are advertised in the late 18th and early 19th centuries and identified as "door stays," "ship hooks," or "ship door hooks" (PEM, Volumes 5, 6, 11, 13). The eyes for these, for both the pivot and hooking, are attached to small plates equipped with fastening holes. The reference to use on ships suggests a non-corroding material such as brass, but this would not preclude use on terrestrial structures as well.

The introduction of wire or round stock for the manufacture of hooks occurred during the 19th century, and the hook and its associated eyes subsequently became relatively plain and simple (Figure 15*e*). Styles offered in the early 20th century (Sargent 1910) consisted of ornamented cast-brass types called "cabin" or "door" hooks, and plain wire types designated as "gate" hooks. The brass types have eyes or staples mounted on plates, whereas the wire types have wire screw eyes.

One form of hook, called a "side hook" by Butter (1968:239), is relatively flat in cross section and, instead of an eye at the pivot end, it has a plate with a perforation for a fastening. The perforation is often countersunk, possibly on both sides, to make the object more versatile. These are intended to be attached with a fastener such as a screw, and can only pivot in one plane. The catch may be a small pin rather than an eye or staple. Such hooks are used on items like boxes and equipment cases where it is preferable to have the hook remain in contact with the surface of the box while pivoting. These hooks are generally small and should not be considered as possible door hardware, although Simmons and Turley (1980:Plate 17) do illustrate a Spanish example used on the door of a wall cabinet.

It has yet to be established if there are significant cultural differences in hand-forged latch hooks. They appear on sites occupied by the English (Priess 1972:Figure 3, 1975:Figure 127), French (Duhamel du Monceau 1767:Plate 13; Dunton 1972:Figures 96, 99; Stone 1974:Figure 145; Dubé 1991:Illustration 4h, i), and Spanish (Simmons and Turley 1980:Plates 19-20) with no significant differences. Simmons and Turley (1980:142, Plate 18) describe "a distinctive Hispanic-style hook," forged from flat stock (Figure 15d). The pivot end is perforated like a side hook and would have been attached with an eye, staple, or nail; the shank is ornamented with stamped designs.

HASPS

A hasp is a latching or locking device generally consisting of a strap or something approximating a strap which pivots at one end and fits over a loop (eye or staple) at the other. A pin or padlock through the loop holds the hasp in place and secures whatever the hasp is attached to. Hasps are used on doors but also appear on various forms of furniture, cupboards, and crates.

A common form of hand-forged hasp is an asymmetrical figure-8 shape fashioned from square or rectangular bar stock (Figure 16a). The smaller end has an eye for pivoting, while the larger end has a lenticular slot. The object is produced by bending a bar in the middle to form the pivot eye, lapping and welding the two ends of the bar, and then forming the slot between the bars. The welded end is generally shaped into a simple scroll. Another hand-forged form is made from flat stock with a pivot hole punched at one end and a longitudinal slot cut near the other (Figure 16c). This form may have the latching end worked into a scroll, possibly to serve as a grasp, and may also have a latch hook attached to provide a means of closure (Figure 16b, d, f). These forms are fairly simple and do not appear to exhibit cultural differences.

An alternate form of hasp has no specific pivot facility but pivots with the door to which it is attached. These are in the form of straps with a slot near one end (Figure 16d). They are intended to be fixed rigidly in place with the slotted end projecting past the door edge. The slot passes over a staple in the door frame

as the door is closed. These are generally large and, in fragmentary form, could be mistaken for part of a hinge. They generally have no taper and none has been encountered with finials or other ornamentation. Such fixed hasps may have two additional features. One of these is a handle attached to the strap (Figure 16d). The other is a latching pin which drops into the staple when the door is closed. Such an arrangement would be best suited for holding the door of a barn or other outbuilding closed when no one is inside.

Machine-made hasps of the 19th century initially duplicate forms hand-forged from flat stock, and include the use of staples for pivot and catch (Figure 16e). They also include forms stamped from thin plate, and are equipped with a multiple-part hinge joint rather than a pivot on a staple (Figure 16g). These are referred to as "hinge hasps" (Russell and Erwin 1865:112). In fragmentary form, the latter could also be mistaken for hinges.

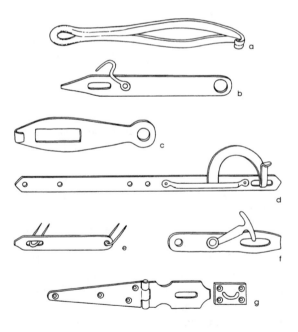

FIGURE 16. Hasps: *a*, common form forged from square or rectangular bar stock; *b*, forged from flat stock with side hook; *c*, forged from flat stock; *d*, forged from flat stock with handle and pivoted latch pin, to pivot with door; *e*, machine-made from flat stock with pivot and catch staple; *f*, machine-made from flat stock with pivoted latch pin; *g*, machine-made "hinge hasp." (*a-b*, unprovenienced; *c-d*, after Harris 1971:Figures 48-49; *e-f*, after Russell and Erwin 1865:144; *g*, after Sargent 1910:1134.)

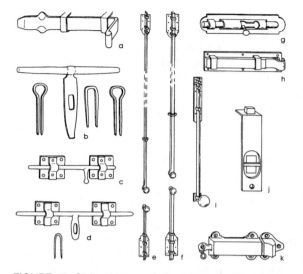

FIGURE 17. Sliding bolts: *a,* forged, flat bolt with staples, mounted directly on door; *b,* forged, round bolt with eyes, attached directly to door, hasp handle; *c,* forged, round bolt with guides, on individual back plates; *d,* forged, round bolt with guides, on individual back plates, hasp handle; *e,* pair of narrow bolts of differing lengths to fit the top and bottom of a door; *f,* pair of wide bolts of differing lengths to fit the top and bottom of a door; *g,* factory-made "barrel" bolt; *h,* factory-made, wrought-iron flat bolt; *i* factory-made, narrow "Canada" bolt; *j,* flush bolt; *k,* chain bolt. (*a,* after Sonn 1928[2]:Plate 116; *b-d,* after Priess 1975:Figures 125-126; *e-f,* after *Recueil de planches* 1764-1766:Plate 34; *g-i, k,* after Russell and Erwin 1865:94-98; *j,* after PEM, Volume 8.)

SLIDING BOLTS

A sliding bolt is a bar which can be attached to a door and slid into a catch on the door frame to hold a door closed. Similar items can also be used on shutters or casement windows. Sliding bolts can be characterized in terms of the method of manufacture, the cross section of the bolt, the methods of controlling its movement, the type of handle, and the method of attaching the bolt to a door. Streeter (1975b:104) summarizes the category as consisting of two types: those secured by staples attached directly to a door, and those affixed to plates nailed or screwed in place. Some of the latter were equipped with springs.

A sliding bolt provides security as it is usually only operable from one side of a door, although Sonn (1928[2]:20, Plate 118) does illustrate a style with a handle that extends through the door and characterizes it as "common to eastern Pennsylvania." Additional security can be achieved by adding some form of lock.

Forged bolts are either rectangular, square, or circular in cross section. A rectangular or square bolt can only slide; a circular bolt can also rotate, thus allowing additional features in its operation.

Bolt handles are quite varied. They may be forged from the end of the bolt, or added to the bolt either at the end or somewhere else along its length. In addition to moving the bolt, the handle may also limit the amount of bolt movement and be a major location for ornamentation. Brass knobs appear to have been used on rectangular bolts by the late 18th century, generally attached to the end of the bolt with a set screw. Ceramic knobs similar to door knobs appear in the 19th century.

The handle may be combined with a hasp (Figure 17*b, d*), thereby providing additional security. Some sliding bolts have long handles which extend well beyond the end of the back plate (Figure 17*e-f*). In fact, some examples have an additional guide and plate attached part way along the handle (Figure 17*e-f*). Such bolts are intended for use at the tops of tall doors, windows, and shutters where the handle has to be brought down within reach of the operator. They appear in the *Recueil de planches* (1764-1766:Plate 34), and Sonn (1928[2]:Plate 122) illustrates an example, from a 1769 Pennsylvania German context, which is slightly over 5 ft. (1.5 m) in length. If found in related archaeological contexts, sliding bolts which are identical except for their length may comprise a pair, one for the top and the other for the bottom of whatever device they were attached to (Figure 17*e-f*).

The bolt is guided by a number of eyes or staples, generally two, and catches in another, possibly matching, eye or staple. The form of the staple is determined by the cross section of the bolt: round for circular bolts and square for rectangular bolts. In the simplest design, the staples are driven directly into the door and frame (Figure 17*a*). A negative consequence of this is that the bolt slides directly on the wood and may cause wear. Bolts with guides attached directly to a door exist only as forged types. Round bolts without back plates are likely to have their handles attached midway on the bolt, between the two staples (Figure 17*b*). The addition of a back plate (Figure 17*c-d*) eliminates wear on the door and stabilizes the guide staples. It also provides a location for ornamentation, as illustrated by Sonn (1928[2]:Plates 118-120).

A sliding bolt used in a vertical position, especially one shot upwards, must have a means of remaining in that position. With round bolts this can be achieved by rotating the bolt and securing the handle behind or in a catch. This is not an option for four-square bolts, however, so these have a spring between the bolt and the back plate. The spring may be a separate piece of metal attached to the back plate, or be fashioned out of the head of the bolt itself. Machine-made versions also have part of the back plate fashioned into a spring.

The nature of the catch on the door frame is determined by how the bolt is attached to the door. A bolt without a back plate would likely have a matching third staple or eye. The catch for bolts with a back plate may be a simple driven staple or a staple attached to a continuation of the plate. In either case, the catch staple would likely match the guide staples in size and shape.

Examples illustrated by Sonn (1928[2]:Plates 116-122) and Streeter (1975b) reveal that back plates were in use during the late 17th century and throughout the 18th century. The late 18th century saw the introduction of rolled plate and the simplification of the production of back plates. The use of these appears to have become more common during the 19th century and is now universal. The use of hollow brass knobs may have begun in the later 18th century. Such knobs are not included in Sonn (1928[2]:Plates 116-122) who illustrates material primarily from the 17th and 18th centuries.

Most sliding bolts were initially forged of wrought iron. Back plates, when present, may exhibit irregularities as a result of being forged from thicker stock. The ends of the staples, where they have been riveted to the back plate, should be irregular as a result of individual hammer blows rather than impact from a mechanized hammer.

Machine-manufactured bolts of the 19th century exhibit greater consistency in form (e.g., staples machine-riveted to back plates are more regular and uniform), and reveal the eventual introduction of short cuts. These include the production of the back plate and guide staples from a single piece of sheeting. This was done for both rectangular and circular bolts.

The term "barrel bolt" (also "socket bolt") appears in catalogues as early as the beginning of the 19th century (PEM, Volumes 3, 5), and generally designates a round sliding bolt with a tube for a guide (Figure 17g) rather than individual staples (Butter 1968:8). The term should only be used to designate a sub-group within the sliding bolt category.

A "flush bolt" is a specialized sliding bolt, so named because it is designed to be let flush into the edge or surface at the top or bottom of a door. If let into the edge, it is used only on double doors, thereby allowing one door to be secured while the other remains operable. As there is no space for a handle in such a case, it must be recessed in the body of the bolt or consist of a pivoting lever.

Flush bolts consist of a flat or L-shaped plate, often made of polished brass, with a sliding bolt attached to its back (Figure 17j). They exist by the early 19th century, at which time the bolt is shown as being rectangular (PEM, Volumes 5, 6). By 1865, the bolt is round or rectangular (Russell and Erwin 1865:95-96).

Another specialized sliding bolt is the "chain bolt." This consists of a bolt with a beveled head enclosed in a housing (Figure 17k). The bolt, which is held in a thrown or latched position by a spring, is withdrawn by pulling on a chain attached to the bolt's tail. It is not known when this type of bolt was introduced. Russell and Erwin (1865:94) illustrate it in their 1865 catalogue.

Sliding bolts machine manufactured in the 19th century have die-stamped back plates and machine-riveted staples, both of which are generally more regular than hand-forged examples. Furthermore, the plates and bolts would likely have been produced from rolled stock which would be more regular in cross section and surface finish.

It seems that the majority of sliding bolts with rectangular cross sections are set with the wide side against the backing plate. Bolts with this configuration could be called flat or wide (Figure 17h), to contrast them with the few which slide on the narrow side and might be termed narrow (Figure 17e). The latter appear on Canadian sites, possibly in 19th-century contexts. A bolt of similar form is illustrated by Russell and Erwin (1865:96) and called a "Canada Bolt" (Figure 17i), a designation defined by Towne (1904:14) as "a box or other bolt the sliding bar of which is prolonged considerably beyond the back plate and provided with a separate guide near its other end." The Russell and Erwin example fits within Towne's definition in that it has the additional guide. Such bolts are similar to a style illustrated in the *Recueil de planches* (1764-1766:Plate 34), suggesting a French origin for them.

One style of sliding bolt, invariably of the wide variety, has a relatively short bolt with a long back plate (vertical measure). These are hand-forged items with a knob handle attached to the middle of the bolt. The back plates are often highly ornamented with extensive pierced work. These are intended to be used on case-ment windows or shutters, situations where only relatively narrow frame components are available for their attachment. Hence, the short bolt and narrow back plate. They are unlikely to have been used on doors and should not be interpreted as door hardware unless additional evidence is available to support such a conclusion.

CREMORNE AND ESPAGNOLETTE BOLTS

Both cremorne and espagnolette bolts serve to secure a door, casement window, or other similar feature. A cremorne bolt (Figure 18*a*) is comprised of "up and down sliding bolts extend-ing the full height of the door and operated by a central handle" (Towne 1904:16; Butter 1968:40). This is presumably what Streeter (1983:Figure 34) refers to as "head and foot bolts." Generally, the two bolts interact with the handle in such a way as to move in opposite directions when the handle is turned. The cremorne bolt could be considered a special form of sliding bolt since it essentially consists of two sliding bolts with extended tails which meet at a common point. The term "cremone" is preferred by Butter (1968:40) and used by the French (actually *crémone*) (Duhamel du Monceau 1767:123), but "cremorne" is more commonly used in North America. Bolts of this type are illustrated by both Duhamel du Monceau (1767:Plates 15, 24) and in the *Recueil de planches* (1764-1766:Plate 34), indicating some antiquity for the concept. Operation of the bolts can be with a rack (Figure 18*c*), an eccentric (Figure 18*d*), or possibly some other means.

An espagnolette bolt (Figure 18*b*) differs somewhat from a cremorne but is intended to accomplish a similar purpose. It consists of a

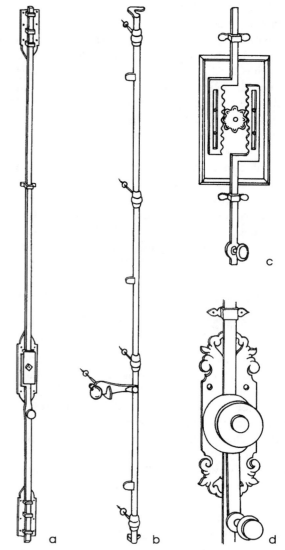

FIGURE 18. Cremorne and espagnolette bolts: *a,* cremorne bolt; *b,* espagnolette bolt; *c,* ratchet method for operating a cremorne bolt; *d,* eccentric method for operating a cremeorne bolt. (*a-b,* after *Recueil de planches* 1764-1766:Plate 34; *c-d,* Duhamel du Monceau 1767:Plates 15, 24.)

single bolt which extends the full height of a door or window and has a hook at either end. When the door or window is almost closed, the bolt is turned by a handle, causing the hooks to engage pins or locking plates on the frame and pulling the door or window completely closed (Butter 1968:64). It may also have "a hinged handle near the center whereby the bar may be rotated to fasten or release the sash [or door] and which also engages with a strike or keeper

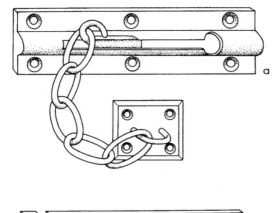

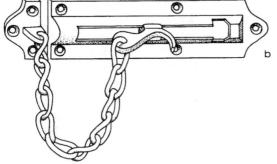

FIGURE 19. Door chains: *a*, early 17th century; *b*, mid-17th century. (*a*, after PEM, Volume 3; *b*, after Russell and Erwin 1865:94.)

which holds the bar in the locked position and further secures the sash [or door] near its center" (Towne 1904:19). Bolts of this type appear in both Duhamel du Monceau (1767:Plate 15) and the *Recueil de planches* (1764-1766:Plate 34), indicating some antiquity for this form of mechanism.

Cremorne and espagnolette bolts are best suited for double doors or windows. No known examples have been recovered from archaeological contexts, and there are presently insufficient data to indicate cultural or temporal differences. Early examples would likely have been forged, with cast and stamped versions probably being introduced some time during the 19th century.

DOOR CHAINS

A door chain is a security device which prevents a door from being opened very far, permitting an assessment of one's callers (Butter 1968:54). One end of the chain is attached to the door frame by means of a small plate, while the other has a fixture which fits into a slotted plate on the door. Such devices have been available since at least the early 19th century (Figure 19*a*). The basic design has changed little since then (Figure 19*b*). Initially forged and then machine made, door chains are presently cast or stamped.

DROP BARS

A simple means of keeping a door closed is to place a stout bar of wood or iron across it (Figure 1*d*). The bar is supported at either end by a staple or L-shaped bracket (Figure 20) driven into the door frame (Streeter 1983:Figure 69). The shanks may be tapered and driven, or bent out and held with fasteners. Using staples is more secure since there is no way to lift the drop bar from the opposite side of the door. Open brackets would be required, however, if there is insufficient room to maneuver the bar into position.

DOOR SPRINGS/DOOR CLOSERS

A door spring or door closer allows a door to close automatically. Streeter (1983:25) describes a type from a late-18th-century context. It consists of a flat spring coiled around a shaft (scroll spring) and enclosed in a housing attached to the door frame. The free end of the spring is attached to an arm which extends horizontally across the door. The end of the arm accommodates a small wheel which rolls along a rectangular plate affixed to the door. When the door is opened, the movement of the arm creates tension on the spring. When the door is released the spring unwinds, exerting pressure on the door, thereby closing it. The roller and plate reduce friction and wear on the door. The same type of door spring is depicted in English hardware sample books around the beginning of the 19th century (Figure 21*a*). A similar type illustrated by Butter (1968:170) is called a "long tail door spring."

The first English patent for a door-closing device (which consisted of a weight and pulleys) was issued in 1786 (GBO 1873:2). The first patent for a device utilizing a spring was issued in 1790 (GBO 1873:3-4), while a patent for the use of a coiled torsion spring within a tube attached to the hinge joint was granted in 1821

FIGURE 20. L-shaped bracket; probable drop-bar support. (After Priess 1975:Figure 128.)

(GBO 1873:9). This may be the first record of such a system, which is similar to modern spring-loaded hinges.

Other examples of door springs include coiled torsion springs (Figure 21c) (Knight 1876:Figure 1688), as well as a simple form consisting of a straight length of heavy wire or rod oriented vertically, with one end attached to the door and the other to the frame (Figure 21b) (Russell and Erwin 1865:375). Opening the door would twist the rod and increase the torsion on it. With the release of pressure, the rod would untwist and close the door. Spring-action door closers combined with a door check system (to prevent the door from slamming) appeared about 1890, first using a pneumatic and then a hydraulic cylinder; the latter was introduced in 1895 (Towne 1904:201-204).

LATCHES

A device for holding a door closed, a latch usually consists of a pivoting bar on the door and a catch on the frame. Unlike a lock, a latch can be operated by anyone who has access to it and it is usually also operable from both sides of a door. It contrasts with a sliding bolt in the manner in which the bolt or bar operates and often also in the complexity of the device. Latches come in a variety of shapes and mechanisms; two major categories are spring latches and thumb latches. Latching components of door locks are discussed in the lock section.

SPRING LATCHES

A spring latch has the various components of the mechanism mounted on a metal plate, with the latch bar held in the latched position by a spring. The latch bar is a pivoting type, often operated with a rotating knob. Butter (1968:15) uses the term "bow latch" for this form. Being attached to the surface of the door, the entire mechanism is exposed to view. Spring latches may be used on doors, but smaller types are also suitable for casement windows or other hinged features.

Two basic mechanisms are illustrated by Streeter (1983:Figures 48-53), each with a differently shaped back or mounting plate. The first mechanism, called a "square spring latch" (Streeter 1983:Figures 48-49), has a knob spindle through the latch-bar pivot (Figure 22c, e). Hence, a turn of the knob (it can only be turned in one direction) is transmitted directly to the latch bar. A handle is attached to the lift bar,

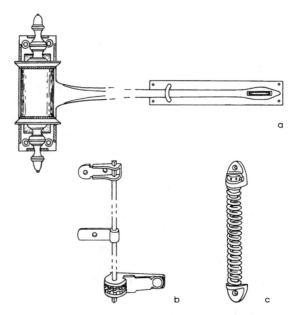

FIGURE 21. Door closures/door springs: *a*, early 17th century, scroll-spring style. (*a*, after PEM, Volume 3); *b-c*, torsion-bar type; *c*, coil-spring type. (after Sargent 1910:556-557.)

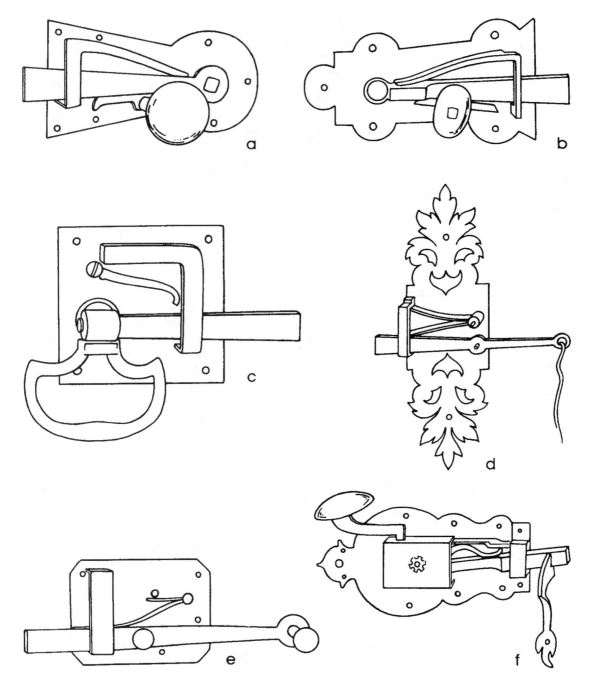

FIGURE 22. Spring latches: *a,* long spring-latch, keyhole-shaped back plate; *b,* long spring-latch; *c,* square spring-latch; *d,* spring latch with vertical back plate; *e,* square spring-latch; *f,* long-latch form from a German context. (*a-c, f,* after Sonn 1928[1]:Plates 98-99, 102; *d,* after Duhamel du Monceau 1767:Plate 15; *e,* after Lunn 1985:Figure 104.)

the mechanisms are relatively short, and the mounting plate is rectangular. Some may have an additional, hand-operated bolt functioning as a night bolt, operable from only one side of the door. The second mechanism, most recently termed a "long spring latch" by Streeter (1983:Figures 50-51), was earlier known as a "wishbone" or "keyhole" latch (Streeter 1954:125). It has the knob spindle passing through a cam positioned under the latch bar

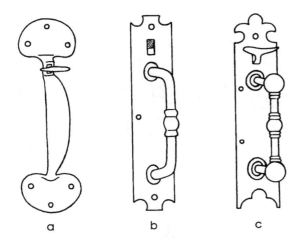

FIGURE 23. Common forms of Suffolk and Norfolk thumb-latch handles: *a,* Suffolk latch with bean-shaped cusps; *b,* Norfolk latch with round cut-out corners; *c,* Norfolk latch with mirror-image ornamentation on the ends of the back plate. (*a-b,* after Priess 1972:Figure 20; *c,* after Sonn 1928[1]:Plate 90.)

(Figure 22*b*). A turn of the knob (it can be turned in either direction) raises one or the other end of the cam which in turn lifts the latch bar. The back plate is relatively long and often has a "keyhole" shape (Figure 22*a*). Both latch mechanisms, including examples with a night bolt, appear in Price's (1856:835) list of available items.

Duhamel du Monceau (1767:Plate 15) and the *Recueil de planches* (1764-1766:Plate 31) illustrate a latch similar in operation to a spring latch, but with a vertical back plate (Figure 22*d*). The latch bar has a pivot near its middle, the pivot point being near the back edge of the back plate. The bar is operated by pulling down on a string attached to a loop at the distal end of the latch bar (the end opposite the catch), thereby lifting the catch end. The use of the string suggests an application beyond the normal reach of a person. A similar latch from a 19th-century Hudson's Bay Company site has a handle instead of the string hole (Figure 22*e*). The specific uses for both forms of these latches are not known, though shutters are a distinct possibility (Duhamel du Monceau 1767:153). It is possible that they were not intended for doors.

Although Butter (1968:Figure 29) illustrates a square spring latch, implying their manufacture

and use well into the 20th century, it appears that both square and long-spring latches, as defined by Streeter, are not common features of 19th-century mass production.

The Germanic variation on a spring latch involves, to some extent, the form of the handle. Latches similar to the long latch, but from German contexts, have a bent handle rather than a knob (Figure 22*f*). This may represent an amalgamation of traditions by North American manufacturers. Other latches from German contexts have the handle and latch bar formed from the same piece of metal, the handle having the scroll or rounded-pad end as found on German locks (Sonn 1928[1]:Plates 98, 100-102).

THUMB LATCHES

A thumb latch consists of a pivoted latch bar attached to one side of a door and operated by a transverse, pivoted lift bar passing through the door. Attached to a handle, the lift bar is pushed down at one end by a thumb or raised at the other end by a finger. The basic components of a thumb latch are a latch bar, lift bar, handle, guide, catch, and occasionally, a latch-bar lock. If security is a factor, a thumb latch may be used in combination with a door lock or other securing device. The inclusion of a latch bar within a door-lock housing obviates the use of two separate hardware items.

Thumb latches exhibit a number of different forms which reflect, in part, changes in technology and have some temporal and/or cultural implications. There are two major categories of forged thumb latches, the main difference between them being the method by which the handle is attached to a door. In the one case, one or both ends of the handle are forged into fastening plates or cusps (Figure 23*a*), while in the other the handle is affixed to a separate plate which can then be attached to a door (Figure 23*b-c*). In English parlance, the former are "Suffolk" latches and the latter are "Norfolk" latches, designations also commonly used in North America. The origin or significance of the names is unknown. The general sense that the Suffolk form preceded the Norfolk and that the latter became popular with the availability of rolled sheet iron is probably an oversimplification.

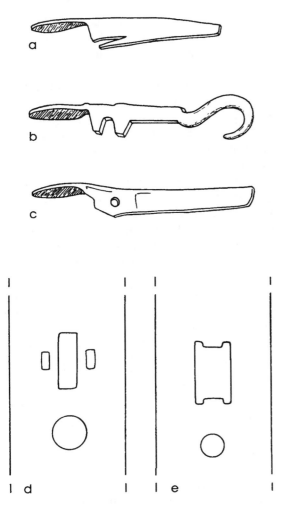

FIGURE 24. Variations in the method of attachment for: *a-c,* lift bars of Suffolk latches, and *d-e,* pivot cheeks on Norfolk thumb-latch back plates. (*a-c,* after Sonn 1928[1]:Plate 93; *d-e,* after Streeter 1971:Figure 6.)

There is a great deal of variety in the shape and size of the cusps, though oval, triangular, and bean-shaped forms are fairly common (Sonn 1928[1]; Streeter 1983:Figures 39-40). In many instances, two cusps are mirror images of each other but, if they are different, the upper cusp will be larger and more elaborate. This is more characteristic of German thumb latches (Streeter 1983:Figure 41).

The lift bar of a Suffolk latch either passes through a rectangular opening in the upper cusp, or through a pivot section positioned between the upper cusp and the end of the handle. In the former instance, the bar would likely be held in position by a cleft in the lower edge (Figure 24*a*) or lugs in the same area (Figure 24*b*); in the latter case it would have a pin through a pivot hole (Figure 24*c*). Mercer (1923:140) suggests that the transition to a separate pivot section took place around the middle of the 18th century, but this is only approximate.

The lift bar can either end in a curved handle, or be straight and cut off short so as to barely extend past the latch bar. Opinions on the significance and dating of these differences vary. Nutting (1921:78) states that lift bars were cut short early in the 19th century, whereas Streeter (1983:Figure 40) notes that lift bars were straight and stubby in the 18th century. Based on examples seen by him, Sonn (1928[1]:29-30) provides what appears to be the most rational perspective. He notes that although many early lifts were straight, there were also longer, curved examples, and concludes that the longer examples may simply be a practical solution to the technical problem of opening a door (Sonn 1928[1]:29). He also observes that local variation would have been a factor, with both types of lift bars being produced and preferred, each in its own area (Sonn 1928[1]:30).

On a Norfolk latch, the handle is attached to a back plate which, in turn, is attached to a door. Common back-plate forms are generally relatively simple and symmetrical, with parallel sides and cut corners (Figure 23*b*), though a range of ornamentation, of the handle as well as the plate, is possible. Streeter (1971:Figure 8) illustrates a variety of forms, including ones which have been sheared, complete with ornamentation, from a continuous strip of stock; consequently, the ornamentation at one end of

The handle of a Suffolk latch may have perforated plates or cusps at one or both ends. If only one cusp is present, it is always the upper one; the lower end of the handle is formed into a shank which can be driven through the door. This form is uncommon on thumb latches from English contexts. North American examples are illustrated by Sonn (1928[1]:Plates 81-83) and identified as Suffolk. At least some of these have non-English associations, and Sonn (1928[1]:Plates 82-83) illustrates a number of comparative examples from France and Quebec.

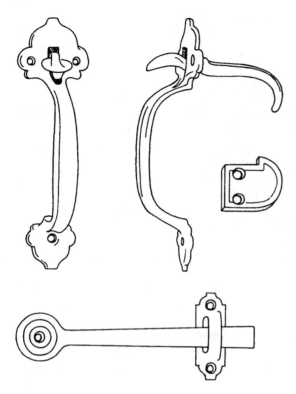

FIGURE 25. Common forms of Blake's-patent cast-iron thumb latch. (After Sonn 1928[1]:Plate 92.)

the back plate is a mirror image of that at the other end (Figure 23c).

It is generally claimed that Suffolk latches preceded Norfolk latches. Any specific example may not fit this scenario, however, since Norfolk-type latches and door handles with back plates, but without the lift bar mechanism, were being produced in England several centuries previously (Chamberlain 1928:106). Furthermore, Streeter's (1983:19) contention that Norfolk latches were introduced into North America "in the early 19th century" is an oversimplification. Such latches appear in 17th- and 18th-century contexts on both this continent (Sonn 1928[1]:Plates 24-26, 91) and in England (Alcock and Hall 1994:26). It is likely that the use of Norfolk latches became more common in North America during the early 19th century because of the availability of rolled bar and plate stock (Streeter 1971:19). This simplified their manufacture and made them economically more attractive than Suffolk types. Consequently, the

Norfolk latch became "the standard cheap door latch of its time" and persisted until well after the introduction of cast iron latches (Streeter 1971:19).

Lift bars for Norfolk-type latches are similar to those for Suffolk latches. According to Sonn (1928[1]:28), early lift bars have straight ends. The bars are usually held in place either by a cleft in the lower edge or a pivot pin through a pivot section. The pivot section usually consists of two small plates or cheeks attached at right angles to the main plate immediately above the upper end of the handle (Streeter 1971:17). The cheeks were initially attached by means of three separate slots through the back plate (Figure 24d); this subsequently changed to a single, H-shaped slot (Figure 24e).

The introduction of casting for the production of thumb latches may reflect a broader shift in technology which also saw the introduction of cast-iron hinges in the late 18th century (Streeter 1971:12). Both Suffolk and Norfolk types were offered in cast form (PEM, Volume 3; Stevens 1969; Streeter 1971:12-13, 15), and these found some application in North America (Streeter 1971:Figures 3, 5). Cast-iron thumb latches, however, did not gain in popularity until the arrival of Blake's patent for a cast-iron latch in 1840 (Sonn 1928[1]:216; Stevens 1969:11). Blake's latch (Figure 25) has a distinctive form which persisted into the 20th century. All components–except for the latch bar and possibly its pivot plate–are cast. The handle has an asymmetrical Suffolk-type shape, with a cusp at either end. The upper cusp is larger, but both are invariably the same shape. The lift bar has a jog at the pivot point so that it is held in place by its position in the handle, without resorting to a pivot pin or cleft edge.

Several 18th-century sources suggest a different tradition for French thumb latches (Duhamel du Monceau 1767:Plate 16; *Recueil de planches* 1764-1766:Plate 31). In both instances, the handle has a one-piece back plate, although not symmetrical as would be the norm for Norfolk latches. The handle is not attached permanently to the plate, however. Instead, the handle has tapered shanks at its ends which pass through holes in the back plate (Figure 26a-c) and are driven through the door and clinched. The upper ends of the shanks have a shoulder which bears on the back plate to hold the latter firmly in place. Specimens from French contexts in North America provide examples of variation of this form. The back plate may relate only to the upper end of the handle, the lower end passing through the door without a plate (Figure 26e-h), or there may be a separate, smaller ornamental plate for the lower end of the handle to serve as a washer and to reduce wear on the door (Figure 26d). The back plate may also be an integral part of the upper end of the handle (Figure 26i). Some of the thumb latches from French contexts also have a lift bar of a different form. The thumb press is a round finial instead of being a flat or curved circular plate (Figure 26g).

Other components of a thumb latch—the latch bar, guide staple, and catch—underwent a transition during the late 18th and early 19th centuries. Initially these various components were attached directly to the door. The latch bar had a perforated finial at its pivot end and was

attached to the door with a nail, screw, or other fastener. The guide was a square staple with tapered shanks driven into or through the door. The catch also likely had a tapered shank which was anchored in the door frame. The catch sometimes had a reinforcing tail that ended in a decorative, perforated finial attached to the door frame with a fastening. The major change was to attach each of the components to a backing plate which would then be affixed to the door or frame with fastenings. This is seen as a feature of Norfolk latches, and the result of the ready availability of rolled plate for the production of back plates (Streeter 1971:19). It should not be automatically assumed, however, that any components with a back plate are associated only with Norfolk latches.

Sonn (1928[1]:Plate 98) illustrates a variation attributed to a mid-18th-century Moravian (German) context. In this instance, the latch bar and guide are both attached to a single back plate (Figure 27a), much like some lock or spring-latch forms. Information concerning the nature of the handle is not provided. Three other examples presented by Sonn (1928[1]:Plates 53-55) are from the second or third quarter of the 18th century (Figure 27b), and are also likely English. Sonn (1928[1]:138, 140, 142, 228) sees this form as being transitional between a latch and a lock.

Late examples of machine-manufactured Norfolk latches include components produced using thinner stock. The catch is formed from such stock bent into a U-shaped cross section, creating the impression of thicker metal and the illusion of greater strength and security. The lift bar may be similarly bent from thin stock. The guide is created by cutting and deforming a single layer of thin metal to provide a slot for the latch bar to pass through and move in. These techniques were used to produce lower-quality materials, but need not have been the only ones used at a particular time.

Although a thumb latch provides little security, it is possible to secure the latch bar. Nutting (1921:78) notes the simple technique of placing a wooden wedge behind the guide staple, above the latch bar, thus making it impossible to raise the latch bar. The more usual arrangement was to place a short latch lock-bar above the

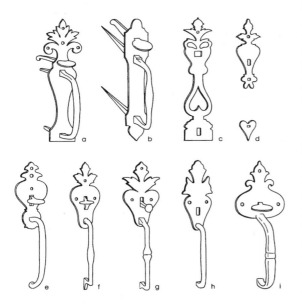

FIGURE 26. Thumb-latch handles or back plates with French or German associations: *a*, mid-17th century; *b*, mid-17th century; *c-d*, probably 18th century; *e*, Quebec, third quarter of the 17th century; *f-g*, France; *h*, early 17th century, Lancaster County, Pennsylvania; *i*, mid-17th century, Moravian. (*a*, after Duhamel du Monceau 1767:Plate 16; *b*, after *Recueil de planches* 1764-1766:Plate 31; *c-d*, after Labonté 1979; *e-i*, after Sonn 1928[1]:Plates 81-83.)

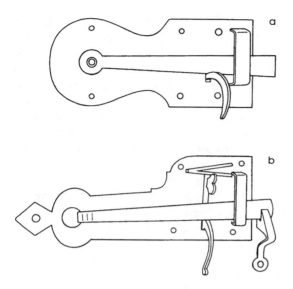

FIGURE 27. Latch bar and guide on back plate: *a*, mid-17th century, Moravian context; *b*, mid-17th century, colonial English context. (After Sonn 1928[1]:Plates 55, 98.)

latch bar. In use, this bar would be positioned vertically above the latch bar, preventing it from being lifted. The lock bar would be positioned on the door so that when not in use it could be pivoted to rest on the guide staple. This was apparently an uncommon feature on thumb latches; it appears on only one of the latch bars illustrated by Sonn (1928[1]:Plate 51). It appears on three latch mechanisms considered to be transitional between latch and lock (Sonn 1928[1]:Plates 53-55). The latch lock-bar on the latter examples is operated with a turn button and held in position by a spring.

BAR LATCHES

A bar latch is a variation that falls between a spring latch and a thumb latch (Streeter 1983:Figures 54-56). The latch bar resembles that of a thumb latch, being pivoted and held down by gravity rather than a spring. Operation of the bar is similar to that of a long spring-latch in that it involves a cam manipulated by a spindle with a knob or handle on one side of the door and a knob attached to the latch bar. In contrast to a spring latch, the various components are mounted on separate back plates (Figure 28), as illustrated by Streeter

(1983:Figures 54-55) and Sonn (1928[1]:Plate 98). These English examples are mostly attributed to the late 18th or early 19th century. They do not appear to persist through the 19th century and are absent from trade catalogues of factory-produced hardware.

RING/KNOCKER LATCHES

A latch bar can also be operated by turning a ring handle on a spindle connected directly or indirectly to the latch bar. According to Sonn (1928[1]:Plates 13-20), there are two basic styles: English (New England) and Dutch. The English style (Figure 29*a*) has a spindle passing through the door and the pivot end of the latch bar. The end of the spindle is split and spread to hold the parts together. The latch bar is guided by a square staple, as for a thumb latch. The Dutch style (Figure 29*b*) is similar, but the end of the spindle engages an asymmetrical cam below the latch bar. A turn of the handle lifts the latch bar, either directly in the English style or indirectly in the Dutch style. In both cases, the ring can only be turned in one direction. The ring may also serve as a knocker but this is not an essential function of the device. Found in an archaeological context, the individual components of a ring/knocker latch, especially the latch bar, may not be recognizable as such since this latch style is similar in its operation to a bar latch. One notable difference is the symmetrical cam of the latter.

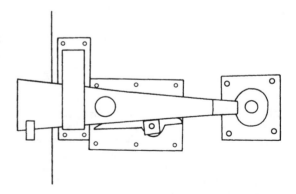

FIGURE 28. Bar latch, late 17th century. (After Streeter 1983:Figure 55.)

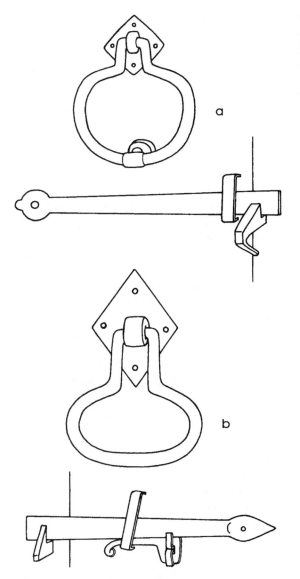

door and clinched. Each shank passes through a slot in a back plate, but does not hold it firmly to the door. A pin protruding from the center of the back of the plate (the escutcheon) extends through the door to the underside of the latch bar. Raising the back plate lifts the latch bar.

Sonn (1928[1]:24) considers this to be "the most unique, and probably the rarest, of the early American latches." A similar latch was recorded in England by Twopeny (1904:Figure 90). The constituent parts, except for the back plate (escutcheon), would not be recognizable individually.

LATCH CATCHES

The most common form of catch for all styles of latches may be characterized as a "figure-4" shape which has a tapered shank to be driven

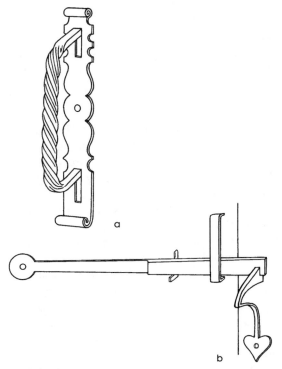

FIGURE 29. Ring/knocker latches: *a,* "English" style; *b,* "Dutch" style. (After Sonn 1928[1]:Plates 14, 16.)

ESCUTCHEON-LIFT LATCHES

On an escutcheon-lift latch (Figure 30), the latch bar and its accessories are the same as for a thumb latch. The difference lies in the nature of the handle and the method of lifting the latch bar. The ends of the handle have tapered shanks which are driven through the

FIGURE 30. Escutcheon-lift latch: *a,* fixed handle with movable escutcheon; *b,* latch bar mechanism. (After Sonn 1928[1]:Plate 22.)

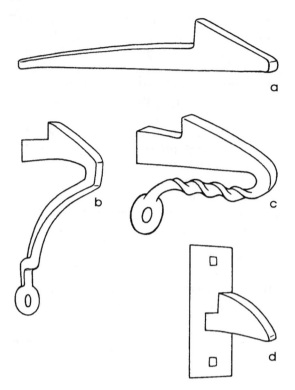

FIGURE 31. Common latch-catch forms: *a,* driven, without reinforcing; *b,* driven, with plain reinforcing; *c,* driven, with twisted-shank reinforcing; *d,* plate mounted. (After Sonn 1928[1]:Plate 94.)

the presence of a German-style lock can only be inferred if supported by the presence of other diagnostic lock components.

LOCKS

The subject of locks used on early American buildings is complex, if their historical development were to be traced through the 17th, 18th, and 19th centuries. There were so many different types and so many varied uses, that such an attempt would fail to be more than a superficial review (Streeter 1974a:41).

A lock is any key-operated device attached to a door and equipped with a bolt or other member to keep the door closed (Butter 1968:163). It provides the ultimate in security by limiting operation to the select few who possess the right "key." Additional security can be achieved by using a lock that is operable from only one side of the door.

Door locks can either be portable, such as padlocks, or permanently fixed to a door. The latter may be attached to the door's surface, set into the door's surface, or let into the door's edge. Those attached to the surface have a variety of designations with major categories being "stock locks" and "rim locks." Those let into the surface are termed "flush locks," while locks let into the edge can all be called "mortise locks." The door lock has a lengthy history extending back to the wooden types used in ancient Egypt and elsewhere in the Middle East (Butter 1968:116-117). A number of lock types were available by the time Europeans began settling in North America in the 16th century. These all had metal mechanisms although some types did have wooden housings. They persisted with little change in form into the 19th century, with changes in design and technology being introduced late in the 18th century.

A door lock can be characterized in terms of the nature of its housing, the number of bolts it has, its method of operation, and the composition or complexity of its internal mechanism. Terminology for the various components is extensive and beyond the limits of the present discussion. For an explanation of the various terms, see Towne (1904:11-32b), Butter (1948; 1968), or Priess (1979:46-73).

into the door frame (Figure 31*a*). The head or catch end may have a tail depending from it which is also attached to the door frame (Figure 31*b-c*), similar to the reinforcing for a pintle. Since the weight of a latch bar is negligible, however, the tail does not serve a reinforcing function but appears to be largely ornamental. The end of the tail is shaped into a finial, often a simple circle, oval, or point. Further ornamentation might include a twisted shank.

Another form of latch catch has the catch device attached to a plate (Figure 31*d*), similar to the treatment of other parts of the latch mechanism. This apparently became common late in the 18th century.

Although most commonly used for various forms of latches, figure-4 catches would also function for German-style locks with a pivoted latch bar. Hence, the presence of such a catch is not an automatic indication of a latch, and

PADLOCKS

A padlock is a portable lock (Reaumur 1767:216; Butter 1968:200) which consists of a mechanism enclosed in a housing and a curved bow or "shackle" which is passed through a loop such as an eye, hasp, staple, or chain link. The shackle may be: (1) loose and slide into the lock, thereby having both ends secured; (2) held in the housing at one end and allowed to slide or rise for a limited distance without becoming separated from the lock; or (3) pivoted at one end with the free end passing into an opening in the housing where it is secured. Padlocks can be used on doors, as well as for various other applications. Although Jousse (1627:15) characterizes them as easy to make because they do not have many parts and are generally easy to break open, Reaumur (1767:216) states that they can be made as large and as strong as regular locks. They can be characterized in terms of the shape of the housing, the manner in which the housing is assembled, and the manner in which the shackle operates. A number of different forms were used in North America up to the beginning of the 19th century. There do not seem to be definite cultural differences as some shapes appear as readily on English sites as on French ones.

Examples illustrated by Frank (1950:Plate 29) reveal that there were various shapes of

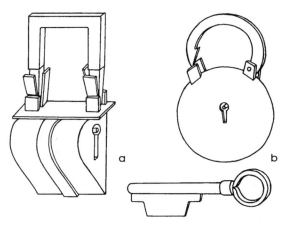

padlocks, at least in early French contexts. Some of these probably correspond to the shapes mentioned by Jousse (1627:15): round, heart, square, and triangle. One of these forms, known to have occurred in both English and French contexts, is best characterized as a "half heart" shape (Reaumur 1767:218; Noël Hume 1969:251), based on the cross section of the housing when viewed from the side (Figure 32a). The back of the housing is flat; the front is bowed. The front often has a vertical reinforcing strip, and the openings for the shackle are usually surrounded by additional plates as well. The shackle is a symmetrical U-shape with both ends thinned. One or more springs are attached to each end; Reaumur (1767:218) mentions two springs. When the ends of the shackle are pushed into the housing, the springs are initially compressed but then spring out, preventing removal of the shackle. To open the lock, a simple key is inserted into the keyhole on the right side of the lock and turned to compress the springs, freeing the shackle. The key is a pipe type which fits over a drill pin for alignment and stability, but otherwise there are likely no additional internal obstructions.

Locks of this type are illustrated in both Duhamel du Monceau (1767:Plate 32) and the *Recueil de planches* (1764-1766:Plate 30). Examples illustrated by Frank (1950:Plate 29) are identical and may be of the same time period or earlier. They have been found in 18th-century French contexts such as the Fortress of Louisbourg (Dunton 1972:Figure 77) and Fort Michilimackinac (Stone 1974:233, Figure 143B). Noël Hume (1969:251-252) considers them to be "fairly common" in 18th-century contexts. They appear on sites of the 1730-1820 period, with the earlier examples having a vertical reinforcing on the back as well as the front. These locks are generally small; Noël Hume (1969:252) gives a size range (body length) of $\frac{7}{8}$ to $2\frac{1}{2}$ in. (2.2 to 6.4 cm) The larger examples could have been used on doors, but the smaller ones likely found other applications, such as trunks.

Other early padlocks, such as the triangular, square, or ball-shaped (semi-spherical; Figure 32b) ones illustrated in various sources (*Recueil*

FIGURE 32. Mid-18th-century padlocks: *a,* "half heart" form with key; *b,* ball form. (After *Recueil de planches* 1764-1766:Plate 30.)

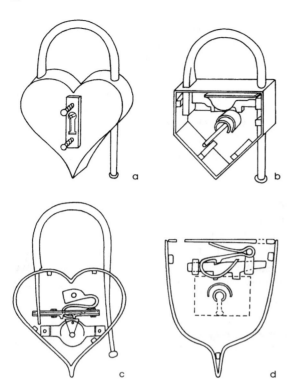

FIGURE 33. Parallel-plate padlocks from French contexts: *a*, heart shaped; *b*, angular; *c*, heart shaped; *d*, rounded-funnel shaped. (*a-b*, after *Recueil de planches* 1764-1766:Plate 30; *c-d*, after Laroche 1988:Figures 17-18.)

de planches 1764-1766:Plate 30; Duhamel du Monceau 1767:Plate 32; Frank 1950:Plate 29), do not appear to be as common in archaeological contexts. Noël Hume (1969:250) indicates that these forms were available in North America during "the first half of the 17th century," with the ball form appearing in contexts as late as the first quarter of the 18th century. These locks, and almost all the other forms yet to be discussed, differ from the half-heart in having a key hole in the front and probably a mechanism with some wards or other obstructions to prevent the use of an incorrect key.

The majority of early padlocks share the characteristic of having their housing constructed of two parallel iron plates joined to a strip of iron by a number of rim rivets (Figure 33*b-d*). The mechanism is attached to the back plate and the keyhole is in the front plate. Variations exist in the shape of the housing (plates) and the nature of the shackle, but in all instances the shackle is secured within the housing. Where only one end of the shackle needs to be secured,

this will invariably be on the left side of the lock (when viewed from the keyhole side). The majority of shackles enter the top of the housing and are secured inside by a horizontal bolt which slides into a notch or slot in the end of the shackle. These shackles are either pivoted on the right side of the lock (Figure 32*b*), or have an extension on the right side that passes through the housing (Figure 33*a-c*). The latter arrangement allows the shackle to rise and fall, moving the free end in and out of the housing. The end of the extension may be enlarged to keep the shackle from falling out of the housing (Figure 33*a-c*).

There are several variations in the shape of the housing, some of which may have cultural affiliations. Two varieties which appear in 18th-century French sources (*Recueil de planches* 1764-1766:Plate 29 Duhamel du Monceau 1767:Plate 32) are heart-shaped (Figure 33*a*), or rectangular with a pointed bottom (Figure 33*b*). Examples of the former are known from Fort Michilimackinac (Stone 1974:Figure 143A) and the Intendant's palace in Quebec City (Laroche 1988:Figures 16-17). A specimen of the latter was found at the Fortress of Louisbourg (Dunton 1972:Figure 77). The Intendant's palace also produced a padlock shaped like a rounded funnel with a small point at the bottom (Figure 33*d*). The nature of its mechanism is unclear, but it may have been a rising shackle with an extended end passing through the housing. Where the mechanism is known, these locks use some form of a one-piece spring and tumbler design as discussed below for French door locks.

Padlocks of similar construction, but with the addition of recognizable ears or lobes at the top, predominate in 18th-century English contexts in North America. Noël Hume (1969:250) indicates they are present "by the late 17th century." They have two lobes, and the housing is usually vertically symmetrical (Figure 34*a*). In all known instances, the bow is pivoted on the right side and the corresponding lobe holds the pivot pin for the shackle. The opposite lobe serves no practical purpose, but provides the symmetry which may have been preferred for aesthetic purposes. In the few instances where the lock is not symmetrical, the upper edge of the housing rises from the right lobe to form a pseudo lobe on the left side (Figure 34*b*). The iron band which joins the front and back plates is a single piece, and begins and ends on the right side at the opening that accommodates the free end of the bow.

Noël Hume (1969:250-251) suggests several trends in shape and design for English locks of the 18th and early 19th centuries. The early locks are supposed to be "bag shaped" (Noël Hume 1969:250); generally rounded and widest near the bottom (Figure 34b). A 17th-century form exists which does not fit into this category (Figure 34a); plus it has virtually no lobes. On later locks, the widest point has moved up, resulting in a housing which is more circular in appearance (Figure 34c). The shape of the lobes varies from near circular (Figure 34c) to pointed or arched (Figure 34e). Some locks

FIGURE 34. Parallel-plate padlocks from English contexts: *a,* symmetrical housing, 17th-century; *b,* asymmetrical housing, hinged keyhole cover; *c,* symmetrical housing, hinged keyhole cover (incomplete); *d,* asymmetrical housing, pivoted keyhole cover; *e,* symmetrical housing, pivoted keyhole cover; *f,* symmetrical housing, pivoted keyhole cover, late 17th/early 17th century; *g,* symmetrical housing, brass escutcheon and pivoted keyhole cover; *h,* symmetrical housing, brass escutcheon and pivoted keyhole cover. (*a,* after Kenyon 1986:Plate 52; *b-e,* after Priess 1975:Figures 115-116; *f,* after PEM, Volume 3; *g-h,* after Russell and Erwin 1865:106-107.)

from the second or third quarter of the 18th century have a single lobe which provides an attachment point for the pivot pin (Figure 34b). This may be an early style which existed alongside double-lobe forms, or it may generally have predated the double-lobe form.

The keyhole cover also changes through time, going from hinged (Figure 34b, d) to pivoted (Figure 34f) and from iron to brass (Noël Hume 1969:250-251). This is partially at variance, however, with a 17th-century lock from James Bay which has a pivoted cover (Figure 34a). The use of brass for keyhole covers is seen as postdating 1840 (Noël Hume 1969:251).

Brass keyhole covers are often stamped and the marks provide an additional means of identifying or dating a lock. The mark may indicate a manufacturer or reveal other pertinent information about the lock type. English locks sometimes exhibit letters which identify the monarch, thus indicating the country of origin as well as providing a date range for the lock. Unfortunately, many of these marks designate Victoria (VR) who reigned from 1837 to 1901, thus limiting their value for dating.

The general shape and construction of padlocks remained the same through much of the 19th century. Most of the locks offered by Russell and Erwin (1865:106-110) are still of the parallel-plate type (Figure 34g). The shapes have changed somewhat, however, in that the housing is widest at the lobes and often has a rounded point at the bottom. Other, more elaborate, shapes are also present (Figure 34h), and the locks often have a loop and chain attached to the bottom (Russell and Erwin 1865:106-108). Similar shapes are also available in brass housings (Russell and Erwin 1865:108), and many of the locks have brass keyhole escutcheons and keyhole covers. The latter all pivot.

Parallel-plate padlocks persist into the 20th century (Sargent 1910:1039-1048). At the same time, cast-brass and bronze types which imitate the shape of earlier locks are also available (Sargent 1910:1030-1031), as are various other types.

An 18th-century padlock from the Fortress of Louisbourg (Figure 35a) resembles other padlocks but is also similar to the embossed door locks discussed below. The lock is square with a housing made of only two plates, the edges of which were apparently riveted together. The back plate is flat, while the front one is embossed (domed) to fit over the mechanism. The right end of the shackle seems to be extended, allowing it to pass into and through the housing as with other padlocks described above. The left end of the shackle is flattened and has a staple-type hasp which fits into a slot in the front plate. The hasp is held in position by a lock bolt inside the lock. The shackle would have to be rotated to remove the hasp from the housing, and the extended right end suggests that it could also rise some distance. The significance of this unusual lock type is presently unknown. Its similarity to the embossed door lock suggests it is French in origin.

A lock style (Figure 35*b-c*) illustrated by Frank (1950) and Simmons and Turley (1980) may be limited to non-English contexts. The housing is a parallel-plate type but, rather than having a moveable shackle, it has a fixed rod attached to the top of the housing. A staple-type hasp slides on this rod and enters the front plate of the housing. A major disadvantage of this arrangement is the possibility that the hasp

may become disassociated and lost. Locks of this form generally tend to be large.

Another style of padlock which appears occasionally has a tubular or barrel housing. The shackle pivots at one end and enters the housing near the other end. The free end of the shackle is held in the housing by various relatively simple systems consisting of a bolt or spring. The lock is opened with a key which simply compresses the spring or pulls back on the bolt (Duhamel du Monceau 1767:Plate 32; Noël Hume 1969:249, Figure 78). Noël Hume (1969:249) presents this type as "the common English padlock of the Middle Ages [which persisted] well into the 18th century." The lock presumably also has French associations as it appears in an 18th-century French technical reference (Duhamel du Monceau 1767:Plate 32) and in the archaeological collections of the Fortress of Louisbourg (Dunton 1972:167, Figure 77).

Early padlocks may not have provided much security. Small locks would have been too fragile to withstand much prying, and the larger locks had more the appearance than the substance of security. The mechanisms are often simple and, as was the case for door locks of the period, did not offer much resistance to picking. The system of internal obstructions (wards) is often simple and the use of variously shaped keyholes provides little advantage. Simple mechanisms, such as the springs to be compressed in half-heart or barrel locks, would likely also not offer any resistance to a determined burglar. Improvements in doorlock technology which began in the late 18th century presumably found their way into padlock manufacture as well. By 1865, padlocks were being offered with tumblers in addition to wards (Russell and Erwin 1865:109).

SURFACE-MOUNTED LOCKS

STOCK LOCKS

A stock lock is a surface-mounted door lock with an iron mechanism set into a wooden housing. The two main subdivisions are "plain" (in which the components of the mechanism are individually attached to the housing) (Figure 36), and "plate" (in which all the parts are first attached to a metal plate which is then affixed

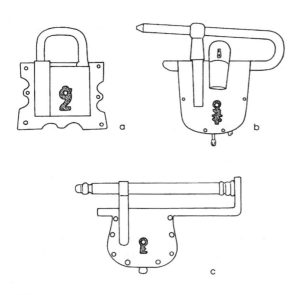

FIGURE 35. Miscellaneous padlocks: *a*, "Embossed" padlock from the Fortress of Louisbourg, probably French; *b*, parallel-plate padlock with hasp, Spanish-American context; *c*, parallel-plate padlock with hasp, possibly French. (*a*, after Dunton 1972:Figure 77; *b*, after Simmons and Turley 1980:Chapter 11, Plate 43; *c*, private collection.)

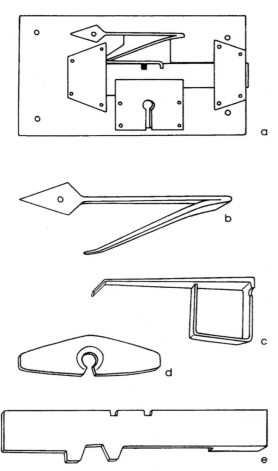

FIGURE 36. Plain stock lock and its constituent parts: *a*, assembled lock; *b*, spring; *c*, tumbler; *d*, main ward; *e*, lock bolt.

ward (Streeter 1970:Figures 9, 11). Other keys (for plate stock locks, rim, or mortise locks) have the collar behind the bit, to contact either the main or cover plate of the lock (Streeter 1970:Figures 9-10).

References to stock locks appear in English documents as early as the 12th century (Hughes 1957:100), suggesting that they could have been used in North America quite early. Streeter (1970:252) contends that stock locks were still being produced in England in 1970. The advantage of a stock lock, especially on an exterior door, appears to be its resistance to weather (Streeter 1970:252).

Stock locks can usually be distinguished from other types in an archaeological context because of their distinctive components. Plain stock locks, which are not likely to be found intact with their wooden housing, have to be recognized from their individual parts. The form of the lock bolt, tumbler, spring, main ward, and possibly also the retaining plates (Figure 36), as well as the distinctive key, is not repeated on other known locks. Hence, the presence of any

to the housing) (Figure 37). They are usually one-bolt (dead bolt) locks (Streeter 1970:251). If a latch were required, it would be provided by a separate mechanism such as a thumb latch. The housing may be ornamented with iron straps (Butter 1968:279; Streeter 1970:Figure 1), and plate stock-locks may have an ornamental brass keyhole escutcheon on the main and cover plates. The escutcheons serve as bearing surfaces since neither of them would have been visible when the lock was attached to a door.

Plain stock locks differ from many other locks in that only the main or bridge ward is available for the attachment of wards and the alignment of the key with the mechanism. The key is kept from passing through the lock by a collar on the shank at the slot in the bit for the main

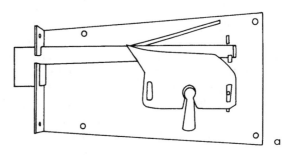

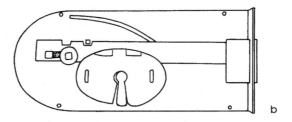

FIGURE 37. Plate stock locks: *a*, common mechanism, trapezoidal main plate; *b*, factory-made, with router-cut housing. (After Priess 1979:Figures 8, 17.)

of these components in a collection reveals the presence of a plain stock lock.

Early plate stock locks also seem to have distinctive, readily recognizable components. The main plate is often trapezoidal, being narrower at the front-plate end. The main plate, even if rectangular, is also recognizable because it will not have any evidence of rim rivets as on rim locks. The lock bolt has a relatively narrow tail, and the cover plate usually has a small spur on an upper corner to hold the lock bolt in place (Figure 37a). The presence of ornamental iron strips (Streeter 1970:Figure 1) at a site may indicate the wooden housing of a stock lock, but other explanations are also possible.

The mechanization of stock-lock production, attributed to the 19th century by Streeter (1970:Figure 8), resulted in several design changes. The lock-bolt tail loses its distinctiveness by becoming wider, with a slot or "lanket hole" (Butter 1968:154, Figure 98) at the end to allow it to ride on a guide, and being held in place with a nut or washer (Figure 37b). This is similar to rim-lock bolts of the period. The cover plate becomes rectangular and loses its spur, and the wards may be of cast brass (Streeter 1970:Figure 8). The main plate is still recognizable because of the absence of rim-rivet holes. Other developments, such as Young's patent of 1825, include the simplification of the creation of the wooden housing by setting the mechanism into a circular rather than a rectangular hole (Price 1856:405-406, Figure 453), the advantage being that the hole could be created with a drill bit rather than a hammer and chisel. The lock mechanism also has a circular main plate rather than the traditional rectangular or trapezoidal one. Similarly, the cut-out for the lock could be done with a router, resulting in a round end on the cut-out and requiring a round end on the main plate (Figure 37b). During the second quarter of the 19th century, a form of stock lock known as Steele's patent (Price 1856:419, Figures 444, 451) was developed wherein the lock mechanism was set into the end of a block of wood, the same as a mortise lock. The lock was intended, however, to be attached to a door's surface and the advantage of the design was that it allowed the lock to be placed on either side of a door without having to turn the lock upside down.

The housing probably did not have ornamental straps on the exterior unless they were added after the lock was attached to a door.

Although stock locks do not appear to have been common in the 19th century, they were still being offered for sale in the United States in 1865 (Russell and Erwin 1865:140) and in England in 1856 (Price 1856:837-843). These sources do not mention any specific advantages of the locks.

RIM LOCKS

The basic requirements for a rim lock are a metal housing and attachment to the surface of a door. The housing minimally consists of a main plate to which the various components are attached, and a rim or sides. Rim locks can be characterized in terms of the method and material of manufacture, the manner in which the housing is assembled, the number of bolts, the manner in which the bolts are operated, the types of obstructions to access, and the proportions of the housing.

The housing is most often made of iron—wrought iron until the 19th century, and then occasionally cast iron. Steel was used later in the 19th century when it became economically feasible. A housing of cast brass could date to the 18th or 19th century. The use of brass for some of the mechanism's components began in the 19th century.

English and French housings are similar to some extent, but possess a few features which often make it possible to differentiate them. On both, the main and front plates are bent from a single piece of iron. The front plate is usually also wider than the other parts of the rim. This allows it to extend onto the edge of the door slightly and provides a means of aligning the lock. On English locks, the back plate is usually also bent from one plate. The English lock then only requires a top and a bottom plate, each of which is a separate strip of iron attached to the main plate with rim rivets. For French locks, as described by Reaumur (1767:160), the three parts of the rim other than the front are made of a single piece of metal bent into a square U and attached to the main plate with rim rivets. Illustrations of 17th- and 18th-century rim locks (Jousse 1627:Figures 25, 28, 31, 34, 36; Duhamel du

Monceau 1767:Plates 16, 17, 20) show this construction clearly. The ends of the rim may also be bent at right angles and riveted to the front plate (Reaumur 1767:168). Housings assembled in this way can be considered as French in origin and thus, in North America, less likely to date to the 19th or late 18th century. Streeter (1973b:Figure 1) illustrates a "cheap" variation in a housing of probable 19th-century American manufacture in which all parts of the rim are bent from the same sheet of iron.

An English alternative to the all-iron housing was the use of cast brass. The brass housing consists of a shallow box, open on one side, which duplicates the main, front, back, top, and bottom plates of the iron housing. In contrast to iron housings, the equivalent of the front plate is the same width as the remainder of the rim. The mechanism for such locks is similar to that of other rim locks. It is attached to a flat, rectangular iron plate which is dropped into the brass housing and held in place by hooks and set screws in the brass. Brass housings are smaller than those of many iron rim locks, and were usually intended for interior doors.

Locks for powder magazines require non-sparking components and, thus, may be made entirely of non-ferrous materials. Such a lock was recovered from the powder magazine at Coteau du Lac, Quebec (Priess 1972:Figure 11). The lock probably dates from the late 18th century, and has a very simple mechanism of wards. The key may also have been of brass.

Since the door lock is a relatively precise machine requiring the proper interaction of a number of components, it is important that all of the parts are properly fitted to each other. With hand-manufacture technology, this would require shaping each component to fit and work properly in a specific housing. To avoid mixing components from several different locks, all parts for the same lock could be given the same number, marked in Roman numerals with a cold chisel.

Technological changes around the beginning of the 19th century are reflected in the manufacture of contemporary rim lock housings. The introduction of rolled plate by the late 18th century (Streeter 1983:3) made it unnecessary to create the flat components by hand hammering. This reduced the amount of work required to produce a housing, and also meant that the material would be smooth and of uniform thickness. Locks showing evidence of individual hammer blows were produced by forge work and are likely earlier than those having smooth plates of uniform thickness. Bar stock with a triangular or channeled cross section was also introduced. This could be used for the top and bottom plate of the housing, giving it less of a box look.

A rim lock can be characterized by the number of bolts in the mechanism. It minimally requires one bolt–a lock bolt–operated at least partly by a key. Often, however, it has a second bolt–a latch bolt–usually operable from both sides of the door by a knob or lever. Additional security may be provided by a third bolt (often referred to as a night bolt or night latch) which is operable only from the lock side of the door.

English rim locks of the 18th and early 19th centuries often have all three bolts and, to a great extent, the various lock examples are similar to each other. The latch bolt is uppermost in the housing, the lock bolt is below it, and the night bolt is on the bottom. The lock bolt can either be a dead bolt, in which case a key is required to move it in and out of the housing, or it can be a latching lock bolt, in which case the head is beveled and the bolt is kept in the locked position by a spring. The beveling on the head allows the bolt to pass a catch on the door frame and to spring back into a locked position once past the catch. A latching lock bolt has to be operated from at least one side of the door by a key, and it may have a handle or other mechanism to work it from the lock side of the door. The head of the latch bar is always beveled and the bar is kept out by a spring. The night bolt is a dead bolt (it must be moved in both directions manually) and is often operated by a brass handle on the bottom plate of the housing. Variations can occur in any of the major components and thus it is difficult to summarize the characteristics of a lock.

The lock bolt of an English rim lock is generally made of a thick strap with one end folded back a number of times and forged into a rectangular block. The head of the latch bolt may be made in the same manner. The latch-bolt tail often has two bends: one to provide it with a surface to ride on the main plate of the housing, and the second to furnish it with a vertical section to interact with the follower from the knob and spindle. The night bolt is often square and uniform in cross section, and has a L-shaped end for attachment of the handle.

Eighteenth-century French rim locks potentially available in North America are known more from historical references than actual specimens. Illustrated examples (*Recueil de planches* 1764-1766:Plates 23-25; Duhamel du Monceau 1767:Plates 17-23) are either one- or two-bolt locks, the second bolt being either a latch bolt or a night bolt. The lock bolt or the night bolt may have a latching head. Something not seen on English locks is the use of multiple heads for a single lock bolt (*Recueil de planches* 1764-1766:Plates 24; Duhamel du Monceau 1767:Plate 22) and the use of multiple lock bolts. Jousse (1627:Figure 36) illustrates a lock with six bolts and a total of seven heads. In this case, however, all the bolts are moved simultaneously by a single turn of the key, considerably lessening the lock's security potential. Known archaeological examples of probable French locks are one-bolt types with a single head on the bolt (Priess 1975:Figures 109-110; Laroche 1988:Figures 13-14).

German rim locks often differ in several aspects from French and English types. The housing seems to be formed the same way as for French locks; the main and front plate are bent from a single plate and the other three sides are a continuous strap attached with rim rivets (Streeter 1983:Figure 23). The tumbler and spring are of one-piece construction (Nägele and Nägele 1836:Plate 4; Streeter 1983:Figure 24), similar to French locks. When present, latch bolts are often pivoted, rather than sliding, and are operated by a lever on the lock side of the door. The lever may be formed as one piece with the latch bolt and enter the lock housing through the top plate. The end of the lever may be finished with a plate or scroll. Springs in these locks often seem to be of the scroll type (Nägele and Nägele 1836:Plates 5, 6, 8). A night latch operated by a knob may also be present on the bottom plate of the lock (Nägele and Nägele 1836:Plate 5).

In all locks, the lock bolt must have a means of stopping when thrown or moved into the locked position. This is partially accomplished by the limitation of how far the key can actually move it. Additional stops are provided,

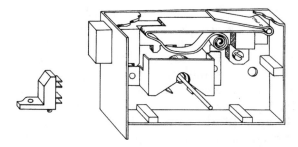

FIGURE 38. French one-bolt rim lock, including detail of a rake ward. (After *Recueil de planches* 1764-1766:Plate 23.)

however. English locks tend to provide this facility somewhere on the bolt tail, either as a widened area or a hook in the end. French locks seem to have a spur on the back of the head (Figure 38). In the case of English locks, the bolt is stopped by an encounter between the mechanism and the bolt tail. On French locks, the encounter is between the bolt head and the housing (front plate). Movement of the lock bolt is usually also restricted by the tumbler catching a notch in the bolt tail up to the early 19th century.

Security in the operation of a lock is provided by several types of obstructions which prevent the use of an incorrect key or the unauthorized movement of the bolt. Lock bolts on early locks, both French and English, have a bar, known as a tumbler, which interferes with the free movement of the bolt. The common tumbler on English locks is a pivoted bar with a lug or "stump" which aligns with one or more lugs on the bolt tail (Figure 39). The tumbler must be lifted out of the way to allow the bolt to move. The tumbler is held in place by a flat, slightly curved spring ("Scotch spring") (Figure 39) which bears on the tumbler near its pivot point. Since it does not move very much, it can be made of iron (Butter 1968:231).

Period illustrations reveal that French locks had two options regarding the form of the mechanism, both of which utilize a combined tumbler and spring. The first option has these two elements in a V-shaped configuration, the upper leg serving as a spring and bearing against the top plate of the housing, with the pivot point being at the apex of the V. Such springs are unknown on North American specimens. The second option utilizes a V-shaped or feather spring. One end of the spring bears against the top plate of the housing, while the other is formed into a rounded or squared P-shaped tumbler (Figure 38). Such spring/tumblers appear on a number of archaeological door locks (Priess 1975:Figures 109-110; Laroche 1988:Figures 13-14), as well as on some padlocks (Laroche 1988:Figures 17-18), and their presence may well indicate the presence of a French lock.

In addition to the tumbler, there are obstructions around the keyhole, theoretically to prevent or hinder the use of an incorrect key. Known collectively as wards, these are often in the form of fixed plates, pins, or other configurations. They are attached to the main and cover plates and a plate known as the bridge ward (Figure 39). The latter is positioned midway between the other two plates, and serves to align the key in the lock and provides another location for the attachment of additional wards. In English rim locks, the bridge ward is held between two vertical plates (cheeks) set perpendicular to the main plate. The cover plate is set on the ends of the cheeks and often held in place with bolts passing into the main plate. The arrangement of cheeks, bridge ward, and cover plate is a relatively rigid structure and provides stability for the operation of the key. In French locks, the bridge ward appears to be attached to the main plate with tabs bent from the end of the ward.

The cover plate is a separate piece with legs and feet straddling the main ward and attached to the main plate (Figure 38). Although Reaumur (1767:163) states that the feet of the cover plate are held in place with screws, they are often attached with rivets, an arrangement that would make it more difficult to remove the cover for repairs. Streeter (1983:13) notes that German locks also had riveted components.

French locks have a number of wards and other obstructions not commonly found on English locks. The ward system often includes a rake ward which consists of a post attached perpendicular to the main plate and has a number of parallel teeth projecting from it (Figure 38). The teeth–the number, spacing, thickness, and length of which vary–interact with slits in the lower edge of the key bit. Additional obstruction was provided by variations in the shape of the keyhole, matched by variations in the cross section of the key bit. A common cross section on French key bits is that of an inverted T, the T being the lower edge of the bit and cut for the rake ward. The cross section of bits on English keys more commonly exhibits straight diverging sides and a rounded end. Additional support for the operation of a key in a French lock may be provided by a tube, often with a round cross section, attached to the cover plate (Duhamel du Monceau 1767:Plate 19, Figures 6,

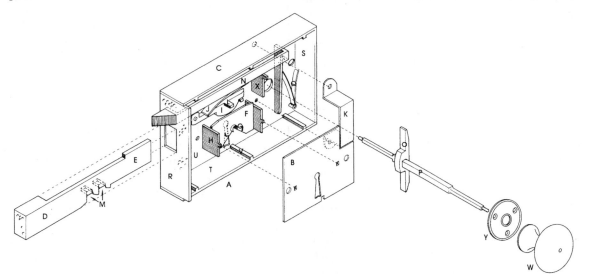

FIGURE 39. Exploded view of a two-bolt English rim lock of the late 18th or early 19th century: *a,* housing (includes main, front, back, top, and bottom plates); *b,* cover plate; *c,* top plate; *d,* lock bolt head; *e,* lock bolt tail; *f,* main/bridge ward; *g,* circle ward; *h,* cheek; *i,* tumbler; *j,* tumbler spring (scotch-spring type); *k,* bolt guide staple; *l,* tumbler stump; *m,* bolt stumps (not visible; behind bolt tail); *n,* latch bolt; *o,* cam/follower; *p,* spindle; *q,* latch bolt spring (feather-spring type); *r,* front plate; *s,* back plate; *t,* bottom plate; *u,* main plate; *v,* rim rivet; *w,* knob; *x,* lock bolt guide; *y,* rose.

9). The tube, which guides the entry of the key into the lock, would extend through the door, its length being approximately equal to the door's thickness. German locks utilized similar tubes (Nägele and Nägele 1836:Plate 5).

A common feature illustrated for French rim locks is the use of a drill pin to guide the key (Duhamel du Monceau 1767:Plate 17, Figure 1, Plate 18, Figure 1). The end of the key is hollow to accommodate the pin. The limitation imposed by this arrangement is that the lock can be operated from only one side. If operation of a lock is required from both sides, it must have a keyhole on either side. These can be aligned so as to access the same mechanism or, as illustrated by Duhamel du Monceau (1767:Plate 22), they can be out of line, thus requiring a separate mechanism (ward system) for either side and involving the use of a drill pin and a pipe key.

Changes in lock security for English locks did not begin to appear until Robert Barron's patent of 1778. One of the initial improvements was the addition of a second tumbler, thereby requiring two parts to be lifted out of the way before the lock bolt could be moved. The second improvement was to introduce a system whereby the tumblers not only had to be lifted to disengage them from the bolt, but they also could not be overlifted. If this were attempted, the tumblers would reengage with other notches in the bolt. A variety of patents followed in an attempt to make locks more secure. The rim locks which had been produced prior to these improvements, however, continued to be manufactured, and seem to be the most common lock found on archaeological sites of the late 18th and early 19th centuries.

Locks resembling the English rim lock were being produced in the United States by the early 19th century (Streeter 1973b:9). A variation from the English design was to shift the latch bolt from above the lock bolt to below it (Streeter 1973b:9). It is further indicated that brass came to be used for some of the parts. Streeter (1973b) also indicates that American-made rim locks are more likely to have marks indicating the manufacturer. English rim locks produced up to the early 19th century do not appear to bear any identifying marks.

Although various lock patents were registered in England and the United States, not all of them caught on. One exception is the 1830 English patent of Carpenter and Young. The specifications for their lock include a number of security measures with tumblers (Price 1856:423), but the most obvious feature is the use of a pivoting latch bar which is held down with a spring and operated with a spindle and cam or follower. Such a concept was not a new idea, however. Pivoting latch bars had been used in spring latches as well as German locks for a considerable time. The so-called "Carpenter lock" gained considerable popularity, being manufactured into the second half of the 19th century (Trump 1954). These locks generally have a circular brass plate or patent seal attached to the outside of the main plate which provides information on the patent, manufacturer, or some other aspect of the lock. Trump (1954) mentions a number of different markings. They are listed in the Russell and Erwin (1865:22) catalogue as "Carpenter Pattern" with the patent seal marked with an eagle and "RUSSEL ERWIN & Co MANUFACTURERS." The box staple for this type of lock is recognizable by the notch which allows the latch bolt head to pass through and drop into the catch. A heavy brass strip reinforces the edge of the staple and provides a sloping surface to lift the latch bolt head. The strip may also be marked with the manufacturer's name or other similar information.

A major transition in lock manufacture took place in the 19th century. This was the eventual, near-complete change to the use of cast iron which, in North America, was accompanied by changes in design as well. These changes were most likely introduced as a result of American manufacturers becoming the major suppliers of locks at this time. The rationale for the shift has not been established, but it involved the housing as well as various components of the mechanism. A major shift in design was in the use of a full cover plate. This completely closed the housing and allowed either side of the lock to be set against the door, eliminating the need for a separate lock for the right and left side of a door as had been the case. There was also a change in lock orientation during this period, the long axis changing from horizontal to vertical.

A possible early example in this transition is a lock with cast-iron housing, including a full cover plate, a cast lock bolt, and tumbler (the latch bolt is missing). The housing still has the equivalent of rim rivets although in this case they are not necessary to hold the housing together. The fake rivets may appear superfluous but they, in fact, provide points on which the cover plate can rest. The front plate is of the old design (longer than the rest of the rim to fit onto the door edge). Hence, the lock is not reversible.

Streeter (1974a:44-45) has suggested that the manufacture of a door lock begins with the key, the size of which also provides the basic unit of measure for the overall lock size. His examination of English locks led him to the conclusion that, using the length of the keyhole as a unit of measure, the height of a lock was about four units, its length was six to seven units, the thickness was about one unit, and the proportion of length to width ranged from one-and-a-half to one-and-three quarters (Streeter 1974a:45). The extent of the validity of such relationships will have to be confirmed through the continuing examination of greater numbers of relevant locks. The indication is that these figures may be generally valid although greater ranges have been observed. A preliminary impression of French locks is that they can be longer relative to their width. During the 19th century, the orientation of locks, rim and otherwise, underwent a shift. It seems that until some time in that century, door locks were horizontal; their horizontal dimension (length) was considerably greater than their vertical dimension (width). The shift reversed this relationship. The vertical dimension became greater and locks of this nature were designated as "upright." The latter term, as defined by Butter (1968:273), applies to locks in which the handle and keyhole are in the same vertical line. As used by Russell and Erwin (1865:10-11), for example, it also refers to locks without handles.

Streeter (1983:Figure 52) and others describe a style of spring latch which requires a key to operate the bolt from one side of the door. The item is a long-latch style with a keyhole-shaped back plate (Monk 1974:43; Streeter 1983:Figure 52). Details of the mechanism are not provided beyond the fact that the key is of an unusual and distinctive form; rather than being affixed to the side of the round shank, the bit is attached to its end by a pin and is designed to pivot. To enter the lock, the bit forms a straight line with the shank. Once inside, however, it pivots to be at a right angle to the shank and functions as a normal bit. This style of key is not known for any other lock styles. Consequently, its presence in an archaeological collection can be taken to indicate the presence of this particular

lock style. Both Streeter (1983:Figure 52) and Monk (1974:43) attribute it to the 19th century.

The catch for a surface-mounted lock, including stock locks, is traditionally called a staple although this does not describe its most common shape. A square staple driven into the door frame provides the simplest catch for a surface-mounted lock. This is inadequate, however, for locks having both a latch and a lock bolt. In this case, the most common catch is a box, still simply called a staple (PEM, Volume 3). These were constructed, as were the locks, by bending a piece of plate to form a top, bottom, and main plate. The back was a separate strap attached with rim rivets. Two sides of the box, the one facing the lock and the one abutting the door frame, were open. The box could be the same width as the lock, the two appearing to form a single object when seen together on a closed door. Operating a latch bolt placed a strain on the edge of the catch. This was compensated for by strengthening the edge, either by rolling it back or adding a strip of thicker metal, sometimes of brass.

Spindles are operated by either levers, knobs, or rings. For German locks with pivoted latch bolts, levers are the norm, often with an ornamental scroll or pad termination. English locks of the 18th century used brass knobs, usually hollow and round or oval in shape (Figure 40a-b). Such knobs were initially attached by passing the spindle completely through them (Figure 40b); one end of the spindle was riveted to hold the knob and the other was threaded for a nut (Streeter 1974a:51). This arrangement left little room for adjusting a knob's position to

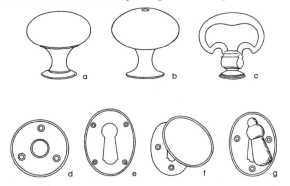

FIGURE 40. Door lock accessories: *a*, round knob; *b*, oval knob with hole for through spindle; *c*, ring handle; *d*, plain, circular rose; *e*, plain, oval keyhole escutcheon; *f*, plain, oval keyhole escutcheon with pivoted oval cover; *g*, plain, oval keyhole escutcheon with pivoted cover. (After PEM, Volumes 5, 6, 8.)

take up slack on the spindle. The spindle had to be close to the required length, allowing for the thickness of the lock, door, and knobs. Later knobs were sometimes held on the shank with a set screw in the neck of the knob (Streeter 1974a:51). Such brass knobs do not necessarily indicate the presence of a two-bolt door lock, however, since they could also have been used on a number of the latch styles discussed previously.

Ceramic knobs were common during the 19th and early 20th centuries, generally being made in three distinct colors: "porcelain" (white), "jet" (black), and "mineral" (mottled brown) (Towne 1904:168). These were attached to iron necks, and usually held on a spindle by a pin or set screw. Glass knobs, attached to metal necks, were also developed during the 19th century. Towne's (1904:168-169) perspective at the end of the 19th century was that ceramic knobs are "used only with the cheapest grades of locks." Cast iron knobs, although "serviceable," are "rarely attractive." Glass knobs, "if properly made . . . are very handsome," while bronze or brass knobs "constitute the best grade and are always used in buildings of the better class." An alternate for English locks of the 18th and early 19th centuries was a brass ring of a relatively standard shape (Figure 40c). They were intended for use on interior doors.

Abrasion damage to a wooden door through the operation of a latch knob was prevented by placing a rose or bearing plate between the knob and the wood. Initially, these were flat, often circular pieces of brass attached to the door with small nails or pins (Figure 40d). Embossed roses came with the introduction of die stamping toward the end of the 18th century (Streeter (1974a:53). Wear at the keyhole was avoided by a brass escutcheon, often oval, attached with three or four fasteners and possibly also having a pivoted cover (Figure 40e-g). Locks having a tubular key guide did not need a keyhole escutcheon.

EMBOSSED LOCKS

A type of door lock which appears in 18th-century French references (*Recueil de planches* 1764-1766:Plate 29; Duhamel du Monceau 1767:215, Plate 32, Figure 1) and on sites with French contexts (Dunton 1972:165-166, Figure 75) is used in association with a sliding bolt with a hasp handle (Figure 41). The lock

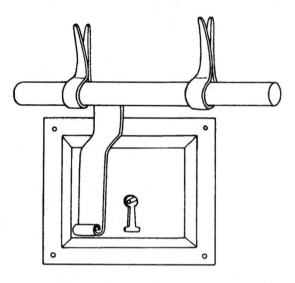

FIGURE 41. Embossed lock. (After Duhamel du Monceau 1767:Plate 32.)

housing consists of two plates: one flat and square; the other also square but embossed with a hollow or depression in the center. The two plates are riveted together to enclose the mechanism, and the housing is attached to the surface of a door. The mechanism appears to be attached to the embossed plate (Duhamel du Monceau 1767:Plate 32, Figure 1). A rectangular slot in this plate permits the entry of a staple-type hasp which serves as the handle for a sliding bolt. The hasp is engaged inside the lock housing by the lock bolt. This type of lock secures the door indirectly since it prevents the sliding bolt from being moved. It differs from an embossed padlock primarily in that it is attached to a door.

Duhamel du Monceau (1767:215) considers the embossed lock to be of great antiquity, usually simply made because it has little value, and seldom used except in the country. Dunton (1972:165) characterizes it as "suitable for cellars." The presence of such a lock in an archaeological collection would suggest a French context predating the mid to late 18th century.

LOQUET À LA CORDELIERE

This is a type of latch which is operated from one side of the door by a specially shaped key (*Recueil de planches* 1764-1766:Plate 31, Figures 151-153; Duhamel du Monceau 1767:136, 138-139, Plate 16, Figures 12-15), hence its inclusion here as a type of lock. The rationale for the name is not clear, but Duhamel du Monceau (1767:136) indicates that they were often used in convent dormitories. The lock bar, guide, and catch may be the same as for a thumb latch. The difference lies in the absence of a handle and thumb-operated lift bar. Instead, the lock bar has a knob attached to its front and a vertical tail affixed to its back. The tail is enclosed in a half tube (Figure 42a) which is attached to the door. From one side, the lock bar is operated by lifting the knob; from the other, it is operated by inserting a key through an escutcheon and lifting it, thereby pushing up on the vertical tail. The shape of the half tube (Figure 42a), the key escutcheon (Figure 42b), and the key (Figure 42c) is quite distinctive, and the presence of any of these components in a collection is conclusive proof of the presence of this type of lock.

English references discuss a lock or latch which, on the basis of key shape, is the same type of lock (Price 1856:Figure 435; Butter 1968:89, Figure 191; Monk 1974:42-43). All the illustrations show the key and keyhole escutcheon, but provide no information concerning the appearance of the latch mechanism. Referred to as a "French latch" (Butter 1968:89) or "French night latch" (Price 1856:Figure 435; Monk 1974:42), it is said to have been invented in 1792 (Butter 1968:89) or "the latter part of the 18th century" (Monk 1974:42) by someone named Odell. This lock type also has English associations although its presence in 19th-century North American contexts is yet to be known. It is known, however, from some probable French contexts (Dubé 1991:Figures 10g, 15f).

MORTISE LOCKS

Mortise locks are set into a mortise on the edge of a door so that only the front plate of the housing is visible. They are similar to rim locks in being one-, two-, or three-bolt locks. The earliest known examples, from the late 18th or early 19th century, have mechanisms similar to those of forged rim locks of the same period.

A major question yet to be answered concerns the inception of the mortise lock. At least one supplier of reproduction hardware claims that a style of mortise lock offered by them has "been used since the early 1700's" (Ball and Ball 1992:77). Neither Moxon (1703:22) nor *The Builder's Dictionary* (1734), however, mention

them in early 18th-century contexts, and Butter (1968:194) notes that mortise-lock makers are not listed in the Birmingham directory prior to 1780. Streeter (1983:11) suggests that they "came into use toward the end of the 18th century," and it is probable that mortise locks found in archaeological contexts do not predate the late 18th century. During the 19th century they were still the less-common lock form, possibly because of the additional work required to cut the mortise. The shift to cast-iron door locks during the 19th century continued to emphasize surface-mounted forms. In 1865, Russell and Erwin (1865) were offering considerably more rim locks than mortise locks. By the beginning of the 20th century, however, mortise locks formed a major portion of the locks offered by such companies as Yale and Towne (Towne 1904:618-673) and Sargent & Company (1910).

As mentioned above, early mortise locks employed the technology and much of the design of rim locks of the same period. The housing is still comprised of a main and back plate bent from a single piece of sheet metal. The top and bottom are attached with rim rivets, and a cover plate is set on the ends of the rim rivets and held down with two or more bolts. The cover plate, however, now completely closes the lock housing. Since it has to be centered on the housing, the front plate is a separate piece of metal, possibly brass. One style, known from various contexts including Price's (1856:Figure 210) listing, is a three-bolt lock type. The bolt arrangement is of the English style with the latch bolt above the lock bolt, but with the

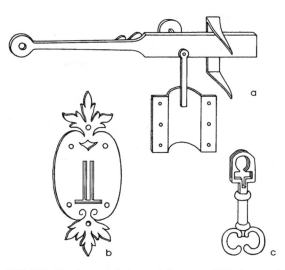

FIGURE 42. *Loquet à la cordeliere: a*, latch bar and half-tube assembly; *b*, key escutcheon; *c*, key. (After Duhamel du Monceau 1767:Plate 16.)

night bolt located between them. The night bolt is operated by a knob, spindle, and cam arrangement; the knob is present on only one side of the door. The two spindles and the keyhole are on a single horizontal line, and the knob roses and keyhole escutcheon are a single plate.

FLUSH LOCKS

A flush lock is recessed into an interior surface, and may be used on drawers or the doors of a cupboard or possibly a closet (Butter 1968:85). This means that the lock is usually out of sight when the drawer or door is closed and may, therefore, not be particularly well finished on the exterior. The main and front plate are bent from a single piece of metal. The mechanism, which is attached to the main plate, is generally smaller than the plate. It is often enclosed by and partly attached to a rim comprised of a single strip of metal which forms the sides, as well as a cover plate which is only slightly larger than the mechanism. The smaller mechanism reduces the amount of wood that needs to be removed to install the lock. A similar lock, identified as a drawer lock, is illustrated in the *Recueil de planches* (1764-1766:Plate 25, Figure 82). Its French origin is apparent in the shape of the spring/tumbler combination, as discussed above. Such locks are operable from only one side, probably using a pipe key. Larger examples which could have been used on room or closet doors are rare (Dunton 1972:Figure 75).

Simmons and Turley (1980:156, Plates 39-40) indicate that flush locks are appropriate in New World Spanish contexts. The lock they illustrate has several features in the mechanism which are similar to those in 18th-century French illustrations; specifically, the shape of the spring and tumbler, and the method of attachment for the cover plate. As mentioned above, latches of similar construction are listed for closets and shutters. Most locks of this type are relatively small and more suited for a drawer or a small door, such as on a cupboard. Larger examples may have served as door locks.

Interpretation of Door Hardware

This report provides an overview of the variety of functions and styles of hardware which may be associated with a door. Cultural and temporal differences exist to some extent and allow more detailed identification or interpretation of specific items, assemblages, or contexts. In an archaeological context, the various parts of a door are likely to become separated and scattered, making structural interpretations more difficult. At the most basic level, the presence of door hardware suggests the presence of a door and, depending on the extent of site disturbance, may provide some indication of the location of doors and the layout of a building. Conversely, the absence of door hardware does not mean that doors were not present. Door hardware, like many other metal artifacts, is salvageable and could have been removed after it was no longer required for its original purpose. Once removed, it could have been reused elsewhere, or reworked to suit other, more immediate needs.

The identification of the material, method of manufacture, and style of a piece of door hardware may provide an indication of its date and cultural affiliation. Wrought iron items may date to any time in the historic period, including the late 19th century. Steel items are less likely to be early. Until some time after the middle of the 19th century, this material was more expensive than wrought iron and its use for door hardware was generally impractical. An object made of machine-rolled stock or using various machine processes to shape or assemble it will date no earlier than the late 18th century. Some objects can be identified as likely having a non-English association. This applies to lock components made in the French or Continental European styles, and may apply to latch handles of some forms. Items produced in one cultural tradition, however, may also find their way to other cultures through trade or other means. Hence, the identification of cultural styles may be misleading.

An archaeological site may occasionally produce a large collection of building hardware, much of which may be door hardware. This permits a more thorough interpretation of the structures involved. In attempting to understand the hardware from a building site, it is important to understand the concept of a hierarchy for the items (Nelson 1980:vii; Chappell 1984:2). Hierarchies exist both within and between buildings. Differences in the quality of the hardware may indicate the social or economic level of a building but, within a building, may simply indicate their location. "In general, the level of expense decreases as one moves from the most to the least public places" (Chappell 1984:2). "In the final analysis, the provenance of hardware within any given building [or archaeological context] must be judged individually and compared with other local examples and [available catalogues]" (Nelson 1980:vii). Hence, what may initially appear to be a diverse collection of items may end up providing a reflection of form and function for a specific structure. Nelson (1980:vii) also makes the important point that "many such studies need to be made before a clearer picture emerges."

REFERENCES

ALCOCK, N.W., AND LINDA HALL
1994   Fixtures and Fittings in Dated Houses 1567-1763. Council for British Archaeology, *Practical Handbooks in Archaeology* 11. London, England.

AMSLER, CORY
1989a   Architectural Hardware, 1700-1860: The Mercer Museum Collection. *Mercer Mosaic: Journal of the Bucks County Historical Society* 6(1):3-17.
1989b   Henry Mercer and the Dating of Old Houses. *Mercer Mosaic: Journal of the Bucks County Historical Society* 6(1):18-28.

ASTON, JAMES, AND EDWARD B. STORY
1939   *Wrought Iron: Its Manufacture, Characteristics and Applications.* A. M. Byers, Pittsburgh, PA.

BALL AND BALL
1992   *Hardware Reproductions* [catalogue]. Ball and Ball, Exton, PA.

THE BUILDER'S DICTIONARY
1734   *The Builder's Dictionary: Or Gentleman and Architect's Companion.* Reprinted 1981, Association for Preservation Technology, Ottawa, Ontario.

BUTTER, F. J.
1931   *Locks and Lockmaking*, 2nd edition. Sir Isaac Pitman, London, England.
1948   *Locks and Builders' Hardware Glossary, Design Manufacture and History.* Josiah Parkes, Willenhall, England.
1968   *An Encyclopaedia of Locks and Builders Hardware.* Josiah Parkes, Willenhall, England.

CHAMBERLAIN, SAMUEL
1928   Notes on Old Wrought Iron. *American Architect* 133:101-107.

CHAPPELL, EDWARD
1984   Looking at Buildings. In "Fresh Advices," Research Supplement to the *Colonial Williamsburg Interpreter*, November. Williamsburg, VA.

D'ALLEMAGNE, HENRY RENÉ
1924   *Decorative Antique Ironwork: A Pictorial Treasury.* Reprinted 1968, Dover Publications, New York, NY.

DOW, GEORGE FRANCIS
1927   The Arts and Crafts in New England 1704-1775. Reprinted 1967 as *DaCapo Press Series in Architecture and Decorative Art* 1. New York, NY.

DUBÉ, FRANÇOISE
1991   La quincaillerie d'architecture de Place-Royale. Ministère des Affaires Culturelle, Les Publications du Québec, Collection Patrimoines, *Dossiers* 71. Québec, Québec.

DUHAMEL DU MONCEAU
1767   *Art du serrurier.* Descriptions des arts et Métiers, faitres ou approuvées par messieurs de l'académie royale des sciences, Paris, France.

DUNTON, JOHN
1972   Building Hardware Excavated at the Fortress of Louisbourg. Department of Indian Affairs and Northern Development, National Historic Parks and Sites Branch, *Manuscript Report Series* 97. Ottawa, Ontario.

ERAS, VINCENT J. M.
1957   *Locks and Keys Throughout the Ages.* Vincent J. M. Eras, H. M. Fracsek, Amsterdam, Netherlands.

FRANK, EDGAR B.
1950   *Old French Ironwork.* Harvard University Press, Cambridge, MA.

GAYLE, MARGOT, AND DAVID W. LOOK
1980   A Historical Survey of Metals. Part I of *Metals in America's Historic Buildings.* United States Department of the Interior, Heritage Conservation and Recreation Service, Technical Preservation Services Division, Washington, DC.

GREAT BRITAIN, OFFICE OF THE COMMISSIONERS OF PATENTS FOR INVENTIONS [GBO]
1873   *Abridgements of Specifications Relating to Hinges, Hinge Joints, and Door Springs. A.D. 1775-1866.* Queen's Printer, London, England.

HARRIS, DONALD A.
1971   Building Hardware from Sainte-Scholastique, Quebec. Department of Indian Affairs and Northern Development, National Historic Parks and Sites Branch, *Manuscript Report Series* 103. Ottawa, Ontario.

HOMMEL, RUDOLF
1944   The Secret Joint Hinge. *Early American Industries Association Chronicle* 4(1):3-4.

HUGHES, G. BERNARD
1957   English Domestic Locks. *The Connoisseur Year Book, 1957,* pp. 100-107. London, England.

JOUSSE, MATHURIN
1627   *La fidelle ouverture de l'art de serrurier.* Georges Griveau, La Fleche.

KELLY, J. FREDERICK
1924   *Early Domestic Architecture of Connecticut.* Reprinted 1967, Dover, New York, NY.

KENDRICK, WILLIAM
1866   Cast Iron Hollow-Ware, Tinned and Enameled and Cast Ironmongery. Frank Cass, London, England. Reprinted 1967 in *Birmingham and the Midland Hardware District*, Samuel Timmins, editor, pp. 103-109. Cass, London, England.

KENYON, WALTER A.
1986   The History of James Bay 1610-1686: A Study in Historical Archaeology. Royal Ontario Museum, *Archaeology Monograph* 10. Toronto.

KNIGHT, EDWARD H.
1876   *Knight's American Mechanical Dictionary.* Reprinted 1979 for The Mid-West Tool Collectors Association and The Early American Industries Association. Riverside Press, Cambridge, MA.

LABONTÉ, COLETTE
1979   Serrurerie Traditionelle. Manuscript, Parcs Canada, Région du Québec, Architecture et Genie, Québec, Québec.

LAROCHE, CHRISTINE
1988   Répertoire descriptive des pièces de quincaillerie d'architecture découvertes sur le site archaéologique du premier palais de l'intendant à Québec (CeEt30) dans les opérations 1 à 17. Université Laval, Québec, *Hors serie* 1. Québec, Québec.

LUNN, KEVIN
1985   Goods on the Bay: Material Culture from Archaeological Investigations of York Factory Hudson's Bay Company Post, 1788-1957. Canadian Parks Service, *Microfiche Report Series* 347. Ottawa, Ontario.

MARTINEAU, F. E.
1866   *Patent Wrought-Iron Hinges.* Frank Cass, London, England. Reprinted 1967 in *Birmingham and the Midland Hardware District*, Samuel Timmins, editor, pp. 610-612. Cass, London, England.

MERCER, HENRY C.
1923   Notes on Wrought-Iron Door Latches. *Old-Time New England* 13(3):139-142.
1924   The Dating of Old Houses. *Old-Time New England* 14(4):170-190.

MONK, ERIC
1974   *Keys: Their History and Collection.* Shire, Aylesbury, Bucks, England.

MOXON, JOSEPH
1703   *Mechanick Exercises. Or the Doctrine of Handy-Works.* Reprinted 1975, The Early American Industries Association, Scarsdale, NY.

NÄGELE, ADAM, AND FERDINAND NÄGELE
1836   *Darstellung der schönen Schlosser-Profession in ihrem ganzen Umfange.* Herausgeben vom Verfasser der Schmied-Profession, n.p.

NELSON, LEE H.
1980   Introduction. In *Illustrated Catalogue of American Hardware of the Russell and Erwin Manufacturing Company*, pp. iii-xiii. Association for Preservation Technology, Ottawa, Ontario.

NOËL HUME, IVOR
1969   *Artifacts of Colonial America.* Alfred A. Knopf, New York, NY.

NUTTING, WALLACE
1921   *Furniture of the Pilgrim Century 1620-1720, Including Colonial Utensils and Hardware.* Bonanza Books, New York, NY.

PEABODY ESSEX MUSEUM (PEM)
Sample Book, Volume 2, watermark 1798. 739.4 S19.2, Peabody Essex Museum, Philips Library, Salem, MA.
Sample Book, Volume 3, watermark 1799. 739.4 S19.2, Peabody Essex Museum, Philips Library, Salem, MA.
Sample Book, Volume 5, watermark 1800. 739.4 S19.2, Peabody Essex Museum, Philips Library, Salem, MA.
Sample Book, Volume 6, watermark 1800; 1806 on cover. 739.4 S19.2, Peabody Essex Museum, Philips Library, Salem, MA.
Sample Book, Volume 8, watermark 1800. 739.4 S19.2, Peabody Essex Museum, Philips Library, Salem, MA.
Sample Book, Volume 9, watermarks 1803, 1804, 1806. 739.4 S19.2, Peabody Essex Museum, Philips Library, Salem, MA.
Sample Book, Volume 10, watermark 1804. 739.4 S19.2, Peabody Essex Museum, Philips Library, Salem, MA.
Sample Book, Volume 11, watermark 1804. 739.4 S19.2, Peabody Essex Museum, Philips Library, Salem, MA.
Sample Book, Volume 12, undated. 739.4 S19.2, Peabody Essex Museum, Philips Library, Salem, MA.
Sample Book, Volume 13, watermarks 1812, 1816, 1817. 739.4 S19.2, Peabody Essex Museum, Philips Library, Salem, MA.
Sample Book, Volume 14, watermark 1814. 739.4 S19.2, Peabody Essex Museum, Philips Library, Salem, MA.
Sample Book, Volume 15, watermark 1815; dated 1817. 739.4 S19.2, Peabody Essex Museum, Philips Library, Salem, MA.
Sample Book, Volume 16, watermark 1812; received 1819. 739.4 S19.2, Peabody Essex Museum, Philips Library, Salem, MA.

PRICE, GEORGE
1856   *A Treatise on Fire & Thief-Proof Depositories and Locks and Keys.* Simpkin, Marshall, London, England.

PRIESS, PETER J.
1972   Building Hardware from the Fort at Coteau du Lac, Quebec. National Historic Sites Service, *Manuscript Report Series* 93. Ottawa, Ontario.
1975   Building Hardware. In Hardware from Fort Beausejour, New Brunswick, by Peter J. Priess, J. Michael Shaughnessy, and Barbara J. Wade, pp. 387-576.

Parks Canada, *Microfiche Report Series* 82. Ottawa, Ontario.

1978 An Annotated Bibliography for the Study of Building Hardware. Parks Canada, *History and Archaeology* 21. Ottawa, Ontario.

1979 A Study of Surface-Mounted Door Locks from a Number of Archaeological Sites in Canada. Parks Canada, *History and Archaeology* 25. Ottawa, Ontario.

PRIESS, PETER J., AND DONALD STREETER
1974 Priess and Streeter Correspondence on Hinges. *Association for Preservation Technology, Bulletin* 6(2):24-33.

PRUDEN, THEODORE (EDITOR)
1974 Historic Hardware in the United States and Canada. *Association for Preservation Technology, Newsletter* 3(3):1-26.

REAUMUR, RENÉ ANTOINE FERCHAULT, SEIGNEUR DE
1767 Des serrures de toutes les especes. In *Art du serrurier*, by Duhamel du Monceau, pp. 159-261. Descriptions des arts et Métiers, faitres ou approuvées par messieurs de l'académie royale des sciences, Paris, France.

RECUEIL DE PLANCHES, SUR LES SCIENCES ET LES ARTS
1764 Serrurerie (Vol. 9). Reprinted 1965, Cercle du livre
-1766 précieux, Paris, France.

RUSSELL AND ERWIN MANUFACTURING COMPANY
1865 *Illustrated Catalogue of American Hardware of the Russell and Erwin Manufacturing Company*. Reprinted 1980, Association for Preservation Technology, Ottawa, Ontario.

SARGENT & COMPANY
1910 *Hardware* [catalogue]. Sargent & Company, New Haven, CT.

SCHIFFER, HERBERT, PETER SCHIFFER, AND NANCY SCHIFFER
1979 *Antique Iron Survey of American and English Forms Fifteenth through Nineteenth Centuries*. Schiffer, Exton, PA.

SIMMONS, MARC, AND FRANK TURLEY
1980 *Southwestern Colonial Ironwork*. Museum of New Mexico Press, Santa Fe.

SONN, ALBERT H.
1928 *Early American Wrought Iron*, 3 volumes. Charles Scribner's Sons, New York, NY.

STEVENS, JOHN R.
1969 Early Cast Iron Latches. *Association for Preservation Technology, Bulletin* 1(3):11-13.

STONE, LYLE M.
1974 Fort Michilimackinac 1715-1781: An Archaeological Perspective on the Revolutionary Frontier.

Publications of the Museum, Michigan State University, Anthropological Series 2. East Lansing.

STREETER, DONALD
1954 Early Wrought Iron Hardware: Spring Latches. *Antiques* 66(2):125-127.

1970 Early American Stock Locks. *Antiques* 98(2):351-355.

1971 Early American Wrought Iron Hardware: Norfolk Latches. *Association for Preservation Technology, Bulletin* 3(4):12-30.

1973a Early American Wrought Iron Hardware: H and HL Hinges, Together with Mention of Dovetails and Cast Iron Butt Hinges. *Association for Preservation Technology, Bulletin* 5(1):22-49.

1973b Some Signed American Rim Locks. *Association for Preservation Technology, Bulletin* (5)2:9-37.

1974a Early American Wrought Iron Hardware: English Iron Rim Locks; Late 18th and Early 19th Century Forms. *Association for Preservation Technology, Bulletin* 6(1):40-67.

1974b Early American Wrought Iron Hardware: Cross Garnet, Side and Dovetail Hinges. *Association for Preservation Technology, Bulletin* 6(2):6-23.

1975a Wrought Iron Hardware for Exterior Shutters. *Association for Preservation Technology, Bulletin* 7(1):38-56.

1975b Early American Wrought Iron Hardware: Slide Bolts. *Association for Preservation Technology, Bulletin* 7(4):104-122.

1976 A Signed American Stock Lock from the Manufactory of J. & J. Patterson. *Association for Preservation Technology, Bulletin* 8(2):76-77.

1980 *Professional Smithing*. Charles Scribner's Sons, New York, NY.

1983 The Historic Development of Hand Forged Iron Builders' Hardware. In *The Technology of Historic American Buildings: Studies of the Materials, Craft Processes, and the Mechanization of Building Construction*, H. Ward Jandl, editor. Association for Preservation Technology. Ottawa, Ontario.

TOWNE, HENRY R.
1904 *Locks and Builders Hardware: A Hand Book for Architects*. John Wiley, New York, NY.

TRUMP, ROBERT TOWNSHEND
1954 The Carpenter-type Lock. *Antiques* 66(6):482.

TWOPENY, WILLIAM
1904 *English Metal Work*. Archibald Constable, London, England.

WOODCROFT, BENNET
1854 *Alphabetical Index of Patentees of Inventions*. Reprinted 1969, Augustus M. Kelley, New York, NY.

PETER J. PRIESS
234 CARROLL ROAD
WINNIPEG, MANITOBA R3K 1H6
CANADA

LYNNE SUSSMAN

Objects vs. Sherds: A Statistical Evaluation

Introduction

This project grew out of a discussion paper on the methodology of using ceramics to interpret archaeological sites. Naturally the subject of object and sherd counts arose. It happens that material culture researchers are singularly unqualified to discuss sherds. Archaeologists almost never deal with them. By this is meant that by the time the material is studied, the forensic science of sherd distribution on a site has already taken place. The archaeologist has presumably studied the material as refuse. We are usually concerned with the character of the material before it was discarded, or rather as if it had never been discarded. We treat the material as objects belonging to the occupants. The distinction between the two approaches is obvious and valuable. You cannot understand your site unless you view the artifacts as garbage (sherds); you cannot understand the occupants unless you view the artifacts as possessions (objects). In this work concern is with ceramics in their roles as possessions.

It will not come as a surprise to anyone who has read numerous archaeological reports that archaeologists are occasionally guilty of blurring the duality of archaeological material. The most irresponsible type of blurring is the failure to establish the links, or the lack thereof, between the refuse and the occupants. (The material found in the ravine all must have belonged to the occupants of the nearest house.) The second type of blurring concerns numbers–counts of sherds indicate the same thing as counts of objects. It is not quite so obvious how heinous the latter practice is. The purpose of this paper is to describe the consequences of treating sherd counts as equivalents to object counts.

The assemblages and their contents as described here are real, so are their physical and cultural attributes (Chism 1972; Sussman 1972). The research questions, however, have been made up purely to explore the object vs. sherd counts (MacLeod 1990; Sussman 1990).

Chi-Square

Archaeologists are well aware of the weaknesses of sherd counts. They know that objects do not neatly break into equal numbers of sherds. They are not blind to the fact that they sometimes recover a complete object and sometimes a tiny fragment. There is published literature on the subject of deriving reliable object counts from sherds (Burgh 1959; Egloff 1973; Chase 1985). To their credit, archaeologists are almost universally in agreement that object counts are desirable, the problem being how to arrive at them. Few are willing to say that one sherd represents one object, a statement that is obvious if sherd counts are used in chi-square statistical tests. A statistician would strongly discourage the comparison of sherd counts using chi-square tests. This test requires that the counts are of independent individuals, not related groups of individuals.

Still, it is tempting to use sherd counts as pretend object counts, especially when they have already been compiled to study deposition on the site. What would happen if the warnings of the statistician are ignored? What would be the ramifications of statistically comparing distributions of artifacts if only sherd counts are used?

Studies in Material Culture Research, 2000:96—103.
Permission to reprint required.

First, to appreciate the effect of sherd counts on site interpretation, one must be reasonably confident that the differences found are not results of cultural or depositional effects, or excavation technique. Comparing ceramics from a 16th-century monastery and a 19th-century landfill site will produce significant differences that far outweigh sherd/object counting.

The ideal test situation would be several rich sites (or distinct components of a site) which shared the same date range, cultural affiliation, depositional character, and excavation techniques. Lower Fort Garry comes as close to this ideal as any site investigated. It was a large Hudson's Bay Company post with buildings that were occupied contemporaneously (Chism 1972). The ceramics in every structure came largely from the Fort Store, and it was almost all tableware or toilet articles made of the same material (transfer-printed white earthenware). Most of it was made by a single manufacturer (Sussman 1972). All structures selected were excavated using the same techniques and recording methods, and all structures were completely excavated. The surface collection, ravine dump, and unprovenienced artifacts were eliminated.

The structures were compared with one another, looking for statistically significant differences in counts of four item types (cups, saucers, plates, and bowls) and separately, in counts of four decorative types (plain, molded, painted, and transfer-printed). This was done once (for each pair of structures) using object counts and again using sherd counts. The chi-square values of these comparisons of item frequencies are presented in Tables 1 and 2.

Even the statistician was surprised at these results. It was expected that the chi-square values would be inflated using sherd counts. After all, there were a lot more sherds than objects. What was not expected were the enormous chi-square values for sherd count comparisons that were absolutely meaningless. Comparisons of the same material using object counts proved to have chi-square values that were much more believable. An extreme example is the comparison between the blacksmith's shop and the fur loft; this comparison has a chi-square value of 199.9 when sherds are counted and a chi-square value of 1.37 when objects are counted.

To grasp the weirdness of the sherd-count comparisons, the chi-square values were divided into four types according to their confidence level. Confidence levels of less than 95% were not considered as being significant. This is Group 1, identifiable in the tables as plain unadorned numbers. Note that only three comparisons out of 45 are not significantly different when sherd counts are used. If really interpreting the site, the researcher would now be obliged to wrestle with the reasons why the counts of the various items were so different in every building. Note also that 32 of the same 45

TABLE 1. CHI-SQUARED VALUES COMPARING FREQUENCIES OF CUPS, SAUCERS, PLATES, AND BOWLS BETWEEN PAIRS OF STRUCTURES– USING SHERD COUNTS

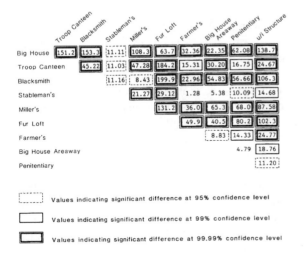

	Troop Canteen	Blacksmith	Stableman's	Miller's	Fur Loft	Farmer's	Big House Areaway	Penitentiary	u/l Structure
Big House	151.2	153.3	11.11	108.3	63.7	32.36	22.35	62.08	138.7
Troop Canteen		45.22	11.03	47.28	184.2	15.31	30.20	16.75	24.67
Blacksmith			11.16	8.43	199.9	22.96	54.83	56.66	106.3
Stableman's				21.27	29.12	1.28	5.38	10.09	14.68
Miller's					131.2	36.0	65.3	68.0	87.58
Fur Loft						49.9	40.5	80.2	102.3
Farmer's							8.83	14.33	24.77
Big House Areaway								4.79	18.76
Penitentiary									11.20

┌──────┐ Values indicating significant difference at 95% confidence level
└┄┄┄┄┄┄┘
□ Values indicating significant difference at 99% confidence level
▣ Values indicating significant difference at 99.99% confidence level

TABLE 2. CHI-SQUARED VALUES COMPARING FREQUENCIES OF CUPS, SAUCERS, PLATES, AND BOWLS BETWEEN PAIRS OF STRUCTURES– USING OBJECT COUNTS

	Troop Canteen	Blacksmith	Stableman's	Miller's	Fur Loft	Farmer's	Big House Areaway	Penitentiary	u/l Structure
Big House	6.92	3.30	1.23	19.9	10.2	3.92	1.95	4.12	4.77
Troop Canteen		4.51	1.25	5.25	12.6	3.82	7.68	3.36	1.24
Blacksmith			3.13	11.42	1.37	5.98	6.46	6.60	3.85
Stableman's				8.16	7.41	0.64	2.21	0.92	1.04
Miller's					20.5	15.5	17.6	12.5	8.86
Fur Loft						12.2	11.3	11.6	7.61
Farmer's							3.96	0.30	1.08
Big House Areaway								3.46	6.32
Penitentiary									1.30

┌┄┄┄┄┄┄┐ Values indicating significant difference at 95% confidence level
└┄┄┄┄┄┄┘
□ Values indicating significant difference at 99% confidence level
▣ Values indicating significant difference at 99.99% confidence level

comparisons are *not* significantly different when object counts are used!

Group 2, distinguished by a broken-line box around the values (7.81 to 11.34), is made up of those comparisons that are different with confidence levels from 95% to just below 99%. Differences at these levels are considered statistically significant.

Group 3, distinguished by a solid-line box around the values (11.42 to 21.11), is made up of those comparisons that are different with confidence levels from 99% to just below 99.99%. These are high confidence levels. A conclusion that the differences are real would be considered very safe for these cases.

Group 4, distinguished by a double line box around the values (higher than 21.11), is made up of those comparisons that are different with confidence levels at 99.99% and higher. The chance of any difference this great occurring randomly is considered almost astronomically remote. Yet note that most of the sherd count differences were this great. Thirty of the comparisons were significantly different at this level when sherds were counted; not one comparison was significantly different at this level when objects were counted.

To say that the chi-square values using sherd counts are inflated is such an understatement as to miss the point. Not only are extremely significant differences found that do not exist, but the real differences are lost in all of the noise. When object counts were used, all of the thirteen significant differences found involved either the miller's house or the fur loft. The fact that something potentially interesting was happening at these structures is not at all apparent when sherd counts were used.

Comparisons of counts for decoration types produce similar results. Of 21 comparisons, 18 are significantly different at a 99.99% confidence level when sherds are counted, whereas only one comparison is significantly different at that level when objects are counted.

Correlational Statistics

Correlational statistics are the perennial favorites of the social and medical sciences. They are meant to answer questions such as "is there a positive relationship between blue eyes and musical genius?" They are often used in an exploratory way, to identify areas of promising research.

For this exercise, it was decided to look for a positive relationship between serving dishes (platters, tureens, gravy boats, etc.) and toiletware (washbasins, ewers, and chamber pots). This is not as farfetched as it may sound. These items can be considered optional household effects, compared to the basic cups, saucers, plates, and bowls.

The statistical analysis used was a Pearson's correlation of frequencies of servers with toilet articles. The frequencies are relative to the combined number of cups, saucers, plates, and bowls. The results of the object-based frequencies and the sherd-based frequencies can be seen in the two scattergrams depicted in Figures 1-2. The object-based frequencies are so different from the sherd-based frequencies, at first it was thought that the scattergrams must be wrong. Each dot represents a structure. The horizontal axis is the percentage of servers found (relative to cups, saucers, plates, and bowls). The vertical axis is the percentage of toiletware found. An ideal positive correlation would lie in a diagonal line from lower left to upper right. The correlation coefficient using objects is +.25, indicating a definite, though not strong, tendency to find servers in the same relative quantities as toilet articles and vice versa. The correlation coefficient using sherds is -.06, indicating absolutely no tendency for the two types of articles to be found together. (Note: correlation coefficients have values ranging from +1 indicating perfect positive correlation, to 0 indicating no relationship between quantities, to -1 indicating perfect negative correlation.) If the scattergrams are again studied it can be seen why there are difficulties in using sherd counts as proportions. As an example, note the dot lying along the bottom axis to the far right. This dot represents a structure wherein no toiletware, but some servers were found. When these servers were counted as objects they made up about 8% of the assemblage, but when they were counted as sherds they made up about 32% of the same assemblage. Obviously one or two servers broke into numerous pieces. It is this variation in the numbers of sherds representing articles which masks any relationship between the articles.

These Pearson's correlation coefficients are intended to provide only an approximate first look at the data. The data were not transformed (as counts or proportions normally are prior to any rigorous statistical analysis) and no statistical

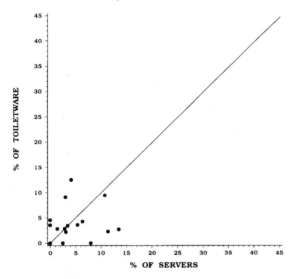

FIGURE 1. Correlation between toiletware and servers: using object counts. (Drawing by Dorothea Larsen.)

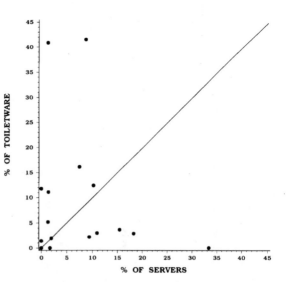

FIGURE 2. Correlation between toiletware and servers: using sherd counts. (Drawing by Dorothea Larsen.)

tests were run to determine the significance of the coefficients. In the normal course of research, relationships would be explored by just such simple analysis. At a preliminary stage, rigor is less important than indications of promising areas of research. This is what is so disturbing about the results of these correlations. If sherd counts had been used, thinking that their proportions were accurate enough for at least indications of relationships, the researcher would have immediately abandoned any exploration of server/toiletware relationship. One could hardly get less encouragement than a correlation coefficient of -.06.

Proportions

Archaeological material is often reported, not as counts, but as proportions of some total. Proportions cannot be compared statistically, unless the numbers (counts) they are based on are considered. Without them, there is no mathematical way of knowing the significance of any differences observed in proportions of two assemblages; one assemblage could consist of two examples, while the other could consist of thousands. This is a fact that, mystifyingly, is ignored in some archaeological reporting. There are reports which carefully tabulate proportions without mentioning counts–as if proportions provided more, rather than less, information.

Initially, because of this, there was no intention of comparing the proportions based on sherds with those based on objects. It was questioned, however, whether the proportions arrived at using sherds even *appeared* to be the same (or close enough to make no difference) as the proportions arrived at using objects. Figures 3-12 depict bar graphs showing proportions of items and decorative types for the five structures with the greatest amount of ceramics. With the understanding that, for comparative purposes, there is no mathematical significance to the sizes of the bars, the results of many of the comparisons were sufficiently *different looking* to be interesting to anyone concerned with a sherd-equals-object hypothesis. Any difference under 25% was considered to be insignificant. That is, if the relative difference calculated as

$$\frac{\text{Difference between object-and sherd-based proportion}}{\text{Object-based proportion}} \times 100\%$$

is *more* than 25%, it is safe to say that this difference is a deformity caused by the sherd counts. On the graphs, the sherd proportions that are unacceptably different from the object proportions are flagged with a thumbs-down hand. Those that are acceptable are flagged with a check-mark. Proportions based on counts of less than ten were not considered; these are the unflagged bars. The numerical code for the items translates as follows: 1=saucers; 2=cups; 3=plates; 4=bowl; 5=pitcher; 6=serving dish; 7=washbasin; 8=ewer; 9=chamber pot; 10=other; 11=unidentified. The numerical code for decoration types translates as follows: 1=molded;

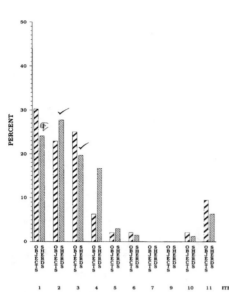

FIGURE 3. Troop canteen: comparison of object and sherd proportions by item (total objects, 96; total sherds, 336). (Drawing by Dorothea Larsen.)

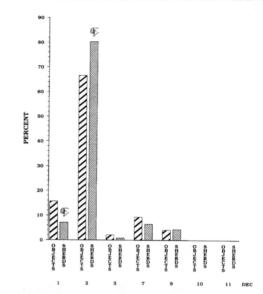

FIGURE 4. Troop canteen: comparison of object and sherd proportions by decoration (total objects, 96; total sherds, 336). (Drawing by Dorothea Larsen.)

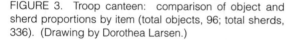

2=transfer print; 3=painted; 7=combinations; 9=plain; 10=other; 11=unidentified.

Looking at these graphs, one has to conclude that sherd proportions are unreliable reflections of object proportions. They may be very close in some cases and highly different in others. The graph of the unidentified structure is an extreme example. If trying to identify the building's function based on proportions of item types, quite different data would be used depending on whether sherd or object propor-

tions were used. The problem with proportions of anything is that an abnormally large or small occurrence of a single type will affect all the other proportions. The proportions of sherds, not surprisingly, seem to be affected by the size of the items–the large serving dishes and toilet articles producing more sherds than their smaller counterparts in the assemblage.

The object and sherd proportions based on decoration are much closer to each other. This is due partly because decoration *on this site*

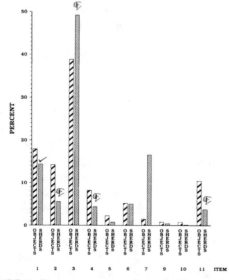

FIGURE 5. Big house: comparison of object and sherd proportions by item (total objects, 134; total sherds, 690). (Drawing by Dorothea Larsen.)

FIGURE 6. Big house: comparison of object and sherd proportions by decoration (total objects, 134; total sherds, 690). (Drawing by Dorothea Larsen.)

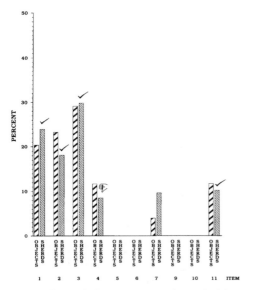

FIGURE 7. Farmer's house: comparison of object and sherd proportions by item (total objects, 103; total sherds, 188). (Drawing by Dorothea Larsen.)

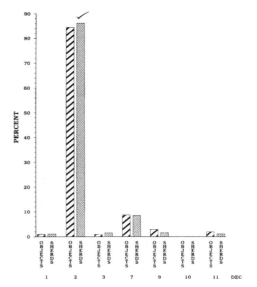

FIGURE 8. Farmer's house: comparison of object and sherd proportions by decoration (total objects, 103; total sherds, 188). (Drawing by Dorothea Larsen.)

is not related to vessel size, and partly to the extraordinary dominance of a single decorative type (60% of all ceramics on the site are transfer-printed). It is not necessary to count either sherds or objects to conclude that every structure's ceramic assemblage is made up largely of transfer-printed pieces.

When the assemblages from all of the structures are combined, the differences between proportions of items based on sherd counts and those based on object counts are smaller. The bar graphs (Figures 13-14) compare proportions

of items based on sherds with those based on objects for the whole site. If questions are asked about the site generally (such as, what are the most common items from the site?), both the sherd counts and the object counts tell the same thing. If conclusions about the site are to be accomplished by comparing proportions of some of the larger items such as washbasins, chamber pots, and servers, then these conclusions are on shakier ground. The data on more than half the item types are unreliable if proportions based on sherd counts are used.

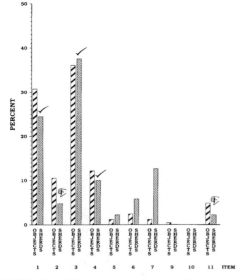

FIGURE 9. Fur loft/store: comparison of object and sherd proportions by item (total objects, 247; total sherds, 1639). (Drawing by Dorothea Larsen.)

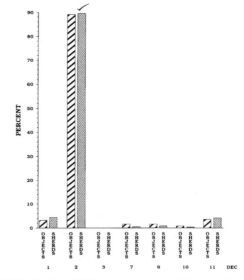

FIGURE 10. Fur loft/store: comparison of object and sherd proportions by decoration (total objects, 247; total sherds, 1639). (Drawing by Dorothea Larsen.)

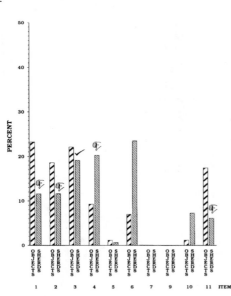

FIGURE 11. Unidentified structure: comparison of object and sherd proportions by item (total objects, 86; total sherds, 345). (Drawing by Dorothea Larsen.)

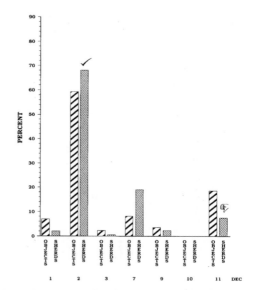

FIGURE 12. Unidentified structure: comparison of object and sherd proportions by decoration (total objects, 86; total sherds, 345). (Drawing by Dorothea Larsen.)

Conclusions

The purpose of this exercise in duplicate counting has been to see what happens when sherd counts are used as the equivalents of object counts. These are the results:

1. When sherd counts are used directly, the results can be truly nightmarish. It is now obvious why statisticians discourage chi-square tests with sherd counts.

2. When sherd proportions are used to compare occurrences of traits between structures

(i.e., between samples that are much smaller than the whole site), the results are alarmingly different from those using object proportions. On the basis of our results, correlation statistics using sherd frequencies are almost as bad as chi-square tests using sherd counts.

3. When comparing proportions by themselves, one can only evaluate the *appearance* of difference or likeness between sherd counts and object counts. Based on this intuitive approach, it is my impression that if using a large sample (7790 sherds equaling 1938 objects have been

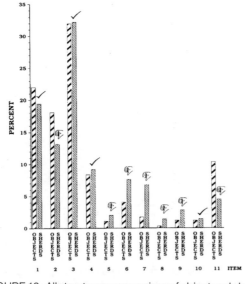

FIGURE 13. All structures: comparison of object and sherd proportions by item. (Drawing by Dorothea Larsen.)

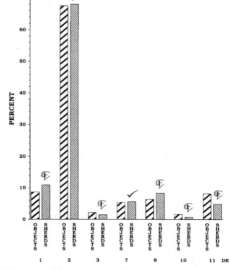

FIGURE 14. All structures: comparison of object and sherd proportions by decoration. (Drawing by Dorothea Larsen.)

recovered from Lower Fort Garry), and if counting traits that are not linked to vessel size (knowing this might be problematical), there is a reasonable hope that the proportions based on sherd counts approximate those based on object counts. On the other hand, these proportions can never be used comparatively because they have no mathematical validity.

The simple statistics and counting described in this work are standards in the repertoire of archaeological research. They are used to demonstrate differences or similarities among groups. When archaeologists report on the quantities of ceramic found at their sites, they presumably are providing information that allows these sites to be compared with others. The numbers they provide are meant to be used rigorously. That is, differences among the ceramic types themselves or among the sites will be looked for using just the techniques used in this paper. The question has been: are groups of sherds equivalent to groups of objects? Yes? No? Sort of? Sometimes? The answer did not prove to be a surprise: no. The surprise lay in the degree of the differences that resulted when the same material was counted as sherds and as objects. Based on what has been seen with the data from a respectably large site, it is concluded that for any serious research purposes, sherd counts cannot be used as substitutes for object counts.

ACKNOWLEDGEMENTS

I am grateful to Duncan MacLeod, the anonymous statistician whose presence is so evident in the text above. I relied not only on his statistical expertise but on his nose for intellectual trickery. Thanks are also due to the computer analyst, Richard Aylesworth and to Dan Pittman who entered the data into an electronically retrievable form.

REFERENCES

BURGH, ROBERT F.
1959 Ceramic Profiles in the Western Mound at Awatovi, Northeastern Arizona. *American Antiquity* 25(2):184-202.

CHASE, PHILIP G.
1985 Whole Vessels and Sherds: An Experimental Investigation of their Quantitative Relationships. *Journal of Field Archaeology* 12:213-218.

CHISM, JAMES V.
1972 Excavations at Lower Fort Garry, 1965-67. *Canadian Historic Sites: Occasional Papers in Archaeology and History* 5. Ottawa, Ontario.

EGLOFF, B. J.
1973 A Method for Counting Ceramic Rim Sherds. *American Antiquity* 38(3):351-353.

MACLEOD, DUNCAN
1990 Analysis of Data to Compare Accuracy of Object-Based and Sherd-Based Information. Manuscript, Parks Canada, Ottawa, Ontario.

SUSSMAN, LYNNE
1972 The Ceramics from Lower Fort Garry. Parks Canada, *Manuscript Report Series* 87. Ottawa, Ontario.
1990 Catalogue of Sherds and Objects Excavated at Lower Fort Garry. Manuscript, Parks Canada, Ottawa, Ontario.

LYNNE SUSSMAN
Low, QUÉBEC J0X 2C0
CANADA

CHARLES S. BRADLEY

Smoking Pipes for the Archaeologist

Introduction

Tobacco consumption had become firmly entrenched in most Western industrial societies by the late 16th century. The popularity of the activity is evidenced by the abundance of smoking pipe remnants which frequent the artifact assemblages of most historical sites. The cheap, fragile, and expendable nature of clay pipes, the standard of the early pipe industry, coupled with the character of the smoking activity which generally deposited discarded pipes where they were consumed, have combined to produce an extensive record from which to draw valuable insight into the social lifeways and material consumption patterns of past cultures. Pipe attributes such as maker's marks, decorative elements, stem–bore diameter, and bowl size, style, and configuration, can help date the contexts from which the artifacts were recovered. Although a clay tobacco pipe can be considered a fragile commodity as a unit, pipe stems, once fragmented, provide an ideal, durable index for dating archaeological contexts prior to the 1760s. The quality and source of the pipes can also reflect the status of the user as well as current trade networks.

This work is not meant to be the definitive word on pipe manufacture, but is designed to provide a succinct and practical field guide for cataloguing and dating smoking pipes from archaeological contexts. It attempts to establish consistent terminology and a rudimentary, yet accurate, descriptive framework for recording the attributes of various types of pipes. The report also discusses the reworking of pipes, and use/wear marks on its various components, as well as such strategies as minimum object counts and bowl-to-stem ratios, and the significance of such analysis.

This study is a compilation of the contributions made by a number of material culture researchers who have worked on smoking pipe

artifacts in the Parks Canada National Reference Collection over the past thirty years. Consequently, emphasis is on the European pipe tradition in Canada. Aboriginal pipes are beyond the scope of this paper.

Pipe Attributes and Characteristics

"Smoking pipe" is the general functional term employed when referring to this artifact class. Labels such as "tobacco pipe" are restrictive in that they represent specific smoking pipe types, and non-tobacco pipes have been encountered in the archaeological record (Figure 1). Furthermore, smoking pipes did not always consume tobacco, especially during times of scarcity; e.g., scraped willow root (Greenhous 1987:140).

Regarding orientation, a pipe should be described from the perspective of the smoker; the portion referred to as the bowl "back" is that section of the bowl that faces the smoker when the pipe is being smoked (Figure 2).

The terminology presented here applies to both clay and component pipes. These can be classified as single- or multiple-unit pipes. Single-unit pipes are of one-piece construction as exemplified by the common molded white clay pipe. Multiple-unit pipes, composed of two or more parts, can be further subdivided into two-unit (two parts) and multi-unit (three or more components) forms (Figure 3). A composite pipe

FIGURE 1. Pipes for substances other than tobacco: **a**, reproduction of an opium pipe bowl recovered from an 1850s context, San Juan Islands, Washington. Note the Chinese characters on the side identifying the maker; **b**, ceramic "toke stone" used in the consumption of marijuana, recovered from the sod layer during excavation of the Ottawa Lock Station, Ottawa, Ontario. (Photo by Rock Chan.)

Studies in Material Culture Research, 2000:104—133.
Permission to reprint required.

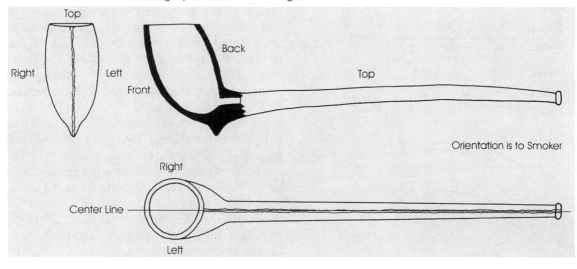

FIGURE 2. Pipe orientation. (Drawing by C. F. Richie.)

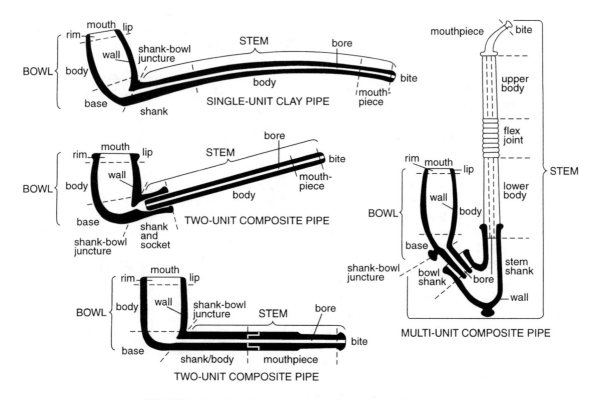

FIGURE 3. Smoking-pipe terminology. (Drawing by C. F. Richie.)

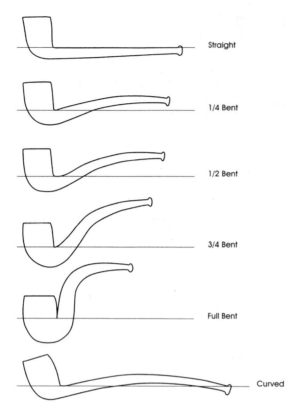

FIGURE 4.   Stem configurations.   (Drawing by C. F. Richie.)

reflecting a Central European tradition, which also became a prevalent form in the United States industry, incorporates a socket-shank that was designed to accept a separate stem of a different material.

A functional pipe consists of a bowl that holds the substance to be smoked, and a stem which transports the smoke to the mouth. The bowl is comprised of several parts which are identified in Figure 3. The point where the bowl and stem meet is the shank/bowl juncture. Feet and spurs are often found at the juncture of the shank and the base of the bowl. On clay pipes, maker's marks may appear on the shanks, bowls, spurs, and feet, while bowl decoration may also extend onto the shank and the stem of some models. The stem (or stem body), which generally tapers toward the bite on white clay pipes, connects the shank to the mouthpiece, the end of which is called a bite or bit. The hole running through the stem is called the bore.

Figure 4 illustrates the standard stem configurations of smoking pipes. Stems range from straight to curved, and include several degrees of bent forms. Although many of these stem styles are generally associated with composite pipes, molded clay imitations of fashionable composite designs were also manufactured. Fragmentary stems may not always conform to the standard. The specimen in Figure 5 is a section of a coiled pipe. Such smoking curios were fashionable novelties during the Victorian era and periodically appear in the archaeological record.

The condition of smoking pipe material can be an important factor in identifying the cause of deposition. For example, the presence of the relatively complete specimens in Figure 6 in latrine fill likely represents accidental loss. Condition encompasses the degree of completeness of the artifact by trait and attribute. Parts of a multi-component pipe should be considered as separate artifacts and described in degrees of completeness relative to the artifact and not to the pipe from which they came. A multi-component pipe is entered as a single artifact, and described as a whole prior to describing each component separately. A *complete* pipe is one with all elements intact as originally manufactured; a *functionally complete* pipe has been reworked to completeness or shows signs of use after breakage. Figures 7 and 8 illustrate the various levels of completeness that may be

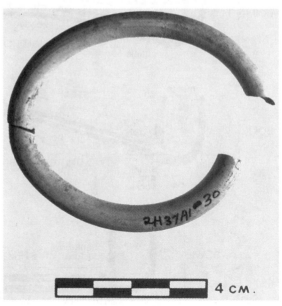

FIGURE 5. Section of a coil pipe from a mid- to late-19th-century context at Fort Wellington, Prescott, Ontario. The presence of a bore indicates that this came from a functional pipe. (Photo by Rock Chan.)

FIGURE 6. Exploded view of two complete composite pipes. The specimen on the left is identified as a half-bent billiard with a military-style mouthpiece. The bowl is not briar but possibly of pearwood. The exterior surface was originally coated with black filler paint, typical of non-briar bowls or briars of inferior quality. The silver-plated brass shank ferrule was secured in grooves on the shank with an interior spring clip mechanism. The hard rubber mouthpiece and the metal tenon jacket were inserted into the ferrule spring clip which is forced over the end of the jacket, securing the mouthpiece to the ferrule. The case (a remnant of which is situated below the pipe) was black leather with a red felt lining and brass furniture. The pipe on the right is a traditional bent wooden style. The short, round briarwood bowl curves into a carved shank to accept the half-bent saddle style, hard-rubber mouthpiece. Elements of a nickel-plated brass ferrule were detected as were remnants of a spark cap. The threaded tenon was incorporated into the mouthpiece design. The mouthpiece is marked NRCo., identified as the mark of the Novelty Rubber Company, a firm that manufactured rubber products in New Brunswick, New Jersey, from 1855 to 1870 (Richie 1981:15). The recovery of these two pipes from 1870 to 1880 latrine fill at Fort Walsh, Saskatchewan, accounts for their relatively intact state. (Photo by Rock Chan.)

encountered within a pipe assemblage. The categories are:

1. Complete pipe: A complete bowl and stem, though the bowl may have portions of less than one major attribute missing.

2. Incomplete pipe: Specimens that do not meet the "complete pipe" criteria. This term should precede the categories listed below:

    a. Whole bowl: The complete bowl without any portion of the stem beyond the shank/bowl juncture. The bowl may have portions of less than one major attribute missing.

    b. Whole stem: The complete stem without any portion of the bowl beyond the stem/bowl juncture.

    c. Incomplete bowl: Any portion of a bowl less than a whole bowl as defined above.

    d. Incomplete stem: Any portion of a stem less than a whole stem as defined above.

Combinations of the whole and incomplete categories can be used except "whole bowl, whole stem" which should be subsumed under "complete pipe."

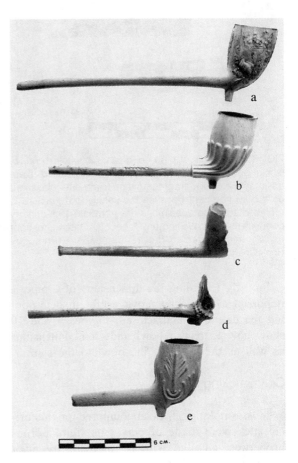

FIGURE 7. Levels of pipe condition: *a*, complete pipe (20th century; Fort Wellington, Prescott, Ontario); *b*, whole bowl/stem fragment (late 19th-early 20th century; Fort Wellington); *c*, bowl fragment/whole stem (mid to late 19th century; Lower Fort Garry, Selkirk, Manitoba); *d*, bowl fragment/whole stem (late 19th century; Fort Wellington, Prescott, Ontario); *e*, functionally complete, incomplete pipe (late 19th-early 20th century; Red Bay, Labrador). (Photo by Rock Chan.)

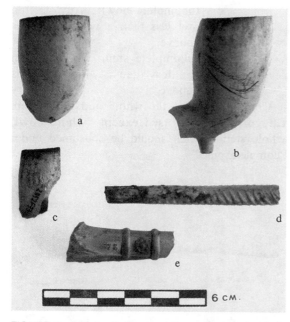

FIGURE 8. Levels of pipe condition: *a*, whole bowl; *b*, whole bowl/stem fragment; *c*, bowl fragment; *d*, stem fragment; *e*, bowl fragment/stem fragment, classified as a bowl fragment because the shank/bowl juncture is represented. The specimens are from late-19th-century contexts at Fort Wellington, Prescott, Ontario, except for *d*, which dates to the 1840s-1850s. (Photo by Rock Chan.)

Properly recording the dimensions of a pipe is important as they can prove useful in determining the date of manufacture. Figures 9 and 10 show how to record bowl and stem dimensions as well as the angle of the bowl to the stem.

Clay Smoking Pipes

Most smoking pipes encountered on historical sites were made of clay. Its light, porous properties, coupled with its malleability prior to firing, made clay an ideal medium for pipe manufacture. Various clays were employed, the most common being a white ball clay, erroneously referred to as "kaolin" in the North American archaeological literature. A range of red to buff to orange clays, as well as occasional dark varieties, were also used. Although the majority of clay pipes were plain, they may also possess polished or glazed finishes.

Manufacturing Marks

A description of the complex process of clay pipe manufacture is beyond the scope of

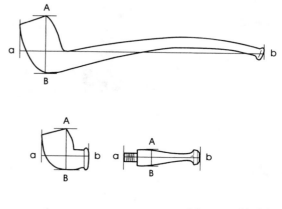

A-B   overall height
a-b   overall length

FIGURE 9. Measuring the overall dimensions of a smoking pipe: top, single-unit pipe; bottom, two-unit composite pipe bowl and stem. Debate exists over the merit of "the overall height" measurement as shown here. Some researchers feel that this should be measured perpendicular to the plane of the bowl rim, similar to bowl dimensions A-B in Figure 10. Either measurement is acceptable, but indicate which*ru are recording. (Drawing by C.F. Richie.)

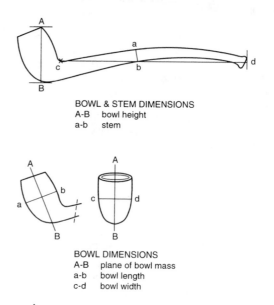

BOWL & STEM DIMENSIONS
A-B   bowl height
a-b   stem

BOWL DIMENSIONS
A-B   plane of bowl mass
a-b   bowl length
c-d   bowl width

ANGLE OF THE BOWL
A-B   plane of bowl mass
a-b   plane of stem
x   angle of the bowl mass away from plane of stem

FIGURE 10. Proper orientations for recording bowl and stem dimensions, as well as the angle of the bowl to the stem. (Drawing by C. F. Richie.)

this report and has been well documented by a number of other researchers (Walker 1971b, 1977; Ayto 1994:19-24). In brief, the prepared clay was placed in a mold, the bowl was reamed with a plunging tool, and a wire was pushed through the stem to form the bore. The latter process usually left a small indentation or scar on the interior of the bowl opposite the bore.

Most clay pipes encountered in archaeological collections were made in two-piece molds, with each piece forming a longitudinal half of the pipe. Seams extend along the top and bottom of the stem and up the front and back of the bowl. The marks were usually removed after the molding process and prior to firing. Trimming marks appear in the form of facets left by the trimming knife. The application of decorative floral sprigs or fronds along the seams was a popular method of masking the mold marks to reduce the labor required to produce a pipe.

Mold marks could also be obliterated by polishing, a burnishing process that applied a uniform, smooth, hard finish to the entire pipe. This step generally identifies better-quality pipes associated with continental, specifically Dutch, manufacture. Evidence of polishing consist of numerous thin striations that follow the contours of the pipe and the resultant dense, smooth surface (Figure 16).

Manufactured Bites

The identification of manufactured bites, also referred to as "bits" in the United States (Weber 1965:169), is important as these can help establish a minimum object count for the pipes in a collection. At least six bite configurations have been encountered at archaeological sites: flared lip, raised lip, plain flat lip, beveled lip, rounded, and rounded flat (Pfeiffer 1982:125). Two types of mouthpieces are generally encountered: in-mold and cut-made; a third type, termed salvaged, appears occasionally:

1. In-mold: Perhaps the most obvious bite style is that which consists of a raised lip around the end of the stem in imitation of the mouthpiece of a composite pipe. A second, more common type of in-mold bite consists of a bulbous or convex contour at the tip, often with a small cylindrical projection at the opening which was created while drawing out the bore wire during production.

2. Cut-made: A flush, cut-made mouthpiece may not be as readily detected. Performed prior to firing, this process involved cutting off the rough end of the stem, usually at an angle so that the very end is tapered. Careful examination of the bite may reveal the cut mark and often a very small projection caused by residual clay adhering to the pipe when the excess material is pulled away.

3. Salvaged: A third type of mouthpiece consists of a pipe stem with a broken end that has been glazed. Broken pipes were glazed and marketed in an attempt to salvage batches of damaged or substandard pipes. Since this was done by the manufacturer, such pipes constitute manufactured bites.

Glazing was one way of treating the bite to keep the smoker's lips from sticking to its surface. The pipe ends were simply dipped in a glaze prior to firing, producing a smooth finish over the porous clay surface. Evidence suggests that yellow/brown and green glazes were employed to a minor degree towards the end of the 1700s, rising dramatically in popularity during the 1800s (Noël Hume 1969:302). Mouthpieces treated with paint and sealing wax, which became popular during the last quarter of the 1800s, have also been recovered archaeologically (Figure 11).

Heels, Feet, and Spurs

Heels and feet were usually associated with early pipes, being replaced by spurs as the pipe form evolved. While the heels and feet on earlier styles enabled the pipe to stand upright on a flat surface, spurs allowed later pipes to be held comfortably while being smoked as the bowl would become very hot. Spike and peg-shaped spurs, located at the base of the bowl at the shank/bowl juncture, were the two principal styles. Some bowl styles did not possess these features.

Decoration and Design

The shape of a pipe bowl may sometimes be considered as decorative, as in the case of effigy pipes (Figure 12) and imitations of meerschaum, calabash, and woodstock styles (Figures 13-14). When describing decorative elements, the method by which they were imparted should be noted.

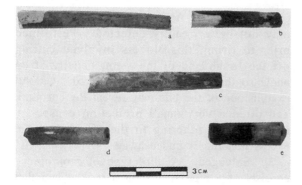

FIGURE 11. Pipe stem bites exhibiting various finishes designed to prevent the smoker's lips from sticking to the porous material: *a*, glazed (Signal Hill, St. John's, Newfoundland); *b*, glazed—note the wear marks where teeth have abraded the glaze (Fort Temiscamingue, Quebec); *c*, red wax (Castle Hill, Placentia, Newfoundland); *d*, red wax (Signal Hill, St. John's, Newfoundland); *e*, black paint (1870s-1880s; Fort Walsh, Saskatchewan). (Photo by Rock Chan.)

FIGURE 12. Examples of effigy bowls: *a*, sometimes referred to as a hussar effigy, there are several varieties of this decorative style ranging from very military-like to an obscure to civilian likeness. Variations are sometimes referred to as a sultan effigy. In the hussar style, a military cap forms the rim and mouth of the bowl. Close inspection may reveal a chin strap indicating the base of a helmet or possible pillbox cap with a puggaree and badge at the front. A high military style of collar can be detected at the junction of the bowl and stem (Fort Coteau du Lac, Coteau du Lac, Quebec); *b-d*, standard variations of a male effigy from post-1840s contexts (Le Vieille Maison des Jesuites, Sillery, Quebec; Fort Wellington, Prescott, Ontario; Signal Hill, St. John's, Newfoundland); *e*, fragmented bowl decorated with a lady's effigy. The fine craftsmanship coupled with remnants of painted detail indicate a pipe of probable French manufacture. The clothing style is suggestive of the latter half of the 1800s (Colonel By House, Ottawa, Ontario); *f*, knight with mailed hood, ca. 1870s. This specimen is unusual in that the effigy faces the smoker (Fort Wellington, Prescott, Ontario); *g*, lady effigy in a socket-stemmed style of probable U.S. manufacture (probably mid 1800s; non-archaeological specimen). (Photo by Rock Chan.)

FIGURE 13. Meerschaum pipe designed and finished to imitate a calabash (late 19th-early 20th century; Fort George, Niagara-on-the-Lake, Ontario). Calabashes, consisting of clay or meerschaum bowls inserted into specially prepared gourds, originated in South Africa and became fashionable in Europe and North America toward the end of the 1800s. (Photo by Rock Chan.)

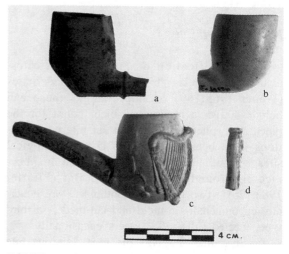

FIGURE 14. Clay imitations of wooden pipe bowl styles: *a*, red clay panel style with a raised ring around the stem simulating the junction of the wood shank and the straight stem (late 19th-early 20th century; Fort Wellington, Prescott, Ontario); *b*, white clay billiard style (Signal Hill, St. John's, Newfoundland); *c*, white clay pipe with a half-bent stem, imitating a popular wooden style (Signal Hill); *d*, white clay bite fragment designed to resemble an articulated bite from a multi-component pipe (1870-1884; Lower Fort Garry, Selkirk, Manitoba). (Photo by Rock Chan.)

FIGURE 15. Some decorative elements on bowls dating from the mid to late 19th century: **a**, crossed lacrosse sticks and ball (Rideau Canal, Ottawa, Ontario); **b**, bowl fragment finished with an egg and claw motif (1870-1884; Lower Fort Garry, Selkirk, Manitoba); **c**, acorn bowl, 1857-1877; Lower Fort Garry); **d**, terra cotta urn bowl with a glazed finish of probable U.S. manufacture (ca. 1860; Fort George, Niagara-on-the-Lake, Ontario); **e**, knob-decorated bowl, sometimes referred to as an imitation corncob style; corncobs were softwood pipes that were developed initially for local consumption in the central United States (Fort George Military Reserve, Niagara-on-the-Lake, Ontario); **f**, thorn-decorated stem (1857-1877; Lower Fort Garry); **g**, scalloped bowl (Signal Hill, St. John's, Newfoundland). (Photo by Rock Chan.)

Furthermore, decoration applied during the manufacturing process should be distinguished from that applied afterwards by the purchaser. Such alteration should be identified as *reworking*.

DECORATIVE CATEGORIES

Seventeenth-century pipes were generally plain, with decoration being restricted to rouletted lines or grape patterns (Figures 22-23) and a Tudor rose design (Figure 22*e*) on the bowl. Bowl decoration became more common during the 18th century, and by the mid-19th century, pipe manufacturers were able to provide innumerable decorative themes to accommodate the great diversification in taste as far as pipe decoration is concerned. The diversity of designs can prove challenging in cataloguing pipe collections (Figures 15-16). The various designs can be documented and classified according to the principal subject of the decoration. Specimens

may be assigned to categories based on broad themes. The perceived themes may change as recording progresses, the researcher finding that what looked like a main decorative theme on a small bowl fragment is actually only a minor theme when seen on a more complete example. Most decorative themes fall into the following five categories:

1. Naturalistic: A realistic, or attempted realistic, representation of an object or scene.

2. Stylistic: A conventionalized representation of an object or scene. This includes abstract and geometric renderings of natural phenomena.

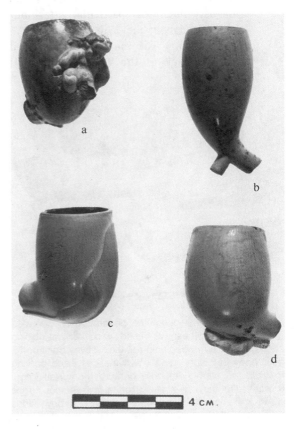

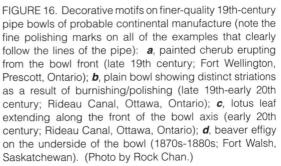

FIGURE 16. Decorative motifs on finer-quality 19th-century pipe bowls of probable continental manufacture (note the fine polishing marks on all of the examples that clearly follow the lines of the pipe): **a**, painted cherub erupting from the bowl front (late 19th century; Fort Wellington, Prescott, Ontario); **b**, plain bowl showing distinct striations as a result of burnishing/polishing (late 19th-early 20th century; Rideau Canal, Ottawa, Ontario); **c**, lotus leaf extending along the front of the bowl axis (early 20th century; Rideau Canal, Ottawa, Ontario); **d**, beaver effigy on the underside of the bowl (1870s-1880s; Fort Walsh, Saskatchewan). (Photo by Rock Chan.)

3. Free-form: The design elements are not representative of natural phenomena and are characterized by non-geometric free forms.

4. Geometric: The design elements do not represent natural phenomena and are characterized by straight lines, circles, triangles, and similar forms (Figure 17).

5. Symbolic: The design elements (including letters, numbers, emblems, etc.) have, or are suspected of having, a meaning derived from their integrated whole. Some examples are:

    a. Ethnic/Patriotic: This category (Figure 18) became a popular form of decoration as pipe manufacturers began to cater to ethnic and national sentiments, which was particularly fashionable throughout the 19th century.

    b. T.D.: The initials "TD" situated on the back of the bowl (Figure 19)

comprise one of the most common decorative categories on clay pipes. There are numerous variations, with the letters raised or impressed on a plain bowl, or within ovals and rounded cartouches, rope wreaths, shields, sunbursts, circles of stars, etc. The significance of the lettering is uncertain. The letters are believed to have appeared in the mid to late 1700s, and are thought to have been the initials of a maker of quality pipes. Through widespread plagiarism, they evolved into a popular symbolic decorative element. By the early 20th century, the firm of Duncan McDougall of Glasgow, Scotland, possessed 22 mold variations of the TD design (Walker 1977:88).

    c. Masonic: Modern Freemasonry was established in England in 1717, and the society had become popular in the United States by the 1730s. The movement was firmly entrenched in the

FIGURE 17. Typical geometric decoration encountered on 19th-century pipes: **a**, raised, wide vertical ribbing encircling the bowl, beginning at the halfway point of the bowl body and continuing down the base and curving towards the stem (late 19th century; Fort Wellington, Prescott, Ontario); **b**, a series of raised vertical ridges within a U-shaped border which covers the bowl sides from the rim to the base (late 19th-early 20th century; Fort Wellington); **c**, raised, beaded paisley decoration around the base of the bowl (1870s-1890s; Fort Wellington); **d**, a series of raised, wide, vertical rectangles encircling the upper portion of the bowl, combined with raised crosshatching on the base (post-1850s; Lower Fort Garry, Selkirk, Manitoba); **e**, pattern of raised panels following the contour of the pipe bowl from the base and extending approximately ¾ of the way up the sides; the panels are crosshatched and alternate with raised ridges (post-1865; Fort Wellington, Prescott, Ontario); **f**, fine raised ribbing which covers the entire bowl and follows its contours (Fort St. Joseph, Ontario); **g**, a series of raised, vertical ridges and facets which alternate around the bowl and follow its contours (Fort Wellington). (Photo by Rock Chan.)

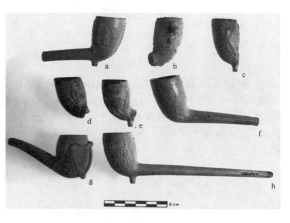

FIGURE 18. Clay pipes decorated with ethnic and patriotic motifs: **a**, flag of Scotland/thistle on bowl sides (late 19th-early 20th century; Fort Wellington, Prescott, Ontario); **b**, crossed flags–Red Ensign and Stars and Stripes–on bowl sides (late 19th-early 20th century; Fort Wellington); **c**, crossed flags, British Flag of the Union and Stars and Stripes, on bowl sides (late 19th-early 20th century; Ottawa Lock station, Rideau Canal, Ottawa); **d**, fleur-de-lis/thistle on bowl sides (1870s-1890s; Fort Wellington, Prescott, Ontario); **e**, Scottish thistle/ Irish effigy harp on bowl sides (1870s-1890s; Fort Wellington, Prescott, Ontario); **f**, maple leaf on bowl sides (late 19th-early 20th century; Ottawa Lock station, Rideau Canal, Ottawa); **g**, Irish effigy harp on the bowl front (post-1840s; Signal Hill, St. John's, Newfoundland); **h**, Wolfe Tone and Irish effigy harp on the bowl sides (late 19th-early 20th century; Fort Wellington, Prescott, Ontario). (Photo by Rock Chan.)

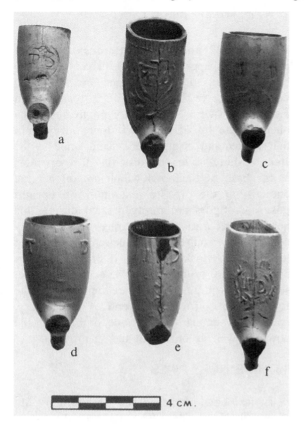

FIGURE 19. A selection of white clay "TD" bowls: **a**, impressed TD within a circular cartouche (ca. 1810; Fort George, Niagara-on-the-Lake, Ontario); **b**, raised TD within a shield with sprigs (ca. 1820s; Fort George); **c**, impressed TD (ca. 1870s; Fort Wellington, Prescott, Ontario); **d**, raised TD (1870s-1890s; Fort Wellington); **e**, raised TD on bowl rim (Fort George); **f**, raised TD within a sunburst (Fort Coteau-du-lac, Quebec). (Photo by Rock Chan.)

2. Impressed: Also applied by molding, the design elements are sunk into the pipe. An effigy pipe bowl is an example of impressed decoration.

3. Incised or Abraded: The design elements are abraded or cut into the pipe with an instrument during the manufacturing process. As mentioned above, this does not include designs added after the pipe has been fired.

4. Color contrast: The design elements are defined by color.

Dating Clay Pipes

Pipes are seldom marked with absolute dates. Specimens do occasionally depict commemorative themes which imply absolute dates and enable the determination of at least a *terminus post quem* for the pipe (Figure 21). Such instances are relatively rare, however, and dates and ascriptions generally need to be determined on the basis of a pipe's attributes. Examination of stem bore diameter, stem thickness, and bowl size and shape should supply a gross assessment of a pipe fragment's chronological position.

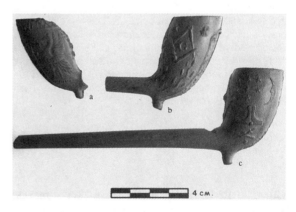

FIGURE 20. Examples of Masonic motifs on pipe bowls: **a**, standard Masonic symbol/bird decorative motif with elk head on the bowl back (Signal Hill, St. John's, Newfoundland); **b**, Masonic symbol consisting of the letter G within a cartouche formed by dividers and a set square. This appears on the bowl side opposite the bird shown in a. The bowl back exhibits the Prince of Wales plumes (early 1840s to early 1850s; Fort Wellington, Prescott, Ontario); **c**, another Masonic pipe style marked W. White, Glasgow. This pipe illustrates a variety of symbols associated with the Order. The design on the bowl back is a sunburst within a Masonic cartouche (late 19th century; Fort Wellington, Prescott, Ontario). (Photo by Rock Chan.)

British military by the early 1800s. The decoration on Masonic pipes can be quite abstract as it often consists of a number of obscure symbols of fraternity and other devices relevant to the organization (Figure 20). One of the more common is the letter "G" set within dividers and a square.

TYPES OF DECORATION

Decorative elements fall into four principal categories, depending on how they were applied to the pipe:

1. Raised: Applied by molding, the design elements appear in relief.

FIGURE 21.   Pipes commemorating events (dating by association): **a**, pipe commemorating Daniel O'Connell, leader and organizer of the Irish Catholic emancipation movement. His election to British Parliament in 1828 led to the passing of the Emancipation Bill of 1829 (Signal Hill, St. John's, Newfoundland); **b**, white clay pipe bowl exhibiting the two sides of a five-franc coin of the Second Republic of France, dated 1849 (Fort Wellington, Prescott, Ontario); **c**, reproduction of a Franklin Pierce presidential campaign pipe.   Pierce, elected 14th president in 1852, was in office from 1853-1857 (San Juan Islands, Washington); **d**, temperance motif commemorating the work of Reverend Theobald Mathew, a leader in the British Temperance Movement (Signal Hill); **e,** white clay pipe bowl commemorating Queen Victoria's 75 years on the throne in 1897 (Ottawa Lock Station, Ottawa, Ontario); **f**, presidential campaign pipe bearing the effigy of Zachary Taylor, elected 12th president of the United States in the 1848 presidential election (non-archaeological specimen); **g,** coronation pipe marking the accession of Edward VII, and dating to the beginning of the 20th century (Fort Wellington). (Photo by Rock Chan.)

Other attributes such as finish, maker's marks, and decoration, if any, are also helpful for this purpose.   Comparing the data recovered from pipe analysis with that derived from other material in an archaeological assemblage will generally also prove useful in dating pipe material.

THE EVOLUTION OF ATTRIBUTES

Clay smoking pipes of British manufacture underwent numerous changes from the 16th to the 20th century.   The following sections highlight the more prominent changes apparent in the evolutionary progression.

17TH-CENTURY PIPES

Figures 22 and 23 illustrate examples of early bowl shapes from the 17th century.   The bowls, bulbous or barrel-shaped, are squat and very small at the beginning of the century but increase in size as the century progresses.   The plane of the lip of the bowl slopes away from the smoker and is at a very acute angle to the stem.   Many styles possess flat feet or heels at the base of the bowl which are often large enough for the pipe to rest on in an upright position.   Spurs are rarely present during this period.   Decoration is also rare and generally consists of a rouletted line encircling the rim of the bowl.   A maker's mark, if present, usually consists of a symbol, initials, or a full name, sometimes within a cartouche, impressed in the foot or heel.   Toward the end of the century, marks also appear on the side or back of the bowl, as well as on top of the shank.

18TH-CENTURY PIPES

Typical bowl shapes of the 18th century are shown in Figure 24.   The plane of the lip of the bowl is parallel to the stem.   The rouletted line encircling the rim has disappeared by this time. The standard of manufacture has improved.   Spurs become fashionable, and many makers begin applying their raised, mold-imparted initials to the sides of these projections.   During the second half of the century, the angle of the axis of the bowl to the stem tends to become less obtuse (more nearly a right angle).   Toward the end of the 18th century, the baroque, heavy style of decoration which would come to dominate the Victorian period begins to appear; fluting and leaves belong either to the end of this century or the beginning of the next.

19TH-CENTURY PIPES

The mass production of clay pipes carried out in many countries–such as England, Scotland, France, Canada, and the United States–resulted in innumerable types and styles (Figure 25). Pipes from this period are heavily decorated, for the most part.   The popularity of meerschaums and briars led to imitations in clay.   Clay bowl shapes, bites, and stem configurations, imitating those of meerschaums or briars, date from the

FIGURE 22. Pipe bowl shapes, ca. 1640s-ca. 1690s: **a,** ca. 1650-1680 (Fort Anne, Annapolis Royal, Nova Scotia); **b,** ca. 1640-1660 (H.M.S. *Sapphire*, Bay Bulls, Newfoundland); **c,** ca. 1640-1700 (*Sapphire*); **d,** ca. 1670-1690 (*Sapphire*); **e,** ca. 1670-1690; this bowl also has a raised Tudor-style rose on both sides of the bowl base (*Sapphire*). (Photo by Rock Chan.)

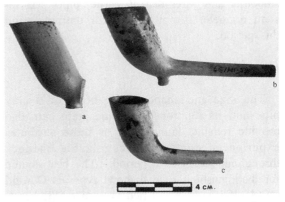

FIGURE 24. Bowl shapes typical of the mid to late 1700s: **a,** ca. 1760 (H.M.S. *Sapphire*, Bay Bulls, Newfoundland); **b,** ca. 1720-1780 (Riviere Richelieu underwater survey to, St-Jean Cantic, Quebec); **c,** a style typical of the North American export trade, a pipe by R. Tippet of Bristol, ca. 1720-1760 (wreck of *Le Machault*, Chaleur Bay, Quebec). (Photo by Rock Chan.)

second half of the 19th century. Effigy pipes had become popular by the beginning of the century. They are certainly represented on sites dating to the first half of the 1800s, as are heavily decorated bowls and stems. Mold-imparted names and ascription on the sides of the shank are also typical of the period. Peg and spike-style spurs are still encountered, many

with marks as before. Old features reappear, such as the plane of the bowl lip once again becoming moderately slanted away from the smoker. On machine-made pipes, the finish of the bowl may be careless (mold lines may not be smoothed off), even though the clay may be

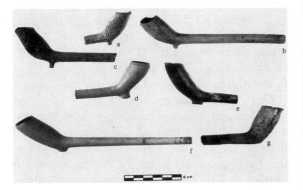

FIGURE 23. Pipe bowl shapes, ca. 1680s-ca. 1740s: **a,** ca. 1680-1710; "mulberry" or "grape" decoration (Castle Hill, Placentia, Newfoundland); **b,** ca. 1680-1710; single rouletted band around bowl back rim (this and the following specimens are all from the 1696 wreck of the H.M.S. *Sapphire*, Bay Bulls, Newfoundland); **c,** ca. 1680-1710; **d,** ca. 1680-1730; **e,** ca. 1680-1730; **f,** ca. 1680-1720; **g,** ca. 1690-1720, with an ambiguous linear decoration extending along the back rim of the bowl (Castle Hill, Placentia, Newfoundland). (Photo by Rock Chan.)

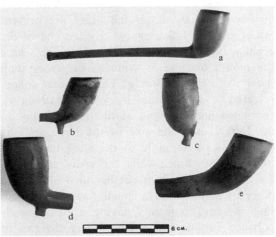

FIGURE 25. Pipe bowl shapes typical of the 1800s. The complete pipe is a short cutty style that became popular during the 1800s. The whole bowl and stem fragment in the lower right is a "woodstock" style which became popular during the latter half of the 19th century. Provenience: **a,** mid to late 19th century (Fort George, Niagara-on-the-Lake, Ontario); **b,** late 19th-early 20th century (Fort Wellington, Prescott, Ontario); **c,** post-1840 (St. Andrew's Blockhouse, St. Andrew's, New Brunswick); **d-e,** mid to late 19th century (Signal Hill, St. John's, Newfoundland). (Photo by Rock Chan.)

smoother and purer than in earlier pipes. Bore-stem diameter is not helpful for dating during this period.

Bowl Shapes

The size and shape of the bowl of a clay pipe and its relationship to the stem can also provide reliable dating clues as these attributes experienced numerous recognizable changes throughout the historic period. The best source for distinguishing English bowl types is Oswald (1961; 1975). A simplified version of his bowl-shape chronology, which is more applicable to North American researchers as it is based on pipes recovered from American sites, appears in Noël Hume (1969:303). It should be noted that as with most typologies, allowances must be made for variations in bowl shape. Departures from the norm will be encountered and should, therefore, be expected throughout any period. The presence, style, and location of the foot or spur may also provide a relative date since spurs begin to appear on the bowl around the early 1700s.

The Dutch clay-pipe industry was initiated around 1600, largely by immigrant English pipemakers, thus, basic similarities in style between English and Dutch pipes are present throughout the 17th century. By the end of the century, bowl shape had changed to one where the mouth became as wide as or wider than the middle of the bowl. This conical shape, referred to as conoidal by Walker (1966a:4), continued until the end of the 19th century in the Netherlands, the size of the bowl and the obtuseness of its angle to the stem tending to increase with time, while the cross section of the bowl changed from circular to oval. Dutch pipes usually exhibit a much finer finish than English ones, frequently having a glossy, well-polished surface and milling along the rim of the bowl (Walker 1971a:90). Dutch bowls often appear to be smaller than English ones. An excellent study of early Dutch pipes in North America is by McCashion (1979). Atkinson and Oswald (1972) and Duco (1976) present more information concerning the identification and dating of Dutch clay pipes.

MAKER'S MARKS

Identifiable maker's marks provide the most dependable means to date clay pipes. These include all marks (such as symbols, names, initials, and numbers) put on a pipe to identify the maker and the place of manufacture, as well as the style and mold number of the pipe. It should be noted that there was a degree of plagiarism within the industry, in that the marks of firms associated with better-quality products were copied by others. These include Peter Dorni pipes, as well as certain Dutch marks synonymous with finer pipes. The ubiquitous "TD" mark, perhaps the most common decorative element on clay pipes, is thought to have originally represented a British maker who manufactured quality pipes (Walker 1966b). There are three types of marks:

1. Raised: The mark appears in relief.
2. Impressed: The mark is sunk into the surface.
3. Incised or abraded: The mark is cut or ground into the pipe with an instrument during the manufacturing process (before firing in the case of clay pipes).

Early pipe marks (dating from the first half of the 1600s) appeared on the base of the foot, the top of the shank or around it, or on the back or sides of the bowl. The marks consisted of initials, a full name, or a combination of the two. Symbols were also employed. With the advent of spurs in the early 18th century, English pipemakers began placing their initials on these features. It was customary to put the initial of the maker's first name on the left side of the spur and the initial of the last name on the right side. It should be pointed out that in these marks, the letter "I" also represents "J" in some cases. Who the initials represent can frequently be determined by consulting Oswald (1975). Cartouches enclosing maker's marks on the sides and backs of bowls persisted throughout this period. One of the more prominent firms to employ this form of identification was the Ford pipemakers of the Stepney area of London. The Fords were principal suppliers to the Hudson's Bay Company and pipes bearing their names within oval cartouches on the bowl back have been excavated at numerous fur trade sites in Canada and the United States. Walker (1983:65) illustrates some typical marks associated with these prominent London makers. Mold-imparted maker's names, usually accompanied by the name of the city where the factory was located, generally began appearing on pipes of British manufacture during the early 1800s, and continued into the 20th century.

Around the middle of the 1800s, a number of British manufacturers began putting marks on the bowls, shanks, or in some cases, the spurs of their pipes. These codes are believed to have identified specific mold patterns or decorations, and could be used to order the desired pipe pattern.

Most Dutch bowls exhibit maker's marks. Unlike the English who tended to use their initials as marks, Dutch makers employed various devices. Their marks were extremely well defined and consisted of very small numbers and letters, often surmounted by crowns, as well as various heraldic and symbolic devices such as windmills, mermaids, milkmaids, etc. These marks were usually located on the base of the foot or heel, and later on the peg-style spur. Dutch pipemakers continued to put their marks in these locations until the end of the 1800s. In the case of a pipe with no spur, the mark was placed on the base of the bowl where the spur would have been or, occasionally, on the back of the bowl. Research on pipe marks registered in the city of Gouda, the major center of the Dutch clay-pipe industry, has resulted in an illustrated catalogue (Helbers 1942). More recently, Don Duco (1976) has conducted extensive research into the identification of Dutch clay pipes and their marks. Although Dutch marks are superbly made with meticulous detail, their use to identify makers and date pipes can be problematic. As these marks could be bought, sold, or inherited, they can be difficult to associate with an individual maker or firm. Nevertheless, the presence of the coat of arms of the city of Gouda on pipes is indicative of manufacture after 1739/1740, when authorization to use this device was granted. The letter "S" for the Dutch word *slegte*, which denotes lesser-quality pipes, was placed above the city's arms shortly thereafter (Walker 1971a:62).

PROMINENT PIPE MANUFACTURERS

CANADA

The Canadian pipemaking industry began in earnest in the 1840s, and lasted into the 20th century. The pipes were produced in the British tradition. Consequently, the maker's name and city of manufacture appeared on the left and right shank sides, respectively, in keeping with the trend in Britain during this period. A list of Montreal pipemakers has been compiled by Robin Smith who is currently researching the clay pipe industry in that city. This listing, "Montreal Clay Tobacco Pipe Makers, 1846-1902," is accessible through the Internet (Smith 1998).

Maker	Location	Date
R. Bannerman	Montreal	1858-1888
Bannerman	Montreal	1888-1907
T. Doherty	Montreal	1850-1857
W. H. Dixon & Co.	Montreal	1876-1894
D. Ford	Montreal	1857-1873
Henderson	Montreal	1847-1876
Henderson's	Montreal	1849-1876
Murphy	Montreal	1859-1886
W&D Bell	Quebec City	1862-1881

SCOTLAND

Five Scottish pipe manufacturers–Alexander Coghill, William Murray, William White, Duncan McDougall, and T. Davidson–monopolized pipe exports during the 19th century.

Maker	Location	Date
Alex. Coghill	Glasgow	1826-1904
Davidson, T & Co.	Glasgow	1861-1910
Duncan McDougall & Co.	Glasgow	1847-1967
Wm. Murray & Co.	Glasgow	1830-1861
John Nimmo	Glasgow	1834-1846
W. White	Glasgow	1805-1955
Thos. White & Co.	Edinburgh	1823-1876
Thos. Whyte	Edinburgh	1832-1864

ENGLAND

As pipe smoking was practiced in England as early as the 1570s (Oswald 1975:4), Great Britain has a long tradition of clay pipe manufacture with thousands of individuals having been associated with the industry. An exhaustive listing was compiled by Adrian Oswald (1975:128-207) which covers pipemakers from the various parts of England as well as Scotland, Ireland, and Wales. When combined with temporal data provided by a pipe's attributes, these lists can be most helpful in identifying the maker of a pipe and its probable date.

Maker	Location	Date
Ford	London (Stepney)	1805-1865
Michael Martin	London (Woolwich)	1847
Posener	London	1866-1899
Swinyard	London	1836-1853
John Williams	London	1828-1842
William Williams	London	1823-1864
Ring	Bristol	1803-1883
Robert Tippet	Bristol	1660-ca.1720
T. Pascall	Dartford	1839-1851
J. Braithwaite	Liverpool	1816-1864
R. Morgan	Liverpool	1790-1845
W. Morgan	Liverpool	1767-1796, 1803
Edward Higgins	Salisbury	ca.1680-1710
C. Carter	Southampton	1720-1750
Reuen Sidney	Southampton	1687-1748

FRANCE

Although this industry has a long history, French pipes only came into their own between the 1850s, and the beginning of the 20th century. French pipes were generally of superior quality, with many of the bowls displaying finely molded effigies and designs. Many of the effigies possessed painted features, such as eyes, hair, hats, scarves, etc., and the clay used for some pipes was dyed red or black, attributes that may help to identify French pipes in a collection (Pfeiffer 1985:117, 1999:personal communication). French pipes were usually marked with the name and place of manufacture on the top of the shank. Two references which illustrate the styles of pipes produced by French pipemakers are Jean-Léo (1971) and Augustin (1980-1981).

Maker	Location	Date
Peter Dorni	St. Omer	ca.1850-ca.1880
Dumeril	St. Omer	1844-ca.1885
L. Fiolet	St. Omer	1746-1920
Nihoul	Nimy	1766-1914
Gambier	Paris	1780-1926
Gisclon	Paris (Lille)	ca.1820-ca.1880

NETHERLANDS

In North America, Dutch pipes appear on sites associated with Dutch and French settlement. One of the principal manufacturers was J. & G. Prince, Gouda (1773-1898).

UNITED STATES

Although Euroamerican smoking pipes have been manufactured in the United States since the 1600s, their production generally constituted a minor portion of a potter's trade and pipes were generally manufactured to fulfill local demand (Sudbury 1979:215). Consequently, few American pipes possess any identifiable maker's marks. The first pipes were crude copies of European designs made in a variety of colored clays, apparently in Virginia and New England (Noël Hume 1969:308). A style of pipe produced in the United States since at least the mid-1700s was the socket-shanked pipe, a two-unit pipe in which the clay portion, consisting of a bowl and shank, was designed to accept a separate stem. Considered the most dominant pipe form manufactured in the United States from the 1840s into the early 1900s, these pipes became synonymous with the later American clay pipe industry (Pfeiffer 1981b:109). This pipe style is believed to reflect a central European tradition (Walker 1971c:30, 1983:40).

Many American pipes were made of terra cotta, a red to orange clay. As with the Aust pipe illustrated in Figure 26, the investigation of pottery and kiln waster sites in the United States is slowly providing information concerning the products of specific pipemakers (South 1964, 1967). Consequently, it is important to record the finish on terra cotta pipes, whether plain or glazed (numerous glazes were used, the most common being salt, or fly ash glaze) and, if glazed, whether the glaze covers only the exterior or both the interior and exterior of the bowl. Sudbury (1979, 1980, 1983, 1986) provides an essential starting point to the very complex problem of identifying American pipemakers. Industrialization within the American pipe industry by the middle of the 19th century prompted large-scale production in areas such as Point Pleasant, Ohio and Pamplin, Virginia.

THE U.S. MCKINLEY TARIFF ACT

The McKinley Tariff Act of 1891 stipulated that all goods imported into the United States henceforth had to bear the name of the country of origin. Often used in dating ceramics, this act also applied to the pipe industry as foreign pipemakers had to comply if they were to compete in the lucrative U.S. market.

STEM-BORE-DIAMETER DATING

Some years ago, North American archaeologists concentrated their efforts on determining the utility of stem-bore diameters to date clay smoking pipes in archaeological assemblages. They concluded that the bores of pipes, measured in increments of 1/64 of an inch, progressively decreased in size until about 1770. Harrington (1954, 1990) gives specifics. The reduction was gradual with the result that three different diameters were often manufactured simultaneously during any given period. Consequently, the mean of the bore diameters derived for a collection of pipe stems provides the probable date for the assemblage, except in the case of the last (1750-1800) period defined by Harrington. The erratic results for samples from sites of this period reveal that the trend towards smaller bores no longer prevailed and demon-

strates the futility of using stem-bore-diameter dating on material postdating the 1750s or 1770s.

As more data were collected, a number of regression formulae were devised in an attempt to date archaeological assemblages. Although it is beyond the scope of this work to describe their mechanics (Harrington 1954, 1990; Binford 1962; Heighton and Deagan 1971) or to assess the accepted dating techniques (Omwake 1956; Noël Hume 1963, 1979:5-7; Walker 1965, 1967; Pfeiffer 1978), some considerations should be raised. The application of the formulae should be restricted to pipes manufactured in England, specifically London and Bristol. Assemblages with a heterogeneous composition tend to provide erratic dates, as do assemblages that predate the 1680s and postdate the 1760s (Noël Hume 1969:300). Therefore, the formulae are not applicable to sites dating from the latter half of the 18th century where a variety of pipes from a number of countries may be present.

A statistically significant sample is needed to obtain good results in stem-bore-diameter dating. Harrington, as the principal proponent of stem-

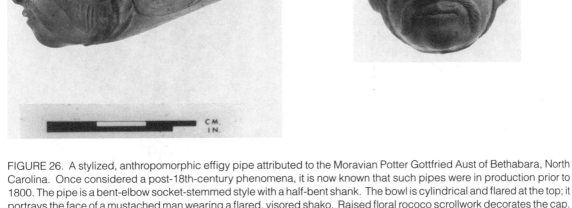

FIGURE 26. A stylized, anthropomorphic effigy pipe attributed to the Moravian Potter Gottfried Aust of Bethabara, North Carolina. Once considered a post-18th-century phenomena, it is now known that such pipes were in production prior to 1800. The pipe is a bent-elbow socket-stemmed style with a half-bent shank. The bowl is cylindrical and flared at the top; it portrays the face of a mustached man wearing a flared, visored shako. Raised floral rococo scrollwork decorates the cap. Recovered from the 1760 wreck of the French privateer *Le Machault*. (Photo by Rock Chan.)

bore-dating, recognized this and the potential for misuse: "I had hoped that no one would be uncritical enough or so literal-minded, that they would attempt to date a single pipe stem fragment, or even a limited number from my chart" (Harrington 1955:12). The formulae also require an even temporal distribution of pipe material. This may not be the case at some sites as samples may be skewed by intermittent occupation. The greatest misuse of the regression formulae, however, has occurred as a result of a researcher's inherent tendency to assign a mathematically derived, absolute date to a pipe sample. Caution must be taken when employing bore diameters to calculate dates for an archaeoological assemblage. Considering the non-regulated nature of the pipe industry, coupled with the extremely gradual evolution of the bore-reduction phenomenon, considerable variation may be expected in stem-bore diameters throughout any given period. The finding of two distinct stem-bore diameters in a wrecked ship's cargo reveals that different-size bore tools were being used simultaneously by a single manufacturer (Higgins 1997:131). Nevertheless, a nominal date for a pipe assemblage can be established in some cases through analysis of the bore diameters of the recovered pipe stems, especially when combined with data derived from other attributes such as bowl configuration and maker's marks.

There is a correlation between time and bore-stem diameter, thus measuring the bore diameters of clay pipe fragments should be a standard cataloguing procedure even though there may be no immediate practical application. As both Pfeiffer (1981a) and Cranmer (1990:73) noted, attributes such as the shape and diameter of stem bores, as well as their frequency in deposits, may prove more useful than for simply determining a mean date. Analysis of these characteristics may provide critical insight into the spatial distribution of a specific site, as well as its occupational phases and their intensity.

Drill bits are ideal for measuring stem-bore diameters. Bits ranging from 4/64 in. to 9/64 in. can be embedded in a rubber stopper, thus forming a handy little measuring device. Another popular tool for measuring bore diameters is the step gauge which incorporates all the required measurements into one implement (Lenik 1971:100-101).

Metal Pipes

Occasional fragments of metal pipes have been recovered from North American sites (Noël Hume 1969:308). One- and two-piece pipes were manufactured from various metals, including silver, iron, brass, and copper. Even some pewter examples are known from Jamestown (Noël Hume 1969:308) and Sainte-Marie among the Hurons (Jeanie Tummon 1990:personal communication). Believed to have been most popular towards the end of the 1700s, these pipes were employed during more robust activities, such as traveling and hunting, where fragile clay pipes might not survive. The forms of the metal pipes mirrored those of contemporary clay pipes. Iron pipes covered with brightly colored enamel are also known, and smokers in remote areas sometimes fashioned pipes from such objects as tin cans (Figure 27).

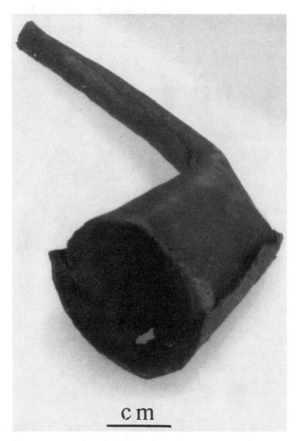

c m

FIGURE 27. Smoking pipe fashioned from a tin can by a member of Franklin's 1845-1848 Arctic Expedition (Eden Point, Devon Island). (Photo by Rock Chan.)

Composite Pipes

Composite smoking pipes possess several components which are frequently composed of different materials such as porcelain, stone, and wood. In addition, composite pipes can also be composed of several clay components, or consist of reworked clay pipes fitted with homemade elements, such as whittled wooden stems. Ehwa (1974) gives a description of various types of composite pipes and their manufacture.

Porcelain

Although documented in the 1700s, porcelain pipes came into fashion around the 1850s (Figures 28-29). Many excavated examples can be identified as the "coffee house" style which consists of a porcelain bowl, usually with a metal spark cap, a porcelain reservoir which connects the bowl to a straight cherry-wood stem of varying length, and a horn, bone, or possibly amber mouthpiece (Figure 30). These pipes were designed for a sedentary, relaxed setting.

Stone

Most European stone pipes are composed of meerschaum, a German term meaning "sea surf" as it was originally thought to be petrified sea foam. The material is, in reality, a metamorphic rock composed of a hydrous magnesium

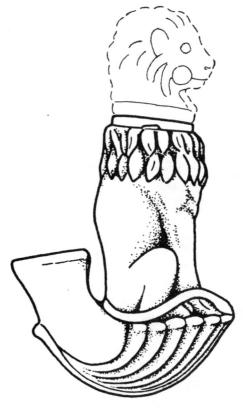

FIGURE 29. Artist's reconstruction of the porcelain lion effigy pipe bowl shown in Figure 28**a**. The spark cap representing the animal's head is based on a similar animal effigy pipe illustrated by Fairholt (1859:201). (Drawing by Dorothea Larsen.)

FIGURE 28. Glazed and painted porcelain pipe bowls: **a,** lion effigy of possible German manufacture (1830-1860; Fort George, Niagara-on-the-Lake, Ontario); **b,** two-tone decorated bowl (late 19th-early 20th century, Rideau Canal, Ottawa, Ontario). (Photo by Rock Chan.)

silicate (Weber 1965:76). The best meerschaum came from Asia Minor, specifically Turkey. It has been carved into pipe bowls since the early 1700s, and such pipes were very much in fashion with the very rich by the 1750s. The discovery of new deposits of meerschaum made this form more affordable and, by the 1850s, meerschaum pipes were a popular smoking medium of the middle classes. Fragile and expensive, meerschaum pipes are occasionally encountered in archaeological contexts.

Meerschaum pipes are composite or multi-component pipes in that the bowl was attached to an amber or horn mouthpiece by a bone tenon and ferrule, or the pipe had a socket style of shank with a tapered hole which accommodated a cork or leather-tipped stem, usually of cherry wood. The bite was generally composed of amber or horn. Pipe bowls of carved meerschaum can be plain or highly decorated (Figure 31). A peculiar quality of meerschaum is that its color changes from chalk white or

FIGURE 30. Porcelain pipe bowl fragments from ca. 1860s-1880s archaeological contexts in relation to an intact coffee house specimen. (Photo by Rock Chan.)

creamy yellow to a rich amber or golden brown as the tars and oils from the tobacco interact with the waxed surface of the bowl.

Fashioned from siltstone, steatite, and catlinite, fragments of stone pipes similar in form to clay pipes have also been encountered on archaeological sites. These generally represent an indigenous pipe industry and probably reflect a Euroamerican pipe tradition (Figure 32).

Wood

Briar pipes, fashioned from the burl of the white heather tree, became popular around the 1850s. As a result, a number of briar-bowl styles came into being during the latter part of the 19th century. Figure 33 illustrates some of the more common forms; billiard, panel, and apple are three of the earlier styles that may be encountered in archaeological collections. Pipe bowls were also made of apple, cherry, and pear wood. Mouthpieces were also occasionally fashioned from wood (Figure 36c).

Other Materials

Composite pipes frequently have components fashioned from such materials as metal, bone and ivory, amber, horn, and synthetic substances.

1. Metal: Metal pipe components were generally in the form of spark caps, ferrules, and filters. *Spark caps*, usually made of copper alloy with a nickel finish, were found on some models of porcelain and wooden pipe bowls (Figure 34).

Ferrules, metal bands or sleeves that covered the join between the pipe shank and mouthpiece, occasionally provide very useful information concerning the origin and date of a pipe. Many better-quality British briar and composite pipes of the 19th century had hallmarked sterling-silver

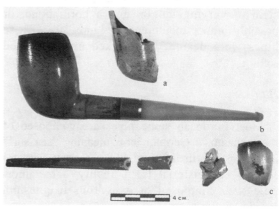

FIGURE 31. Meerschaum pipes and a white clay meerschaum imitation (late 19th-early 20th century): *a,* plain meerschaum bowl fragment. The light color suggests that the pipe was not heavily smoked, despite attempts to prolong the life of the piece by reaming out the broken shank to accept a makeshift stem (Fort Walsh, Saskatchewan); *b,* complete composite meerschaum pipe. The color of the plain bowl indicates that the piece was well-smoked. The pipe possesses a straight-stemmed amber mouthpiece. Note the hallmarks on the silver pipe stem ferrule (non-archaeological specimen); *c,* four fragments of a white clay pipe manufactured by Fiolet of France, and finished with a baked varnish finish to imitate a well-smoked meerschaum. Note the uniform color on the stem, the same amber-colored hue as a meerschaum, and the darker color of the rim and base of the bowl fragment in imitation of the well-smoked pipe in the center. The detailed figure on the bowl back is typical of the style encountered on meerschaums (Fort Wellington, Prescott, Ontario). (Photo by Rock Chan.)

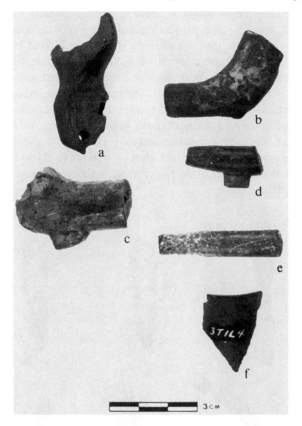

FIGURE 32. Fragmentary stone pipes: **a,** traditional indigenous style (Fort Amherst, Prince Edward Island); **b,** unfinished siltstone whole bowl/stem fragment (Fort St. James, British Columbia). This and the remaining fragments reflect Euroamerican pipe manufacture; **c,** siltstone bowl fragment/stem fragment (Yuquot, Nootka Island, British Columbia); **d,** steatite bowl fragment/stem fragment which includes the stem/bowl juncture as well as a rectangular spur (Fort St. James); **e,** steatite stem fragment, note the teeth marks (Fort St. James); **f,** bowl fragment, unidentified stone (Fort St. James). (Photo by Rock Chan.)

ferrules. The marks consisted of a maker's mark, a mark indicating the guild/city, and, most importantly, a date mark. By comparing these marks to references on the subject (Bradbury 1927), it is possible to determine the year of manufacture. Less expensive pipes with plated copper-alloy ferrules often had the maker's initials stamped within a number of cartouches that were reminiscent of hallmarks (Figure 35).

Filters, small metal fittings found within some stems, served to remove tars, oils, and other substances from the smoke. As the volatized material encountered the filters, it was trapped on the fittings which absorbed the heat, causing the substances to condense on the metal.

FIGURE 33. Wooden bowl styles: **a,** billiard bowl (probably 20th century; Fort Wellington, Prescott, Ontario); **b,** undesignated squat, panel, or faceted bowl style (Lower Fort Garry, Selkirk, Manitoba); **c,** bulldog bowl (Fort Anne, Annapolis Royal, Nova Scotia); **d,** panel bowl (1870s-1880s; Fort Walsh, Saskatchewan); **e,** small "prince" bowl (ca. 1848-1911; Lower Fort Garry, Selkirk, Manitoba). (Photo by Rock Chan.)

2. Bone and Ivory: These materials usually appear in composite pipes in the form of mouthpieces or tenon inserts in pipe shanks (Figure 36a-b, e; 38a-b).

3. Amber: Mouthpieces were also made from amber (Figures 36f, 37), and it was also periodically employed as a decorative element.

4. Horn: This substance was usually used for mouthpieces.

FIGURE 34. Metal spark caps, also known as wind caps or pipe-bowl covers, from component pipes. Note the hinge which allows the cap to swivel and the curved metal clips which secure it in the closed position. Both specimens appear to be nickel-plated brass and date to the 1870s-1880s (**left**, Lower Fort Garry, Selkirk, Manitoba; **right**, Fort Walsh, Saskatchewan). (Photo by Rock Chan.)

FIGURE 35. Marked metal pipe ferrules from the Fort Wellington latrine, Prescott, Ontario: **a,** cylindrical silver ferrule with a remnant of a briar shank. The marks include the maker's initials "HF," the mark designating Birmingham, and the date code for 1903; **b,** cylindrical silver ferrule with marks including the maker's initials "HM," the mark for Chester, and the date code for 1903; **c,** fragmented diamond-faceted ferrule with remnants of an associated wooden shank (late 19th-early 20th century). Maker's marks appear within a series of cartouches in imitation of hallmarks on a better-quality pipe. "EP" within the diamond-shaped cartouche indicates a silver, electro-plated finish on copper alloy. (Photo by Rock Chan.)

5. Synthetics: Vulcanite, a form of hard sulfurized rubber, was made into mouthpieces for briar and several other component pipes (Figures 36d, 38). Although Walker (1983:39-40) stated that Vulcanite mouthpieces came into use around 1878, a small number of pipe stems recovered from the 1865 wreck of the steamboat *Bertrand* possessed poorly molded, hard-rubber mouthpieces (Pfeiffer 1986:86), indicating that they were in use at least thirteen years prior to that date. Pfeiffer (1986) goes on to say that the use of Vulcanite mouthpieces on a variety of composite pipes had been firmly established by 1875. Plastic has also been used to manufacture mouthpieces since at least the 1950s.

Tenon Styles

The tenon united the shank with the stem component of a composite pipe. There are three principal types:

1. Threaded Tenon: This consists of a carved insert, generally of bone, that threads into the stem/mouthpiece and the shank body. It can also be molded into the mouthpiece as in the case of Vulcanite, or carved as in the case of some wooden examples.

2. Push Tenon: These generally consist of a smooth tube projecting from the mouthpiece which slips into the wooden shank and is held in place by a combination of friction and expansion caused by the heat generated during smoking.

3. Military Tenon: Sometimes termed a military stag tenon, the military tenon consists of a tapered form of push tenon, and was held in place by the same forces. The style's name derives from the fact that it was easier for a soldier to repair it rather than a threaded tenon in the field.

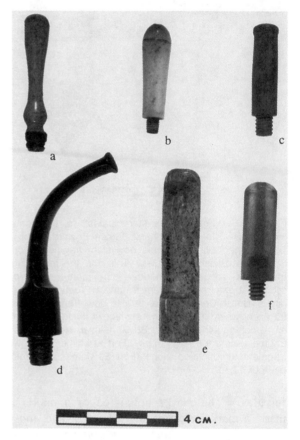

FIGURE 36. Mouthpieces from composite pipes: **a,** bone mouthpiece held in place by a crimped copper-alloy ferrule. It was probably for a multi-unit coffee-house style pipe (1870-1884; Lower Fort Garry, Selkirk, Manitoba); **b,** ivory example with a carved tenon extension (1870-1884; Lower Fort Garry); **c,** wooden mouthpiece with an integral carved tenon; **d,** Vulcanite, half-bent saddle-style mouthpiece with integral threaded tenon (1870s-1880s; Fort Walsh, Saskatchewan); **e,** ivory saddle-style mouthpiece (1870s-1880s; Fort Walsh); **f,** amber mouthpiece with threaded bone tenon insert (Fort St. James, British Columbia). (Photo by Rock Chan.)

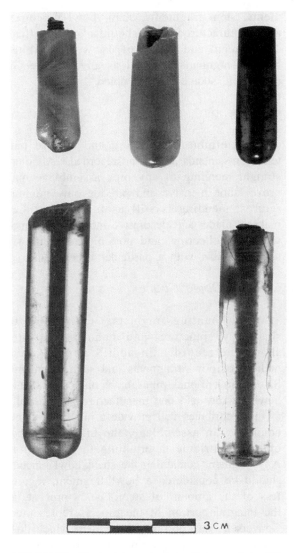

FIGURE 37. Flush-style amber mouthpieces (late 19th-early 20th century). The color varies from red to gold to yellow and from translucent to opaque. The hand carved nature of the bites accounts for the subtle differences in form. (Photo by Rock Chan.)

Composite-Pipe Bites

The weight of composite pipes necessitated a change from the traditional round clay-pipe style mouthpiece to a wider and flatter one which enabled the smoker to better clench, balance, and support the heavier pipe in his teeth (Walker 1983:39). The two most common mouthpieces used with composite pipes are known as "flush," where the mouthpiece is flush with the adjoining shank, gradually tapering to the bite, and the

"saddle" or "cut back" style where the pipe is symmetrically reduced on both the upper and lower planes, giving a popular streamlined look.

Cigar/Cigarette Holders

These are included here as they have the form of tobacco pipes (Figure 39), but are smaller in size and were intended to have a cigar or cigarette inserted into the bowl, rather than shredded tobacco.

British soldiers were first exposed to cigars during the Peninsular campaign of the Napoleonic Wars. The fashion did not become affordable to any but the upper classes before the 1840s (Dunhill 1954:25), and probably did not

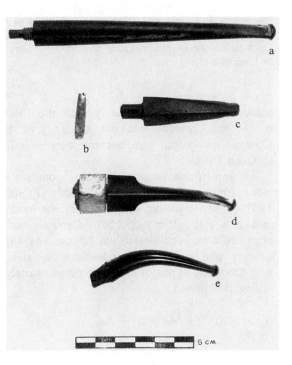

FIGURE 38. Hard rubber mouthpiece styles: *a,* straight-tapered flush stem with a threaded bone tenon insert (late 19th-early 20th century; Fort Wellington, Prescott, Ontario); *b,* threaded bone tenon from a composite mouthpiece (late 19th-early 20th century; Rideau Canal, Ottawa, Ontario); *c,* diamond-sectioned straight stem with a push-style tenon. Note the pattern of teeth marks (1870s-1880s; Fort Walsh, Saskatchewan); *d,* bent saddle-style mouthpiece. The threaded tenon is integral with the mouthpiece. Note the electro-plated ferrule with imitation hallmarks (late 19th-early 20th century; Fort Wellington); *e,* tapered, half-bent, military-style mouthpiece pared down to fit snugly into a pipe shank (late 19th-early 20th century; Rideau Canal, Ottawa). (Photo by Rock Chan.)

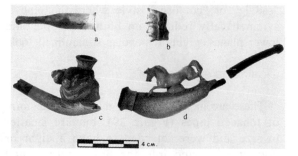

FIGURE 39. Typical forms of cigar/cigarette holders, latter half of the 19th century: **a,** glass cigar holder (1870s-1880s; Fort Walsh, Saskatchewan); **b,** small grenadier effigy white clay cigarette pipe. The cigarette was inserted in the bowl and smoked in a vertical position (late 19th-early 20th century; Fort Wellington, Prescott, Ontario); **c,** fragmented meerschaum cigarette pipe in the form of a woman's head. Worn features on the example indicate that the pipe was subjected to heavy handling (non-archaeological specimen); **d,** fragmented cigarette pipe with a more horizontal orientation of the bowl, indicating the direction of evolution (non-archaeological specimen). (Photo by Rock Chan.)

achieve a degree of popularity until the 1860s or 1870s. Cigarette smoking, a legacy of the Crimean campaign, also became very popular in Great Britain.

As in Britain, cigars became popular in North America during the early 1800s (Pfeiffer 1983:43), and cigarettes came into fashion around mid-century (Pfeiffer 1985:114). Certainly, both practices were well-established by the late 19th century, and cigar/cigarette holders co-existed with the many types of smoking pipes available during this period.

Analyzing Pipe Material

Examination of such physical attributes as bowl shape, maker's marks, decoration, and stem-bore diameter should reveal information concerning a site's overall temporal placement. The second phase of analysis is to examine the pipe material collectively in order to place the assemblage within the cultural context of the site, identifying the nature of the occupation as well as activity areas, thereby shedding light on the lifeways of the occupants.

Once the recovered pipe material has been sorted by material (clay, stone, porcelain, etc.), the fragments should be sorted and counted by provenience. The number of bowl frag-

ments, stem fragments, shank/bowl junctures, and manufactured bites should also be tallied. The amount and nature of use/wear exhibited by the fragments, as well as any evidence of reworking, should also be noted.

Crossmends

To determine distribution and discard patterns, crossmends should be recorded. Although straight mending of any pipe assemblage may prove labor-intensive and provide only minimal returns, mending is still useful to determine maker's marks and decorative motifs represented within a collection, and possibly associating a specific maker with a particular decoration.

Minimum Object Count

When counting fragments, the number of shank/bowl junctures and manufactured bites should be recorded in addition to the total number of bowl fragments and stem fragments. Since conventional pipes have only one shank/bowl juncture and one manufactured bite, a tally of these attributes will provide a minimum object count for an assemblage, the highest number of either attribute determining the population. Any fragment containing the shank/bowl juncture should be considered a bowl fragment, regardless of the amount of stem that is present, as the integral portion of the pipe is represented. Conversely, any portion of the stem which does not include the shank/bowl juncture should be classified as a stem fragment.

Bowl-to-Stem Ratio

Determining the bowl-to-stem ratio of a clay-pipe assemblage may provide insight into the nature of pipe use on site, indicating where smoking took place, and possibly identifying disposal patterns (Richie 1978:136). The ratio is based on the premise that a pipe can still be functional even after the stem has been broken. A pipe's stem can be reduced through breakage several times during its life, resulting in a higher recovery of stem fragments than bowl fragments at most sites. Theoretically, the longest clay pipe style of the first half of the 18th century had a 12-inch stem which will produce a ratio of one bowl fragment to four stem fragments

(Richie 1978:135). The bowl to stem ratio for pipes manufactured after 1780, which had shorter stems, should not be less than 1 bowl fragment to 1.5-2 stem fragments for a typical distribution. This reduced ratio is based on the regulated and relatively short "Virginia" pipe style which was exported to North America in an attempt to alleviate the high rate of stem breakage in transit (Jackson and Price 1974:83, 85).

Pipe assemblages from sites with highly transient populations and no nearby source of pipes should have a low number of bowls in proportion to stems because functional bowls were removed from the site in spite of attrition in the form of stem breakage. Conversely, a site with a population close to its source of pipes should exhibit a higher proportion of bowl fragments as the probability of bowls being discarded would be higher. For example, statistics approaching a 1:1 ratio of bowls to stems indicate a somewhat restricted smoking population close to its source of pipes, a typical distribution expected in, for example, military garrisons.

As with stem-bore diameters, caution should be exercised in determining bowl-to-stem ratios. The presence of pipe stems may not necessarily represent smoking activity. Some fragments may represent merchandise damaged in transit, or possibly some form of reuse. Since the ratios are based on postulated stem length, adjustments need to be made to the formula because stems shortened over time. Also, variations in stem length will be encountered throughout any given period. Only an approximate size can be reflected in archaeological material. An ideal assemblage for such analysis would be English pipes, especially those made in Bristol, representing isolated events or limited occupations during the latter half of the 18th century.

Use/Wear Marks

Clay pipe fragments should also be examined for use/wear marks and evidence of reworking as such information will help to determine the nature of the material and consumption patterns. For example, a lack of teeth marks and smoking stains on broken pipes may be indicative of damaged cargo, rather than personal possessions, and extensively repaired and reworked pipes might suggest that pipes were not readily available.

Teeth marks on pipe stems are caused by clenching them between the teeth, an activity that gradually abrades the surface of the stem. Classic patterns consist of an upper bite which is a little further forward than the lower bite. Evidence of idiosyncratic behavior can also be defined on occasion, such as chewing or twirling the pipe while in the mouth. Finding a relatively intact pipe which exhibits the reverse of the classic pattern indicates that the owner either smoked or held the pipe upside down. Teeth marks on the end of a clay stem fragment indicate that the owner either intentionally shortened the stem of his pipe to suit his needs, or continued to smoke a pipe after its stem broke accidentally (Figure 40). Such stems often exhibit score marks or rings which helped to snap the stem at the desired location (Figure 41).

Smoking stains found within the bowl and, in some cases, radiating out from the bore of the stem are clear evidence that a pipe was used. The degree of staining can reveal how much a pipe was smoked. The stains can range from a light gray color to blue to black, depending on how much the pipe was smoked. This dark discoloration is caused by the oils and tars being absorbed by the clay. On extremely heavily smoked specimens, the outer rim of the pipe–especially the area around the back of the rim–can become quite black from use. The staining substances are water soluble so care must be taken not to remove them when washing pipe material after excavation. It should also be noted that some types of soil and exposure to sunlight can eradicate smoking stains, as can burning.

Other use/wear marks noted primarily on clay pipes include:

1. Charring/burning: Exposure to high heat, as in a house or trash fire, can cause clay pipes to become semi-vitrified, approaching a near-porcelain-like state. This can also cause slag/cinders to adhere to the fragments (Figure 42).

2. Chipping: Found on the bowl interior and resulting from ash extraction.

3. Spalling: Pock marks caused by exposure to fire, salt, or freeze/thaw (Figure 43).

4. Abrasion: Marks imparted to a pipe fragment after being discarded, as gouged surfaces caused by grinding underfoot.

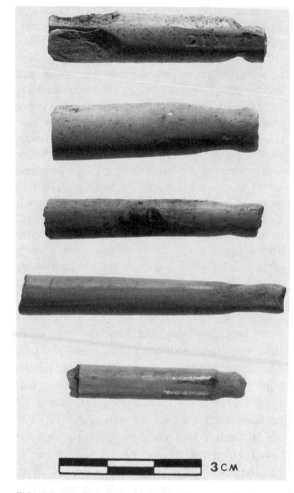

FIGURE 41. Pipe stem scored to facilitate snapping at the desired point (1750–early 1800s; Beaubassin, New Brunswick). (Photo by Rock Chan.)

to prolong the life of a pipe; and (3) to adapt the pipe or pipe fragment for alternative uses. Instances of reworking tend to be higher on sites where the populace has limited mobility or is some distance from a source of pipe supply, such as remote military and fur trade posts. With the advent of more-expensive composite pipes, instances of reworking components to prolong the life of a pipe would be expected to be higher. Some of the most common examples of reworking include: (1) stems fashioned into bites (Figure 44); (2) stems and bowls altered to accommodate reed or wooden stems (Figure 45); (3) repairs to such components as ferrules (Figure 46); (4) initials and/or designs applied by the owner (Figure 47); and (5) pipe stem fragments reworked into such objects as beads

FIGURE 40. Classic teeth-mark patterns on the stems of mostly 19th-century smoking pipes. The lower examples reflect idiosyncratic habits. The patterns on the lower-most stem fragments, in particular, indicate habitual chewing and twirling of the pipe while in the mouth. The other examples demonstrate the range of wear, from slight abrasion to pronounced teeth marks indicative of hard use. (Photo by Rock Chan.)

    5. Trowel marks.

When recording such evidence, the main objective should be to determine whether the artifact was deposited as the result of loss or discard and, in the case of the latter, whether primary or secondary deposition is involved.

Reworking

Reworking marks found on pipe fragments indicate purposeful alteration after the manufacturing process. This was done for three reasons: (1) to customize an individual pipe; (2)

FIGURE 42. Evidence of charring and exposure to extreme heat on smoking pipe fragments: **a,** charred bowl; **b,** charred stem; **c–f,** burned bowl and stem fragments. (Photo by Rock Chan.)

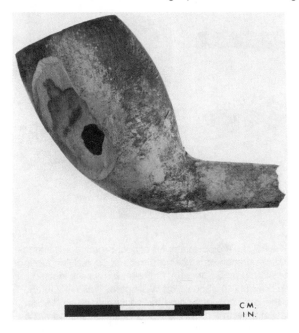

FIGURE 43. White clay bowl/stem fragment exhibiting classic evidence of frost spalling (mid-1800s; Mount Beaufort, Devon Island, Northwest Territories). (Photo by Rock Chan.)

and hairpipes (Figure 48) (Walker 1976:124-127; Sudbury 1978:105-107).

Conclusion

Smoking became so rapidly entrenched after its mid-16th-century introduction into European

FIGURE 44. Examples of bites fashioned on clay pipe stems. The two uppermost specimens have definite carved bites. The other examples have been altered into mouthpieces by abrasion. The one in the lower right was carved prior to abrasion and could also represent alteration to accommodate a makeshift stem. (Photo by Rock Chan.)

FIGURE 45. Broken pipes reworked by abrasion in an attempt to extend their life. Although the majority of these appear to have been altered to friction-fit in a wooden or reed stem, the bowl fragment in the top right has been reamed out to accept a stem insert. (Photo by Rock Chan.)

society that few other artifacts are as indicative of occupation by Northern Europeans. Consequently, fragmented smoking pipes invariably occur on most historical sites in North America. Large-scale industrialization in the pipemaking industry in both Europe and North America, coupled with recognition of pipes as a medium of decorative expression, resulted in the production of an innumerable variety of styles and designs, many of which can help to date and interpret their archaeological contexts.

Although smoking could be described as a highly social activity, it is also very personal, as evidenced by variations in use, the idiosyncrasies of wear, ingenuity in repair, and acts of personalization detected on many pipe fragments. An apt statement in the frontispiece of Iain Walker's monumental work on the Bristol pipemaking industry was an observation made by Sir Arthur Conan Doyle's fictional detective, Sherlock Holmes: "Pipes are occasionally of extraordinary interest–nothing has more individuality save, perhaps, watches and bootlaces" (Walker 1977:iii). The researcher should document any details of use and wear in pipe assemblages as they may prove helpful in expanding a record of past lifeways.

The advent of composite-pipe styles during the latter half of the 19th century fostered a radical change in smoking habits as smoking

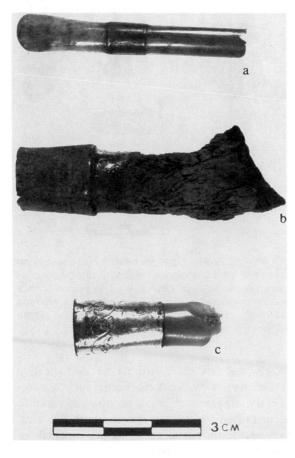

FIGURE 47. Typical examples of post-production markings and decoration on smoking pipes: **a,** scored line around the stem (Fort St. Joseph, Ontario); **b,** crosses incised on the bowl (1840-1850s; Fort Wellington, Prescott, Ontario); **c,** the letter "A" incised on the socket shank (Fort Walsh, Saskatchewan); **d,** painted decoration on the bowl (Fort St. Joseph, Ontario); **e,** series of intermittent incised lines encircling the pipe shank (Fort St. Joseph, Ontario). (Photo by Rock Chan.)

FIGURE 46. Reworked pipe stem fragments illustrating the range of makeshift ferrules: **a,** this homemade stem and mouthpiece represents a lot of effort to repair a pipe. The stem body was fashioned from a hollow bird bone, while the mouthpiece was carved from more dense bone. The two components are joined by a silver ferrule crimped around the juncture. The success of this repair is revealed by the dense pattern of teeth marks on the mouthpiece (1870s-1890s; Fort Wellington, Prescott, Ontario); **b,** shank of a wooden pipe with an improvised ferrule fashioned from the base of a .410-gauge shotgun shell (1870s-1880s; Fort Walsh, Saskatchewan); **c,** remnant of an amber mouthpiece with a decorated white-metal ferrule crimped around one end (1870s-1880s; Fort Walsh). (Photo by Rock Chan.)

unit pipe elements that are recovered archaeologically often exhibit evidence of reworking, showing that the owner attempted to prolong the life of his pipe.

Other forms of tobacco consumption during the latter half of the 19th century must also be considered by the researcher. Cigars, cigarettes, and chewing tobacco represent expressly expendable tobacco products which have left only a very subtle trace in the archaeological record.

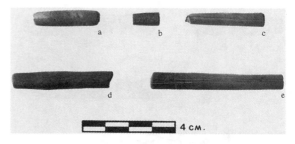

pipes were no longer considered a cheap and expendable commodity. The increasing popularity of composite forms should be reflected in late 19th-century disposal patterns, as the more-durable and expensive composite pipes were kept for longer periods than were traditional clay forms, often lasting throughout the occupation of a site and leaving very little trace. Those multi-

FIGURE 48. White clay pipe stem fragments reworked into beads: **a,** definite bead, tapered at both ends; **b,** possible wampum-style bead; **c,** possible bead preform consisting of the manufactured bite and a scored and snapped opposite end; **d-e,** long beads or possible hairpipes. All specimens are from H.B.C. Nottingham House, Lake Athabasca, Alberta (1802-1806). (Photo by Rock Chan.)

Although much has been learned about smoking-pipe assemblages, the potential to learn more is incredible as archaeologists have really only just begun to appreciate the potential of this artifact class.

REFERENCES

ATKINSON, D. R., AND ADRIAN H. OSWALD
1972   A Brief Guide for the Identification of Dutch Clay Tobacco Pipes Found in England. *Post-Medieval Archaeology* 6:175-182.

AUGUSTIN, NIELS
1980-81 *The European Picture Book of Clay Pipes*. Icon-Ceramisch Museum, Willemstad, Netherlands.

AYTO, E.G.
1994   Clay Tobacco Pipes. *Shire Publication* 37. Shire Publications, Aylesbury, Bucks, England.

BINFORD, LEWIS R.
1962   A New Method of Calculating Dates from Kaolin Pipe Stem Samples. *Southeastern Archaeological Conference Newsletter* 9(1):19-21.

BRADBURY, FREDERICK
1927   *Bradbury's Book of Hallmarks*. Reprinted 1988, J. W. Northend, Sheffield, England.

CRANMER, LEON E.
1990   Cushnoc: The History and Archaeology of Plymouth Colony Traders on the Kennebec. *Occasional Papers in Maine Archaeology* 7. Augusta.

DUCO, DON H.
1976   *Gouda Pipemakers' Marks*, L. T. Alexander, translator. Privately printed, Amsterdam, Netherlands.

DUNHILL, ALFRED H.
1954   *The Gentle Art of Smoking*. G. P. Putman's Sons, New York, NY.

EHWA, CARL, JR.
1974   *The Book of Pipes & Tobacco*. Random House, New York, NY.

FAIRHOLT, FREDERICK W.
1859   *Tobacco: Its History and Associations*. Chapman and Hall, London, England. Reprinted 1968, Singing Tree Press, Detroit, MI.

GREENHOUS, BRERETON
1987   *Guarding the Goldfields: The Story of the Yukon Field Force*. Dundurn Press, Toronto, Ontario.

HARRINGTON, J. C.
1954   Dating Stem Fragments of Seventeenth and Eighteenth Century Clay Tobacco Pipes. *Quarterly Bulletin, Archeological Society of Virginia* 9(1).

1955   A Comment on "A Critique and Rebuttal of the Paper Dating Stem Fragments of 17-18 Century Clay Tobacco Pipes" by John F. Chalkley. *Quarterly Bulletin, Archeological Society of Virginia* 9(4):11-12.

1990   Dating Stem Fragments of Seventeenth and Eighteenth Century Clay Tobacco Pipes. *Quarterly Bulletin, Archeological Society of Virginia* 45(3):123-128.

HEIGHTON, ROBERT F., AND KATHLEEN A. DEAGAN
1972   A New Formula for Dating Kaolin Clay Pipestems. *The Conference on Historic Site Archaeology Papers 1971* 6:220-229. Columbia, SC.

HELBERS, G. C.
1942   De Merken en het Merkenrecht van de Pijpmakers te Gouda. In *Goudsche Pijpen*, by G. C. Helbers and D. A. Goedewaagen. *Monographiae Nicotinae* 4. Gouda, Netherlands.

HIGGINS, DAVID A.
1997   The Identification, Analysis and Interpretation of Tobacco Pipes from Wrecks. In Artefacts from Wrecks: Dated Assemblages from the Late Middle Ages to the Industrial Revolution, Mark Redknap, editor, pp. 129-136. *Oxbow Monograph* 84. Oxford, England.

JACKSON, R. G., AND R. H. PRICE
1974   Bristol Clay Pipes: A Study of Makers and Their Marks. *Bristol City Museum Research Monograph* 1. Bristol, England.

JEAN-LEO
1971   *Les pipes en terres Françaises du 17me siècle à nos jours*. Les Grenier du Collectionneur, Brussels, Belgium.

LENIK, EDWARD J.
1971   The Step Gage: A New Tool for Measuring Pipestem Bore Diameters. *Historical Archaeology* 5:100-101.

McCASHION, JOHN H.
1979   A Preliminary Chronology and Discussion of Seventeenth and Early Eighteenth Century Clay Tobacco Pipes from New York State Sites. In The Archaeology of the Clay Tobacco Pipe: II; The United States of America, Peter Davey, editor, pp. 63-150. *British Archaeological Reports International Series* 60. London, England.

NOËL HUME, AUDREY
1963   Clay Tobacco Pipe Dating in Light of Recent Excavations. *Quarterly Bulletin, Archeological Society of Virginia* 18(2):22-25.

1979   Clay Tobacco Pipes Excavated at Martin's Hundred, Virginia, 1976-1978. In The Archaeology of the Clay Tobacco Pipe: II. The United States of America, Peter Davey, editor, pp. 3-36. *British Archaeological Reports International Series* 60. London, England.

NOËL HUME, IVOR
    1969   *A Guide to Artifacts in Colonial America.* Alfred
            Knopf, New York, NY.

OMWAKE, H. G.
    1956   Date-Bore Diameter Correlation in English White
            Kaolin Pipe Stems, Yes or No? *Quarterly Bulletin,
            Archeological Society of Virginia* 11(1).

OSWALD, ADRIAN H.
    1961   The Evolution and Chronology of English Clay
            Tobacco Pipes.   *Archaeological Newsletter*
            7(3):55-62.
    1975   Clay Pipes for the Archaeologist.   *British
            Archaeological Reports* 14. London, England.

PFEIFFER, MICHAEL A.
    1978   The Utility of Clay Tobacco Pipes and Stems as
            a Time Marker in the Pacific Northwest. Paper
            presented at the 31st Northwest Anthropological
            Conference, Pullman, WA.
    1981a   Clay Tobacco Pipes from Spokane House and Fort
            Colvile. *Northwest Anthropological Research Notes*
            15(2):221-235.
    1981b   Notes on Unusual Clay Tobacco Pipes Found in
            Seattle. *Historical Archaeology* 15(1):109-112.
    1982   The Clay Pipes. In Kanaka Village/Vancouver
            Barracks 1975, by David Chance, et al., pp.
            113-127. Office of Public Archaeology, Institute for
            Environmental Studies, University of Washington,
            Reports in Highway Archaeology 7. Seattle.
    1983   Clay Tobacco Pipes from Five Archaeological Sites
            in Nebraska. *Historic Clay Tobacco Pipe Studies*
            2:39-47. Bryon Sudbury, Ponca City, OK.
    1985   Tobacco. In Archaeological Investigations at the
            Cabinet Landing Site (10BR413), Bonner County,
            Idaho, by Keith Landreth, Keo Boreson, and Mary
            Condon. *Eastern Washington University Reports
            in Archaeology and History* 100-45:114,116-120.
            Cheney.
    1986   Tobacco Pipes from the Arrowtown Chinese
            Settlement, Central Otago, New Zealand. *Historic
            Clay Tobacco Studies* 3:79-88. Bryon Sudbury,
            Ponca City, OK.

RICHIE, CLARENCE F.
    1978   Nineteenth-Century Clay Tobacco-Pipes from the
            High Arctic. *Canadian Journal of Archaeology*
            2:123-137.
    1981   Tobacco Pipes from Fort Walsh, Saskatchewan:
            A North-West Mounted Police Post, 1875-1883.
            Manuscript, Parks Canada, Ottawa, Ontario.

SMITH, ROBIN
    1998   Montréal Clay Tobacco Pipe Makers 1846-1902.
            <http://www.virtlogic.ca/pipe/mtlmake.html>29
            January 1998.

SOUTH, STANLEY
    1964   Eighteenth Century Clay Pipes from the Kiln Waster
            Dumps in the Moravian Town of Bethabara, North
            Carolina. *North Carolina Department of Archives
            and History Newsletter.*
    1967   The Ceramic Forms of the Potter Gottfried Aust
            at Bethabara, North Carolina, 1755 to 1771. *The
            Conference of Historic Site Archaeology Papers
            1965-1966* 1:33-52. Columbia, SC.

SUDBURY, BYRON
    1978   Additional Notes on Alternative Uses for Clay Tobacco
            Pipes and Tobacco Pipe Fragments. *Historical
            Archaeology* 12:105-107.
    1979   Historic Clay Tobacco Pipemakers in the United States
            of America. In The Archaeology of the Clay Tobacco
            Pipe: II. The United States of America, Peter Davey,
            editor, pp. 151-340. *British Archaeological Reports
            International Series* 60. London, England.
    1980   *Historic Clay Tobacco Pipe Studies*, Vol. 1. Byron
            Sudbury, Ponca City, OK.
    1983   *Historic Clay Tobacco Pipe Studies*, Vol. 2. Byron
            Sudbury, Ponca City, OK.
    1986   *Historic Clay Tobacco Pipe Studies*, Vol. 3. Byron
            Sudbury, Ponca City, OK.

WALKER, IAIN C.
    1965   Some Thoughts on the Harrington and Binford Systems
            for Statistically Dating Clay Pipes. *Quarterly Bulletin,
            Archeological Society of Virginia* 20(2):60-64.
    1966a   Identification and Dating of Clay Pipes.
            Manuscript, Parks Canada, Ottawa.
    1966b   TD Pipes: A Preliminary Study. *Quarterly Bulletin,
            Archeological Society of Virginia* 20(4):86-102.
    1967   Statistical Methods for Dating Clay Pipe Fragments.
            Post-Medieval Archaeology 1:90-101.
    1971a   An Archaeological Study of Clay Pipes from the
            King's Bastion, Fortress of Louisbourg. *Canadian
            Historic Sites, Occasional Papers in Archaeology and
            History* 2:55-122. Ottawa, Ontario.
    1971b   The Manufacture of Dutch Clay Tobacco-Pipes.
            Northeast Historical Archaeology 1(1):5-17.
    1971c   Note on the Bethabara, North Carolina, Tobacco
            Pipes. *The Conference on Historic Site Archaeology
            Papers 1969* 4:26-36. Columbia, SC.
    1976   Alternative Uses for Clay Tobacco Pipes and Tobacco
            Pipe Fragments: Some Notes. *Historical Archaeology*
            10:124-127.
    1977   Clay Tobacco-Pipes, with Particular Reference to
            the Bristol Industry. Parks Canada. *History and
            Archaeology* 11. Ottawa, Ontario.
    1983   Nineteenth-Century Clay Tobacco-Pipes in Canada.
            In The Archaeology of the Clay Tobacco Pipe: VIII;
            America, Peter Davey, editor, pp. 1-87. *British
            Archaeological Reports International Series* 175.
            London, England.

WEBER, CARL
1965   *Carl Weber's The Pleasures of Pipe Smoking.* Bantam Books, New York, NY.

CHARLES S. BRADLEY
MATERIAL CULTURE RESEARCH
ONTARIO SERVICE CENTRE
PARKS CANADA
1600 LIVERPOOL COURT
OTTAWA, ONTARIO K1A 0M5
CANADA

GÉRARD GUSSET

A Preliminary Annotated Bibliography on Electrical Artifacts

Introduction

Devices which produce or use electricity do not often spark an archaeologist's enthusiasm. They often look unusual and hard to identify, and no one seems to know much about them. While some, like the ubiquitous insulator, are often simple to identify, others are far more intriguing and complex. Since expertise is not available and most archaeologists do not have the time or resources to learn about them, these objects often do not get the same degree of attention that other artifacts do. At the end of many excavations, they are often piled together and eventually classified and recorded as "electricals."

Electrical artifacts can tell us a lot; not only about the production and use of electricity in a specific context, but also about the way a specific electrically driven activity or trade was organized and conducted. These artifacts are useful because of their highly specialized nature: most of them were designed and manufactured for a very specific purpose or a very limited number of uses. For example, a "barrel-shaped glass jar Edison primary battery" was probably used for railway signaling purposes; a "200-ampere, 125-volt angled dial rotary switch" was likely used in a heating appliance, such as a cooking range. Electricals are generally found well preserved because they are often made of stable or durable materials such as porcelain, stoneware, glass, bakelite, gutta-percha, copper alloys, and aluminum. They are also relatively easy to identify and date since most of them were patented and well described in catalogues.

This short bibliography is intended to guide the user to a basic corpus of information on those electrical artifacts most often found in archaeological sites. It includes products manufactured or sold in Canada, and emphasizes source documents that meet the following criteria: (1) published material widely available and relatively easy to find; (2) well illustrated to assist with identification and dating; (3) not too

technical; and (4) plentiful detailed information with direct relevance to the interpretation of domestic and small industrial archaeological sites. Machinery and supplies from large industrial plants and highly specialized equipment could obviously not be covered here. Documents are grouped under thirteen headings: Bibliographies; Patents; History, Sociology, and Economics; Trade Catalogues; Power Production and Distribution; Batteries and Accumulators; Insulators; Fixtures, Receptacles, and Wiring; Lighting; Domestic Appliances; Motive Power; Electroplating; and Communication and Recording.

The section on trade catalogues is the largest. These documents are a major source of information on brand name electrical supplies. They normally contain detailed illustrations, manufacturers' names, standard trade names and marks, model numbers, materials, dimensions, specifications, and prices. They also often provide useful information in the form of wiring diagrams, technical descriptions of innovative products, directions for installation, explanations of intended purpose and use, and safety precautions. Catalogues from large companies were generally published yearly. By consulting them chronologically, one easily gets a sense of the improvement and evolution of supplies and machines through time. The present selection covers the vast majority of general domestic and industrial supplies marketed from the 1880s to about 1950. Monographs provide a more in-depth explanation on how devices work and how electrical components are put together to function in properly designed setups.

This bibliography is intended for the beginner who wants to learn the basics of electrical technology as it was understood from the 1880s to the 1940s. As the second half of the 20th century unfolded, electricity was no longer a separate alternative in technology. It permeates most modern trades and many new technical activities. Electrical and electronic machinery can no longer be described and understood on the basis of a limited number of discrete electrical components and circuits. Due to the higher degree of specialization and integration, and because of the huge amount of information that has been published, a different approach becomes necessary. Each activity, field, and subfield should then presume a separate and specific quest for information.

Historical Archaeology, MCR 2000:134—140.

Bibliographies

LOWOOD, HENRY
1992 Current Bibliography in the History of Technology (1990). *Technology and Culture* 33:1-211.

Energy conversion: hydraulic engineering, steam-electrical stations, power transmission, lighting, heating and ventilation, refrigeration, and direct-conversion power plants. Electronics and electro-mechanical technology: tools, machines, instruments, timekeepers, and automatic controls. Communication and records: telegraph, telephone, radio, phonographs and recorders, and photography.

THE SOCIETY FOR THE HISTORY OF TECHNOLOGY
1991 An Annotated Index to Volumes 1 through 25 of Technology and Culture 1959-1984. *Technology and Culture* 32(2).

Lighting, railroads, communications, engineers and scientists, industry, power production and transmission, electrical technology and science, electrochemical technology, electrocution, electrohorticulture, and electronics industry.

Patents

FISET, RICHARD
1993 *Record of Canadian Patents 1824-1891– Electricity.* Nessy Publications, Quebec, Quebec.

Canadian patent numbers 1,670 to 37,956, with line illustrations, list of inventors, and index by subject.

History, Sociology, and Economics of Electricity

DENIS, LEO G.
1918 *Electric Generation and Distribution in Canada.* Commission of Conservation Canada, Ottawa, Ontario.

Electrical plants by province, with a brief description of equipment, power, fuel, value of assets, rates, and the distribution network, photos, drawings, maps, and index.

HALL OF HISTORY FOUNDATION
1989 *The General Electric Story: 1876-1986.* Schenectady, NY.

Illustrated history of the company, history of electrification, bibliography, and index.

HAUSMAN, WILLIAM J., AND JOHN L. NEUFELD
1989 Engineers and Economists: Historical Perspectives on the Pricing of Electricity. *Technology and Culture* 30(1):83-104.

The economics of the electrical utility industry, contrasting view of engineers and economists, cost and fare structures, fixed costs, and differential rates.

HUNTER, P. V.
1916 Development of Electric Power Stations. *The Electrician* 77(24):838.

A concise history of power production in Europe.

INSTITUTE OF ELECTRICAL AND ELECTRONICS ENGINEERS-CANADIAN REGION
1985 *Electricity: The Magic Medium.* The Institute of Electrical and Electronics Engineers, New York, NY.

Commemorates the achievements of the Canadian electrical industry over the past 100 years or so. Historical highlights, electrical engineering and technology education, and production of electricity; past, present, and future.

NYE, DAVID E.
1990 *Electrifying America: Social Meanings of a New Technology.* Massachusetts Institute of Technology Press, Cambridge.

Social and economic impacts of electrification.

SCHURR, SAM H., CALVIN C. BURWELL, WARREN D. DEVINE, AND SIDNEY SONENBLUM
1990 *Electricity in the American Economy: Agent of Technological Progress.* Greenwood Press, Westport, CT.

A history of the technological and economic impacts of electrification on many fast-evolving trades in the United States, such as mining, transportation, and entertainment.

WALKER, DAVID F., AND JAMES H. BATER
1974 *Industrial Development in Southern Ontario.* University of Waterloo, Waterloo, Ontario.

Many chapters on the electrification of various manufacturing processes.

Trade Catalogues

AMALGAMATED ELECTRIC
1956 *Wiring Supplies Catalogue, Bulletin No. 1–Wiring Devices.* Amalgamated Electric Corporation Limited, Montreal, Quebec.

Wiring devices, domestic lighting, and switches.

ARMY AND NAVY STORES
1969 *Yesterday's Shopping: The Army and Navy Stores Catalogue 1907*, introduction by Alison Adburgham. David and Charles, Newton Abbot, Devon, England.

Domestic appliances, batteries, bells, games, fans, heating, flashlights, lamps and parts, time pieces, medical supplies, shaving mirrors, hair brushes, toys, machine models, electricians' tools, telephones, and electroplated goods.

BENJAMIN ELECTRIC MANUFACTURING COMPANY OF CANADA

1926 *Benjamin Electric Products–Catalogue C25.* Benjamin Electric Manufacturing Company of Canada, Toronto, Ontario.

General catalogue; domestic and industrial supplies.

CANADIAN GENERAL ELECTRIC

[1915] *Electrical Supplies–Catalogue No. 15.* Canadian General Electric Company, Toronto, Ontario.

General catalogue; all domestic and industrial supplies with index.

1927 *The CGE Farm Book–Electricity in the Farm.* Canadian General Electric Company, Toronto, Ontario.

Lighting, motors, dairy machines, brooders, ranges, irons, and other domestic appliances; battery chargers, radios, and wiring devices.

1929 *Electrical Merchandise–Catalogue No. 29.* Canadian General Electric Company, Toronto, Ontario.

General catalogue; all domestic and industrial supplies; index.

1940 *Motors. Catalogue 40M.* Canadian General Electric Company, Toronto, Ontario.

Illustrations of all CGE motor types, applications of motors and controls, DC generators, and induction motor-generators.

1949 *Wiring Devices–Catalogue 49WD.* Canadian General Electric Company, Toronto, Ontario.

Lampholders and accessories, wiring devices, switches, signaling, terminals and boards, indoor bus supports, power line hardware, fluorescent lighting, and insulators.

1952 *Wiring Supplies, Power Apparatus–Catalogue 53G.* Canadian General Electric Company, Toronto, Ontario.

Air conditioning, domestic appliances, aviation equipment, power tools, water treatment, conduits and fittings, electronic equipment, flashlights, batteries, generators, rectifiers, welding equipment, insulators, meters, lighting, locomotives, motors, controls, magnets, power line hardware and tools, raceways, signaling equipment, switches, transformers, wires and cables, and wiring devices.

CANADIAN WESTINGHOUSE ELECTRIC COMPANY

1960 *Canadian Westinghouse Industrial Apparatus–Catalogue H-30-000.* Canadian Westinghouse Electric Company, Hamilton, Ontario.

Descriptions, specifications, and illustrations of motors, controls, switches and breakers, ducts, panelboards, transformers, and lighting devices.

GENERAL ELECTRIC

1930 *General Electric Catalogue GEA-600A.* General Electric Company, Schenectady, NY.

Generators, converters, motors, domestic and industrial fuses, switches, lighting, resistors, wiring devices, steel furnaces, controls, conduits, and glazes for crucibles.

[1935] *Electric Equipment for Industry. Catalog GEA-621.* General Electric Company, Schenectady, NY.

Motors types, generators, and specifications.

GRAYBAR ELECTRIC COMPANY

1948 *General Catalog No. 103.* R. R. Donnelly & Sons, Chicago.

Domestic and industrial supplies.

NORTHERN ELECTRIC COMPANY

[1917] *General Catalogue No. 3–Wire and Cables, Telephone Apparatus, Electrical Supplies.* Northern Electric Company, Montreal, Quebec.

Domestic and industrial supplies; index.

[1921] *General Catalogue No. 4–Electrical Supplies.* Northern Electric Company, Montreal, Quebec.

Domestic and industrial supplies; index.

[1925] *General Catalogue No. 5.* Northern Electric Company, Montreal, Quebec.

Domestic and industrial supplies; index.

1937 *Electrical Supplies–Catalogue No. 7.* Northern Electric Company Limited, Montreal, Quebec.

Domestic and industrial wiring, lighting, and insulators.

1940 *Electrical Supplies–Catalogue No. 2241.* Northern Electric Company, Montreal, Quebec.

Domestic and industrial supplies and their specifications.

1953 *Illumination–Industrial: Catalogue I-53.* Northern Electric Company, Montreal, Quebec.

Incandescent, mercury, and fluorescent tubes and bulbs.

n.d. *Materials and Tools for Line Construction and Maintenance, Overhead and Underground.* Northern Electric Company, Montreal, Quebec.

Power lines: tools, wiring, insulators, and poles.

SEARS, ROEBUCK & CO.

1897 *Sears Roebuck Catalogue 1897.* Sears, Roebuck & Co., Chicago, IL. Reprinted 1993, Chelsea House, New York, NY.

Electrical bells, motors, batteries, rings, switches, and other goods; index.

1908 *The Great Price Maker, Catalogue no. 117–1908.* Sears, Roebuck & Co., Chicago, IL. Reprinted 1971, Digest Books, Northfield, IL.

Domestic appliances, toys, batteries, small motors, telephony, bells, wiring supplies, magnets, electricians' tools, insulators, meters, lightbulbs, and lightning arresters; index.

1927 *The 1927 Edition of the Sears Roebuck Catalogue.* Reprinted 1970, Crown Publishers, New York, NY.

Domestic appliances and accessories; index.

T. EATON COMPANY
1927 *Eaton's Spring and Summer Catalogue 1927.* T. Eaton Co. Toronto, Ontario. Reprinted 1971, Musson Book Company, Toronto, Ontario.
Lightbulbs, cookers, wiring devices, lamps, sewing machines, curling tongues, and washing machines; index.

WESTINGHOUSE ELECTRIC & MANUFACTURING COMPANY
[1906] *Detail and Supply Apparatus–Perpetual Catalogue No. 3001* (1906-1916). Westinghouse Electric & Manufacturing Company, Pittsburgh, PA.
All domestic and industrial supplies, their description and specifications; index.
1939 *General Catalogue 1939-1940.* Westinghouse Electric & Manufacturing Company, East Pittsburgh, PA.
Specifications, technical information and prices for domestic insulators, fuses, motors, wiring, lighting (bulb and tubes), domestic appliances, batteries, medical supplies and X-ray equipment, power line equipment, switches, speed reducers, vacuum tubes, battery chargers, rectifiers, and radios; index.

WOOD, ALEXANDER & JAMES
[1923] *Jobbers of Electrical Supplies–Catalogue No. 23.* Wood, Alexander & James, Hamilton, Ontario.
General catalogue of industrial supplies.
[1938] *Wholesale Electrical Supplies–Catalogue No. 38.* Wood, Alexander & James, Hamilton, Ontario.
General catalogue of domestic and industrial supplies.

Power Production and Distribution

BLACKWELL, F. O.
1906 The Power Plant of the Electric Development Company of Ontario. *The Electrician* 57(19):746.
General technical description of the plant; construction, equipment, and operation.

BUCK, H. W.
1906 The Electrical Plant of the Canadian Niagara Power Company. *The Electrician* 57(19):738.
General technical description of the plant; construction, equipment, and operation.

U.S. DEPARTMENT OF AGRICULTURE
1956 *Description of Units, Specifications and Drawings for 7.2/12.5 KV Line Construction.* Washington, DC.
Many drawings of aerial lines: poles, cables, guy wires, insulators, and related equipment.

Batteries and Accumulators

CRAWTER, FRANK
1916 Some Accumulators of the Past. *The Electrician* 77(24):829.
Principles and operation of some types of chemical accumulators.

SCHALLENBERG, RICHARD H.
1982 *Bottled Energy–Electrical Engineering and the Evolution of Chemical Energy Storage.* American Philosophical Society, Philadelphia, PA.
The evolution of the technology and industry of batteries and accumulators in the U.S. between 1880 and 1970. Commercialization, the role of batteries in transportation, electrical cars, and alkaline batteries.

Insulators

BROWN, GERALD
1972 *Collectible Porcelain Insulators.* Gerald Brown, Two Buttes, CO.
Insulators for power lines and telegraph, mainly pin-type insulators, notes on electrical porcelain, drawings for each specimen, dimensions, model numbers, some descriptions from trade catalogues, and marks.

CANADA, DEPARTMENT OF ENERGY, MINES AND RESOURCES
1968 *Ceramic Plants in Canada.* Mineral Resources Division, Department of Energy, Mines and Resources, Ottawa, Ontario.
A listing of ceramic plants and their products; mostly insulators.

CRANFILL, GARY G.
n.d. *The Collectors' Guide for Glass Insulators–Revised,* 2 volumes. Gary G. Cranfill, Sacramento, CA.
Various types of glass insulators: markings, dimensions, and drawings.
n.d. *Dictionary of Glass–Ceramic Insulators.* Gary G. Cranfill, Sacramento, CA.
Various types of ceramic insulators: markings, dimensions, and drawings.

CRANFILL, GARY G., AND GREG A. KAREOFELAS
1973 *The Glass Insulator–A Comprehensive Reference.* Gary G. Cranfill and Greg A. Kareofelas, Sacramento, CA.
Glass insulators: markings, dimensions, and drawings.

LAUCKNER, MARK
1995 *Canadian Railway Communications Insulators: 1880-1920.* Gyote Publishing, Mayne Island, British Columbia.
A brief history of Canadian railway communications, insulator design, glass insulator

manufacturing, glass mold development, porcelain insulator manufacturing, threading, numbering system, marks, color pictures for classifying colored glass insulators, other references, bibliography, rarity, and value guide.

McINTOSH, COLIN
n.d. *Canadian Insulators & Communication Lines.* Colin McIntosh, n.p.
Descriptions, drawings, and photographs of several types of telegraph and power insulators. Short notes on companies across the country.

MILHOLLAND, MARION C.
n.d. *Glass Insulator Reference Book.* Marion C. Milholland, Sequim, WA.
Various types of insulators: markings, dimensions, and drawings.

MILLS, BRENT
1970 *Porcelain Insulators and How They Grew.* Canfield and Tack, Rochester, NY.
Various insulators: markings, dimensions, and drawings.

PARMELEE, CULLEN W.
1951 *Ceramic Glazes.* Industrial Publications, Chicago, IL.
Insulating properties of glazes, electrical porcelains, and leadless glazes.

WOODWARD, N. R.
1988 *The Glass Insulator in America—1988 Report.* N. R. Woodward, Houston, TX.
Discusses most common brands of American insulators from about 1865. Short histories of Brookfield, early Boston-area production, Hemingray, Witall, Tatum, Armstrong and Kerr, Gayner and Lynchburg, Pyrex insulators, production in the Denver area, and production on the West Coast. Identification of and basic information on little-known company names, telegraph and telephone company names, high-voltage insulator names, supply companies, glass insulators in Canada and other countries, and insulator styles and marks. Section drawings and dimensions of selected models, and U.S. Patents for molded glass insulators.

Fixtures, Receptacles, and Wiring

BLACK, ROBERT M.
1983 *The History of Electric Wires and Cables.* Peter Peregrinus/Museum of Science, London, England.
Early telegraph cables, lighting cables, paper insulated cables, three-phase cables, house-wiring cables, telephone cables, enameled wires, special purpose cables, etc.

COOK, ARTHUR L.
1933 *Electric Wiring for Lighting and Power Installation.* John Wiley & Sons, New York, NY.
Lighting systems, power systems, and interior wiring.

GRAHAM, FRANK D.
1946 *Audels Handy Book of Practical Electricity with Wiring Diagrams—Ready References for Students and All Electrical Workers.* Audels, New York, NY.
Electrical theory, batteries and cells, wires, cables, insulators, electrolysis, electroplating, transformers, converters, rectifiers, DC apparatus (internal and external), underground wiring supplies, marine wiring, signs, lighting (fluorescent and neon), AC and DC motors, dynamos, alternators, winding and repairs, power stations, power tools, welding, ignition, vehicles, pumps, elevators, cranes, bells, telegraphs, telephones, radios, motion picture projectors, heating and refrigeration, compressors, and resuscitation equipment.

SCHROEDER, FRED E. H.
1986 More 'Small Things Forgotten': Domestic Electrical Plugs and Receptacles 1881-1931. *Technology and Culture* 27(3):525-543.
Domestic wiring (1881-1931): accessories, plugs, and receptacles.

UNDERWRITERS' NATIONAL ELECTRIC ASSOCIATION
1908 List of Electrical Fittings that have been Examined and Approved by the Underwriters' National Electric Association for Use under the Rules and Requirements of the National Board of the Fire Underwriters for the Installation of Electric Wiring and Apparatus. Underwriters' National Electric Association, Chicago, IL.
Product names for many wiring devices, model numbers for approved products, American manufacturers, and UL labels.

Lighting (Incandescent Lamps, Arc Lamps, Gas Discharge Lamps)

ANDREWS, LEONARD
1906 Long Flame Arc Lamps. *The Electrician* 57(3):87; 57(4):51; 57(4):129; 57(5):164.
A series of short articles on the development of arc-lamp machines.

BOHM, C. R.
1906 Modern Forms of Electrical Incandescent Lamps. *The Electrician* 57(23):894.
A brief survey of the latest bulb designs, bulb shapes, and filament material.

BRIGHT, ARTHUR
1949 The *Electric-Lamp Industry: Technological Change and Economic Development from 1800 to 1947.* Macmillan Company, New York, NY.
Technological evolution in the manufacture of incandescent, arc, and ionization lighting in America.

Cox, Henry Bartholomew
1979 Hot Hairpin in a Bottle: The Beginning of Incandescence. *Nineteenth Century* 5(3):45-49.
History of incandescent lighting in the United Kingdom and the United States; discusses the various substances used for filaments.

Davis, Pearce
1949 *The Development of the American Glass Industry.* Harvard University Press, Cambridge, MA.
Brief history of the technology and manufacturing of lightbulbs.

Dubuisson, Bernard
1968 *Encyclopédie Pratique de la Construction et du Bâtiment*, Tome 2. Librairie Aristide Quillet, Paris, France.
General and industrial engineering, public works, public lighting, and public transportation.

The Electrician
1903 Westinghouse Bremer Arc Lamps. *The Electrician* 51(15):615.
Development of a new type of arc lamp.

O'Dea, W. T.
1958 *A Short History of Lighting.* Science Museum, London, England.
History and construction of lighting devices: incandescent, arc, and ionization lamps.

Paterson, Clifford C.
1916 The Evolution of the Electric Lamp. *The Electrician* 77(24):822.
A short technological history of early-20th-century incandescent lamps. Discusses bulb shapes and new material for filaments.

Phillips, Charles John
1960 *Glass—Its Industrial Applications. Reinhold,* New York, NY.
Technology and manufacture of various types of electrical lightbulbs and electron tubes: incandescent, vapor discharge, projection, photography, heating, radio receiving, power tubes, cathode ray, and television.

Shand, E. B.
1958 *Glass Engineering Handbook.* McGraw-Hill, New York, NY.
Technology, manufacture, and properties of glass for lightbulbs, electron tubes, and insulators.

Steinmetz, P.
1903 The Mercury Arc. *The Electrician* 51(4):171.
Brief description of the design and operation of the mercury vapor lamp.

Woodhead, E. I., C. Sullivan, and Gérard Gusset
1984 Lighting Devices in the National Reference Collection, Parks Canada. Parks Canada, *Studies in Archaeology, Architecture and History.* Ottawa, Ontario.
A short history of lighting devices; description of operating principles; terminology of components; and incandescent, arc, and ionization lamps. Some archaeological specimens included.

Domestic Appliances

Artman, E. Townsend
1996 *Toasters 1909-1960.* Schiffer, Atglen, PA.
Describes and illustrates many forms by type: perchers, pinchers, flatbeds, floppers, etc. Includes novelties and discusses all major brands and some rarities.

Gordon, Bob
1984 *Early Electrical Appliances.* Shire Publications, Aylesbury, England.
Photographs and drawings of appliances for heating, refrigeration, cooking, water heating, cleaning and washing, health and beauty, etc., with brief descriptions and historical comments.

Miller, Gary, and K. M. Scotty Mitchell
1991 *Price Guide to Collectible Kitchen Appliances.* Wallace-Homestead, Radnor, PA.
Coffee makers, combination appliances, cooking appliances, irons, mixers and whips, novelties, toasters, waffle irons, sandwich grilles, and bibliography; index.

Peet, Louise J., and Lenore E. Sater
1934 *Household Equipment.* John Wiley & Sons, New York, NY.
Description and illustration of common electrical equipment in the standard household including ranges, small equipment, refrigerators, cleaning equipment, and lighting; index.

Motive Power

Fynn, V. A.
1906 The Classification of Alternate-Current Motors. *The Electrician* 57(6):204; 57(8):284; 57(9):329.
Series of articles on the design and operation of the best known types of AC motors, with wiring diagrams. Lists advantages and disadvantages of each type.

Kline, Ronald
1987 Science and Engineering Theory in the Invention and Development of the Induction Motor, 1880-1900. *Technology and Culture* 28(2):283-313.

Theoretical background and invention of the induction motor, engineering, research, and development from 1888 to 1891.

PARSHALL, H. F.
1916 Electric Traction. *The Electrician* 77(24):824.
Motive power and transportation.

PENN, E.
1987 Fifty Electric Motors. *Electronics & Technology Today* (Sept.):11-13.
Short discussion of the various type of electric motors normally found in a typical modern home with some theory.

WALKER, MILES
1916 Dynamo-Electric Machinery, 1878-1916. *The Electrician* 77(24):817.
New developments in direct-current machines.

WORMELL, R.
1897 *Electricity in the Service of Man–Popular and Practical Treatise on the Application of Electricity in Modern Life.* Cassell and Company, London, England.
Many engravings and descriptions of machines and apparatus, both domestic and industrial, including the history of power producing machines for AC and DC, dynamos, alternators, transformers, batteries, accumulators, lighting, motive power, electrochemistry and metallurgy, and telephone and telegraph.

Electroplating

HASLUCK, PAUL N.
1908 *Electroplating–With Numerous Engravings and Diagrams.* Cassell and Company, New York, NY.
Illustrates and describes shop equipment such as vats, batteries, dynamos, measuring devices, shop machines and accessories, and hand tools; also explains procedures.

REETZ, HENRY C.
1911 *Electroplating–A Treatise for the Beginner and for the Most Experienced Electroplater.* Popular Mechanics Company, Chicago, IL.
Principles and apparatus, shop equipment, cleaning, copper-, nickel-, silver-, and gold-plating.

Communication and Recording (Telegraphy, Telephony, Wireless, Sound and Picture Recording)

BRIGHTS, CHARLES
1916 The Story of the Submarine Cable. *The Electrician* 77(24):801.

A short history (including new developments) of submarine cables for communication.

COHEN, B. S.
1916 Long-Distance Telephony. *The Electrician* 77(24):814.
The operation of long-distance telephone systems; new designs and schematic diagrams.

FLEMING, J. A.
1916 Radiotelegraphy: A Retrospect of Twenty Years. *The Electrician* 77(24):831.
A short history of technological advances in early-20th-century wireless telegraphy transmitters, receivers, and related apparatus.

HARRISON, H. H.
1916 The Story of Land Telegraphy. *The Electrician* 77(24):798.
Overview of telegraph systems on land including technical descriptions and schematic diagrams.

KINGSBURY, J. E.
1916 The Story of the Telephone. *The Electrician* 77(24):812.
Overview of telephone systems with technical descriptions and schematic diagrams.

KNAPPEN, RON, AND MARY KNAPPEN
1978 *History and Identification of Old Telephones.* R. Knappen, Galesville, WI.
Terminology, history, description, and illustrations of typical phones; description and identification by parts; switch boards; bell boxes; index of manufacturers many period illustrations.

MARCONI, ELECTRONIC TUBES AND COMPONENTS DIVISION
1951 *Radiotron Characteristics Manual.* Marconi, Electronic Tubes and Components Division, Toronto, Ontario.
Interpretation of technical data, classification, characteristics, and ratings of receiving tubes, special-purpose tubes, television picture tubes, non-standard tubes, outline drawings of tubes and tube sockets, and typical circuits.

READ, OLIVER, AND WALTER L. WELCH
1959 *From Tin Foil to Stereo.* Howard W. Soms, Indianapolis, IN.
Description and illustration of electrical apparatus and machines for telegraphy, telephony, radio, motion pictures, and sound recording.

GÉRARD GUSSET
MATERIAL CULTURE RESEARCH
ONTARIO SERVICE CENTRE
PARKS CANADA
1600 LIVERPOOL COURT
OTTAWA, ONTARIO K1A 0M5
CANADA

OLIVE R. JONES

A Guide to Dating Glass Tableware: 1800 to 1940

Introduction

Between 1800 and 1940, the glass industry production method in North America and Europe changed from predominantly mouth-blown to predominantly machine-made. At the beginning of this period, successful glass production was based on practical observation and experience but, step by step, the knowledge base changed to mechanical and scientific expertise. Hand-in-hand with changing production methods came changes in tableglass decorating technologies and new glass formulas. Increased mechanization and innovations provided lower-priced tableglass which significantly increased the number of consumers who could afford glass and, at the same time, increased the choices available to consumers.

Tableglass was made and purchased not only to be used but to be seen, motivations similar to those for choosing ceramic tablewares, furniture, and other domestic furnishings. Motifs and tableglass shapes often reflected the decorative arts movements of the 19th and early 20th centuries. At the same time, some motifs and shapes remained in production regardless of fashion. For example, tumblers decorated with vertical panels were made throughout the entire 1800-1940 period. Some tableglass was made with no surface decoration; some was completely covered with decoration; some motifs were pictorial, others were geometric or abstract. Increasingly, between 1825 and 1940, consumers could choose from a number of different styles and a variety of price ranges. Prestigious and expensive hand-cut or hand-engraved motifs were imitated in inexpensive mold-blown, pressed, or acid-etched glasses while inexpensively cut and engraved tableglass competed with pressed and acid-etched glasses. Consumers chose tableglass that reflected their purchasing power, aesthetic preferences, and social position. However, in any one household, the tableglass probably represented a range of prices, a variety of styles, and different levels of service. In the same household, as with ceramic tablewares, one might also expect to find a mix of older and newer glassware.

During the 140 years covered by this guide, the goods produced by glass manufacturers reflected changes in drinking patterns and in food service. For example, tumbler usage increased as non-alcoholic drinks–such as soda water, water, lemonade, and fruit juices–became the drinks of choice for many consumers. The American habit of drinking tea from the saucer led to the production and use of glass cup plates between the late 1820s and about 1860. Celery glasses reflected the practice of serving celery stalks at the table. Salt shakers were introduced in the 1860s, and gradually became the dominant form for serving salt, although small individual open salts continued to be sold. Inns and taverns had always served food and drink but it was not until the 1840s that glass manufacturers started offering "bar tumblers" and decanters with "bar lips" for commercial use. By the early 20th century, suppliers offered a wide range of wares specifically for commercial use by restaurants, hotels, clubs, ocean liners, and railroads (Budde & Westermann 1913).

At the beginning of the 19th century, American markets were supplied with some domestically made glass and with glass imported from continental Europe and Britain (Lanman 1969:15-48; Wilson 1994[2]:769-772). Although glass manufacturers in the United States faced fierce competition from Europe and a shortage of experienced workmen, they were able to establish the basis for a successful American glass industry during the first 25 years of the 19th century. During the second quarter of the century, American glass factories began to compete seriously with foreign producers (Davis 1949:35-41, 50-64, 65-71) and by mid-century, the industry was firmly established. However, imported glasswares continued to be an important part of the American marketplace, particularly in mouth-blown and hand-decorated wares.

From the 1760s until the 1840s, the Canadian market was served almost entirely by British-made products, but after Great Britain adopted

Historical Archaeology, MCR 2000:141—232.
Permission to reprint required.

free trade in 1845, the Canadian market was opened to American and European products (Jones 1986a, 1986b, 1986c, 1986d, 1992). Attempts to manufacture glass in Canada began in the 1840s, but the companies survived only briefly. In the 1870s, a glass factory in Hamilton, Ontario, was able to operate successfully for a number of years, but it was not until the 1890s that the Canadian glass industry truly became established (King 1987:front and back flyleaves). The primary tableglass products were pressed and machine-blown tablewares. Canadian cut glass firms operating in the early 20th century used imported blanks; Henry Birks & Sons, for example, used French and American blanks (Henry Birks & Sons 1903:8).

While the country of origin was sometimes used as a selling point, it is important to understand that the glass industry of the 19th and early 20th centuries was an international one (Great Britain 1907). Successful technological advances, decorative innovations, and decorative motifs were immediately copied by manufacturers and decorators in other countries, not just by rival firms. After the success of the 1851 London Great Exhibition, subsequent international exhibitions encouraged the diffusion of technology and styles throughout the western world.

From 1800 to 1940, the tableglass industry was one of innovation, invention, eclecticism, revivals, and imitation, particularly after about 1850, when interest in industrial design led to the establishment of design schools and of museums such as the Victoria and Albert Museum in London and the Musée des arts décoratifs in Paris. This interest led glassware designers to pillage the past for inspiration. For example, engraved glassware shown at the Paris Exhibition in 1878 highlighted classical motifs, but also included Arabian, Assyrian, Byzantine, Egyptian, Persian, Indian, Chinese, Japanese, Celtic, Medieval (Gothic Revival revisited), Renaissance, and 18th-century styles (Morris 1978:95-96). Colonial, Adam, or Georgian revival styles, which imitated patterns of the first 30 years of the 19th century, began to appear in the early 20th century and continued well into the 1930s. At the same time, the glass industry was a conservative one, with many shapes and motifs staying in production for decades. While it is possible to give introductory dates for many changes, it is more difficult to establish end

dates. Certain types of decorative motifs faded but never entirely disappeared, or they survived in a simplified form, or reappeared in a modified version or as a conscious revival which never quite matched the original. It is safest to assume that no motif or style disappeared for good. Nevertheless, it is possible to identify trends and to place individual pieces of tableglass within a context.

Technological innovations were also an integral part of the manufacturing and decorating techniques introduced between 1800 and 1940. However, while one part of the industry adopted new technology other parts did not, depending on the markets served by the manufacturer. Hand-blown and hand-decorated glassware existed alongside pressed glassware and, finally, machine-blown tablewares. For example, from about 1820 to 1860, trailed glass threads as decoration were applied to wares made in window and bottle glass factories in the United States. The process was mechanized in the 1860s, but hand-trailing continued to be used on glassware at the high end of the market (see Glass on Glass).

Morris (1978:14) summarizes the table glass industry at the end of the 19th century as follows:

> Towards the end of the Victorian period production had crystallized into three main streams catering for different social strata with widely differing tastes. At the top end of the scale were richly cut and engraved table glass and expensive novelties such as "cameo" glass, for the high class trade and for export. Plainer, simpler glass, often historically based on earlier styles catered for those of aesthetic taste and for devotees of the Arts and Crafts movement. The third stream, the cheapest end of production, included pressed glass (sometimes in imitation of the current styles of cut glass, but often in entirely independent styles) and innumerable styles of fancy glass and novelties catering for the vast mass of the public.

With the large volume of detailed information available on tableglass manufactured between 1800 and 1940, no attempt has been made to duplicate these details. Instead, this guide will summarize datable attributes, introduce the primary and secondary sources, and provide guidance as to which sources have additional information on a specific decorative or manufacturing process. Discussion centers on American, British, and Canadian glass, with some information given on Bohemian and other continental

European glass. Emphasis is placed on less expensive tablewares as these are found most frequently in archaeological contexts.

The guide is organized in three sections. The first introduces the secondary and primary literature available for research. The second concentrates on method of decoration, providing introductory dates for technological innovations, and, where appropriate, discusses the motifs popular in different time periods. The third section discusses tableware forms, illustrates examples of these forms, and, for stemware and decanters, provides additional dating information.

Researching Glass Tablewares

Secondary Sources

Numerous books and articles have been written on the tableglass produced during the 1800-1940 period. However, coverage is uneven and reflects the interests and needs of 20th-century collectors. It is often difficult to follow the history of a specific type of tableware if it is not considered collectible. For example, a great deal of research has been done on American mold-blown tableglass of the first half of the 19th century, but very little on glassware decorated this way in Britain at the same time or in either country during the second half of the century. Most books concentrate on glassware made in a specific country, such as the United States, Canada, or Ireland, and frequently on production at a specific factory or in a specific region. However, most pay little attention to the types of glassware used in a region or country, regardless of manufacturing origins. While it is difficult to get a complete picture of glassware used in a particular country or region from these sources, they nevertheless offer useful dating information for archaeologists.

Fueled by interest in Colonial and Federal America, collectors and dealers in the early 20th century began researching the history of "early American glass." Many researchers, like Knittle (1927), Lee (1944, 1958), and McKearin and McKearin (1948), sought to identify the products of known American factories of the 19th century. Both Palmer (1993a:13-39) and Wilson (1994[1]:17-20) provide useful discussions of the early history of glass collecting in the United

States, and the often symbiotic relationships between dealers and collectors. Researchers such as Revi (1959, 1964), Wilson (1972, 1994), Innes (1976), Heacock and Bickenheuser (1978), Spillman (1981, 1982), Welker and Welker (1985), and Palmer (1993a) have expanded on the earlier work by refining and redefining the conclusions reached by earlier researchers and by studying other parts of the industry. In the 1970s, collecting interests expanded to include common tableglass of the 1920s and 1930s, and books began to appear on this glass (Weatherman 1974; Florence 1995a, 1995b, 1996). Within the last twenty years researchers have begun publishing on tableglass produced in the United States after 1940 (Weatherman 1978; Florence 1992; Rogove and Steinhauer 1993; Measell 1994b). The high end of the glass market, such as brilliant cut glass and art glass, has also been the subject of much study in the last 30 years (Revi 1965; Farrar and Spillman 1979; Spillman 1989, 1996). Dozens of publications exist on individual American companies that made glassware in the late 19th and 20th centuries and whose products are of interest to collectors (Stout 1972; Fauster 1979; Husfloen 1992:130-148, 186-190). Organizations, such as the Early American Glass Club and the Sandwich Historical Society have active publishing programs which encourage new scholarship; these two produce *The Glass Club Bulletin* (Spillman et al. 1993) and *The Acorn*, respectively.

Academic studies of American glass production have primarily been in the economic and labor history tradition and generally lack details concerning products made by the industry (Scoville 1948; Davis 1949; Zembala 1984). These are important resources for understanding the context in which the American glass industry operated, although they are less useful for identifying and dating individual objects. Theses by American curators trained in decorative arts offer a great deal more information on objects produced in American factories (Lanman 1968; Baker 1986; Leinicke 1986; Nelson 1988; Blaszczyk 1995).

Organized or systematic research into Canadian glass production began under the impetus of Stevens (1967) and MacLaren (1968) and continued with work by Unitt and Unitt (1969), Holmes (1974, 1987), King (1987), and others (Holmes and Jones 1978). Although Stevens and MacLaren had begun researching the history of Canada's glass industry in the early 1960s, it was the Canadian centennial (1967) which spurred wider interest in Canadian-made glass. As the Canadian industry did not even begin until the 1840s, and was not on a firm footing until the 1870s, the bulk of the glassware discussed dates from the 1870s to 1920. Since the demise of the *Glasfax Newsletter* in the late 1970s and the *Canadian Antiques Collector* in the late 1980s, there is no obvious publishing venue for new research on Canadian tableglass.

For most of the 20th century, researchers studying glassware manufactured in Britain and Ireland had little interest in tableglass made after 1830. The first book on British Victorian glass appeared in 1961 (Wakefield 1961), but it was virtually the only one until the late 1970s, when several important studies began to appear (Morris 1978; Lattimore 1979; Wakefield 1982; Slack 1987; Thompson 1989; Hajdamach 1991). In the late 1980s British researchers began to publish work on 20th-century British glass (Tyne and Wear County Council Museums 1983; Dodsworth 1987; Crowe 1989; Jackson 1997; Launert 1997). Both British glass collectors' organizations, the Glass Circle and the Glass Association, publish newsletters and periodic journals (*The Glass Circle* and *Glass Cone*, respectively) which are encouraging new research.

Continental European studies on the glass of the 19th and early 20th centuries have tended to concentrate on the high end of the market or on specific factories, such as Baccarat and Lalique in France or Val St. Lambert in Belgium (Philippe 1975). The cheaper wares, which were certainly sold in North America (Lanman 1969), have received less attention and very little has been published in English. However, some publications are available (Charleston 1965; Lanman 1969; Buchwald and Schlüter 1975; Mucha 1979; Drahotova 1983), and comparative discussions in both Hajdamach (1991:81-94) and Wilson (1994[2]:523-526) highlight the key role Bohemian glass styles played in British and American glass production and decoration in the 19th century.

Documentary Sources

TECHNICAL BOOKS

Books written by practicing glassmakers such as Pellatt (1849), Jarves (1865), and Bontemps (1868) provide much useful and accurate information on glassmaking practices of their own time. They are less trustworthy when discussing manufacturing techniques and products from earlier eras, such as Roman or Venetian glass.

NEWSPAPER ADVERTISEMENTS

Advertisements published in newspapers have been heavily used by such researchers as Wilson (1972, 1994), Jones and Smith (1985), and Palmer (1993a) for understanding products either made or used in North America during the 18th and early 19th centuries.

PATTERN BOOKS, PRICE LISTS, AND GLASSWARE CATALOGUES

Some illustrated pattern books exist from the early 19th century, although most of them are undated (Charleston 1965; Lanmon 1969:29-47; Westropp 1978:232-233, Plates x-xiv; Wolfenden 1987, 1992; Hajdamach 1991:45-56; McFarlan 1992; Pattern Book n.d.). Unillustrated price lists dating to the first half of the 19th century give an idea of the range of products that were made by different branches of the glass industry, although it is difficult to be certain what the glasses looked like from the descriptions (e.g., the 1829 list in Hughes [1958:24-25] and Sullivan [1985]). It was only in the 1840s that published, illustrated glassware catalogues began to appear (Wakefield 1968; Spillman 1983). In the 1860s, several American companies making pressed glass published illustrated catalogues (Watkins 1970 [or Spillman 1997]; Innes 1976:298-311; M'Kee and Brothers 1981). From the 1870s onward, more catalogues were published and/or have survived. Several glass catalogues were reprinted in the 1970s, and parts of others are available in various publications. Microfiche or microfilm copies of catalogues are available from The Juliet K. and Leonard S. Rakow Research Library of The Corning Museum of Glass (Corning 1987), the Winterthur Library (McKinstry 1984), and the Peabody Essex Museum (1794-1819) in Salem, Massachusetts.

RETAIL CATALOGUES

These generally date from the 1890s onward. Wholesale distributors, such as Butler Brothers, assembled glassware assortments for retail stores and their catalogues generally show a wider range of glassware than the large North American catalogue shopping stores such as Sears Roebuck, Montgomery Ward, or T. Eaton Co. (Toronto). For example, glassware offered in Eaton's catalogues between 1889 and 1940 tended to be conservative, generally offering only one or two choices in either object or style, with essentially two price ranges; one for the low end and one for a moderately high end market. English catalogues include Silber and Fleming (1990), *The Victorian Catalogue of Household Goods* (1991), and *Yesterday's Shopping* (Army and Navy Stores 1969). Price lists and retail catalogues provide useful comparative data concerning price variations between differently manufactured and/or decorated glasswares.

DESIGN REGISTERS

In 1839, the British Patent system began to include designs and, in 1842, the British Design Register system was set up (Morris 1978:190; Slack 1987:21-22). In subsequent years many glass designs were registered. Thompson (1989) extracted the glass designs registered between 1842 and 1908, and has itemized, and often illustrated, patterns registered by the principal manufacturers of pressed glass. Slack (1987:135-198), whose typewritten list for the years 1842 to 1883 is easier to read than the photocopied originals shown in Thompson, has also listed the design registers until 1900. Edgley (1996) compiled a list of glass registration numbers for the years 1908 to 1945. From 1842 to 1883, the design mark embossed in the glass is diamond-shaped like those on ceramics and metalwares. After 1883, the mark is simply "Rd" followed by a number.

PATENTED DESIGNS AND PROCESSES

From the late 1820s, submissions to the American patent office have contained information about the pressing process (Zembala 1984; Wilson 1994[1]:265-285) and, from the late 1860s (Innes 1976:299), pressed glassware designs. Among the authors who have published design patent illustrations are Revi (1964), Innes (1976), and Welker and Welker (1985). Along with catalogues, these records form the basis for dating American pressed patterns of the late 1860s to 1890s. Descriptions and illustrations of several different decorative processes developed in England can be found in Hajdamach (1991).

GOVERNMENT DOCUMENTS

Other government documents providing information on the glass industry include reports on industries, and investigations into tariff regulations, child labor, and excise administration (Britain between 1745 and 1845). Examples include Great Britain (1835, 1865, 1907), Weeks (1886), and United States Senate (1911). These reports are useful for understanding how the glass industry operated and occasionally offer details useful for dating.

ARCHIVAL MATERIAL

Archival materials from glass factories, including design books and business correspondence, are available and much new work is continuing to be done using these sources. Three examples of new work are Spillman (1996) on recently available material from the T. G. Hawkes firm in Corning, New York; Evans et al. (1995) on the Whitefriars factory in London, England; and Blaszczyk's (1995) work in the Corning Glass Company archives, Corning, New York, on the development of Pyrex.

EXHIBITION CATALOGUES

Beginning with the 1851 exhibition in London, exhibition catalogues illustrated and commented on the glass entries from many different countries. While these entries usually featured the finer, more elaborate end of the market, less expensive ordinary glassware echoed the themes shown at the world's fairs. As one commentator noted, concerning the Pellatt and Company products shown at the 1862 exhibition:

> Their costlier works are of rare excellence: these are to be regarded, however, rather as examples of what they can do than what they continually produce, for Messrs. Pellatt are extensive manufacturers of every class and order of "table glass;" and the same good taste and sound judgement that have produced more expensive objects, have been exercised to form and decorate such as are within the reach of persons of ordinary means (*The Art-Journal* 1862:128).

TRADE JOURNALS

Beginning in the mid 1870s, trade journals such as the English *Pottery Gazette and China and Glass Trades Review*, subsequently referred to as the *Pottery Gazette*, and the *American Crockery and Glass Journal* began to appear. Welker and Welker (1985:490-491) summarize the publishing histories of American glass trade journals. *The Canadian Pottery and Glass Gazette* was published briefly in the first decade of the 20th century.

Glassware

COMPANY NAMES AND TRADEMARKS

Embossed company names in blown-molded glassware appeared in wares manufactured by Irish glass factories, dating from ca. 1790 to 1820 (Figure 64*a*) (Warren 1981:71-98, 199-200). Several pressed salts made in the late 1820s had company names embossed on them (McKearin and McKearin 1948:Plate 165, Nos. 1-3, Plate 142, No. 4; Wilson 1994[1]:295-297). English trademark legislation came into effect January 1876, and shortly afterwards several English pressed-glass firms used trademarks embossed in the glass to identify their wares (Slack 1987:133-134). Peterson (1968) illustrates American glass marks, who registered them, and how they were applied: embossed, etched, stamped, or labeled. Acid-etched marks were used primarily by cut-glass firms around 1900. Pullin (1986) includes European and North American marks, and King (1987:247-250) shows Canadian marks, primarily for containers. Dodsworth (1987:109-110) illustrates early-20th-century English marks.

ARCHAEOLOGICAL EXCAVATIONS

Dated archaeological contexts provide information on glassware used at the same time and place and may contribute to refinements in dating. However, the chief contribution archaeological material makes is for understanding social contexts in which glassware was used, such as work groups (Jones and Smith 1985) or ethnic affiliation. Studied in combination with ceramic and metal tablewares, food and beverage storage containers, and food preparation items, glassware helps in understanding food and beverage choices and different levels of service at the table of consumers.

Excavations on glass factory sites have also been a technique used in the United States and Canada to identify products from specific factories (Stevens 1967; MacLaren 1968; White 1974; Starbuck 1986). With the exception of Starbuck's work at the New England Glassworks in Temple, New Hampshire, a great deal of this work has, unfortunately, consisted of digging holes on the sites, finding glass fragments, and concluding that whatever was found was made at the factory. Glass batches require the use of cullet, which can come from anywhere, thus this may or may not be a valid conclusion. Sheeler (1978) discusses the thorny issue of cullet and how many sherds of a specific pattern or bottle style are needed to state that it was made at the factory. Certainly glass scrap from manufacturing processes is more likely to reflect wares made at the factory, rather like wasters found during excavations at ceramic factories.

GLASSWARE

Handling and closely examining glassware is one of the best ways to develop expertise concerning manufacturing and decorating techniques, and how glass from different periods looks and feels. Archaeological collections provide the best context but often are too fragmentary to provide information concerning the appearance of complete pieces. Museum collections (Spillman 1981; Palmer 1993a; Wilson 1994), private collections, and antique shops and shows all provide opportunities to refine our knowledge of how to date glass and are particularly useful for hands-on knowledge of glassware illustrated in secondary sources.

Decorative Techniques

Colored Glass

Although many different glass colors were known and used by glassmakers, colorless glass has been the primary choice for tableware for 500 years. Nonetheless, colored tableglass has been fashionable at different periods.

Coming into the 19th century, colors in production were cobalt blue, amethyst, emerald green, and opaque white. Early-19th-century tablewares made in bottle and window glass factories in the United States also came in aqua, dark green, and amber shades (Figure 8) (Wilson 1994[1]:73-88, 153-160. These colors were caused by iron and other impurities in the sand, not by deliberate attempts to create them. On the other hand, colorless glass *is* a deliberate choice achieved partly by adding certain metallic oxides to the glass batch which change or mask the colorizing effects of any impurities (Jones and Sullivan 1989:12-13).

In the late 1820s, Bohemian glassmakers began to experiment with color and developed a gold ruby glass (an intense transparent red), as well as black, opaque sealing-wax red, cornflower blue, opaque white, apple green, and turquoise. By the early 1830s, glassmakers had learned how to use uranium which gives glass a distinctive lime-yellow or lime-green color. In the 1840s, translucent colors, sometimes called alabaster or clam broth, in white, pink, aqua, and green were introduced. Although these colored glasses were introduced at the high end of the market, some were also made in pressed glass. Most distinctive of all were the cased glasses composed of two or three layers of differently colored glass which were cut or engraved to expose the colors under the surface layer. In archaeological contexts, these layered glasses are usually window glass or lighting devices, particularly lampshades, although vase and tableware fragments are occasionally encountered, and usually date closer to 1900. Yellow and red stains introduced in the 1830s were used as cheaper versions of cased glass. For colored illustrations, see Spillman (1981:Plates 1-16), Drahotova (1983:166-167, Plates 122-128), Hajdamach (1991:81-94, 104), and Wilson (1994[1]:249-263).

In the 1880s, colored glass once again became fashionable, from the cheapest to the most expensive wares, with an astonishing array of colors made possible by the introduction of new glass formulas and new decorative techniques, including many which are outside the scope of this guide (Revi 1959; Hajdamach 1991:249-329). The prevailing theme from the 1880s onward seems to have been "more is better." Exuberantly decorated glass stayed popular into the 20th century, as can be seen by the water and lemonade sets offered by Butler Brothers in 1910 (Figure 1). Colored glasses made in this period include the following:

1. Transparent colors. In the 1880s, red became a very popular color but uranium yellow/green, amber, aqua, pale blue, and grass green (ca. 1900) were also produced.

2. Opaque colors (Figure 2). Opaque white pressed glass was relatively common before the 1870s, but in the later 1870s, British and American manufacturers expanded the opaque glass repertoire to include yellow, ivory, greens, blue, turquoise, and black (Spillman 1982:185, 190; Slack 1987).

3. Heat-sensitive glasses (Figure 3). For batches containing arsenic, uranium, or gold, the glass was cooled slightly and then reheated to change its color wherever the heat was applied and the glass was thickest. This meant that shaded colors could be made in transparent or opaque glass, shading from ruby to amber, pink to yellow, transparent blue to opalescent blue, or vice-versa. Pressed glass patterns sometimes had protuberances, such as hobnails, so that the tips would be a different color than the base. Developed in the United States in 1883, the formulas spread like wildfire, with many different color combinations tried out, including cased glasses in which the outer layer changed color but the inner did not. Even in fragments, the graduated colors of heat-sensitive glass make it easy to identify.

4. Cased or flashed glasses. New in this period was the treatment of layered glasses using hot glass techniques, which took advantage of the transparent and translucent properties of glass and of the new heat-sensitive glasses. Cutting, engraving, and acid-etching continued to be used on layered glasses. Extremely complex technical processes were used. For example,

FIGURE 1. Selection of jugs from the 1910 Butler Brothers catalogue which illustrates the variety of decoration offered from the 1880s until World War I, including colorless, green, blue, and ruby glass; opalescent and iridescent glass; enameling; and gilding as well as pressed, engraved, and etched patterns in geometric, naturalistic, and abstract motifs. With almost no exceptions, the glass is covered in decoration. One of the characteristic jug shapes in the early 20th century was a small handle placed in the center of the tall body which was often waisted (wider at the top and base and narrow through the middle) (Butler Brothers 1910:401). (Courtesy of Collins Kirby Art & Antiques, Fort Payne, Alabama.)

FIGURE 2. Opaque glassware: **left**, creamer in opaque turquoise blue, called Vitro-Porcelain glass, introduced ca. 1885, made by Tyne Flint Glass Works, South Shields, England (Slack 1987:107); **right**, creamer in opaque white glass, probably English. (Photo by Peter Lockett, private collection; digital image by Rock Chan.)

shaded opalescent glassware (Figure 1, center, bottom two rows), which featured opalescent white patterns such as coin dots, swirls, and hobnails against a colored ground, was accomplished by layering a heat-sensitive colorless glass over a colored ball of non-heat-sensitive glass. The vessel was blown in a pattern mold, the glass cooled slightly and then reheated to "strike" the opalescent white (Revi 1959:32-34; Spillman et al. 1994:70,74-75). Cased glass

refers to two or more layers of glass of equal thickness; flashed glass refers to a thin layer of colored glass over a thicker layer, usually colorless (Jones and Sullivan 1989:52-53).

5. Marbled glasses (Figure 4). In the late 1870s, English pressed-glass manufacturers reintroduced marbled glasses–generally opaque white mixed with transparent purple, blue, green, pink, and brown–which are characterized by swirled color variations (Slack 1987:34, 51, 93, 94). These types of glasses were also made in the United States.

6. Solarized glasses. Colorless pressed glass tableware made after 1864 in the new soda-lime glass (see Glass Composition) can be found with a purplish tint. Manganese, used to decolorize the glass, produces a photo-sensitive glass which begins to turn purple after prolonged exposure to ultraviolet rays. Solarized glass is most common from the 1870s to World War I, but some 18th-century French table glass is also affected. Although also decolorized with manganese, colorless potash-lead glasses are not affected by sunlight.

In the late 1920s, a new color palette was developed for the U.S. and Canadian market: transparent pastel colors in pink, green, yellow, and blue; transparent dark blue and deep red;

FIGURE 3. Pressed creamers made in heat-sensitive glass patented in 1889, by George Davidson & Co., Gateshead-on-Tyne, England (Slack 1987:74, 76-80): **left**, Primrose Perline, a yellow transparent glass shading into translucent/opaque yellow; **right**, Blue Perline, an "electric" transparent blue glass shading into translucent/opaque blue. (Photo by Peter Lockett, private collection; digital image by Rock Chan.)

FIGURE 4. Pressed salt in marbled glass, called Blue Malachite, introduced in the late 1870s by Sowerby's Ellison Glass Works, Gateshead-on-Tyne, England. (Photo by Peter Lockett, private collection; digital image by Rock Chan.)

and black. These colors are distinctive and, combined with motifs from the period, can easily be distinguished from earlier colors after some experience with real examples (Weatherman 1974; Spillman 1982:15, 90; Florence 1995a, 1996).

Applied Colors

Glass could also be colored by enameling, gilding, or staining, which are cold techniques that do not need to be done in a glasshouse, and by exposing hot glass to metallic chlorides which is done at the time of manufacture.

ENAMELING

In this process, vitreous colors combined with an adhesive are applied to a glass surface and then reheated between 700° and 900° F (370° and 480° C), fusing them to the surface and burning off the adhesive. The technique is an old one which was particularly favored by decorators in the German/Bohemian regions of Europe. Enameling was one of the popular decorative techniques used from the 1880s into the early 20th century (Figure 5).

Beginning in the late 1920s, enameling once again became popular for beverage wares in North America (Figures 14, 69) and was done partly by hand and, after the mid 1930s, also

by machine. Several techniques were used, including turning glass against a wheel filled with paint, using a rubber stamp, rolling glass in paint or enamel dust, by silk screen technique (Weatherman 1978:5-6), or by using a transfer to outline the pattern which was filled in by hand (Golledge 1987:29-30, 56-59). Motifs used in the 1930s, and often later, included colored horizontal or swirled bands in red, yellow, black, white, jade green, or navy blue; playing card motifs (hearts, clubs, diamonds, and spades); sailboats, checkerboards, tulips, polka dots, Spanish dancers, "Mexican theme," polar bears, fighting cocks (cocktails), and Scotty dogs. Generally at least two colors were used. One pattern, which had raised frosting on the lower half of the pitcher and tumblers with a narrow red band above it, was described in this way: "The frosting gives this Beverage Set a very cold appearance and the red bands give a colorful cheerful effect . . ." (Weatherman 1978:91). "Colorful cheerful effect" sums up this whole range of wares.

GILDING

Gilding is done by applying a layer of gold leaf, paint, or dust to the glass surface, which may then be fired or unfired (Newman 1977:131-132). Unfired gilding can be easily rubbed off and appears to be the type used in the 1890s and later for cheaply decorated wares (Figures 5, 89) where it was applied around the rim, in bands, or to highlight parts of pressed patterns (Measell 1994a:127-130, 165). As an alternative to gilding, some used iridescent gold (Figure 93).

STAINING

Using silver chloride to produce a yellow stain was developed in 1820 and a red stain in 1840 (Newman 1977:293). The technique was a cheap imitation of cased or flashed glasses. From the late 1880s and into the 20th century, red and yellow stains became popular ways to color cheap pressed wares (Figure 6). The stains do not adhere well to the glass surface and are usually worn or scraped off. Ruby staining was often used for cheap souvenir wares which exhibit crudely engraved designs and wording that celebrate famous attractions, special occasions, and sentiments.

IRIDESCENT GLASS

In the 1870s, another distinctive color development was iridescent glass which was produced by exposing hot glass to metallic chlorides. Depending on the color of the base glass and the composition of the fumes, the surface of the glass became iridescent in colors such as ambers, blues, or greens. As pressed-glass manufacturers were usually prompt to imitate more expensive techniques, it is puzzling that pressed iridescent glass, called "carnival" by collectors, was not made until 1905 (Figure 1) (Spillman 1982:51, 65, 286-289; Measell 1994a:132-136, 153-155, 163-168). After that date American, European, and even Australian glass companies made carnival glass and it continued to be a well-known product past the 1930s.

DEPOSIT-WARE

Bonding silver onto glassware was being done by 1880 (Revi 1959:198-201; Hajdamach 1991:287-289), and continued into the 1930s. Patterns offered in the T. Eaton Co. catalogues around 1914 were in sinuous art-nouveau styles, while those in the 1930s resembled acid-etched patterns of the period.

Glass Composition

The basic glass compositions of potash-lime, potash-lead, and soda-lime continued during the 1800-1940 period. Potash and soda are fluxes added to the glass batch to lower the melting point of sand. Lime and lead are also fluxes but their primary purpose is to make glass stable after it is cool (Jones and Sullivan 1989:10-12). However, determining glass composition is difficult without expensive time-consuming tests. Although shortwave and longwave ultraviolet lights are useful tools for archaeologists to sort glass fragments of different composition (Jones and Sullivan 1989:12), determining what the fluorescences actually mean is impossible without further tests. For example, in contexts dating to the second half of the 19th century, a purple fluorescence in colorless glass fragments probably indicates the presence of lead in the composition. However, no chemical analyses have been done to confirm this. Purple fluorescence has been found on both tablewares and lamp chimneys. Be cautious when reading documentary material as words such as "flint" and "crystal" are sometimes used to suggest higher quality glass than is justified, such as the "pure crystal glass" offered by Montgomery Ward & Co. (1901:45). These terms describe colorless glass of good quality but not necessarily with any lead content. Only if the source states that the glass contains lead can one assume that it does; e.g., "Pure thin lead blown glass" (Butler Brothers 1905:147). Another term found in early-20th-century literature is "pot metal" which refers to glass melted in a pot furnace rather than a tank furnace. Pot metal was of better quality (Rosenhain 1908:109-110).

It is impossible to use glass composition to determine date and country of origin because of the international nature of the glass trade in the 19th and 20th centuries and the lack of hard base-line data. Some datable composition changes are known, most of which are related to color, such as the introduction of heat-sensitive glasses and uranium for yellow/green glass (see Colored Glass).

One important composition change is related to American pressed glass. From the introduction of mechanically pressed glass in the late 1820s, American manufacturers used potash-lead glass. Lead glass has a high refractive index which was considered desirable in pressed glassware. Its luster compensated for deficiencies in pressing technology, particularly in the early years, and it echoed the luster and weight of cut glass. Lead glass, however, sets up slowly; that is, it remains fluid longer than soda-lime glass which meant that in the pressing process, glass had to remain in the mold longer for the glass to "set." The ingredients for lead glass were also comparatively expensive. In 1864, William Leighton in West Virginia developed a formula for soda-lime glass. The formula substituted bicarbonate of soda for the type previously used. It produced glass which resembled lead glass, but was lighter in weight, and could be made for one-third the cost of lead glass (Wilson 1994[2]:522). Within a few years, most American pressed-glass factories had switched to the new formula. Patterns made from the 1840s into the late 1860s and early 1870s can be found in both lead and soda-lime glasses, depending on the date of manufacture. Patterns introduced after the late 1860s, however, were only made in soda-lime glasses.

English manufacturers also altered their pressed-glass formulas, as an 1888 article in the *Pottery Gazette* indicates, by retaining a small

FIGURE 5. Jug decorated with pink, white, blue, and brick red enameling; gilding; optic molding; and a crimped rim. Crimping tools were introduced about 1874, but came into widespread use in the 1880s (Hajdamach 1991:297-300). The handle was first applied at the base and pulled up to the rim. The jug has optic-molded panels on its interior (see Optic-Molded Glass). The absence of mold lines indicates that the second, full-size, mold was a turn mold. There is a rough pontil mark on the base, demonstrating that the pontil continued in use in the tableglass industry long after the mid 19th century, when alternative tools had come into use (Hajdamach 1991:34-36). Based on the combination of decorative techniques and overall style, the jug dates from the 1880s to early 20th century, and was probably made in Bohemia, although American firms also made similar wares (Measell 1994a:127). (Photo by Rock Chan, Parks Canada collection.)

amount of lead in the formula (Slack 1987:47, 50).

HEAT-RESISTANT GLASSES

Borosilicate glasses have a low coefficient of expansion which makes them suitable for coping with extreme temperature changes. Formulas for this type of glass were developed in the early 20th century to make specialty products such as railway lanterns and battery jars.

PYREX

By 1910, Corning Glass Works had developed several different borosilicate glass formulas for

railway signal lenses, lantern globes, and battery jars. The new formulas were so effective that the rate of breakage dropped dramatically and sales of replacement lenses and globes plummeted. The company began searching for alternative uses for its borosilicate glasses. Between 1911 and 1915, Corning Glass Works concentrated on developing a chemically stable, safe, chip-proof glass suitable for baking, on determining the right product mix, and on developing a product with consumer appeal (Blaszczyk 1995:489-521). In 1915, after four years of research, the company had perfected its formula and began to sell casseroles and baking dishes, custard cups, loaf pans, cake dishes, and pie plates (Rogove and Steinhauer 1993:70-83). Other items followed, such as teapots in 1922, measuring cups in 1925, and refrigerator dishes in 1929. Sales were brisk from the beginning. In its 1917 fall catalogue, the T. Eaton Co. showed the new baking dishes, placed in a silver-plated holder: "Silver plated casserole, lined with transparent oven glass, cut glass cover. Glass will stand heat of the oven, fitted in silver-plated pierced design bright burnished seven-inch frame" (T. Eaton Co. 1917-18:289).

FIGURE 6. The Red Block pattern, introduced in the mid 1880s, was made by several American firms and reissued several times during the 1890s by the United States Glass Company (Jenks and Luna 1990:432-433). This is a sugar bowl in colorless glass with a scratched and worn red stain around the rim and on the top of the blocks; the handles were pressed at same time as the body. (Photo by Rock Chan, Parks Canada collection.)

Pyrex Casserole, Cut-glass Cover

30-1601. Handsome Casserole with a real **Pyrex** glass lining, cut glass cover, pierced design frame with conventional ornamentation, wood handle diameter about 8 ins. **Pyrex** glass is transparent and will stand the heat of the oven. Would be appreciated as a gift; most moderately priced. Price, delivered **7.25**

FIGURE 7. An early offering of Pyrex by T. Eaton Co., with cut decoration on the cover, and placed in a silver-plated holder for service at the table. (T. Eaton Co. 1918-19:359; reproduced with the kind permission of The T. Eaton Company Limited, Toronto; digital image by George van der Vlugt.)

The 1918 Spring/Summer catalogue noted that the glass casserole would not chip or break from the heat, that it did not absorb odors, was easy to keep clean, and "with proper care will last indefinitely" (Figure 7) (T. Eaton Co. 1918:225). The casserole and its electro-plated frame cost $6.00. Eaton's catalogues continued to offer both pie plates and casseroles until 1940, with frequent design changes. In the Eaton's catalogues, Pyrex competed with, and soon replaced, white-lined brown earthenware baking dishes called Guernseyware.

In 1922, Corning had plants in Europe and Britain manufacturing Pyrex (Tyne and Wear County Council Museums 1983:8), but Canadian production did not begin until 1946 (King 1987:192).

Pyrex sales slowed down in the 1920s for a number of reasons: high prices, stagnant designs, and breakage which resulted when Pyrex was not treated properly. It was considered expensive and had not reached lower income consumers except as wedding presents. Company research showed that the middle-class market was saturated (Blaszczyk 1995:649-651; 660-662). Through the 1930s, the company worked at lowering its prices, at redesigning products, and at developing a glass that could be placed directly on the burner.

PYREX FLAMEWARE

Alterations in glass formulas produced an aluminosilicate glass which could be used on top of the stove. It was made from 1936 to 1979. Between 1936 and 1946, the glass had a bluish tone to it to distinguish it from Pyrex (Rogove and Steinhauer 1993:100).

Molded trademarks and green stamped marks for Pyrex and Flameware can be found in Rogove and Steinhauer (1993:67-69), although they do not date most of them.

FIRE-KING GLASSWARE

Borosilicate glasses were also developed by other firms. "FIRE-KING" is the trademark used by the Anchor Hocking Glass Corporation between 1942 and 1976. Kilgo et al. (1991) illustrate and date the different forms and decorations produced under this trademark, but the most familiar product is the translucent white or green coffee mug.

Glass on Glass

Placing glass onto glass can be part of the process of making an object, such as attaching a stem, foot, or handle, or it can be a decorative technique. It was a common decorative technique during two periods: initially during the first half of the 19th century and again, at the higher end of glass production, during and beyond the 1880s.

DOUBLE GATHERS

With the exception of cased or flashed glass, double gathers were usually done on the lower part of the body and could be plain or decorated by ribbing or tooling (Figures 8, 42 [nos. 16 and 21], 48, 74*f*). Often combined with a flaring rim, objects decorated by this technique echo classical Greek-urn shapes. Pillar molding, which has bold protuberant ribs, does not have an obvious second layer, and dates from the 1830s to ca. 1870 (Wilson 1994[1]:195-196).

LOOP OR FESTOON GLASS

"A thread–generally opaque white but sometimes blue or red, was trailed horizontally around

FIGURE 8. Glass threading and "lily pad" decoration applied to the lower body of hollowares, such as bowls, pitchers, and vases, was done in bottle- and window-glass houses in New England, New York state, and possibly, in 1840, in a short-lived factory at Mallorytown, Ontario. As a group, the tablewares manufactured in these factories were made in shades of aqua, green, and amber, and date from ca. 1820 to 1860 (Spillman 1982:Nos. 122-123; Palmer 1993a:174-179; Wilson 1994[1]:46, 142-144). (Courtesy of The Corning Museum of Glass, Corning, New York.)

the body of a piece and then, after reheating, pulled up and then down" (Wilson 1994[1]:94, 147-150). The technique was used in the 18th century and again in the United States around 1840.

THREADED GLASS

This is another old technique which continued in use in the early 19th century in North America, primarily for tablewares made in bottle and window glass factories. The threads used were the same color as the body of the glass and were applied by trailing a thin stream of glass onto the object as it was rotated by the glassmaker (Figure 8, far right). In 1876, a machine for threading was patented in England and subsequently several other machines were developed. Usually in a different color from the base glass, these threads are distinguished by their consistent size, the mechanical regularity of application, and were used to cover all or parts of an object (Figure 9). Combining threading with other decorative techniques, glassmakers produced amazing variations on the

theme over the next few decades (Hajdamach 1991:273-283).

TRAILED GLASS

In the 1880s, under the influence of Rustic styles and Japonism, and at the higher end of the glass market, glassmakers applied asymmetrically crude (often decorated by ribbing) trails or irregularly shaped buttons of differently colored glass over a glass piece already decorated in other ways. Sometimes they added pointy feet or handles (Hajdamach 1991:Color Plate 30).

Blown Glass

Mouth-blown glassware is shaped by blowing air through a blowpipe into hot glass and manipulating it with various types of tools into whatever style is desired. *Free-blown* glassware is made without using molds but may still be decorated in some way by tooling or adding glass (Figures 8, 39 [tumblers]), or by cold techniques like cutting, engraving, acid-etching, enameling, or gilding. *Mold-blown* glass is shaped and decorated by the use of some type of mold (Jones and Sullivan 1989:50-54, 23-33). *Semi-automatic machine-blown* tableware production began in 1897 for tumblers, finger bowls, lemonade glasses, and stemware using a machine developed originally for blowing light bulbs and lamp chimneys (Scoville 1948:97-98, 133-135, 152-154, 195-196). These were turn- or pastemold machines so they left a highly polished surface with no visible mold lines. The role of *automatic machines* in blown tableware production in the 1920s and 1930s has not been discussed in detail in the sources used (Scoville 1948; Weatherman 1974; Dodsworth 1987), but it is doubtful if details of manufacturing technology will provide much refinement in dating objects whose patterns can be dated and assigned to specific factories.

Even after the introduction of machines, mouth-blown glassware continued to be made because, as Davis (1949:227) points out in connection with the pressed-glass trade, hand production is profitable for items not made in large enough quantities to justify mechanized production and also to supply a market which values "hand-made" glassware. For example, from the late 1930s and into the 1950s, American industrial designer Russel Wright used American hand factories to manufacture his designs for department stores catering to middle-class shoppers (Blaszczyk 1993:2-22). Unfortunately most of these American hand factories faced financial difficulties in the 1940s and 1950s, and many had closed by the early 1970s. Not without difficulties, hand production continues in Britain, Ireland, and parts of continental Europe.

It is frequently difficult to determine how individual pieces of tableglass were made if there are no obvious signs of mold use. Glassmakers made free-blown wares, and used fire-polishing or turn molds to eliminate mold lines and dulled surfaces, resulting in glasses with the same look. It is likely that products blown in semi-automatic or automatic machines can be identified with more research.

PATTERN-MOLDED GLASS

Pattern molding, in which the glass parison is blown into a patterned mold and then removed and blown to full-size, is not a technique which translates to machine production. It is a very old technique and was still in use in the first

FIGURE 9. Footed goblet with an engraved bowl, a colorless applied frill at the stem and bowl junction, and a foot decorated with cranberry threads applied by machine. Based on these decorative methods, the goblet dates no earlier than the 1880s. (Photo by Peter Lockett, private collection; digital image by Rock Chan.)

half of the 19th century for tablewares, particularly tumblers, and jelly and wine glasses (Figures 10, 85). Although various types of diamond patterns were used in the 18th century, the 19th-century motifs are primarily ribs, rib/flutes, and rib/panels. The technique, which gives a diffuse look to motifs, was still a useful decorative technique for art glass in the last quarter of the 19th century. Pattern molding can be identified by the corresponding profiles on the interior and exterior surface: a rib on the outside can be felt as a rib on the inside.

CONTACT-MOLDED GLASS

In this process, glass is blown into a full-size open-and-shut mold which can shape and

FIGURE 10. Wine glasses with drawn stems with bowl, knop, and step decorated by pattern molding. This style of drawn stem–with a knop and a step–is shown in the 1840 Apsley Pellatt catalogue as a "six-fluted ball stem" (Wakefield 1968:52). (Photo by Olive Jones, private collection.)

decorate it at the same time. In comparison to labor-intensive techniques such as cutting and engraving, it produces a decorated item with minimum effort and can imitate cut and engraved motifs successfully, although the resulting pattern is more diffuse. Contact molding can be identified by comparing the profiles of the interior and exterior surface: a rib on the outside corresponds to a depression on the inside. With some exceptions, the role of contact molding in forming and decorating tableglass was not discussed in the sources used.

From ca. 1790 to ca. 1820, several Irish glasshouses used a full-size partial mold for decorating the base and lower body of decanters, finger bowls, and other vessels. Generally, the lower body is decorated with ribs/flutes which, on the base, become rays encircling an undecorated center which may or may not have a molded company name on it (Figure 64a) (Warren 1981:71-98, 199-200). Warren is unclear as to whether a dip mold or a hinged mold was used for these objects, although both are feasible.

"Blown three mold" is an American collectors' term for a wide range of decorated tablewares blown in full-size open-and-shut molds from about 1810 to 1840s (Figures 11, 48). The molds usually consisted of three vertical parts

and a base part (Wilson 1994[1]:168-171, 205, 214-247). The earlier patterns imitated cut-glass styles, primarily vertical rib/diamond combinations. In 1814, Rundell stated in her book on domestic cookery: "Those who wish for trifle dishes, butter stands, &c. at a lower charge than cut glass, may buy them in molds, of which there is a great variety that looks extremely well if not placed near the more beautiful article" (Wilson 1994[1]:170).

From the 1820s to 1840s, there appeared densely packed vertical ribs and patterns with more flowing lines consisting of scrolls, fans, arches, guilloches, peacock eyes (or comets), and rosettes. Characteristic of all these patterns is overall coverage in the molded parts. McKearin and McKearin (1948:240-331) provide comprehensive analysis of the blown three-mold patterns and have assigned numbers to each pattern which subsequent authors continue to use. Colors produced were colorless, aqua, amber, cobalt blue, purple, and olive green.

Fully mold-blown Anglo-Irish tablewares made during the first half of the 19th century have not been studied as thoroughly as American ones. Anglo-Irish factories made tablewares with vertical rib/diamond patterns, possibly earlier than the American examples (Warren 1981:200-212; McNally 1982:112-113; Jones and Smith 1985:32, 73). The factories, however, also seem to have produced other types of patterns, particularly for tumblers. Included in an 1829 list of prices for the English flint-glass trade are a number of molded items: cruets and castors, decanters, blow-over and blow-back dishes and salts (see Blow-over Molds), liquor bottles, and tumblers with "molded, star or ornamental bottom" (Hughes 1958:24-25). Tumblers with molded ribs, with star bursts on the base, are examples of this type of decoration (Figure 12) (Brooks 1987:11, 15, 18) and were probably blown in a partial full-size mold similar to the marked Irish pieces. The discrepancy between American and British coverage of the "blown three-mold" group makes it difficult to compare products. Was this a decorative technique little used in the English glass industry or, as seems more likely, is its absence in the secondary literature based on a lack of interest by English researchers and collectors? Did much of this type of glassware find its way across the Atlantic from the 1920s to the 1950s,

FIGURE 11. Examples of blown-three-mold glass attributed to New England and Midwestern factories. The creamer and decanter on the left are in the "baroque" style while the other decanter and sugar bowls are in the "geometric" style which imitates cut glass motifs of the early 19th century (Figure 40). The colorless decanter is of lead glass. Both covers on the sugar bowls have pontil marks on top of the finial. (Courtesy of The Corning Museum of Glass, Corning, New York.)

and become transformed into "early American glass?"

After the mid-19th century, the use of contact molding for decorating tableware becomes less clear. Some American products can be identified, such as molasses cans, bar bottles, or colognes made in bold patterns similar to pressed patterns of the 1850s and 1860s (Wilson 1994[2]:523, 540-545). From the 1870s onward, the principal type of contact molding used seems to have been optic molding (below) although some contact molding continued (Figure 13). It is likely that pressing (see Pressed Glass) had become the dominant technique for making and decorating cheaper tablewares, a position pressed wares held until the development in the late 1890s of semi-automatic machines to make blown-molded, but undecorated, tumblers and stemware. A commentator in the *National Glass Budget* made the following observations on the new machine, which Michael J. Owens had developed and the Rochester Tumbler Company had bought the rights to use:

When the Owens machine was introduced and it was proven that the output of punch tumblers could be greatly increased and the cost of production radically reduced, there was no alternative left the Rochester Company between acquiring the right to use the machine, or practically abandon, not only the hand manufacture of punch tumblers, but, since the machine blown punch tumbler contains less metal, is of lighter weight, (freight advantage), and can therefore be made and sold much cheaper than a pressed tumbler, also abandon the manufacture of pressed tumblers, their specialty, or sink all their investment and possessions in vainly competing for a few brief years with a more formidably equipped, and unconquerable antagonist, or turn their entire plant over, for the manufacture of such specialty as did not exist (*National Glass Budget* 1897:1).

The commentator went on to compare the output of each system: a hand blower could make about 700 punch tumblers in the same period as the machine made between 1800 and 2000 tumblers. Comparative costs were 50¢ per hundred compared to less than 6¢ per hundred. As this was a semi-automatic machine there was still considerable human involvement but it was

FIGURE 12. Colorless lead glass tumbler decorated by contact molding on the base and body and by sketchily-done engraving on the upper body, similar in execution to Bohemian-style engraving often found on tumblers. As this is of lead glass and the ribs and flutes were executed by contact molding, the tumbler was likely made in England sometime during the first half of the 19th century. Similar Bohemian-style tumblers would have been made in potash-lime glass and decorated by pattern-molding (Figure 85). The pontil mark consists of rough bits of glass around the resting point. (Photo by Rock Chan, private collection.)

less skilled and lower-paid work. It is likely that the tumblers shown in the Butler Brothers (1914:324A) catalogue were made in a semi-automatic machine: "9 ½ oz. LEAD BLOWN TABLE TUMBLERS. Just think of it! We have a half million of these tumblers in stock and we'll sell them all before the month is out. Are you one of the lucky buyers?" The tumblers were tapered, completely plain, thinly blown, and cost 23 ½ ¢ cents per dozen.

The next obvious group of tableware decorated by contact molding is found in the late 1920s and 1930s. In the Butler Brothers (1929, 1930) catalogues, thin blown tumblers, stemware, and water sets are offered in greater variety than in

previous catalogues and the term "thin blown" is highlighted (Figure 14). Designers of the period used the flexibility offered by contact molding to produce patterns with distinctive modern looks (Weatherman 1974:48; Florence 1995a:182).

BLOW-OVER MOLDS

In this technique, glass is blown into the mold and then burst off, which leaves a thinner edge, or blown over, which leaves a thicker edge (Figure 15) (Pellatt 1849:96). The technique was used to make objects in which the rim could be cut and polished, such as salts or open dishes, or ground for a fitment, such as castor and cruet bottles. The finish or rim was ground or polished when the glass was cold, thus it was not necessary to use a pontil to hold the object while it was being made. On small dishes the glass can be so thick that the inner surface is smooth, without the concave/convex relationship between the interior and exterior surface so characteristic of contact molding (Wilson 1994[1]:205). Using descriptions in American period documents, Wilson (1994[1]:171-173, 205-213) dates the technique ca. 1810 to ca.

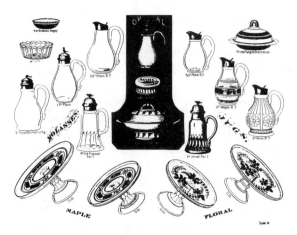

FIGURE 13. The pint Rose pattern jug (center right) was blown in a mold while the jugs adjacent to it in Maple and Jewel patterns were pressed (Pennsylvania Glassware 1972:30). Molasses or syrup jugs are characterized by metal covers, often of Britannia metal and often patented, which regulated the flow of viscous liquid (Spillman 1982:192-194). They were introduced at least as early as the 1850s (Figure 22), and continued to be offered into the 1930s (Butler Brothers 1930:n.p.). Salvers in Maple and Floral patterns are also shown on this page. (Courtesy of the Juliet K. and Leonard S. Rakow Research Library of The Corning Museum of Glass, Corning, New York.)

1830. Its inclusion in Pellatt's book suggests, however, that it was still in use, at least in British glasshouses, into the 1840s. For vessels with glued-on fitments or screw tops, such as molasses jugs, or salt and pepper shakers, the burst-off technique continued to be used into the 20th century. For this use it was not always necessary to grind the finish and without the metal covers, one can sometimes note the horizontal mold line at the top and the thin burst

off remnants (Spillman 1982:No. 185; Jones and Sullivan 1989:91; Lyon 1994:71-74).

TURN-MOLDED GLASS

It is likely that some tablewares from the 1870s onward were blown in turn molds. The turn mold is a full-size multi-part mold that is coated with a paste which is moistened before blowing the object. During the blowing process,

FIGURE 14. The majority of the jugs and tumblers in these water and beverage sets are described as "blown" and clearly the horizontal-rib patterns, such as IC-1851 and IC-1047, are best made by blowing into a full-size mold. Technically, the horizontal nature of these patterns would make it feasible to blow the jugs and tumblers in turn or paste molds, to eliminate mold lines. In the same catalogue, berry bowls and nappies, and cream and sugar sets are all pressed, mostly in older, less-adventurous patterns than these (Figure 61) (Butler Brothers 1930:n.p.). (Courtesy of Collins Kirby Art & Antiques, Fort Payne, Alabama.)

FIGURE 15. Glass dish made in the blow-over method. Its roughly ground rim and undecorated surface indicate that it was to be used as a liner, probably for a silver or silver-plated dish. Generally open vessels made in this technique have a flat or decorated and polished rim. (Photo by Rock Chan, Parks Canada collection.)

the object is rotated, riding on a thin cushion of steam which imparts a shiny surface and eliminates mold marks (Figure 5) (Jones and Sullivan 1989:30-31). The technique is suitable for mouth-blowing or machine production, and was used for making bottles, lamp chimneys, and light bulbs as well as tablewares.

OPTIC-MOLDED GLASS

Optic molding is a technique in which the glass is blown into a small patterned mold and then transferred to a full-size undecorated mold and blown. The pattern, usually consisting of panels, ribs, or circular protrusions, is transferred to the inside of the object (Jones and Sullivan 1989:32-33). When the full-size mold is a turn mold or dip mold, no mold lines appear on the piece. Tumblers blown in this way have been found on 18th-century French colonial sites in North America, but the major use of the technique in tableware dates from the 1880s into the 20th century where it was used principally for drinking glasses and jugs (Figures 5, 14) (Diamond Flint Glass Company 1904:25; Butler Brothers 1910:408; Wilson 1994[2]:605-974). It is one which translates into machine production as it involves the use of two molds, a process familiar to 20th-century glass manufacturers. In addition to optic molding, glasses are often decorated with enameling, gilding, needle etching, and light cutting. In the 1905, 1910, and 1914 Butler Brothers catalogues, optic molding was not common; however, in the 1925, 1929, and 1930 catalogues, for both tumblers and stemware, it is the dominant decorative

technique. Continental European glassmakers are still making optic-molded tableware.

COMPRESSED AIR

In the early 1830s, Robinet–a glassblower at Baccarat in France–invented a mechanical pump which supplied sufficient air pressure to enable French manufacturers to produce complex patterns with crisp definition. This technique was largely used in European glass houses, particularly in France. Air was used rather than a plunger, thus it may be possible to feel the characteristic surface on blown contact molding (Spillman 1982:164). The French patterns are generally very detailed and often resemble American pressed lacy patterns. Examples of this type of glass from Launay Hautin & Cie ca. 1840 catalogues are published in Innes (1976:299-300) and copies of complete catalogues are available on fiche from The Juliet K. and Leonard S. Rakow Research Library of The Corning Museum of Glass. English manufacturers also used this technique (Figure 16) (Hajdamach 1991:96-97).

Pressed Glass

PINCHING

During the 18th century, specialized branches of the British glass industry used hand-held pinchers to form small objects such as chandelier drops and fob seals. By the end of the century, vessel manufacturers used the technique to form decanter stoppers and feet for salts and bowls (Figure 17) (Jones and Sullivan 1989:33-35). These techniques continued to be used at least into the late 1820s. In 1828, Thomas Leighton, of the Boston & Sandwich Glass Company, sent examples of articles to his colleague in Scotland: "We make them the Same as you Make the Square feet. the Mould Lifts with 2 ha[n]dles and opens at the Corners" (Spillman 1992:6). The surface was ruffled, hence the pinched elements were decorated, usually with ribbing, and flat parts, such as edges and resting surfaces or feet, were cut and polished.

MECHANICAL PRESSING

Pressed glass is formed in a multi-part mold in which glass is pushed into the mold by a plunger powered by a screw or lever mechanism. At its simplest, the whole object can be shaped and decorated quickly and cheaply with very little skill as only the correct amount of glass needs to be dropped into the mold. Initially mechanical pressing was developed in the United States in the mid-1820s to manufacture glass furniture knobs. By 1828, however, the technique was being used to make a variety of tableware forms, and firms making the new wares were already having to protect their designs from competitors (Nelson 1988:48-62, 98). Both the technique and the products spread quickly. By 1831, Apsley Pellatt in London was taking out a patent for pressed glass and in 7 June 1832, the *Brockville Gazette* (Ontario), advertised "75 Casks American pressed Glass Ware, consisting of Sugar bowls, Creams, Salts, Preserve Dishes, Fruit, and Stand dishes, 3, 4, 5, 6, 7, 8, and 9 Inch Plates, 110 Dozen Glass Knobs" (Jones 1992:11). Plates and open bowls or dishes

FIGURE 16. Cream or milk jug in thick, heavy lead glass may have been formed by compressed air as the inner surface follows the contour of the outer surface. The top has been fire-polished, however, to form the pouring lip which may have altered the relationship between the inner and outer surfaces. As well, the glass is close to 1 cm (0.4 in.) thick which may also affect the profile of the inner surface as thick glass retains heat longer than thin glass. Handle was applied first at the rim and then looped down to the lower body; it has a cut and polished base with impressed starburst and scalloped rim. Probably English, mid-19th century. (Photo by Rock Chan, Parks Canada collection.)

had not been a strong product line in the glass industry prior to mechanical pressing but open forms, including salts, were particularly suited to the pressing technique. Rectangular and square objects require effort to make freeblown, however, along with blown contact molding (Figure 64d), pressing expanded the range of angular forms which could be made quickly and cheaply. Until the late 1830s, the traditional backbone products of the glass industry–stemware, tumblers, and decanters–were not made by pressing because of difficulties in making a vessel with a thin upper part (see Tumblers) as well as narrow-mouthed vessels.

Manufacturers very quickly figured out how to make multi-part objects, such as lamps and even decanters, by attaching different parts to each other with thin wafers of hot glass, sometimes by pressing one part and blowing another, or by using multi-part open-topped molds with subsequent retooling to form the object (Figures 18, 19) (Wilson 1994[1]:278-280). Throughout the 19th century glass manufacturers, machinists, and engineers continued to invent time-saving and cost-cutting improvements in the process of pressing (Scoville 1948; Davis 1949:226-229; Zembala 1984; Slack 1987:14-20; Wilson 1994[1]:265-285). Wilson (1994[1]:289-517) documents manufacturing processes in his descriptions of pressed pieces in the Toledo Museum, one of the few authors to do so. In 1917, automatic feeders were introduced to the pressed-glass trade and bit by bit, other parts of the process were mechanized. However, hand plants continued to make pressed specialized products whose production runs were too small for machines (Davis 1949:226-229).

Pressed glass is usually described by its decorative motifs because pressing not only shaped the object but also decorated it. The motifs possible in this technique ranged anywhere from plain to highly decorated; they could mimic simple or complex geometric cut-glass patterns or the realism of engraved patterns. Complex cut and engraved patterns took hours to make; pressed imitations took seconds.

PRESSED GLASS, 1827-CA. 1850

Pressed glass of this period is generally covered in decoration; the decoration is bold,

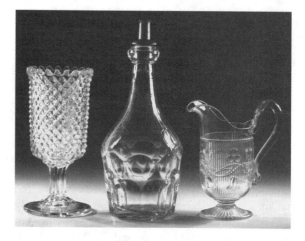

FIGURE 17. Decanter stopper made by pinching. (Photo by George Lupien, Parks Canada collection.)

FIGURE 18. Pressed glass made in multi-part open-topped molds (from left to right): *Celery* in the Diamond Point or Sharp Diamond pattern which was made from the late 1840s to ca. 1870. Three mold lines, hidden in the pattern, extend from foot to rim although they were eliminated at the rim when it was fire-polished. Made in colorless lead glass, the piece is very heavy. As no pontil mark appears on the piece, a snap case or other holder was used to hold it while the rim was fire-polished. *Decanter* in the Ashburton pattern which was introduced at least as early as 1848, and continued to be made into the 1880s (Watkins 1970:151-152, 157-159; Husfloen 1992:32; Wilson 1994[1]:280, 285, n. 69). Narrow-mouthed vessels like this were pressed in a mold with a plain, flat base part, three or four body parts bearing the decoration, and above them an undecorated one-piece cylindrical mold part (Wilson 1994[1]:478). Held by a pontil, the cylindrical part was reheated and tooled to form the shoulder, neck, and lip. Mold lines encircle the heel and follow the edges of the body pattern and across the top of the design. As this piece was empontiled, the pontil mark has been ground away and then polished, resulting in a smooth, circular depression. The one-piece cylindrical upper part in the mold made it possible to make complex objects without mold lines showing on the undecorated part and was adaptable to different forms, including stemware bowls and feet. An American patent illustrating this concept was taken out in 1847 (Wilson 1994[1]:271), and pressed items, such as goblets, shown in this guide with no mold marks on the upper undecorated surface were made in this type of mold and subsequently fire-polished. *Creamer* in Ribbed Leaf pattern (Figure 24) in which the upper part was initially formed in the same way as the Ashburton decanter, reheated, and tooled to form the pouring lip. Three vertical mold lines are hidden on the vertical ribs and extend down over the foot where a fourth mold part was used to shape the bottom of the foot. A horizontal mold line encircles the top of the pattern. The handle was initially applied at the top and looped down to be attached on the lower body. No pontil was used. Made of lead glass, the piece dates 1864 to ca. 1875. (Photo by Rock Chan, Parks Canada collection.)

detailed, and well-defined, with crisp edges. The glass sparkles because it is made of lead glass, which has high refractive qualities, and because it is covered by over-all patterns which provide many surfaces for light to catch. The dense patterns also serve to hide imperfections left by the pressing technique such as shear marks, which appear as cracks in the glass, and dulled surfaces caused by under-heated molds.

The earliest pressed glass, dating 1827 to ca. 1830 or 1835 (Spillman 1981:37-44; Wilson 1994[1]:276, 292-312), was decorated with imitation Anglo-Irish cut motifs: strawberry diamonds, crosscut waffle squares, and fans. Dating for these patterns is based on the absence of mold lines associated with the use of a cap ring, introduced about 1830, which was a mold part that formed and controlled the thickness of an object's rim (McKearin and McKearin 1948:345; Nelson 1990:44-48).

From about 1830 until ca. 1850 (Figure 20) (Wilson 1994[1]:278), the patterns are known as "lacy" because of the presence of dots, diamonds, or lines on the background. Thousands of pattern variations exist which imitate cut and

FIGURE 19. Narrow-mouthed vessels made in cut-and-shut molds were pressed upside down with a large band of undecorated glass at the base of the object. After withdrawing the object from the mold, the glass at the base was tooled inward and cut off which left a swirled crease on the base. The technique was developed in the 1870s (Innes 1976:66-67) and is most commonly found on cruets and molasses jugs. (Photo by Rock Chan, Parks Canada collection.)

engraved patterns and/or reflect decorative arts movements of the period. Motifs include classical (acanthus leaves, palmettes, cornucopia, oak leaves, shells and scrolls, feathered leaf shapes), gothic revival (arches, rosettes, quatrefoils, lancets, hairpins), folk art (hearts, tulips), historical/realistic (ships, eagles, buildings), peacock eye (later called comet), guilloches, thistles, and pineapples (McKearin and McKearin 1948:Plates 144-175).

Lacy-type patterns were also made in Europe, either by pressing or compressed air, and their production continued past mid-century (Spillman 1981:358-359).

PRESSED GLASS, CA. 1840-1870S

Pressed panel tumblers, introduced in the late 1830s (see Tumblers), seem to have been the first products made in a new style, now called geometric. During the 1840s, many new patterns were introduced in both the United States

FIGURE 20. Covered sugar bowl, open dish, cup plate, salt, and plate decorated by "lacy"-type pressed patterns produced in American factories between 1830 and ca. 1850. They are characterized by crisp, well-defined patterns against a textured ground and are of lead glass. The cup plate, center front, shows the *Chancellor Livingston* which operated between New York City and Providence, Rhode Island, until 1834, when it was decommissioned (Spillman 1981:137) (Courtesy of The Corning Museum of Glass, Corning, New York.)

FIGURE 21. Page from the O'Hara Flint Glass Works catalogue which illustrates examples of geometric styles, sizes, and different functions of the stemware made by this firm (O'Hara Flint Glass Works 1861:3). Patterns are: No. 1 - Huber; No. 2 - Hotel; No. 3 - New York; No. 4 - Bohemian; No. 5 - Ashburton; No. 6 - Cincinnati; No. 7 - St. George; No. 8 - Huber; and No. 9 - O'Hara. Several patterns of this type continued to be made past the 1870s. Patterns resembling New York, for example, were still being made into the 1920s. (Courtesy of the Juliet K. and Leonard S. Rakow Research Library of The Corning Museum of Glass, Corning, New York.)

and Britain which imitated cut-glass motifs, particularly panels, flutes, round or oval facets, hexagons, diamonds, cross-hatching, and miters (Figures 21-23). During the 1850s, advertisements in Montreal newspapers by the Boston & Sandwich Glass Company and other American glass manufacturers showed both the range of objects and the range of patterns in the new style (Figure 22) (Jones 1992:10, 13-15). One piece of evidence suggests that the new styles in pressed glass competed head to head with cut glass and may even have forced the lowering of some cut-glass prices. An advertisement in the *Montreal Transcript* (1842) stated that it had "English Cut Dishes, as cheap as American pressed." The geometric style was produced in both Britain and the United States (Morris

1978:190-197; Spillman 1982:416-417; Slack 1987). Although its patterns were less detailed than the lacy ones, they nevertheless tended to cover all or most of the vessel surface up to the rim. The glass is thick, heavy, and of potash-lead composition. It is not clear if lacy patterns continued to be made during the 1850s and 1860s in the United States.

PRESSED GLASS, CA. 1865-1880S

In 1864, William Leighton developed a new soda-lime formula (see Glass Composition) which was considered a satisfactory visual substitute for potash-lead glasses. Most American pressed glass manufacturers had switched to the new formula within a few years because it was so

American Pressed Glassware,
ON ACCOUNT OF THE
Boston and Sandwich Glass Company.

THE Subscribers will Sell by Auction, at the Stores of the Agents, Messrs, MILLAR, GLASSFORD & CO., No., No. 5, St. Sacrament Street, on TUESDAY, 28th September—

106 casks ASSORTED GLASSWARE, first quality manufactured at the Works of the Boston and Sandwich Glass Company, comprising :—

Punty Bowls on Feet
Spangle and Pannel Dishes
Do Bowls on Feet, Jugs
Bedford, Providence, and other Lamps
Cone, Egg, and Concave Hall Lamps, Bronze Mountings
Napies, with or without Covers
Quart, half-gallon and gallon Specie Jars
Ice Cream Glasses, Salts
Mo-flu. and Spangle Bitter Bottles, Brit. Tubes
Astor and Revere Champagne Goblets
Egg Cups, Jellies, and Cellaries
Gothic, Arch and Ashburton Lemonades
Astor and Ashburton Wines
Spoon Holders, Cup Plates and Candlesticks
Punty and Sp. Knob Ale Glasses
Spangle and other Pat. Decanters
Castor Bottles, assorted
Molasses Jugs and Mustards, Brit. Covers
Tumblers in great variety of weight and pattern, &c. &c.

—ALSO,—

An assortment of Druggists' Ware

Terms :—Six months credit on all amounts exceeding £25.

Catalogues will be ready for delivery, and samples on view, on the 20th September.

☞ Sale at TEN o'clock.

157 JAMES SCOTT & CO.

FIGURE 22. Named patterns from the Boston & Sandwich Glass Company include Punty, Spangle, Panel, Astor, Revere, Gothic, Arch, and Ashburton. The list includes a wide range of tablewares, including specialized forms with Britannia-metal tubes or covers (Montreal Gazette 1852:3).

much cheaper to produce. A comment in the *Crockery and Glass Journal* in 1879 about a newly introduced pattern extolled the visual appeal of pressed glass: "Every line in the design is a component part of an exquisite group and when this entire set of twenty-four pieces is placed on a well-spread table, the crystalline effect is beautiful" (Wilson 1994[1]:281).

Several different types of motifs were introduced during the ca. 1865-1880s period (Figures 24-25). Generally, the orientation of the patterns was horizontal; they circled the object rather than going from rim to base. *Geometric patterns* from the 1850s and 1860s continue, particularly honeycomb, facets, panels, and V-shaped ribs. *Plain patterns* left most of the object undecorated except for decorative elements on the rim, finial, stem, or foot. Blank areas could be decorated with engraving (Figure 49) or, from the 1880s onwards, by staining. *Naturalistic patterns*, such as fruit, flowers, leaves, animals, hands, shells, baskets, and people, were used on finials, stems, and on the main body of the piece. The motifs stood out from the background and most typically went around the object. *Textured patterns* had stippled grounds with raised dots or frosted areas in contrast with smooth shiny areas. This type of design began in the mid 1860s (Morris 1978:194-196), and the effect was achieved by molding, acid-etching, engraving, or sandblasting. Many of these types of patterns continued to be made into the 1890s and later. Beginning in the 1870s, handles began to be pressed in the mold, rather than being applied by the glassmaker in a separate operation.

PRESSED GLASS, 1880S AND LATER

During the 1880s, color innovations became an important feature of pressed glass, including not just the glass (see Color), but also ruby and yellow stains, enamels, and gilding. Motifs introduced in the 1870s continued to be made, but several design changes were introduced in the late 1870s and early 1880s (Figures 26-29). The most prominent change concerned the orientation of patterns which switched from a horizontal to a vertical orientation. *Naturalistic patterns* featuring fruit and flowers, birds, animals, people, and scenes had a vertical orientation and were often confined in panels. Many new floral and leaf designs were shallower and less sculptured than the 1870s ones. Patterns in *contrasting textures* continued to be popular. *Rustic* designs were characterized by handles, feet, and finials disguised as twigs or branches. *Hobnails*, featuring protuberant rounded or pointed circles on the body of vessels, were often made in heat-sensitive glass. *Japonism* motifs were asymmetrical, with designs enclosed in parallelograms rather than squares or rectangles, and included such things as fans, butterflies, and swallows. Square bowls and plates were made under the same influence. *Plain* patterns often had a heavy band of decoration at the base in sharp contrast to an undecorated

FIGURE 23. Called Comet in period catalogues, collectors also call this type of pattern Horn of Plenty or Peacock Eye (Wilson 1994[1]:483). It dates mid-to-late 1850s into the 1870s. This group illustrates the range of shapes produced in a single pattern, including lamps. (Courtesy of The Corning Museum of Glass, Corning, New York.)

body. Some earlier *Geometric* patterns continued to be made. *Brilliant patterns* imitated brilliant cut patterns (Figure 26) (see Cut Glass). They were in production almost immediately after 1882, and continued to be a dominant style in pressed glass for much of the 20th century.

Patterns produced in English factories followed themes similar to those produced in American and Canadian factories, such as imitation cut patterns (Figure 52), rustic and Japonic patterns, contrasting textures, and naturalistic patterns. The naturalistic patterns tend to have a crisper, more sculptured look to them than North American examples, and often include realistically shaped vessels (Figures 2-4) (Slack 1987). Evidence for English production in the late 1870s and 1880s comes from the design registers, trademarked pieces, catalogues, and *The Pottery Gazette*. Partly because so much of the production is easily identified, and partly because of its attractiveness, glass from this period has been popular for both collectors and researchers.

PRESSED GLASS, 1890S AND LATER

In 1891, 18 companies in the American Midwest amalgamated to become the United States Glass Company although, after a devastating strike between 1893 and 1896, several of the original factories closed. By 1904, only six remained, plus three additional specialized plants (Revi 1964:306, 308). Production from this new company included new designs and reissues of many older patterns from its member factories (Figures 27-29). Catalogue pages from the U.S. Glass Company are illustrated throughout Revi (1964), in *Pennsylvania Glassware* (1972:133-156), and Heacock and Bickenheuser (1978). These catalogues serve as a snapshot of American pressed glass production in the 1890s, for both patterns and vessel shapes. A number of independent glass firms, however, continued to make pressed tablewares during the 1890s and first decade of the 20th century (Husfloen 1992:130-146).

During the 1890s and the first decade of the 20th century, consolidation also took place in the Canadian industry with several smaller factories being taken over by Diamond Glass which became the Dominion Glass Company in 1913 (Figure 30) (King 1987:84, 107-126).

Although a good variety of new patterns was issued, dozens of best-sellers from previous decades continued in wide production. Sometimes they were given a face lift by the addition of color, such as ruby and amber staining, and the application of flashy gold or colored enamel trim to highlight the design" (Husfloen 1992:102-103).

Colored glassware, including transparent and opaque colors and "marbled" colors, continued to be popular. Introduced into pressed-glass production in the early years of the 20th century was "Carnival glass" which featured iridescent golds, blues, and greens (Figure 1), and was often decorated with fruit or flower motifs.

From the patterns shown in the catalogues of the U.S. Glass Company, of Butler Brothers (Figures 1, 79), and of retail firms such as Montgomery Ward & Co. and T. Eaton Co., it is clear that imitation cut patterns and geometric patterns dominated the pressed-glass market

FIGURE 24. Although the Ribbed Bell-Flower or Ribbed-Leaf pattern has been attributed to several manufacturers and even to a ca. 1850 date, the 1864 M'Kee catalogue is the first dated documentary evidence for its production (M'Kee and Brothers 1981:29-31). The pattern does not appear in M'Kee's 1859-1860 illustrated catalogue, while the 1864 catalogue illustrates 42 pieces, strongly suggesting a new pattern. The style of decoration, with naturalistic motifs going around the object, as well as the contrast between a smooth pattern against a heavily patterned background, supports the view that this is a pattern introduced in the mid 1860s. Objects shown here include the "set" consisting of creamer, covered sugar, spooner, and covered butter, as well as a tumbler, different stemware, a plate, and pitcher. (Courtesy of The Corning Museum of Glass, Corning, New York.)

FIGURE 25. Examples of pressed-glass patterns of the 1870s (from left to right): *Footed sugar i*n the Princess Feather or Rochelle pattern which appears in the ca. 1875 catalogue of Bakewell Pears & Co. It has three feathered medallions with a crosshatched center and a stippled ground. Patterns of this type bear some resemblance to lacy pressed patterns of the second quarter of the 19th century. *Goblet* with patterns similar to Nova Scotia Grape and Vine or Grape Band were introduced about 1870 and exhibit typical 1870s realistic decoration going around the vessel (Maple and Floral salvers in Figure 13). *Goblet* in a plain panel pattern of a type in production for decades. *Goblet* in Lion Head pattern, introduced ca. 1877, which consists of a plain undecorated bowl with panels supporting the bottom of the bowl, three lions' heads on the stem, and a cabled foot rim. The stem and foot are frosted by acid etching. *Creamer* in the Jacob's Ladder pattern which was patented in 1876, and was in production as late as 1907, in both Canada and the United States (Jenks and Luna 1990:297). This pattern has a vertical orientation which presages the patterns introduced in the 1880s. *Jug* in Victor or Shell and Jewel pattern was introduced in the 1870s but continued in production into the 20th century, and in Canada into the 1920s although the later Canadian versions have a flat rim (Figure 30). It is characterized by bold, high-relief glossy motifs against a stippled ground. (Photo by Rock Chan, Parks Canada collection.)

FIGURE 26. The Daisy and Button pattern, in imitation of the brilliant-cut Russian pattern, was a perennial favorite produced by many companies. Note the square celery and bowl in the lower left corner, an 1880s design change which reflected the angular forms of Japanism (Hobbs Glass Company n.d.). (Courtesy of The Winterthur Library, Printed Book and Periodical Collection.)

FIGURE 27. Examples of tumbler patterns offered by the United States Glass Company (1894) in an undated catalogue of the 1890s as reissues of patterns originally produced by member companies in the 1880s (Revi 1964:18-22, 54-61, 67-68, 86-90, 125-127, 148-151, 163-171, 216-223, 270-276). In this group, the patterns cover most of the body. Some have stiff, formal repeats (**top far right, bottom center**). Other motifs include imitation cut diamonds, swirled ribs, swirled rosettes, a meander (in the **far right of the last row** called Ribbon Candy), and one naturalistic vertical pattern enclosed in a frame which is called Fan and Butterfly. (Courtesy of the Juliet K. and Leonard S. Rakow Research Library of The Corning Museum of Glass, Corning, New York.)

from the 1890s to the 1920s. In the early 20th century, several American firms marketed these patterns under trade names such as Prescut (M'Kee; patented 1904), Plunger-cut (Heisey; patented 1906), and Nu-cut (Imperial; patented 1914) (Wilson 1994[2]:642). Although some new patterns featuring plants and flowers were introduced during these 30 years, usually for iridescent-glass patterns, they were far fewer in number, and "realistic" patterns, featuring such things as coins, were even fewer (Husfloen 1992:104). As a rule, patterns were oriented vertically on the piece, and as they tend to be narrower than patterns from earlier periods, the necessary repeats around the object often give a stiff, formal look to the patterns (Figures 27, 31).

Brilliant cut patterns included stars, pinwheels, Xs, strawberry diamonds, buzz-saws, fans, curved miter cuts, and crosshatching (Figure 32). In 1905, Butler Brothers offered a new pressed pattern: "Heavy pure crystal glass in beautiful new deep cut pattern copied from the latest genuine cut glass design, brilliantly fire polished" (Butler Brothers 1905:141). *Vertical ribs and panels* (Figure 29) were a common motif, sometimes plain, sometimes decorated, sometimes alternating plain and decorated, and were often outlined in

FIGURE 28. More from the 1890s U.S. Glass Company catalogue. The top row features (left to right): Magic, a rosette-type pattern, Fish-scale or Coral with alternating matte and shiny surfaces, and Brazil or Paneled Daisy which is a naturalistic pattern with vertical orientation and enclosed in a panel. The other patterns are largely imitation cut motifs including, in the middle row, diamond or square patterns composed of deep V-shaped grooves. (Courtesy of the Juliet K. and Leonard S. Rakow Research Library of The Corning Museum of Glass, Corning, New York.)

notches, beading, or cross-hatching. *Swirled ribs and panels* (Figure 29) helped give movement to an otherwise repetitive and stiff pattern. *Squares and diamonds* (Figure 28) created by V-shaped grooves formed a comparatively plain group of patterns. *Rosettes* (Figure 27), a round "floral" pattern consisting of a center and "petals," were also made during this period. *Meander, serpentine, and guilloche* (Figure 31) formed sinuous patterns, often combining both vertical and horizontal movement. *Naturalistic* patterns (Figure 27), featuring flowers, vines, leaves, or fruit, were oriented vertically and usually confined within panels although some patterns were placed over the panel edges. *Rococo revival* styles (Figure 33) appeared in both

pressed and acid-etched glassware in the early 1890s, with designs characterized by curving asymmetrical figures, scrolls, shells, and patterns with names such as "Louis XV" (Revi 1964:269). Beginning in the early 1900s, relatively plain paneled patterns, called "colonial" (Figures 34, 93), represented a growing interest in plainer patterns associated with Colonial revival aesthetics.

PRESSED GLASS, CA. 1920-1940

From the early years of the 20th century, in response to Colonial revival tastes, some pressed glass had been offered in comparatively plain patterns. The bulk of pressed glass, however, carried the heavily patterned look of the late

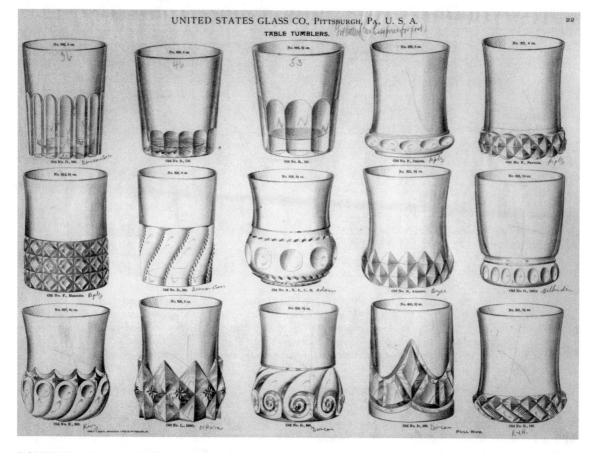

FIGURE 29. This page from the 1890s U.S. Glass Company catalogue features tumblers with plain upper bodies and imitation cut patterns on the lower body which often swells out at the base, a characteristic feature of this time period. (Courtesy of the Juliet K. and Leonard S. Rakow Research Library of The Corning Museum of Glass, Corning, New York.)

FIGURE 30. A group of Canadian patterns produced ca. 1900 to 1920s (Rottenberg and Tomlin 1982). From left to right: *Covered butter* in Stippled Swirl and Star is an example of the swirled-rib type of pattern; *Jug* in Maple Leaf pattern is a naturalistic-type pattern with a large well-defined motif, reminiscent of patterns from the 1880s; *Sugar bowl* in Nugget pattern, a Canadian version of Victor first produced in the 1870s, and reissued by the U.S. Glass Company in the 1890s, and still in production in the United States in the early 20th century and in Canada until the 1920s (Figure 25); *Covered sugar* which illustrates the vertical-type patterns (Beaded Oval and Fan No. 1) with an undecorated oval outlined by beading, another characteristic feature of the ca. 1900-1920 period; *Footed nappy* in Beaded Oval and Fan No. 2 pattern which is a brilliant-cut imitation; Jug in Athenian pattern which has a large bold motif placed on a textured ground and, like Maple Leaf, harks back to patterns of the 1880s; *Covered butter* in Bow Tie pattern, consisting of overlapping vertical ovals and small horizontal ovals decorated with crosshatching which form a horizontal row through the center of the vertical ovals. (Photo by Rock Chan, Parks Canada collection.)

Victorian period. By the late 1920s and into the 1930s, however, it was largely replaced by a lighter look which, although often profusely decorated, was achieved through the use of light colors, thinner transparent glass, shallow decoration, and clean lines (Figures 35-37). Pressed patterns tended to echo acid-etched or engraved designs, the lighter cut patterns introduced around 1910, and even blown glassware. Interest in the Colonial or Georgian period brought revivals of cut and pressed patterns of the 1820-1840 period and reinterpretations of neo-classical motifs. New vessel forms introduced during this period were serving plates with handles in the center, grill plates with three dividers molded in the glass, cups and saucers, soup bowls, and dinner and salad plates (Figure 59). Although introduced before the turn of the century, specialized plates or trays for such things as cheese and crackers, spoons, bonbons, olives, and mayonnaise were common. The impression from the Butler Brothers catalogues is that by 1929-1930, machine-blowing had become more prominent than pressing for making jugs, tumblers, and stemware.

Beginning in the mid to late 1920s, pressed glass (and blown glass) is most easily recognized by its color palette: pastel pinks, ambers, lime and emerald greens, blues, deep intense blue and red, amethyst, and opaque colors including white, custard, and black (Florence 1995a, 1996). "Carnival" glass also continued to be made. *Brilliant cut patterns* (Figures 38, 61) continued to be offered although in much smaller variety and were commoner in "company" pieces, such as berry bowls, vases, and sugar and cream sets. Often referred to as "colonial," *vertical panels* were staple patterns, in varying heights, widths, with rounded or square tops, or going from top to bottom of the object (Figure 34). *Horizontal panels/ribs*, sometimes combined with vertical ribs, were completely new to pressed tableware and reflected art deco aesthetics. This type of combination was also found in blown glassware (Figure 14). *Squares* or *hexagons* assumed more of an art deco look although they had been introduced earlier (Figures 28, 36). Overall patterns, such as *bull's-eyes, hobnails, and crackle*, continued to be produced (Figure 55). *Acid-etched* designs featuring florals, borders, festoons,

OUR "BIG BRILLIANT"
TABLE SET ASSORTMENT.
Large full size sets at a price usually charged for small ones.

C1030—Asst. comprises: 6 sets each of 3 patterns, all footed, one with large double handles. Each set consists of covered butter dish, sugar bowl, spoon holder and cream pitcher, all in rich new crystal patterns. Total 18 sets in bbl. (Bbl. 35:.)
Per set. 16⅝c

NEW "MAGNIFICENT" TABLE SET ASST.
Positively the most beautiful set ever offered at a 50c price.

C1034—Three elaborate and brilliant genuine cut glass patterns, all extra large, heavy and massive, richly finished and polished. 4 sets of 3 patterns. Total 12 sets in bbl. (Bbl. .')
Per set. 32c

FIGURE 31. Selections from the 1905 Butler Brothers catalogue: *upper*, intertwined-type pattern contrasted with one of the stiff vertical patterns; *lower*, pattern featuring guilloche with central rosette, a meander-type pattern and a brilliant-cut-type pattern (Butler Brothers 1905:142). (Courtesy of Collins Kirby Art & Antiques, Fort Payne, Alabama.)

hanging pendants, medallions, and other vaguely neoclassical-inspired designs were shallowly pressed and imitated popular acid-etched motifs (Figures 35, 37, 82). *Lacy* patterns imitating pressed lacy glass of the 1830-1850 period were part of Colonial revival esthetics.

Cut Glass

Cut glass is a cold decorating technique and as such can be done in a glass factory, in a cutting shop, or by individuals (Kaellgren 1993; Palmer 1993b, 1993c; Spillman 1996). It was a decorating technique favored by, but not exclusive to, the English, and enhanced the lustrous light-transmitting properties of potash-lead glass.

The surface of the glass is cut away by grinding with wheels and grit. Polishing is accomplished by using increasingly finer abrasives and polishing wheels. In the 19th century, the edges of the cut motif are generally crisp, the cut surface is shiny, and the wheel marks can be seen on some pieces. For most cut glass, there is a difference in surface texture between the cut and uncut areas. In the early 20th century, however, acid baths began to be used for polishing, replacing the laborious and time-consuming wheel work (Hajdamach 1991:178; Wilson 1994[2]:640). As acid removes the surface, it also removes the marks of the wheel and softens the sharp edges so characteristic of earlier cutting. Motifs in cut glass tend to be geometric, based on straight line cuts, although curved lines and ribs are possible.

"Rich cut glassware" or "elegant cut glassware" were phrases used over and over in 19th-century Canadian newspaper advertisements because cut glassware, whether consisting of elaborate designs or simple panels, had an immediately recognized prestige which it still retains. From the 1790s onward, the constant imitation of cut-glass-inspired motifs in both contact-molded patterns and in the pressed glass industry attest to the popularity of the cut-glass look. Cut glass imported from Great Britain and Bohemia or made in the United States served the American market while Canadians used British cut glass almost exclusively. By the early 20th century, several Canadian firms were using imported blanks from Europe and the United States to make cut glass. Blanks are pieces of glass produced to be decorated by cutting or engraving.

For much of the 19th century, glassware cut in simple motifs, such as panels, flutes, miters, and facets, was the standard offering in the market. More elaborate cut patterns, however, were fashionable in different periods.

Variously called Georgian, Regency, or Anglo-Irish, patterns featuring V-shaped miter cuts were characteristic of British and American cut glass from ca. 1800 to the 1840s (Figures 39-42). In addition to flat cuts forming panels, cutters used

FIGURE 32. Jug in imitation brilliant-cut design which exhibits its characteristic complex motifs and the overall exuberance of decoration. (Photo by Rock Chan, Parks Canada collection.)

designs were shown at the 1851 exhibition, but these were certainly not bread-and-butter wares (*The Art-Journal* 1851:32, 70, 138-139, 174-175). As glassware became lighter in the late 1860s and 1870s, cut motifs tended to be shallow and simple (Figure 44) (Boston & Sandwich Glass Co. 1992).

From 1882 until 1915 and later, elaborately cut glass, known as brilliant cut glass, was fashionable. The first of it, in the Russian pattern, was patented in 1882, by a cutter working for T. G. Hawkes & Co. of Corning, New York, although many other glass companies also made it (Figure 26) (Spillman 1982:29; 1996:239-241). Brilliant cut glass featured stars, hobstars, strawberry-diamonds, fans, sunbursts, pinwheels, Xs, and curved V-shaped miters deeply cut into thick, heavy blanks and, in the earlier years, covering the entire object. "The characteristic feature of the work itself was the exact mathematical precision to which the cutters aspired. Usually composed of bold groupings of relatively small elements, the decoration gave an effect of great richness" (Wakefield 1982:45). Cut in the United States, Canada, Britain, and Bohemia, brilliant cut glass became a standard of social and material success

a V-shaped wheel to produce a repertoire of motifs consisting of V-shaped grooves, fields of plain diamonds or strawberry diamonds, blazes (straight or diagonal), fans, splits, and swirls (McFarlan 1992:1-12).

Beginning in the late 1820s and 1830s, a new vertical look was introduced into cut glass. This style had broad flute cuts which tended to go all the way up the body of the vessel to meet similar cuts coming down the neck and shoulder (Figure 42).

By mid-19th century, cut glass was characterized by simple bold motifs such as broad panels, large facets, and deep miter cuts (Wilson 1994[2]:523), similar to those seen in pressed glass (Figures 21, 23), generally on thickly blown glass (Figure 43). "Between 1851 and 1860 Stevens and Williams, for example, recorded over 1,000 cut glass designs in their pattern books. The majority of these patterns consisted of flutes, hollows, miters, prisms and fan scallops . . ." (Figure 87) (Hajdamach 1991:359). Vessels covered with elaborate cut

FIGURE 33. Covered sugar in opaque white glass in a rococo-revival-type pattern, although it is a subdued and rather stiff rendition in contrast to some of the acid-etched versions (Figure 56). (Photo by Rock Chan, Parks Canada collection.)

FIGURE 35. Bowl, 4 in. (10 cm), in lime green glass in Cloverleaf pattern which was made between 1930 and 1936 by the Hazel Atlas Glass Company (Florence 1996:38-41). (Photo by Rock Chan, Parks Canada collection.)

FIGURE 34. Innumerable patterns with vertical panels, called Colonial, were made by many companies from ca. 1900 onward, and they are one of the long-lived "looks" of the 20th century. These patterns were part of the Colonial revival movement and both the names used and the shapes made echoed early 19th-century styles. For example, the high squared handles on the compote imitate early-19th-century Georgian silver forms. Two forms offered as a parfait or egg glass and as a sundae or grapefruit glass suggest that the same shape could be used for different purposes. Dessert glasses, particularly individual serving bowls, become far more obvious in early-20th-century catalogues. For example, in addition to the six sundae variants on this page, the company also offered three other styles in different sizes (Stevens 1967:164-167). Figure 34 is taken from an undated catalogue of the Jefferson Glass Company, a Canadian company which operated from ca. 1912 to 1925 (Rottenberg and Tomlin 1982:10). (Photo by Rock Chan; original in Dominion Glass Company Limited papers in the National Archives of Canada, Ottawa.)

both technological innovations and changes in the patterns lowered the price of brilliant cut glassware (Farrar and Spillman 1979:13-15; Wilson 1994[2]:635-643). In the 1880s, the patterns on individual pieces tended to consist of a single motif, but later ones generally had a mixture of motifs. "On glass with a repeat design, . . . it is especially important that the cutting be perfectly even, the lines parallel, and that all points of the design meet properly. With mixed motifs, you may overlook poor cutting . . ." (Spillman 1982:262). Blown or

FIGURE 36. Footed sherbet in pink glass showing an imitation cut pattern in which V-shaped grooves intersect to form diamonds. This is the Waterford pattern made by Anchor Hocking between 1938 and 1944 (Florence 1996:225-226), although it resembles patterns from the 1890s shown in Figure 28. (Photo by Rock Chan, Parks Canada collection.)

and was popular as giftware, particularly for weddings. For example, in the early years of the 20th century, Henry Birks & Sons of Montreal offered "ATTRACTIVE WEDDING GIFTS IN CUT GLASS" which featured boxed versions of water sets comprising a carafe and six tumblers, cream and sugar sets sometimes in combination with a berry bowl, or a berry bowl with six small bowls (Henry Birks & Sons 1906:94-95). Over the next 20 years,

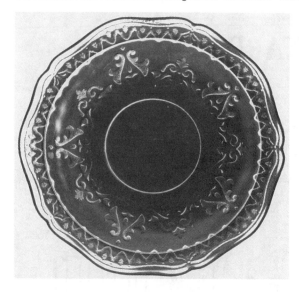

FIGURE 37. Saucer in pale amber glass with a pattern imitating acid-etched designs, including the frosted surface. This is the Patrician pattern made by Federal Glass Company, 1933 to 1937 (Florence 1996:168-169). (Photo by Rock Chan, Parks Canada collection.)

molded blanks with patterns already roughed out virtually eliminated the preliminary roughing process. Pressed glass imitations of brilliant cutting were a successful part of the marketplace from the 1880s into the 1920s (Figure 32), and, in the opinion of some, were partly responsible for the demise of brilliant cut glass (Wilson 1994[2]:643).

About 1900, brilliant cut styles were joined by a light, shallow cut style with simple floral/fruit/leaf and stem designs which left most of the surface uncut (Figure 45). Flowers were stylized, facing outward with a round center and petals coming out from it. Sometimes this type of cutting was offered in a "gray" finish; it was left unpolished, like copper wheel engraving or acid-etched designs. Shallowly cut glass could be done on the thin light glass so widely used up to and during the 1930s, and on Pyrex (Figures 7, 82, 94). This type of cutting significantly lowered the price of cut glass, offering its prestige to a lower economic range, but it also appealed to consumers who wanted a lighter look. Conscious imitations of early 19th-century glasswares also affected cut glass (Figure 46).

Engraved Glass

As with other cold-decorating techniques, engraving can be done independently from the glass factory. It was a technique favored by, but not exclusive to, German/Bohemian decorators.

Like cutting, engraving involves the cutting away of glass by using abrasives and wheels, but the wheels are smaller and capable of producing a much greater variety of motifs than the cutting process. Generally, the surface is left unpolished, providing a matte surface in contrast to the original glossy surface. As engraving is flexible, it can be shallow to accommodate very thin glass or deeply incised for a rich carved look. Many different levels of engraving were done, from simple motifs (Figures 44, 46-51, 88) to complex scenes covering the whole vessel; from sketchy quickly-done motifs (Figures 12, 85) to superbly executed imitations of period prints requiring hundreds of hours of work. Engraving was so adaptable, it could be used to produce personal mementoes as well as large-scale commercial works.

In the early 19th century, Bohemian engravers favored motifs in the Federal or neoclassical style, such as swags, festoons, knots, hanging tassels, stars, bouquets, closely packed rows of tiny vertical flowering plants, narrow bands with small oval or round cut and polished facets, and floral sprays (Lanman 1969:29-47; Spillman 1982:No. 101; Pattern Book n.d.). Similar motifs were adapted by engravers working in the United States and were produced up to ca. 1840 (Figure 47) (Innes 1976:166-171). Also in the first 40 years of the 19th century, engravers working in Britain and the United States made commemorative glasses for places, events, ships, buildings, and clubs, as well as for individuals, engraving people's names or initials, and dates. They also engraved words such as "wine" or "spirits," and idyllic scenes (Wakefield 1982:80-86; Hajdamach 1991:149-156).

Most authors discuss high-end engraved glassware of the mid to late 19th century, which featured complex, finely executed patterns done by famous engravers, often for international exhibitions (Morris 1978:76-100; Hajdamach 1991:156-173). Rock crystal engraving, which has polished surfaces, was introduced in the 1880s, and "intaglio" engraving, which is deep engraving done by stone wheels and produces larger bolder patterns, came in about 1900 (Wakefield 1982:94, 98, 102). Elaborately engraved glassware was still being made in the 1920s and 1930s (Farrar and Spillman

FIGURE 38.   Selection of jugs from the Butler Brothers (1925) catalogue showing pressed designs.   Note the variety of vertical panels offered, all called Colonial.   The distinctive short, squat jug in the center of the top row was shown in their 1914 catalogue as was an ice water pitcher featuring a bent-in lip designed to hold back ice, which became generally available as refrigerators became more common.   (Courtesy of Collins Kirby Art & Antiques, Fort Payne, Alabama.)

1979; Spillman 1982:No. 33, No. 275, No. 307; 1996).

In the 1870s, it is possible to pick up the threads of less expensive engraved glasses through catalogue illustrations and glassware (Figures 49-51) (Bakewell, Pears & Co. 1875:43, 44; Boston & Sandwich Glass Co. 1992). Borders, horizontal bands of floral/leaf/fruit motifs, sprays of flowers, and monograms enclosed in wreaths seem to have been standard ware. The role of simpler engraved patterns past 1900 is not clear as simple cut, acid-etched, and enameled patterns seem to have fulfilled the role

they had played in the past. Although Butler Brothers included some engraved tumblers in their 1905, 1910, and 1914 catalogues, there seems to be no engraving in the 1925, 1929, and 1930 catalogues (Butler Brothers 1905:147, 150, 1910:403-404, 1914:318-319).

Frosted Glass (Textured Glass)

Terminology for these techniques is difficult to sort out as both period documents and 20th-century authors have used the same terms inconsistently.

FIGURE 39. Lynn-molded and cut glassware (from left to right): Both *tumblers* are decorated by a hot-glass technique known as Lynn molding which leaves irregularly spaced, shallow, horizontal grooves around an object. Examples have been found in archaeological contexts in Canada dating from the late 18th to early 19th century. *Decanter* decorated with cut panels on the shoulder and lower body, as well as tiny vertical V-shaped grooves. Although the cutting elements are vertical, they are placed in bands around the object, which, when combined with the applied neck rings, give the decanter a squat horizontal look. Ringed decanters with this tapered-body shape date from the late 18th century into the 1840s (Figure 64 *left*); *Stemware* with a centrally knopped stem and a bucket bowl was the dominant style during the first half of the 19th century and continued to be made during the second half of the 19th century, although in far fewer numbers (Figure 74). Two glasses are decorated with cut panels, and the large goblet on the right has angled blazes as well. All cut glassware from archaeological sites of this period tends to be comparatively plain. (Photo by Rock Chan, Parks Canada collection.)

ROUGHED GLASS

A fashion for contrasting textures began in the 1840s and 1850s (Morris 1978:25-26). It consisted of a gray granular ground with shiny pattern superimposed on it or of a textured pattern against a shiny ground (Figure 51). Several different techniques were used to achieve these results:

1. Grinding the glass surface with a wheel and leaving it unpolished, like engraving, or by using stone wheels normally used for cut glass but eliminating the polishing steps (Figure 52). In some examples, the horizontal lines left by the wheel can be seen. This technique was superseded by pressing and acid etching beginning in the late 1860s and 1870s.

2. Acid etching, in which the surface etched by the acid was left matte, leaves "a very fine, uniform, flat texture" (Hajdamach 1991:184). A "white" acid finish, which results in a frosted silky surface, is achieved by neutralizing hydrofluoric acid with an alkali salt (Figure 53). As acid cuts into the glass evenly, if the pattern has sufficient depth, one can observe an almost right-angled edge to the roughed surface leading up to the smooth surface.

3. Sand blasting, in which sand is directed against glass by air pressure, was developed in the late 1860s and early 1870s. The areas to be left undecorated were protected by an overlay resist and a stencil or cut-out design was used to make the pattern. The technique was used to decorate or label windows, lampshades, and

FIGURE 40. Jug, attributed to a New York glasshouse, decorated in the Anglo-Irish style of cutting which features horizontal and vertical miter cuts, diamonds with crosshatching, and flat panels. Inexpensive imitations of these motifs were done by contact molding. (Courtesy of The Corning Museum of Glass, Corning, New York.)

drinking glasses and generally left a coarser surface with less detailed design than other methods (Figure 54) (Hajdamach 1991:374-378).

4. Pressing, in which the texture was molded into the glass (Figures 25, 30).

CRACKLED GLASS

Fissures or cracks in the glass were made by several techniques:

1. During the manufacturing process, the hot glass is plunged into cold water, reheated, and expanded. The process produces glass "irregularly veined, [having] marble-like projecting dislocations, with intervening fissures" (Pellatt 1849:116-117). Although the resulting glass is full of cracks it is, as Pellatt states, "perfectly sonorous." Called crackled glass, or sometimes ice-glass, Pellatt introduced it to the English market in the mid-19th century as an imitation of an earlier Venetian technique.

2. During manufacture, the object is rolled in crushed glass which adheres to the exterior surface and, when expanded by blowing, forms a rough surface with smooth veins (Revi 1959:61-64; Spillman 1982:95). Collectors have

FIGURE 41. Cut glass attributed to the Pittsburgh area, ca. 1820 to 1850, which shows different combinations of motifs associated with the Anglo-Irish repertoire. The cut motif on the celery vase, second from the left, was imitated by an English firm in the 1930s (Figure 69). (Courtesy of The Corning Museum of Glass, Corning, New York.)

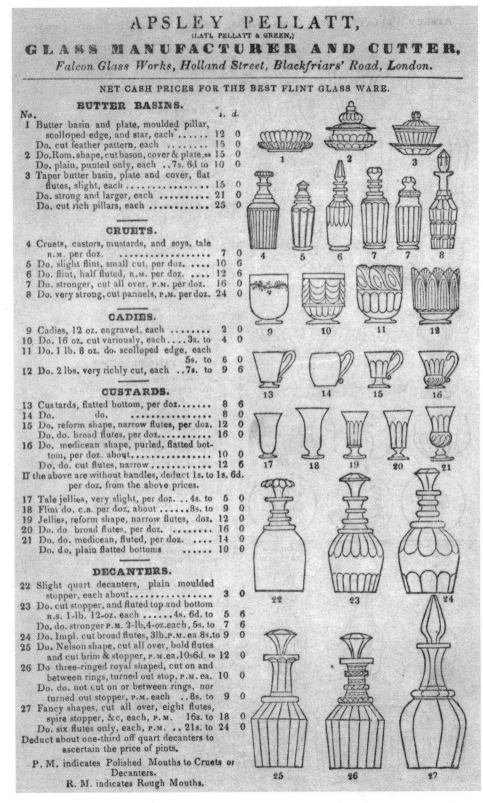

APSLEY PELLATT,
(LATL PELLATT & GREEN,)

GLASS MANUFACTURER AND CUTTER,
Falcon Glass Works, Holland Street, Blackfriars' Road, London.

NET CASH PRICES FOR THE BEST FLINT GLASS WARE.

BUTTER BASINS.

No.   s. d.
1 Butter basin and plate, moulded pillar,
   scolloped edge, and star, each 12 0
  Do. cut feather pattern, each 15 0
2 Do. Rom. shape, cut bason, cover & plate, 15 0
  Do. plain, punted only, each ..7s. 6d to 10 0
3 Taper butter basin, plate and cover, flat
   flutes, slight, each 15 0
  Do. strong and larger, each 21 0
  Do. cut rich pillars, each 25 0

CRUETS.

4 Cruets, castors, mustards, and soys, tale
   n.m. per doz. 7 0
5 Do. slight flint, small cut, per doz. 10 6
6 Do. flint, half fluted, n.m. per doz. 12 6
7 Do. stronger, cut all over, p.m. per doz. 16 0
8 Do. very strong, cut pannels, p.m. per doz. 24 0

CADIES.

9 Cadies, 12 oz. engraved, each 2 0
10 Do. 16 oz. cut variously, each ....3s. to 4 0
11 Do. 1 lb. 8 oz. do. scolloped edge, each
                        5s. to 6 0
12 Do. 2 lbs. very richly cut, each ..7s. to 9 6

CUSTARDS.

13 Custards, flatted bottom, per doz....... 8 6
14 Do.   do. 8 0
15 Do. reform shape, narrow flutes, per doz. 12 0
  Do. do. broad flutes, per doz........... 16 0
16 Do. medicean shape, purled, flatted bottom, per doz. about................. 10 0
  Do. do. cut flutes, narrow 12 6
If the above are without handles, deduct 1s. to 1s. 6d.
per doz. from the above prices.
17 Tale jellies, very slight, per doz. ..4s. to 5 0
18 Flint do. c.n. per doz. about ......8s. to 9 0
19 Jellies, reform shape, narrow flutes, doz. 12 0
20 Do. do. broad flutes, per doz. 16 0
21 Do. do. medicean, fluted, per doz. 14 0
  Do. do. plain flatted bottoms 10 0

DECANTERS.

22 Slight quart decanters, plain moulded
   stopper, each about................. 3 0
23 Do. cut stopper, and fluted top and bottom
   r.s. 1-lb. 12-oz. each ......4s. 6d. to 5 6
  Do. do. stronger p.m. 2-lb. 4-oz. each, 5s. to 7 6
24 Do. Impl. cut broad flutes, 3lb. p.m. ea 8s. to 9 0
25 Do. Nelson shape, cut all over, bold flutes
   and cut brim & stopper, p.m. ea. 10s 6d. to 12 0
26 Do three-ringed royal shaped, cut on and
   between rings, turned out stop, p.m. ea. 10 0
  Do. do. not cut on or between rings, nor
   turned out stopper, p.m. each ..8s. to 9 0
27 Fancy shapes, cut all over, eight flutes,
   spire stopper, &c, each, p.m. 16s. to 18 0
  Do. six flutes only, each, p.m. ..21s. to 24 0
Deduct about one-third off quart decanters to
ascertain the price of pints.

P. M. indicates Polished Mouths to Cruets or
Decanters.
R. M. indicates Rough Mouths.

FIGURE 42. First page of Apsley Pellatt's 1840 catalogue showing three decanters in the bottom row which are decorated with a broad flute-style of cutting. (Courtesy of the Juliet K. and Leonard S. Rakow Research Library of The Corning Museum of Glass, Corning, New York.)

FIGURE 43. Decanter and stopper in heavy lead glass with deep-cut finger flutes on the body alternating with a curved uncut surface, cut vertical panels on the neck, and a deeply cut star on the base. This decanter resembles some produced in Britain in the late 1830s and 1840s (Hajdamach 1991:52; Morris 1978:19, 28). (Photo by Rock Chan, Parks Canada collection.)

called this technique "overshot," but Nelson (1992:13, 15, 17-18) notes that the Boston & Sandwich Glass Company called glassware decorated by this technique "frosted;" ground surfaces were called "roughed;" vessels with ground surfaces decorated by wheel-polished designs were called "Frosted and Bright;" and the term "etched" was used for acid-etched designs.

3. Using pressed patterns to imitate glassware decorated by either of the above methods. The Tree of Life pattern, resembling overshot technique, was introduced in the late 1860s, and versions of it continued in production into the 1890s (Jenks and Luna 1990:524-525). Twentieth-century versions included Spider Web in carnival glass (Spillman 1982:197) and crackle glass (Figure 55).

Acid-etched Glass

A glass object is coated with a compound which resists the action of hydrofluoric acid; a design is incised through the resist; and the glass is placed in an acid bath or in fumes where the acid attacks the exposed glass surface. Afterwards, the resist is removed from the glass. Depending on the mixture in the acid bath, the surface can be made silky smooth, shiny, frosted, textured, or granular, and, depending on the time in the acid, the glass can be etched shallowly or deeply. More complex designs can be done by etching sequentially.

The discovery of hydrofluoric acid and its effect on glass dates to the 18th century, but until the middle of the 19th century, it was regarded more as a curiosity than a viable commercial proposition. In the 1850s, both Benjamin Richardson and John Northwood began experimenting with different parts of the process, including the resist material, ways of transferring the pattern through the resist, and the acid mixture itself. In those early years, and later, acid-etching could involve a great deal of handwork, sometimes making it as expensive as engraving (Morris 1978:113-126; Hajdamach 1991:175-201).

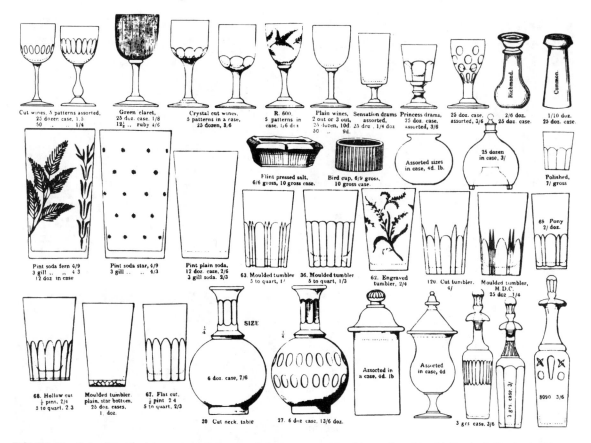

FIGURE 44. Selection of plain, cut, and engraved stemware and tumblers offered by M. Davis & Co. in the *Pottery Gazette* (1881:near 817). Bicolored glasses, like the claret glass in the top row, third from the left, with green or red bowls and colorless stems and feet, date from ca. 1850 to World War I. In marked contrast to brilliant-cut glass, these designs are plain, traditional, and vary little from earlier periods. It is not clear if the molded tumblers are pressed or blown-molded. Also shown in the lower right corner are three castor and cruet bottles decorated by cutting (Courtesy of The British Library, London; digital image by George van der Vlugt.)

NEEDLE ETCHING BY TEMPLATE

In 1861, Northwood developed a template machine for tracing patterns through the resist, which made it possible to produce complex patterns of great delicacy, comparable to engraving (Figure 56) (Morris 1978:116, 118; Hajdamach 1991:179-182).

NEEDLE ETCHING BY LATHE

In the mid 1860s, Northwood developed a geometric etching machine for incising a design through the resist (Hajdamach 1991:182-184). The apparatus resembled a lathe and was capable of producing repeating patterns, such as a Greek key design or a continuous band of overlapping circles (Figure 57) (Boston & Sandwich Glass Co. 1992:Plate 27). A host of repeating patterns

followed and were still in production in the 1930s. This type of decoration was particularly suited for thinly blown glassware popular from the 1870s into the 1930s, and is often found in conjunction with optic molding (Figure 94, *bottom left*).

PLATE ETCHING

Through a complicated process similar to transfer printing on ceramics, the resist was put on paper and transferred to the glass, leaving the pattern open. The rest of the glass was then covered in the resist as well so that the vessel could be dipped in acid. This process was developed in the 1850s (Hajdamach 1991:196-197). A simpler process, in which the acid pattern was put on paper and then applied to the glass, was developed in the 1870s

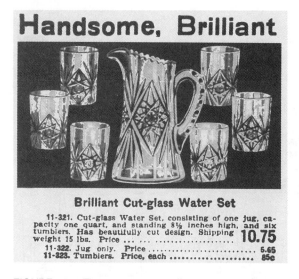

Handsome, Brilliant

Brilliant Cut-glass Water Set

11-321. Cut-glass Water Set, consisting of one jug, capacity one quart, and standing 8½ inches high, and six tumblers. Has beautifully cut design. Shipping weight 15 lbs. Price **10.75**
11-322. Jug only. Price **5.65**
11-323. Tumblers. Price, each **85c**

Sparkling Cut-Glass

Handsome Grape-design Water Set

11-324. Seven-piece Water Set, with a handsome grape design cut on clear blanks. Light-weight tumblers. Set consists of 6 tumblers and 1 jug, capacity 3 pints. Shipping weight 7 lbs. Price **2.50**
11-400. Extra Tumblers, per half-dozen. Price.... **1.00**

FIGURE 45. Three water sets offered by T. Eaton Co. (1918/19:514) showing the difference in price between the brilliant-cut set (**upper left**), which is a comparatively plain pattern, the simple-cut style (**upper right**), and the brilliant-pressed pattern (**right**). The new style of cutting tended to be done on lighter glass, not only cutting costs at the factory and cutting shop, but also shipping costs. The cut grape water set continued for a long time in Eaton's catalogues, being offered intermittently until 1930-31 when the price had fallen to $1.25 per set. The pattern also appeared on individual tumblers, fruit bowl and nappy sets, and decanter or cordial sets. (Reproduced with the kind permission of The T. Eaton Company Limited; digital image by George van der Vlugt.)

7-piece Water Set

11-336. Seven-piece Crystal Glass Water or Lemonade Set; made of extra heavy, clear crystal Glass with an attractive and handsome "Prescut" design. Set consists of 1-qt. jug and 6 tumblers. Shipping weight 12 lbs. Price, per set **1.75**

(Hajdamach 1991:197-198). Patterns done by this type of process tended to be pictorial (Figure 58).

Tableware Forms

Glass tableware is part of a whole group of objects of different materials that are used to serve and consume food and beverages. Identifying their function from fragments, therefore is important for archaeologists interested in studying foodways. This section of the guide briefly discusses tableware forms made between 1800 and 1940, and, when appropriate, provides guidance for dating attributes.

Glass tableware was used in a variety of settings. Different meals and occasions, such as breakfast or dinner, afternoon tea or evening tea, formal or informal, required different assemblages (Williams 1985). If the meal were eaten at

home, it may have had a different composition than meals eaten at the workplace, taverns, restaurants, or hotels. As well, social class influenced both the selection of objects and the cost level of the choice:

"Fortunately," replied Monsieur, to whom this aside had been addressed, "the persons who consider Champagne, japonicas, and attar of roses necessaries of life are very well able to provide cut-glass receptacles for them. But isn't it worth one's while to be proud of a country where every artisan's wife has her tumblers, her goblets, her vases, of pressed glass, certainly, but 'as good, to her mind, as cut,' to quote our friend? And don't you think it better that twenty-two thousand dozen pressed tumblers should be sold at ten cents apiece than one-third that number of cut ones at thirty cents, leaving all those who cannot pay the higher

E 9686
GOBLET
Height 5½"
12/- each

E 9686
CHAMPAGNE
Height 4⅜"
10/- each

E 9686
CLARET
Height 4½"
9/- each

E 9686
COCKTAIL
Height 4½"
7/6 each

E 9686
PORT
Height 4"
7/- each

E 9686
SHERRY
Height 4"
7/- each

E 9686
LIQUEUR
Height 3¼"
6/- each

E 9686
FINGER BOWL
Dia 5"
11/6 each

E 9686
½-PINT TUMBLER
Height 3¾"
7/6 each

E 9686
GRAPE FRUIT GLASS
Dia. 4"
9/- each

E 9686
CELERY OR FLOWER VASE
Height 8"
21/- each

E 9686
QUART DECANTER
Height 11½"
90/- pair

E 9686
QUART JUG
Height 6½"
30/- each

FIGURE 46. This type of design, with the bowl bulging out over a constricted base, is reminiscent of Anglo-Irish styles of the 1820s (Figure 74*e*) and is a good example of the top-heavy look in glass which came in with Colonial revival and art deco styles, and which, to a certain extent, still persists. Hillston Crystal produced a variety of 18th- and 19th-century styles as revivals or as reproductions (Hill-Ouston Co. 1936:81). Virtually the same pattern, without the engraving, was produced in pressed glass by Hocking about 1930, and called "Georgian" (Figure 95) (Weatherman 1974:140). (Author's collection; digital image by George van der Vlugt.)

price to drink out of . . ." (Austin 1991:84).

The structure of a meal, such as one with a soup course, followed by one or two meat and vegetable courses and finally a dessert, necessitated the use of different vessels. Until about the middle of the 19th century, it had been customary to place the serving dishes on the table in a balanced and aesthetic manner so that guests served themselves and each other. Beginning about mid-century, however, a new style was introduced into North America, called *service à la russe*, which had the serving dishes placed on a side table and the food carved and brought to the table by servants (Williams 1985:149-155). Flowers, ornaments, vases, or ornamental scenes were placed in the center of the table. Although the method of service changed the location of the serving pieces, it did not necessarily affect their number or variety. At the other end of the scale, individuals or households living a marginal existence may have had little or no glass.

Beverage service also varied from situation to situation, depending on place, the consumers, and the occasion. It was not necessarily associated with the consumption of food or even with a table.

Sets or services of glassware decorated in the same way and with the same motifs were available in the early 19th century (Warren 1981:224-239; Gray and Gray 1987:11-18). Until the middle of the 19th century, sets tended to be confined to things that were used together, such as paired decanters, drinking glasses, cruet sets, dessert glasses, glassware for traveling

FIGURE 47. The engraved motifs of swags, bows, stars, and hanging pendants were typical neoclassical motifs favored by Bohemian engravers of the first half of the 19th century, as was the contrast in texture between the polished leafy branches and flower against the matte surface of the unpolished swag. The three-ring decanter shape, pressed mushroom stopper, lead-glass composition, and ground and polished pontil mark point either to an English origin for the decanter or to an American imitation of an English style. As with all cold-decorating techniques, like cutting and engraving, the decoration could be done anywhere and was not necessarily part of a glass factory operation. Independent cutters and engravers operated in cities such as New York, Philadelphia, and Baltimore, decorating domestic and/or imported glass, or whatever glass their customers wanted (Palmer 1993b, 1993c). Although this decanter is attributed to the American Midwest, as Wilson (1994[1]:197) points out in connection to a similarly engraved celery in lead glass, attributions to specific areas have been based on the presence of glass houses capable of producing this type of ware and on the fact that in the early days of collecting, from the 1920s to the 1950s, objects of this type were being found in certain locations. (Courtesy of The Corning Museum of Glass, Corning, New York.)

FIGURE 48. A group of engraved glasses, attributed to the Pittsburgh area, dating ca. 1815-1840s (Innes 1976:154-164; Spillman 1982:71, 130), from left to right: *Covered sugar bowl* with galleried rim. The bowl is decorated with an engraved berry-and-leaf design; the cover with a leaf-wreath design. *Celery* decorated with a blown-three-mold baroque-style design on the lower body and engraved with daisies and leaves. *Celery* with a ribbed double gather of glass at the base of the bowl, and above it, an engraved scene with house, pots of flowers, and birds. Below the scene is a rough band decorated with shallow cut and polished round facets, and beneath that a swag with pendants and stars. *Jug* decorated by 12 contact-molded ribs and an engraved floral/leaf/berry design. The handle is hollow and the pontil mark unground. (Courtesy of The Corning Museum of Glass, Corning, New York.)

chests, and matching bottom plates for butter tubs or finger bowls. When one considers the similarity of cut, engraved, or blown-glassware patterns available in the first half of the 19th century, however, consumers certainly had the choice to purchase different forms in the same or similar patterns if they wished to do so. As the century progressed, larger groups of matching glassware became more common, particularly in pressed glass where as many as 42 different pieces were offered in a single pattern (Figures 23-24) (Jenks and Luna 1990). Although the compositions of the groups sometimes changed over time, forms used together continued to be sold together, including pressed glass "sets" consisting of butter, sugar, creamer and spooner, cruet and castor sets, salt and pepper shakers, beverage sets consisting of a jug and six glasses, decanter sets of a decanter and six glasses, or a large berry bowl with six nappies.

It was not until the late 1920s and 1930s, that the equivalent range of tableware forms found in ceramics was made in glass (Florence 1995a, 1996). During this period, glass manufacturers introduced cups and saucers for hot beverages as well as dinner and salad plates in the same patterns as other glass tableware. Nevertheless, it is clear from catalogues of the period, such as those of T. Eaton Co., that serving pieces did not have to match each other or the drinking glasses or plates. Hostesses could use their prized glassware pieces, perhaps received as wedding gifts, as special embellishment for the table. Another group introduced in the early 20th century (Butler Brothers 1910:407), although not included in this guide, were matched kitchenwares used in the storage and preparation of food, such as pantry jars, measuring cups, and, later, refrigerator dishes and mixing bowls (Florence 1995b), some of which may have ended up on informal dining tables.

Specific dating factors for glass tableware forms are more difficult to develop than for the manufacturing and decorative techniques for a number of reasons. Most glass publications, with the exception of Spillman (1981; 1982), Warren (1981:105-198), Jones and Smith (1985), and Palmer (1993a), are not organized by functional form. Establishing date ranges for specific forms requires one to piece together information from a number of sources–dated examples in the secondary literature, and primary sources in both published literature and in documentary collections. Information found in documents is not straightforward, however. It is frequently impossible to match glassware shapes with those mentioned in unillustrated documents. Nouns and their modifiers vary from one document to another both in the same period and over time. American and British usage varies. It is not clear how closely the names used in documents reflected how consumers used that form. Manufacturers even offered different uses for the same form (Figure 34).

With some exceptions, most tableglass forms made in 1800 were still in production in 1940. Starting in the 1880s, however, a number of specialized shapes were introduced which were seldom entirely new but were rather an adaptation of forms already in production. While some shapes underwent stylistic changes, became static, and then changed again, others remained relatively static for long periods of time. Some shapes, such as plates, were in production throughout the whole period under discussion, but their roles on the dinner table changed. Other forms became more specialized over time. As with the decorative motifs, once a form was introduced, it tended to remain in production although sometimes its use became far more

FIGURE 49. Page from the King, Son & Company catalogue, early 1870s, which shows simple engraving on glassware made in plain pressed patterns such as Mitchell. The motifs are horizontal and some echo the swags, floral sprays, hanging pendants, and bands seen on Bohemian-style engravings of the early 19th century (*Pennsylvania Glassware* 1972:38). (Courtesy of the Juliet K. and Leonard S. Rakow Research Library of The Corning Museum of Glass, Corning, New York.)

FIGURE 50. Blown cruet decorated with cut vertical panels on neck, a small cut facet on top of the handle, a cut starburst on base, and engraved fern pattern on the body. Ferns were a long-lived and popular engraved motif from the 1860s onward, after publication in the late 1850s of John Moore's book on ferns (Morris 1978:82). Sketchy fern motifs like this one show up in catalogues of the 1870s and 1880s (Figure 88). As indicated by the swelling at the base of the handle, it was attached first at its base and then brought up and attached at the neck. This method was introduced in the late 1860s and became the dominant technique by the 1880s (Spillman 1982:79; Hajdamach 1991:274). The earlier method was to attach the upper part of the handle first (Figure 16) and pull it down towards the base. The squat jug style of cruet with handle and globular body was in production by the 1880s (Spillman 1982:190-191) and became the common cruet style in the 20th century. (Photo by Rock Chan, Parks Canada collection.)

restricted, such as with open salts, or its production faded away, such as with the celery vase. In the following discussions, more-detailed dating guides have been offered for stemmed drinking glasses and decanters as these are forms likely to be found in archaeological contexts. Other forms are discussed generally as they are found less frequently.

Bowls, Dishes, and Trays

As a general guide, *bowls* have curved sides, *dishes* have straight sides and are usually shal-

lower than bowls, and *trays* are flat or almost flat (footed examples are called salvers); all three styles were made without a foot, with a foot, with a foot and stem, and with or without a cover. Bowls were made throughout the period but in increasing variety and quantity after the mid-19th century, particularly in pressed glass (Figures 13, 20, 23, 26).

This group of glassware was used primarily for food service, but it also included pieces for individual use. Common throughout the 1800-1940 period was the use of bowls for serving cold food such as salads, vegetables, or different types of desserts. Bread trays, often with wheat themes, were made in the 1870s and 1880s. Celery trays were introduced in the 1890s, and spoon trays, oval pickle dishes, small olive or bonbon dishes (often with a single small round handle), and mayonnaise bowls appeared at about the same time (Figure 59) (Spillman 1982:248-289). A standard offering in 20th-century catalogues was the berry set consisting of a bowl with six matching nappies but the same bowl, without the nappies, was also sold as a salad bowl (Figures 60-61).

Castors, Cruets, and Covered Pots

Serving vessels for condiments included a range of vessels (see Salts). *Cruets* were for

FIGURE 51. Page from early 1870s King, Son & Company Catalogue showing engraved patterns (Figure 49), including sprays and an initial enclosed in a wreath, and "frosted and cut" patterns (bottom half) (*Pennsylvania Glassware* 1972:39). (Courtesy of the Juliet K. and Leonard S. Rakow Research Library of The Corning Museum of Glass, Corning, New York.)

FIGURE 52. Sugar bowl made by Percival Vickers & Co. of Manchester in design registered 7 May 1873 and marketed as St. Petersburg into the 1880s (Slack 1987:161; Yates 1987:35). The bowl was completely pressed and the exterior surface roughed by wheel grinding, as evidenced by horizontal striations left by the wheel visible in the close-up. (Photo by Rock Chan, private collection.)

sugar, cayenne, and were fitted with a perforated top (Figure 49). The exterior upper neck surface was usually ground so that the top could be glued on; later versions had screw threads to accommodate a threaded cover. *Covered pots* were for wet condiments such as mustard, horseradish, and pickles. Specific forms were made for mustards and pickles during the 19th century (Wakefield 1968:50-51; Jones and Smith 1985:69-70, 74-77). In the late 19th and early 20th century, other *specialized forms* were

FIGURE 53. Pressed goblet in Lion Head pattern in which the stem and foot have been acid etched, leaving a frosted surface that is satiny to the touch. Pattern dates to the late 1870s. (Photo by Rock Chan, Parks Canada collection.)

liquids such as oil and vinegar, and prepared sauces, and had a pouring spout, a stopper and ground (or ground and polished) bore, and sometimes a handle (Figures 44, 50). *Castors* were for powdered substances such as pepper,

ILLUSTRATIONS OF SAND BLAST ENGRAVINGS.

FIGURE 54. Sand-blasted designs from a ca. 1900 United States Glass Company catalogue. (Courtesy of the Juliet K. and Leonard S. Rakow Research Library of The Corning Museum of Glass, Corning, New York.)

offered, including a bowl for mayonnaise (Spillman 1981:Bowls), elaborate stands for highly decorated pickle jars, and a small single-handled dish for olives or bonbons. Commercially prepared foods could be placed on the table in their original *bottles or jars*, and by 1900, some silverware firms even offered special holders for things such as Maclaren's Imperial Cheese jars, and Lea and Perrins, Tabasco, or Harvey's Sauce bottles (Rainwater 1973; Langbridge 1975). It was, of course, practical to leave food in its original container, but the commercial package with its label and distinctive look also attested to the quality of the condiments being served.

Although condiment containers were used by themselves, the popular and acceptable way for most of the 19th century was to put them together in a stand made of wood, silver, silver plate, or Britannia metal. After electroplating was introduced in the 1840s, the market for silver-plated cruet stands expanded, and they became standard on middle-class tables. The condiments offered varied, depending on the meal and household, so that stands held different assemblages of containers. Newspaper advertisements, production and sales documents, and numerous patterns in catalogues attest to the popularity of cruet stands and specialized glasses for condiments (M'Kee and Brothers 1981; Wilson 1994[1]:228). In Canadian newspaper advertisements in the mid-19th century, they are mentioned frequently; e.g., "Cruet stands with 3,4,5,6,7 bottles of surpassing elegance, being quite new designs" (*Montreal Gazette* 1867).

Two types of stands were available. The first had a flat base and cage-type holders for straight-sided castors, cruets, and pots (Figures 42, 44). These types were made throughout the 19th century. About 1880, a squat bottle with a globular body and handle was introduced and also put in this type of holder (Figure 50) (Spillman 1982:190-191). This shape became the standard one for oil and vinegar. The second type of stand had the castors, cruets, and pots suspended in a holder, either a flat circular piece with holes for the bottles or an open frame. Containers for this type have a narrow cylindrical lower body and an upper body that swells out over the holder (Figure 49). This type was probably introduced during the mid-19th century as examples are shown in the 1858 catalogue of the Rogers Brothers Mfg. Co. (*Victorian Silverplated Holloware* 1972:34-36). Although early 20th-century catalogues, such as the 1901 Montgomery Ward & Co. catalogue, show elaborate cruet stands, they were on their way out for middle-class households.

During the early 20th century, cruet stands were replaced by smaller sets or by individual dishes, such as salt and pepper shakers, mayonnaise bowls, pickle dishes, pickle jars in elaborate stands, small handled oil and vinegar cruets sometimes in a stand, or salt and pepper shakers with one vinegar or oil cruet in a small handled stand, often made of glass (Butler Brothers 1910:406). For example, T. Eaton Co. (1914-1915:219) advertised a simple stand holding both a vinegar and an oil bottle, and salt and pepper shakers. On the same page were illustrated a stand holding two jam dishes, and an elaborate stand holding a covered pickle jar. Individual pieces or small sets were ideal candidates for presents or wedding gifts so that a relatively modest table might sport one or two more elaborate and expensive condiment dishes.

Celeries

Celeries–substantial footed vases with a tall bowl–were used to serve celery on the table (Figures 18, 23, 48). The first dated evidence for their production appears in 1820, in an

FIGURE 55. Examples of crackled glass offered by Butler Brothers (1929:255) although the method used to achieve the effect is ambiguous as they describe it as "embossed cracked effect" or as "all-over genuine crackled design." (Courtesy of The Fenton Art Glass Company, Williamstown, West Virginia.)

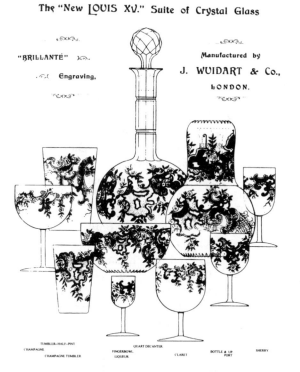

The "New LOUIS XV." Suite of Crystal Glass

"BRILLANTÉ"
Engraving,

Manufactured by
J. WUIDART & Co.,
LONDON.

TUMBLER—HALF-PINT
CHAMPAGNE
CHAMPAGNE TUMBLER
FINGERBOWL
LIQUEUR
QUART DECANTER
CLARET
BOTTLE & UP
PORT
SHERRY

FIGURE 56. Drinking glass set with a needle-etched design, probably using a template, in a rococo revival design called "New Louis XV" (*Pottery Gazette* 1894:before 49). (Courtesy of The British Library, London; digital image by George van der Vlugt.)

advertisement from Virginia which offered celery stands along with a variety of other products (Wilson 1994[1]:173). From that period on, they became standard offerings in advertisements, glassware price lists, and catalogues. For much of the 19th century, growing celery was a labor-intensive task, making it expensive, and its presence on a table was a sign of prestige. Commercially grown, self-blanching celery was available by the 1880s, however, so that its status diminished thereafter (Williams 1985:109-111). Although the tall, footed celery glass was still offered around 1900 and later, it had become old fashioned:

> Why does not some inventive woman give us a pretty celery glass? asks a society writer. The old tall vase is, I am told, 'out of fashion,' and it is now supposed to be more correct to hand it round upon a flat dish, which, from every point of view, is a mistake (*Pottery Gazette* 1893:4).
> Who . . . has not mentally anathematized the old fashioned tall celery glass, from which it is almost impossible to remove one stalk without dragging two

or three more out upon the spotless damask? (Palmer 1993a:270).

Flat dishes for celery were shallow, rectangular or oval (Figure 59) (Higgins & Seiter 1899:27). Vertical celery glasses were still offered, however, without stem and often unfooted, and sometimes with a shorter body, more closely resembling spoon holders (Figure 62). As late as 1936, this later style of "flower or celery vase" was still available (Hill-Ouston Co. 1936:39).

Cups

Small handled cups usually with hemispherical bowls, sometimes footed, were in production throughout the 140-year period discussed in this guide and were used in a variety of ways. The

FIGURE 57. Blown tumbler decorated around the rim with needle-etched pattern typical of the relentless repeats of the lathe-type process and on the lower body by cutting. This glass is thin and light, of a type introduced in the 1870s, but far more pervasive in North American markets between 1900 and into the 1930s, after the introduction of semi-automatic machines. (Photo by Rock Chan, private collection.)

FIGURE 58. Pressed goblet decorated by plate etching. Detailed patterns were possible using this technique. Although the etching has no depth there is a discernible difference in surface texture. (Photo by Rock Chan, Parks Canada collection.)

(Figure 59). Mugs in opaque white or green heat-resistant glass for drinking coffee appeared in the 1930s (Spillman 1982:69).

Decanters

Decanters were produced throughout the 1800-1940 period (Figures 64-69). As temperance became more and more acceptable, however, many households made the choice not to drink liquor, replacing alcohol with tea or cold beverages, such as water or lemonade, for social and family occasions (Williams 1985:134-140). The T. Eaton Co., whose founder Timothy Eaton was a staunch opponent of both alcohol and tobacco, generally did not include decanters in its catalogues although they did sell wine glasses as late as 1908. In the catalogues of the late 1920s and early 1930s, after the repeal of prohibition in Canada, the company sold a set labeled "cordial set" or "decanter set" which consisted of a "Seven-Piece Decanter Set of generous size in the popular cut grape design. Bottle and six glasses for . . . $1.00" (T. Eaton Co. 1930:286). The accompanying tumblers, also sold separately, were "Bell-shaped Optic Tumblers. Strong, fine glass in graceful optic cut grape design. Have smoothly rounded edges. Popular tall, slender shape. Price dozen . . . 84¢" (T. Eaton Co. 1930:286). In comparison, one or more lemonade or water sets, consisting of a jug and a half dozen tumblers, were always included in the catalogue and the design changed regularly. Eaton's customers, from personal experience, included a large clientele which chose to serve their guests tea or cold non-alcoholic drinks. In comparison, the Army and Navy Store catalogue for 1907 offered over two dozen different "table glass services" consisting of decanters, stemware, and finger bowls as well as one and one-half dozen spirits bottle styles, and another two dozen jug styles for drinks such as claret cup, champagne, etc. (Army and Navy Stores 1969:923-924, 936-938). These offerings ranged from plain thicker wares for regimental and naval messes to elaborately cut and engraved wares. It is clear from the glassware offered in this catalogue that their clientele included those who expected formal and elaborate table settings and who served alcohol as a matter of course, a well-established British military tradition (Jones and Smith 1985). Drinking sets,

most common seems to have been for desserts, primarily custard or, by the late 19th century, for sherbet (Figure 63). Cups or small handled mugs were also used for drinking lemonade, and, starting around 1900, were part of punch sets with a large matching bowl. There do not seem to be any obvious differences in the illustrated documents between dessert cups or cups for drinking. In the late 1920s, cups and saucers for hot beverages were introduced

FIGURE 59. Selection of serving pieces from the 1930 Butler Brothers catalogue as well as cups, saucers, and plates for individual service (Butler Brothers 1930:n.p.). (Courtesy of Collins Kirby Art & Antiques, Fort Payne, Alabama.)

with decanter and matching glasses or decanter and matching tumblers, were also offered in American catalogues in the 20th century but in fewer numbers (Figure 38). Only a handful of the late higher-end 1920s and 1930s drinking sets shown in Florence (1995a) had decanters, although a few had cocktail shakers and some had ice buckets. This glassware catered to a middle-class clientele which shopped in department and gift stores and might be expected to use decanters. On the other hand, all the traditional drinking sets (Figure 46) in the English 1936 Hill-Ouston Co. catalogue had decanters, although cocktail sets in trendier designs (Figure 69) were also featured in the catalogue. Cocktail shakers, with a wide mouth, cover, and pouring lip, were introduced in the 1930s.

From the late 1840s onward, *pressed decanters* were made for both domestic and commercial use including those made with bar lips and a

specialized stopper suitable for pouring (Figure 18, caption for decanter). Most bar-lipped decanters are associated with the geometric-style patterns which came in during the late 1840s and early 1850s. Without a pouring stopper of some type, it is very difficult to pour liquid successfully from these vessels. From the 1870s onward, decanters appear in far fewer numbers in the catalogues, if at all, and seem to have been made primarily for use in bars and restaurants. For example, in 1868, M'Kee and Brothers (1981:123-154) offered decanters in ten patterns but only one was shown with a glass stopper, and five had patent cork stoppers with bar lips. In the 1880 catalogue, only one decanter was shown (in the Huber pattern, introduced around 1850) and it is on the same page as bitters and bar bottles, suggesting it was used in the same setting (Stout 1972:85). The Bakewell Pears & Co. Glass Catalogue (1875:10-11) offered four decanters but, again,

FIGURE 60. Berry set offered by T. Eaton Co. (1918-19:514) in the lighter style cutting. The pressed set offered on the same page cost only $1.40. (Reproduced with the kind permission of The T. Eaton Company Limited; digital image by George van der Vlugt.)

these were placed with bitters and bar bottles. In the lists of vessels made in each pressed pattern in Jenks and Luna (1990), decanters are seldom mentioned but when they are, the patterns were introduced prior to 1870. Virtually none of the pressed-pattern sets made in the late 1920s and 1930s included decanters (Florence 1996).

Bar bottles appear to have been intended for use in commercial settings like bars and restaurants. They had tall bodies, with short necks, sometimes with bar lips and patented cork stoppers or sometimes with flanged lips and glass stoppers. Later examples were shaped more like bottles (Figure 68). Some catalogues show them with names such as Brandy or Whiskey cut or engraved on them, but most appear to have been plain. *Bitters bottles* were in production at least as early as the 1850s (Figure 22) and continued into the 20th century. They tend to be smaller than bar bottles because they contained strong flavorings such as peppermint, ginger, or bitters.

Comprehensive glassware drinking sets included different stemware shapes and sizes

FIGURE 61. Selection of berry bowls from the 1930 Butler Brothers catalogue in which older, heavily patterned pressed styles predominate, in contrast to the more modern designs offered in water and beverage sets (Figure 14) (Butler Brothers 1930:n.p.). Two new colors (pink and emerald green) join colorless and iridescent glass which were the only choices offered by the company in their 1925 catalogue. (Courtesy of Collins Kirby Art & Antiques, Fort Payne, Alabama.)

Spoon Holders and Celery Glasses

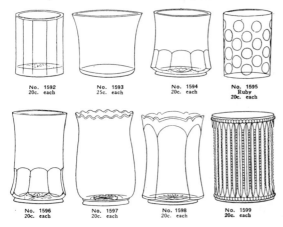

FIGURE 62. Shorter spoon holders and taller celery glasses from the Budde & Westerman (1913:45) hotel wares catalogue. In the 20th century celery glasses tended to be made without the stem and foot found on 19th-century examples. (Courtesy of George Miller.)

for different beverages, tumblers, finger bowls, water bottles or carafes, and sometimes matching tumblers set upside down over the top of the bottle (Figure 56), and sometimes narrow-mouthed "claret" jugs or wide-mouthed jugs for hard liquor.

The implications of finding decanters on sites need to be considered in both temporal and cultural contexts. Decanters are storage and serving containers, not commercial packages, thus they represent a level of service above the minimum, particularly during the 1800-1940 period when bottled wines, beers, and distilled liquors were commonplace. As the 19th century progressed, decanters represented an increasing level of formal service in either domestic or public settings, or, at least, a continuing level of service at certain strata of society. Depending on the time period and context, decanters may represent a masculine setting, such as a club, or army or navy mess, or may reflect different ethnic or socio-economic groups. Judging by the early-20th-century documentary evidence, Britons may have been more inclined to use decanters than either Americans or native-born Canadians. The decreasing presence of decanters in pressed glass, in comparison with the host of examples offered in cut, engraved, or acid-etched styles, suggests that, by the end of the 19th century, they were not used by lower-income groups. Finally, families and groups who did not drink

FIGURE 63. Handled sherbet cups from Butler Brothers (1914:319); footed sherbets without handles were also offered. (Courtesy of the Juliet K. and Leonard S. Rakow Research Library of The Corning Museum of Glass, Corning, New York.)

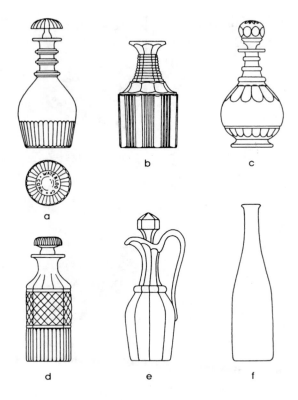

FIGURE 64. Examples of decanter styles, 1800 to ca. 1850: **a,** classic Anglo-Irish decanter shape between 1800 to 1840s. It is characterized by a pronounced flanged lip, tapered body, three applied and tooled neck rings, and came with a mushroom, lozenge, or target stopper. It may be undecorated or decorated by cutting, engraving, and contact molding. This example is decorated by contact-molded ribs on the lower body and base, on which is molded the words "Waterloo Co. Cork," one of many Irish glasshouse products marked in this way (Warren 1981:54-55, 71-98). This company was in business between 1815 and 1835. In British and American factories the shape continued in production after the mid century but the rings had basically disappeared by the 1850s (Figure 65**f**). The form with neck rings continued to be made, however, in Swedish and Danish glass factories after 1850 (Buchwald and Schlüter 1975:37-116 [16-18]; based on Warren 1981:91); **b,** by the mid to late 1820s, decanters with more cylindrical bodies were available as were examples without neck rings. This decanter illustrates the shape suited to the vertical broad-flute cutting style introduced in the late 1820s. The body is decorated with cut ribs alternating with ribs decorated with flutes. The decoration, however, still retains the elements of earlier horizontal bands on the shoulder and neck. Illustration based on WHR drawings discussed in Wolfenden (1987:22). Real example shown in Wakefield (1982:30); **c,** American style consisting of globe-shaped body on a foot, with or without the three applied neck rings, made undecorated, or with contact molded, cut and/or engraved decorations. This style was illustrated in several American newspaper advertisements between 1823 and 1831 (Innes 1976:139; Palmer 1993a:138; Wilson 1994[1]:176) and is considered to date ca. 1815 to 1840s. Without the neck rings, slenderized versions of the footed spherical body were made in the mid-19th century (Wakefield 1982:40; Hajdamach 1991:134). Based on Wilson (1994[1]:199); **d,** squared decanters decorated by engraving or cutting, or blown in plain or patterned contact molds were made for liquor stands and for cases or traveling trunks. Those for cases and trunks were usually decorated on the shoulder. Square decanters are very conservative forms and can still be found in late-19th-century catalogues. Based on mold-blown decanter in McKearin and McKearin (1948:252, GII-28, Plate 10, 264-265); **e,** claret decanter decorated with cut panels from base to lip in the broad flute style which dates from the late 1820s onwards. Claret decanters with taller, narrower bodies, tall narrow necks, pouring lips, and handles became a fixture in glass production from the 1840s onwards. This example is based on one in Pellatt's 1840 catalogue (Wakefield 1968:51; Warren 1984:122); **f,** tall narrow decanter dating from the 1840s onward. Dated examples in the literature are colorful and decorated in many different ways. Based on yellow opaline example decorated with transfer print in Hajdamach (1991:104). (Drawings by Dorothea Larsen.)

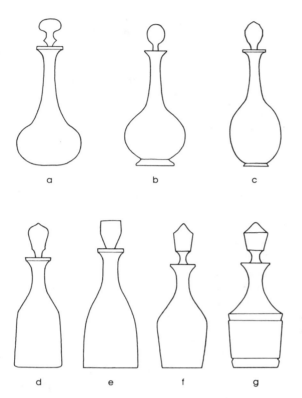

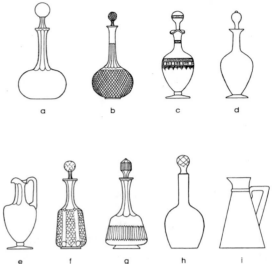

FIGURE 65. Examples of decanter styles ca. 1850-1870: **a,** decanters with long necks and spherical bodies continued in production from ca. 1850 into the 20th century (Figure 67). They often had vertical cut panels on the neck which emphasized the squatness of the body. Based on a decanter exhibited at the 1851 exhibition *(The Art-Journal* 1851:175); **b,** similar in style to a but with an applied foot. Based on a decanter made in London for the Viceroy of Egypt, 1854-1863 (Warren 1984:131); **c,** long-necked decanter with an ovoid body and applied foot (The Art-Journal 1851:175); **d,** decanter with body sloping outward towards the base, based on a decanter made in England about 1850 (Morris 1978:28); **e,** a pressed version of d with a less-defined neck as it curves into the long sloping shoulder; based on an illustration in the 1861 James B. Lyon & Company catalogue (Innes 1976:345); **f,** pressed decanter with body widening towards the shoulder. This form was in style from the early 19th century and continued in production at least as late as 1869 (based on Watkins 1970:158; Spillman 1997:95); **g,** pressed decanter with body widening towards the shoulder and an abrupt body and shoulder junction. This variant of **f** was introduced in the late 1840s (based on Watkins 1970:153; Spillman 1997:79). (Drawings by Dorothea Larsen.)

FIGURE 66. Examples of decanter styles 1870-1890: **a,** the long-necked decanter with globular body continued to be produced during this period and appears to have been the commonest shape. Decorated with cut panels, a subdued and slightly everted lip, and a globe-shaped stopper. This shape was also made as a claret jug, with a high handle and pouring spout. Based on Smart Brothers (1885:3); **b,** similar to a but with a foot. Based on M. Davis and Co. advertisement in Pottery Gazette (1881); **c,** shapes derivative of Greek pottery shapes, such as this one, were first introduced in the late 1840s and many examples were shown at the 1851 exhibition (Wakefield 1982:68). The decanter has an egg-shaped body, the characteristic trifoil lip, a cushion knop separating the body and foot, and a globe stopper. Based on Smart Brothers (1885:3); **d,** similar to c but without the cushion knop and with a plain everted lip. Based on Smart Brothers (1885:3); **e,** claret jug with handle and pouring lip imitating another Greek pottery shape. This style can be found with or without the cushion knop separating the body and foot. Based on Smart Brothers (1885:3); **f,** body widens from shoulder to base, the lower body curves in towards the foot, although on other examples in the catalogue the angle is much more abrupt. Based on Smart Brothers (1885:3); **g,** A squatter version of **f** and a style which appears to start in the 1880s. This example has a different stopper style, one which reflects the body shape. Based on Smart Brothers (1885:4); **h,** Not all decanters had an everted lip. In this example the lip is simply left flat on top. Based on example in the ca. 1874 Boston & Sandwich Glass Co. catalogue (1992:Plate 37); **i,** decanters with this straight tapered body were often decorated with vertical trails of glass. The shape was apparently introduced in the Stourbridge area in the early 1870s and continued in production until the end of the century (Wakefield 1982:117-118). Based on Smart Brothers (1885:5). (Drawings by Dorothea Larsen.)

alcohol had little need of decanters. It appears that North American glass manufacturers and retailers had already responded to changing drinking patterns before the advent of prohibition in 1919.

Figures 64-69 are guides only to changing decanter styles, particularly after the middle of the 19th century when innovations in decoration became commonplace. It is clear that a strong conservative element resulted in the production of some decanter styles for over 60 years.

Dessert Glasses

Dessert glasses encompass a number of forms for individual service: small handled custard or sherbet cups (Figure 63), jelly glasses (Figure 42), small bowls or nappies, plates, and footed sherbets or sundaes (Figure 70). Serving pieces include large bowls and salvers (see Bowls), and plates (Figure 59).

Finger Bowls and Wine Glass Rinsers

There is some confusion as to how finger bowls and wine glass rinsers were used at the table. It is clear from English glass manufacturers' documents of the first half of the 19th century that they thought of finger bowls and wine glass rinsers as different. In his 1840 catalogue, Pellatt, for example, illustrated three styles of "finger-cups" but noted that the price for monteiths or wine coolers was an additional 10% (Wakefield 1968:51). In period illustrations and commentaries, however, the finger bowl style was also being used as a wine glass rinser.

These bowls held water which was used in three ways (Warren 1981:244-245; Lole 1993:2-4). According to some observers, it was a custom in England, dating from the mid to late 18th century, to rinse out one's mouth at the table using the water in the bowl and then spitting it back into the bowl. A second use was to rinse one's fingers before dessert was served. The third use was to rinse or cool a wine glass in the water. The latter use is one often seen in period illustrations where wine glasses are upended in bowls of water (Jones and Smith 1985:55-57). This practice continued at least into the early 1860s, as a photograph in the National Archives in Ottawa shows a table set at the governor's house in Halifax with each

place setting provided with a water bottle and tumbler turned upside down over it, two wine glasses (one colored), and a third resting in a bowl. During the second half of the 19th century, however, the only usage which remained was to rinse fingers, although even as late as 1865, an American etiquette guide still felt it necessary to caution diners not to rinse out their mouths (Williams 1985:41-42). Etiquette books suggest that the finger bowl be presented on a doily on a plate before the dessert course (Fenwick 1948:279). By the late 19th century and into the 20th century, their presence on a table suggests the presence of either servants or waiters.

The first style of bowl, generally considered wine-glass rinsers, is essentially a cylinder about 4 in. (10 cm) high and 4 in. (10 cm) in diameter. Some have one or two pouring lips or notches (Spillman 1982:272) which were used to support the stem of one or two wine glasses. Examples of this style in both glass and faience have been found on mid-18th-century French colonial sites in Canada. Both historic illustrations and documents make it clear they were intended to be used as wine glass rinsers or coolers. It is possible that the practice of rinsing or cooling wine glasses originated in France and was adopted in England during the 18th century. This style disappeared sometime during the first half of the 19th century.

The second bowl style, generally considered finger bowls, was a hemispherical bowl about 3 to $3\frac{1}{2}$ in. (7.5 to 9 cm) high with a rim diameter of about 5 in. (13 cm). Period price lists often offer finger bowls in colored glass, and several examples found in early-19th-century contexts in Canada are in colorless, blue, or green glass. Finger bowls matched other tableware pieces (Figures 34, 56) (Weatherman 1974:278-279). By the early 20th century, finger bowls were about $\frac{1}{2}$ in. (1.3 cm) shallower.

Pitchers, Jugs, and Beverage Sets

Pitchers and jugs were used to serve milk (see Sets), water, cider, beer, wines, and other alcoholic beverages. The two terms seem to have been used interchangeably. Their use increased dramatically in the 19th century and by the early 20th century, pitchers and jugs appear to have become the dominant form

CUT GLASS DECANTERS   CUT GLASS DECANTERS

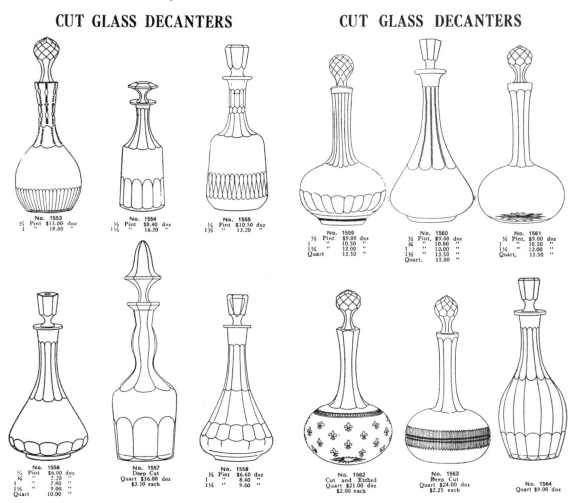

FIGURE 67. Decanters illustrated in Budde & Westerman (1913:39-40) showing the long-lived nature of some decanter shapes and decoration. (Courtesy of George Miller.)

for serving beverages. Water, lemonade, and other non-alcoholic beverages had replaced alcoholic beverages in many homes and public settings, and manufacturers and retailers responded by offering the water, lemonade, or beverage set, consisting of a half-gallon pitcher and six glasses, and sometimes a tray. These sets were decorated in an astonishing array of patterns and decorative techniques (Figures 1, 14, 38, 45) and were obviously comparable in both status and use to ceramic tewares. Guests who might not expect a meal would certainly expect to be offered a drink and perhaps a little snack.

Plates

Although glass plates were made from the 18th century onward, they were not common and, at least in the first half of the century, tended to be used as under-plates for butter tubs (Figure 42) or covered pickles, or as "ice plates" for serving ices, a popular dessert. In the 1830-1860 period, pressed-glass plates, called toddy plates by collectors, were made in 5 and 6 in. (13 and 15 cm) sizes, but their precise use is not clear. A common pressed or blown plate that was made between the late 1820s and

FLINT GLASS WORKING BOTTLES

(Capacity 26-28 oz.)

FIGURE 68. Examples of bar bottles in Budde & Westerman (1913:42). (Courtesy of George Miller.)

about 1860, was the *cup plate* for which more than 800 pressed patterns have been identified (Figure 20) (Wilson 1994[1]:274-275). Between 3 and 4 in. (7.5 and 10 cm) in diameter, cup plates held the cup while a person sipped tea from the saucer (Spillman 1971:128-133). Visitors to the United States often commented on this habit. In comparison to the large number of shallow bowls or dishes, the ca. 1874 catalogue of the Boston & Sandwich Glass Company (1992:Plates 5, 19, 21, 24, 31, 37, 39) offered very few plates. These included plates for serving ice cream, those with a domed cover for serving cheese or butter, and under-plates for cracker jars and butter tubs. Plates in pressed

patterns from the 1870s onward tended to be serving plates. In the late 1920s, however, individual eating plates were introduced in a full range of sizes, including ones divided into three sections (Figure 59). Also introduced during this period were serving plates with central handles which were either molded in the glass or made of metal and detachable (Spillman 1982:Nos. 212, 217, 218, 219).

Salts and Salt Shakers

Small open dishes for salt are one of the commoner tableware forms recovered from archaeological sites, at least until the 1870s (Figures 71-72). Some salts were made in the same patterns as other tableware pieces; others were made in distinctive patterns. Smaller individual salts began to appear in the catalogues in the 1860s. As salt and pepper shaker combinations became more common in the 1880s, larger open salts disappeared but individual salts, or "salt dips," continued to be offered, primarily in catalogues selling cut glass. They became the sign of formal service instead of everyday service. Salts were not traditionally part of the cruet or castor set, although pepper castors (or dusters) were. Salt shakers began to be made in the late 1850s, and by the 1880s, salt and pepper shaker sets had become common in both utilitarian pressed or blown glass and in expensively decorated pairs suitable for gifts.

Peterson (1970:50) outlined the steps which led to successful salt shakers and their common use: (1) molded screw threads for the finish, beginning in the late 1850s and early 1860s, which made it easier to keep salt away from the metal top; (2) mechanical devices to keep salt from caking and to facilitate the flow of salt, beginning in the late 1850s; (3) altering the nature of salt to keep salt from caking, beginning in the 1880s; and (4) changing the metals used in tops to ones less subject to corrosion.

Sets (Creamer, Sugar Bowl, Butter Dish, Spoon Holder)

Pressed "sets" are illustrated in many catalogues and consist of a *cream jug*, *sugar bowl*, *butter dish*, and *spoon holder* (Figure 71). The butter dish was often referred to as a covered

(text continues on p. 224)

8508	**7447**	**8257**	

8659 DECORATED COCKTAIL SHAKER	Height 8⅜"	**14/6** each
8508 ,, ,, GLASS	4"	**42/-** doz.
7447 ,, ,, ,,	3⅛"	**42/-** ,,
8257 ,, ,, ,,	4⅛"	**42/-** ,,

Plain Gilt-edged Tray for above. Dia. 10½" **6/6** each

8689
8-PIECE COCKTAIL SET
Coloured " Horse-Racing " Decoration

Glasses	Height 3½"	**6/-** each
Shaker	9½"	**21/-** ,,
Gilt-edged Tray	Dia. 10½"	**13/-** ,,

70/- per 8-piece Set

9275
8-PIECE SHERRY SET
Jade Green and Platinum Decoration

Decanter	Height 9¼"	**19/-** each
Tray	Dia. 11¼"	**17/-** ,,
Glasses	Height 3¾"	**4/-** ,,

60/- per 8-piece Set

9276
8-PIECE JADE GREEN AND PLATINUM LIQUEUR SET
to match
50/- per 8-piece Set

E 9241
ENGLISH CUT CRYSTAL 7-PIECE SHERRY SET

Decanter	Height 11¼"	**30/-** each
Glasses	3½"	**4/6** ,,

57/- per 7-piece Set

E9241
ENGLISH CUT CRYSTAL 7-PIECE LIQUEUR SET

Decanter	Height 9¼"	**21/-** each
Glasses	2¾"	**4/-** ,,

45/- per 7-piece Set
Matching Suite E9241 Page 75

FIGURE 69. Examples of cocktail and wine sets from Hill-Ouston (1936:105). Three of the sets are decorated with enameling and the cut set is an imitation of cut patterns of the second quarter of the 19th century (Figure 41). (Author's collection; digital image by George van der Vlugt.)

FIGURE 70. Examples of footed sherbets from Butler Brothers (1929:253). In this catalogue the sherbets are closer in style and decoration to the beverage glasses and sets than they are to berry bowls. In the 1930 catalogue (Figure 82) they are placed with other stemware. One possible explanation is that food was brought to the table already in sherbet dishes, whereas with berry bowl sets, food was presented first in the large bowl and served into individual bowls at the table. Although individual footed nappies or footed jellies were available as early as the 1870s (*Pennsylvania Glassware* 1972:35) it was not until the 20th century that the form became dominant and offered in such wide variety. (Courtesy of The Fenton Art Glass Company, Williamstown, West Virginia.)

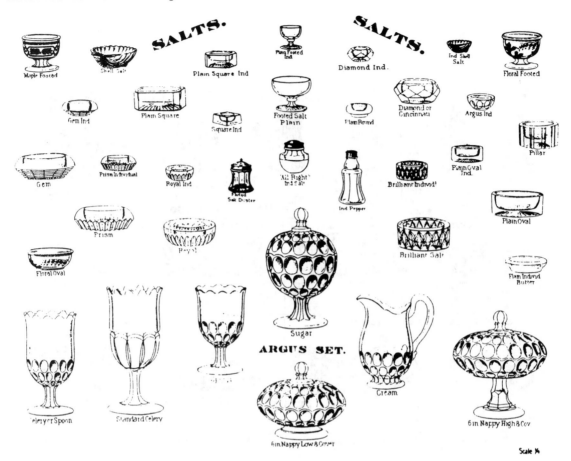

FIGURE 71. Selection of salts from the early 1870s King, Son & Company Catalogue (*Pennsylvania Glassware* 1972:29). Note the presence of "master salts" which were shared between diners, individual salts, salt dusters, and an individual pepper which matches neither of the salt dusters. Maple and Floral patterns were part of large tableware sets. (Courtesy of the Juliet K. and Leonard S. Rakow Research Library of The Corning

FIGURE 72. Salt and pepper shakers offered in the 1930 Butler Brothers catalogue showing both utilitarian sets in Colonial pattern and more decorative ones. Toothpick holders were introduced in the 1880s. (Courtesy of Collins Kirby Art & Antiques, Fort Payne, Alabama.)

FIGURE 73. Cream and sugar sets from Butler Brothers 1930 catalogue offered a mix of modern and older styles. By this time the paired cream and sugar were commoner than the four-piece sets including the butter and spooner, although one is still offered here in the center of the bottom row. Top right shows "new modernistic colonial design" with strong art deco elements including the inverse-shaped conical body with largest diameter at the rim, squared handles, and the squared motif. Although the look is more strongly associated with art deco, inverse cone-shaped bowls placed directly on the foot appear as early as 1916 in the Bryce Brothers' (1916:246) catalogue. (Courtesy of Collins Kirby Art & Antiques, Fort Payne, Alabama.)

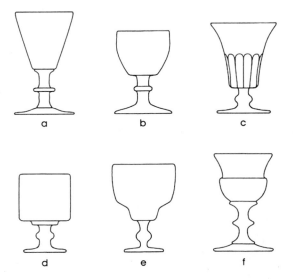

FIGURE 75. Drawn stemware styles, late 1770s to 1840s. The stem was generally drawn out from the bowl and attached to the foot. In contrast to earlier 18th-century drawn stems, this group is short, ranging from 9.5-12.0 cm ($3\frac{3}{4}$- $4\frac{3}{4}$) in height: *a,* plain drawn stem with conical bowl, decorated by vertical cut panels, a type of decoration done from the 1780s onward (Jones and Smith 1985:39, 46). Based on Apsley Pellatt's 1840 catalogue (Wakefield 1968:52); *b,* plain stem, cup-shaped bowl, unfinished pontil mark, folded foot. Folded feet, with the edge of the foot folded under, were called "welted" in price lists, and were still being offered as late as 1832 (Sullivan 1985). Based on example in Wilson (1994[1]:187, No. 162) dated ca. 1815-1830; *c,* drawn stem with knop, conical bowl, decorated by pattern-molded panels (Figure 10). This is one of the newer stemware styles included in the 1840 Pellatt catalogue. Based on glasses in private collections and archaeological examples. (Drawing by D. Larsen.)

FIGURE 74. Centrally knopped stemware styles, ca. 1780-1840s. Called "button" stem in the documents, the style occurs with V-shaped, bladed or rounded knops, with or without a step at the foot, with or without a collar (or merese) under the bowl, and with different bowl shapes: *a-b,* bucket; *c,* bell; *d,* cylindrical; *e,* ogee; *f,* thistle. The bowls were decorated by cutting, usually panels, pattern-molding, contact-molding, engraving, and enameling. Although the basic style is simple, the different combinations of shape and decoration make it a complex group. It is not clear how datable the different combinations are. The picture is complicated by the fact that European glassmakers continued to make this type of stemmed drinking glass into the second half of the 19th century, generally in non-lead glass, and that it may never have entirely died out in English production (Figure 44) before revivals of the style were introduced in the 20th century (Spillman 1982:Nos. 8-9). Detailed descriptions: *a,* bucket-shaped bowl with engraved crest for the 13th Regiment of Foot who were stationed in Canada during the War of 1812-1814 (Jones and Smith 1985:114). Collar under the bowl, step at the stem, and ground and polished pontil mark. Height 11.0 cm ($4\frac{1}{2}$ in.) (Parks Canada collection); *b,* incurved bucket with no collar or step, unfinished pontil mark. Height 8.5 cm ($3\frac{1}{2}$ in.) (Parks Canada collection); *c-e,* based on Samuel Miller Waterford Glass House Patterns, dated ca. 1820-1830 (Warren 1970:41-42, 48). Several of the designs offered by this factory included star cuts on the base; *f,* the thistle shape is achieved by a double gather of glass on the lower part of the bowl and a strong outward curve on the upper part. The bowl resembles classical urns and is found on other glassware items such as jellies (Figure 42, nos. 16, 21) and celery vases (Figure 48) which date ca. 1830 to 1840s. Step and collar are present, pontil mark is unfinished. Height 10.0 cm (4 in.) (Parks Canada collection; drawing by D. Larsen.)

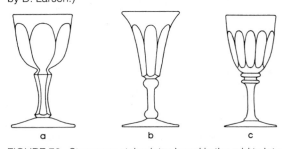

FIGURE 76. Stemware styles introduced in the mid to late 1830s. The point of interest on these stems has shifted from the center to below the bowl and at the foot. Although Hajdamach (1991:47-48) and Spillman (1989:39) suggest these styles were in production in the late 1820s, other evidence supports a late 1830s introductory date. For example, dated English price lists for 1829 and 1832 offer only button stems and plain stems and Irish factory drawings thought to date to the 1820s (Warren 1981:43-51) do not show this style. However, *b* resembles one style in the 1840 Pellatt catalogue and *a* reflects the long flute cuts going from foot to bowl also included there. Both *a* and *b* resemble stems styles from a Manchester factory catalogue hand dated to 1846 (Yates 1987:32, 39). All three drawings are based on examples in a Webb Richardson pattern book thought by Hajdamach (1991:47) to date between 1829 and mid 1830s, but which probably dates no earlier than the mid to late 1830s: *a,* curved stem which swells out under bowl and above foot. Vertical cut panels on the stem, going up onto the lower part of the bowl in the broad flute style of cutting; *b,* straight stem with knops at bowl and stem junction. Cut panels on bowl; *c,* straight stem with collar and knop under bowl and slight step at foot. Cut oval-shaped panels on bowl. (Drawing by D. Larsen.)

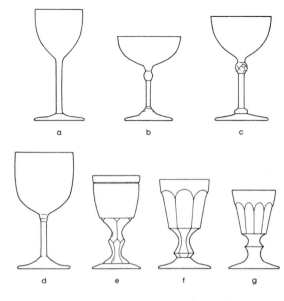

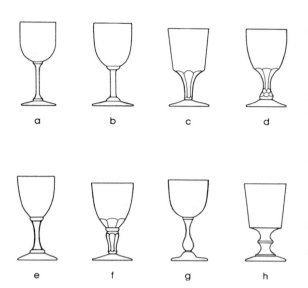

FIGURE 77. Examples of stemware styles 1850-1870: **a,** thin straight stem with rather flat foot and oval bowl. Profile of a wine glass accessioned at the Conservatoire National des Arts et Metiers in Paris in 1851, made by Apsley Pellatt's firm in London (based on Warren 1984:128, Figure 15); **b,** champagne glass characterized by an open shallow bowl, a style introduced about the middle of the 19th century and still associated with champagne. Profile of a glass given by Pellatt and Company to the Royal Scottish Museum in Edinburgh in 1864 (based on Warren 1984:128-129, Figure 17**d**); **c,** oval bowl on a thin straight stem with a knop near the bowl (and decorated by cut facets) and pronounced step at the base of the stem. The foot is relatively flat. Part of the same group as **b** (based on Warren 1984:129, Figure 17e); **d,** cylindrical bowl with curved bottom and a thin straight stem with a step at the foot. Part of the same group as b (based on Warren 1984:130, Figure 18**c**); **e,** stem is decorated by pressed vertical flutes which break at the central knop to form a serrated pattern. American pressed stemware of all types often has the knopped stem decorated in this way or with hexagonal facets. Based on Sharp Diamond pattern champagne glass made by the Boston & Sandwich Glass Company and shown in their 1868-1869 catalogue (Watkins 1970:153; Spillman 1997:79); **f,** bucket-shaped bowls continued in production in this period but definitely had lost their dominant position. Even in pressed glass, stems in this period had knops or swellings lower on the stem or near the bowl. Shown in the same catalogue as **e** (Watkins 1970:160, Figure 12; Spillman 1997:94); **g,** pressed New-Orleans-pattern cordial glass, one of the last remnants of the centrally knopped stems with bucket bowls so common during the first half of the 19th century. Shown in the same catalogue as e (Watkins 1970:160, Figure 12; Spillman 1997:94). (Drawings by Dorothea Larsen).

FIGURE 78. Examples of stemware styles 1870-1890. Not shown in this group is the hollow-stemmed champagne glass with saucer bowl which was introduced in the mid 1870s (Innes 1976:352; Boston & Sandwich Glass Company 1992:Plates 27, 37): **a,** stem is straight and thin with a collar under the bowl that in many illustrated examples is quite thin and sharp and with a step at the base of the stem (Figure 44) (based on *Pottery Gazette* 1881:817); **b,** stem is slightly thicker than the previous example, the collar and step correspondingly larger and rounded (Figure 44) *(Pottery Gazette* 1881:817); **c,** relatively straight stem that widens considerably under the bowl. Whether cut or pressed, the panels on the stem go just onto the base of the bowl, making a kind of base for the bowl to rise from. This is in contrast to the earlier styles where the panels extended onto the bowl, sometimes as much as three quarters of the way up (based on King, Son & Company catalogue dated early 1870s [Pennsylvania Glassware 1972:38]); **d,** similar to **c** this glass has a swelling, a pronounced step at the base of the stem, which could be decorated. The stem profile is curved rather than straight (based on King, Son & Company catalogue dated early 1870s [Pennsylvania Glassware 1972:38]); **e,** a common style for this period was the curved stem sometimes ending with a collar and/or step (Figure 44) *(Pottery Gazette* 1881:817); **f,** the inverted baluster stem was also made during this period, sometimes in a vestigial form (based on King, Son and Company catalogue, dated early 1870s [*Pennsylvania Glassware* 1972:38]); **g,** true baluster stem, with the swelling at the base of the stem, not just a step before the foot, is common in this period. The stem can be plain or decorated with panels or facets. The domed foot is unusual (Figure 44) (*Pottery Gazette* 1881:817); **h,** although examples of the centrally knopped stem with bucket bowl were rare, they were still in production; based on Greek Champagne glass in Bakewell Pears & Co. (1875:8).

Wine Glasses, Etc. *265

775, 28c Doz. C86, 28c Doz. C79, 29c Doz. C83, 29c Doz. C76, 30c Doz. C73, 31c Doz.

	Doz.
C75, **"Diamond" Wine**—Imitation cut pattern...........	30 28
C86, **"Beaded Wine"**—Beaded pattern with plain edge, cut stem...	28
C79, **"Bright" Wine**—For wine and mantel.............	29
C83, **"Popular" Wine**—You can double your money......	29
C76, **"Mirror" Wine**—Dot mirror pattern...............	30
C73, **"Plain" Wine**—Cut stem...........................	31

282, 33c Doz.   C80, 33c Doz.   C87, 35c Doz.   C88, 38c Doz.   C78, 40c Doz.

C82, **"Beaded Panel" Wine**—Brilliant flared top........	33
C80, **"Pressed Band" Wine**—Three mold bands....	33
C87, **"Satin Cut" Wine**—Cut glass pattern, fancy stem, star base...	35
C88, **"Shapely" Wine** — Panel patteen, flaring shape, fancy stem..	38
C78, **"Sherry" Wine**—For wine or toothpick glass	40

C95, 41c Doz.   C81, 41c Doz.   C84, 42c Doz.   C89, 42c Doz.   C366. 80c Doz.

C95, **"Figured Panel" Wine**—Figured and plain panels, fancy stem..	41
C81, **"Cut Pattern" Wine**—Cut stem	41
C84, **"Floral Engraved" Wine**— Regular size....	42
C89, **"Elite" Wine** — Cut panel, fancy stem...	42
C366, **"Reflector Wine Glass"**— Burnished gold band.............	80
C85, **"Gold Prism" Wine** — Gold lines and panels.	80
C367, **"Gold Band" Cut Pattern Wine**—Imitation cut stem and ½-in. band of 18 karat gold top	80

C85, 80c Doz.   C367, 80c Doz.

Cup Foot Wine Glasses. *254

C90, 39c Doz.   C91, 39c Doz.   C92, 41c Doz.   C94, 42c Doz.   C77, 43c Doz.   C93, 43c Doz.

C90, **"Engraved Band"**—One wide and two narrow engraved bands..................	39
C91, **Cut Stem Cordial Glass**—Plain. imitation cut stem. cup foot.......................................	39
C92, **Cut Stem Wine Glass**—Medium size, plain. fancy stem...	41
C94, **Plain Wine Glass**—Unique stem.............	42
C77, **"Banded Wine"**:—Cup foot. seamless banded wine.	43
C93, **"Hoffman House" Wine Glass**—Low shape. plain, slender stem, cup foot................................	43

Assortment of Wine Glasses. *243

C641, 29c Doz.   C640, 30c Doz.

C641, **"Staple" Wine Glass**—1 doz. each of four patterns: colonial flute, bead panel, plain and flute and pressed band. Total 4 doz. in box, no charge for box .	29
C640, **"Fancy" Wine Glass**— Rich cut patterns, finished and fire polished. 1 doz. each of 4 patterns. 4 doz. in wood case, no charge for case...........................	30

FIGURE 79.   Pressed wine glasses offered by Butler Brothers (1902:124). (Courtesy of the Juliet K. and Leonard S. Rakow Research Library of The Corning Museum of Glass, Corning, New York.)

PORT AND SHERRY WINE GLASSES
Fine French and Bohemian Cut and Plain

No. 1156	No. 1157	No. 1158	No. 1159	No. 1160	No. 1161
1¼ oz	1¾ oz	1½ oz	1½ oz	1¾ oz	1¾ oz
$2.75 doz	$3.50 doz	$2.75 doz	$2.50 doz	$2.00 doz	$2.00 doz
		2 oz $2.75 doz			

No. 1162	No. 1163	No. 1164	No. 1165	No. 1166	No. 1167
1¾ oz	1¾ oz	2½ oz	2½ oz	1¾ oz	1½ oz
$1.75 doz	$1.30 doz	$2.00 doz	$1.25 doz	$1.25 doz	$1.25 doz
					2 oz $1.25 doz

No. 1168	No. 1169	No. 1170	No. 1171	No. 1172	No. 1173
1¾ oz	1½ oz	1¾ oz	2 oz $1.25 doz	1½ oz	1¾ oz
$1.25 doz	$1.25 doz	$1.25 doz		$1.25 doz	$1.25 doz

Dock Trial Glasses

No. 1174	No. 1175	No. 1176	No. 1177	No. 1178	No. 1179
1¾ oz	2 oz $1.25 doz	2¼ oz	1¾ oz	3¼ oz	5 oz $1.50 doz
$1.25 doz		$1.25 doz	$1.25 doz	$1.25 doz	

Special prices by the gross and original packages.

PORT AND SHERRY WINE GLASSES
Domestic Pressed

No. 1180	No. 1181	No. 1182	No. 1183	No. 1184	No. 1185
1¼ oz 60c. doz	1½ oz 85c. doz	2 oz 75c. doz	1½ oz	2 oz 85c. doz	2 oz 85c. doz
			$1.00 doz		

COCKTAILS AND CREME DE MENTHES
Domestic Pressed

No. 1186	No. 1187	No. 1188	No. 1189	No. 1190
2¼ oz 75c. doz	2¾ oz 75c. doz	2¼ oz 75c. doz	2¼ oz 75c. doz	2¼ oz 75c. doz

No. 1191	No. 1192	No. 1193	No. 1194	No. 1195
2¾ oz 75c. doz	2½ oz 75c. doz	2¼ oz 75c. doz	3 oz 75c. doz	2¼ oz 75c. doz

Imported, Thin Blown

No. 1196	No. 1197	No. 1198	No. 1199	No. 1200
2½ oz	2½ oz	2½ oz	2¾ oz	2½ oz
$1.25 doz	$1.25 doz	$1.25 doz	$1.25 doz	$1.25 doz

Special prices by the gross and original packages.

FIGURE 80. Selection of stemware from 1913 Budde & Westerman catalogue for hotelware. The catalogue illustrates the difference in price between blown, cut, and pressed wares. For example, No. 1159 plain blown cut stem cost $2.50 dozen, No. 1170 plain blown stem cost $1.25 dozen, No. 1183 plain pressed stem cost $1.00 dozen. Many of the stemware styles shown here and in other catalogues of the same period, such as Bryce Brothers (1916), continue to show styles first introduced between ca. 1850 and 1880 (Budde & Westermann 1913:11-12). A shift in styles is beginning to appear, however, in the number of conical, ogee, or trumpet-shaped bowls being offered. The look is more open and echoes 18th- and early-19th-century bowl shapes. (Courtesy of George Miller.)

FIGURE 81. Blown stemware in pink glass, decorated by optic molded panels and lightly cut motif which has been left unpolished. This glass has a large bowl, with the bowl rim diameter of $3\frac{1}{2}$ in. (9 cm) considerably larger than the foot rim diameter of $2\frac{3}{4}$ in. (7mm), and a comparatively long stem. Total height is almost 7 in. (17.2 cm). These proportions are characteristic of stemmed drinking glasses from the 1920s onward. The cut pattern was done by a gang wheel, introduced about 1913, which had a serrated surface so that a single cut could make a petal or leaf.   The resulting pattern–which consists of a group of narrow parallel grooves or, when cut again at right angles, creates crosshatching–is distinctive (Farrar and Spillman 1979:14, 21).   (Photo by Rock Chan; Parks Canada collection.)

FIGURE 82. Selection of stemware offered by Butler Brothers (1929:254). Notable features for the late 1920s and 1930s were the preference for thin glass, large open bowls decorated by different optic molded patterns and then by cutting, acid etching, or gilding. Different dark-colored feet or stems and feet (such as "Tiffin" stemware) were introduced in this period. The stemware offered includes goblets, wines, and sherbets, plus tumblers for iced tea. Stems are thin, plain, and comparatively tall. Several patterns have decorated feet. (Courtesy of Fenton Art Glass Company, Williamstown, West Virginia.)

FIGURE 83. Heavy goblet with molded stem applied to bowl and foot, neither of which have mold lines. No pontil mark, lead glass. Total height is 5 in. (12.5 cm). Probably English, mid-19th century (Morris 1978:108, 111). (Photo by Rock Chan, Parks Canada collection.)

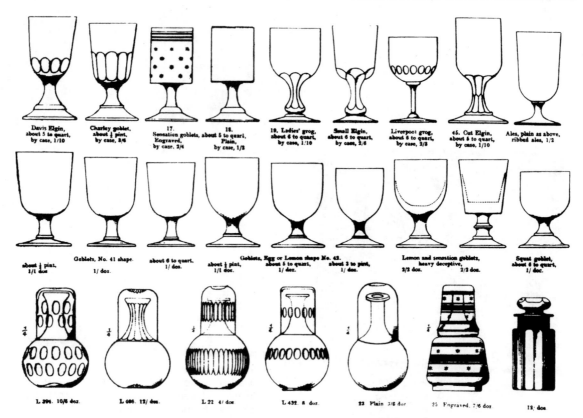

| Davis Elgin, about 5 to quart, by case, 1/10 | Charley goblet, about ½ pint, by case, 2/6 | 17. Sensation goblets, about 5 to quart, Engraved, by case, 2/4 | 18. Plain, by case, 1/2 | 19. Ladies' grog, about 5 to quart, by case, 1/10 | Small Elgin, about 6 to quart, by case, 2/6 | Liverpool grog, about 6 to quart, by case, 2/3 | 45. Cut Elgin, about 5 to quart, by case, 1/10 | Ales, plain as above, ribbed ales, 1/2 |

| about ½ pint, 1/1 doz. | Goblets, No. 41 shape. 1/ doz. | about 6 to quart, 1/ doz. | Goblets, Egg or Lemon shape No. 42. about ½ pint, 1/1 doz. about 5 to quart, 1/ doz. | about 3 to pint, 1/ doz. | Lemon and sensation goblets, heavy deceptive, 2/2 doz. 2/2 doz. | Squat goblet, about 6 to quart, 1/ doz. |

| ¼ L 394. 10/6 doz. | ¼ L 406. 12/ doz. | ¼ L 22 4/ doz | ¼ L 432. 8 doz. | ¼ 23 Plain 3/6 doz. | ½ 25 Engraved. 7/6 doz. | ½ 12/ doz. |

FIGURE 84. A selection of goblets and water bottles with their tumblers, called tumble-ups, inverted over the neck. The sizes of the bowls are indicated by how many would be needed to hold a quart of liquid–"about 5 to quart" (*Pottery Gazette* 1881:before 817). (Courtesy of The British Library, London; digital image by George van der Vlugt.)

FIGURE 85. Example of a Bohemian-style tumbler with pattern-molded panels and ribs, and sketchy engraving at the rim. Made of non-lead glass which, when compared with the heaviness of the tumbler in Figure 12, makes this tumbler extremely light. One feature which has been found on mid-18th-century examples excavated from French colonial sites in Canada is the rough grinding around the pontil mark. Tumblers such as this date from the mid 18th century into the early years of the 19th century. (Photo by Rock Chan, private collection.)

2 　　　　　　　　PRICES OF TUMBLERS, per Box of 6 doz. each. (See Plate.)

No.	Description.	Cut. made	Punty.	Flat. bought 6 D.L.	Post.	No.	Description.	Cut. made	Punty.	Flat. bought 6 doz.	Post.
30	Third quart, Huber, hdld., in in bt.	400	--		40	47	Half pint, Cincinnati table, handled,	450		53	
31	Half pint, Gaines, pillar flute,	400			46	48	Gill, Huber,	450		24	
31	Half pt. Gaines, pillar flute, handl'd	450	--	50		48	Gill, Huber, handled,	450		27	
32	Half pint, New Orleans bar,	575		49		49	Third quart, N. E. 9 flute, Heavy,	550		73	
33	Half pint, Astor, plain, large,	550	--	42		50	Half pint, large, Cincinnati, footed,	400		40	
34	Half pt. 8 flute, Heavy, taper bar,	550	--	70		51	Half pint, Cincinnati, footed,	400		54	
35	Half pint, Huber, taper,	550	--	54		52	Half pint, Mioton bar,	550		65	
35	Half pint, Huber, taper, handled,	400	--			53	Half pint, Sage, 6 flute,	550		61	
36	Half pint, Tyrrell Ale, plain,	575		52		54	Third pint, Brooklyn, plain,	400		38	
37	Half pint, plain taper, Heavy,	550		47		54	Third pt. Brooklyn, plain, handled,	450		44	
37	Half pint, plain taper, Punch,	600		36		55	Third pint, Cincinnati table,	500		35	
38	Third pint, Saloon, plain, Heavy,	400	--	41		55	Third pt. Cincinnati table, handled,	450		41	
38	Third pint, Saloon, plain, Punch,	600		30		56	Gill, Cincinnati table,	550		23	
39	Half pint, Mobile bar, Heavy,	550		48		56	Gill, Cincinnati table, handled,	450		26	
40	Pint, Soda, 6 flute, tall, 4 doz. in box,	400	--	94		57	Half pint, Huber, 10 flute,	575		47	
41	Third pint, Philadelphia bar,	400		38		57	Half pint, Huber, 10 flute, handled,				
42	Pint, Astor Julep, 4 doz. in a box,	450		74		58	Third pint, Western bar,	400		43	
43	Third quart, Astor Julep,	475		58		59	Half pint, O'Hara, footed,	400		40	
44	Gill Saloon, plain, Heavy,	700		29		60	Pint, Gauche, 6 flute, large,	450		14	
44	Gill Saloon, plain, handled,	450		33		61	Pint, Gauche, 6 flute,	450		75	
45	Half pint, Water Bottle, per doz.	650		48		62	Half pint, New York table,	500		50	
46	Third pint, Mobile bar, Heavy,	550		50		63	Gill, New York table,	500		22	
47	Half pint, Cincinnati table,	500		47		63	Gill, New York table, handled,	450		25	

JAS. B. LYON & CO. Manufacturers, No. 116 Water Street, PITTSBURGH, PA.

FIGURE 86. Text and accompanying illustrations from the 1861 catalogue of the O'Hara Flint Glass Works in Pittsburgh. The text lists capacity, pattern name, and other distinguishing features such as handled, heavy, table, or bar. Although 63 tumblers are illustrated in the catalogue, most are paneled patterns, along with two hexagonal patterns. Lists such as this one frequently mention bar tumblers, generally heavy and with a thicker base. Handled tumblers or mugs were offered throughout the 140 years covered by this guide. (Courtesy of the Juliet K. and Leonard S. Rakow Research Library of The Corning Museum of Glass, Corning, New York.)

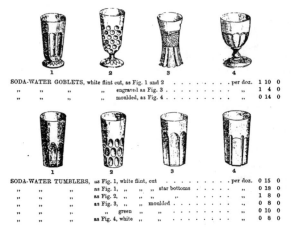

FIGURE 87. Soda water glasses are taller and slimmer than other tumblers. The 1840 Apsley Pellatt price list illustrates an example (Wakefield 1968:52) so they were in production at least that early. Specialized glasses for soda water reflect the growing popularity of this type of beverage. In American sources, however, they were often referred to as lemonades and in the 20th century as iced tea glasses. This group, decorated by cutting, engraving, or molding, appears in S. Maw & Son (1866:260). (Private collection.)

FIGURE 88. A group of engraved tumblers offered by M. Davis, many of which exhibit the rather stiff vertical orientation of patterns introduced in the 1880s. The pattern in the bottom row with the swallows was inspired by Japanese motifs (*Pottery Gazette* 1884:before 817). (Courtesy of the British Library, London; digital image by George van der Vlugt.)

FIGURE 89. Tumbler in aqua glass decorated by optic molding, enameled floral/leaf sprays around a decal of Niagara Falls put on a white enamel ground, and gilding on the rim. The body surface has been lightly acid-etched to provide a matte surface for the enameling and to hide its less attractive back view. This tumbler represents Bohemian-style taste both in decorative techniques and motifs around the turn of the 20th century. It also represents a whole group of inexpensive souvenir ware produced at the same period. Although decals were introduced in North America during the 1890s, they were in use in continental Europe in the 1870s. The flat ground rim, disguised with gilding, is also a Bohemian feature found on drinking glasses. English glassblowers preferred to cut excess glass off from wide-mouthed wares, such as wine glasses or tumblers, with a pair of shears in a single operation. "In Bohemia and Germany, generally, the workmen are said not to be sufficiently skilful to use the shears; but the edges of bowls are blown in the rough, and cut smooth by the glass-cutter when cold, which leaves a flat and unsightly finish, far inferior to the round, smoothed edge of fire-polish after shearing" (Pellatt 1849:82). (Photo by Rock Chan, private collection.)

FIGURE 90.   Jelly glasses for storing preserved jellies were in production at least by the early 19th century.   Early examples were tumbler-shaped with a folded-in, slightly everted lip which held the oiled-paper or cloth covering in place (Wilson 1994[1]:186-187).   These early 1870s examples from the King Company had glass or tin covers, and were intended for domestic use (*Pennsylvania Glassware* 1972:22).   (Courtesy of the Juliet K. and Leonard S. Rakow Research Library of The Corning Museum of Glass, Corning, New York.)

FIGURE 91. Packer's tumblers made by Dominion Glass Company were sold filled with mustard, jelly, and other foods, and then the consumer could use them as tumblers afterwards. These were suitable for Anchor Caps (with fine vertical ribs), lugged closure, or slip top (Dominion Glass Company 1915:74-77). The Anchor Cap was introduced in 1908 under the Sure Seal trade name and with some variations continued to be made into the 1960s (Bender 1986:77-79). Even fragments of these lips are easily identified. (Papers of Dominion Glass Company Limited, National Archives of Canada, Ottawa.)

BAR OR WHISKEY TUMBLERS

Thin Blown, Plain

No. 1001
1½ & 1¾ oz
45c. doz

No. 1002
2 & 2¼ oz
45c. doz

No. 1003
2½ & 2¾ oz
45c. doz

No. 1004
3 & 3¼ oz
45c. doz

No. 1005
3½ & 3¾ oz
45c. doz

No. 1006
5 oz
55c. doz

Any of the above banded, 10c. per dozen extra.

Thin Blown, Cut Flute

No. 1007
2½ & 2¾ oz
65c. doz

No. 1008
3 & 3¼ oz
65c. doz

No. 1009
3½ & 3¾ oz
65c. doz

No. 1010
4¼ oz
70c. doz

No. 1011
4¾ oz
70c. doz

No. 1012
5½ oz
80c. doz

Cut Flute and Polished Bottom

No. 1013
4½ oz
$1.00 doz

No. 1014
5 oz
$1.25 doz

No. 1015
5½ oz
$1.35 doz

No. 1016
6½ oz
$1.50 doz

No. 1017
4½ oz
$1.25 doz

No. 1018
4½ oz
$1.75 doz

Thin Blown, Etched

No. 1019
2½ oz
90c. doz

No. 1020
3½ oz
90c. doz

No. 1021
4 oz
90c. doz

No. 1022
3 oz $1.50 doz
5 oz $1.65 doz

No. 1023
4 oz
$1.10 doz

No. 1024
4 oz $1.60 doz
5¾ oz
$1.90 doz

Heavy Pressed Whiskies

No. 1025
1½, 2 & 3 oz
50c. doz

No. 1026
1½, 2 & 3 oz
50c. doz

No. 1027
2½, 3 & 3½ oz
50c. doz

No. 1028
1¼, 1¾, 2½ oz
50c. doz

No. 1029
2½ oz
80c. doz

No. 1030
5 oz
80c. doz

Special prices by the gross and original packages.

FIGURE 92. Selection of tumblers offered to the restaurant and hotel trade which includes thinly-blown wares, heavy pressed wares, and cut or acid-etched decorations. The extra-thick glass in the two tumblers on the lower right in the last row is often found on pressed tumblers and probably dates as early as the mid-19th century (Budde & Westermann 1913:1). (Courtesy of George Miller.)

FIGURE 93. Tumbler in Athenia or Paneled 44 pattern, introduced by the United States Glass Company in 1912 (Peterson 1973:127-129). The T. Eaton Co. included a 4-piece table set in their 1914 catalogue (1914:110) which describes the pattern as "a combination of Colonial and Grecian border pattern with small floral design." Except for the flowers, the back to back 4s resemble Arts and Crafts motifs. The plain panels are decorated by gold iridescence. (Photo by Rock Chan, private collection.)

FIGURE 94.   A selection of tumblers from Butler Brothers 1930 catalogue showing range of pressed and blown tumblers decorated by enameling, cutting, and acid-etching.   (Courtesy of Collins Kirby Art & Antiques, Fort Payne, Alabama.)

POPULAR STYLE WATER GLASSES

EXTRA HEAVY MACHINE MADE WATER GLASSES

2K1902 9 oz. Heavy Pressed Cupped-in Top and Fluted Bottom. Ht. 4 in. In lots of 24 doz. Packed in cartons of 6 doz. Wt. 48 lbs. Factory Shipments from Penna.

2K2203 9 oz. Heavy Pressed Cupped-in Top and Fluted Bottom. Ht. 3⅞ in. In lots of 24 doz. Packed in cartons of 6 doz. Wt. 48 lbs. Factory Shipments from Penna.

EITHER STYLE AT THESE PRICES

Factory Direct Shipment In 24 Doz. Lots Only Net Per Doz.	Our Stock Shipment In 24 Doz. Lots Only Net Per Doz.	In Single Doz. Lots From Our Stock Only Net Per Doz.
45c	50c	60c

IN CARTONS OF 6 DOZ. From Our Stock Only. Net Per Doz. 55c

LUNCH ROOM OR RESTAURANT SERVICE

2K1920 Plain Style. Ht. 3¾ in.

2K1925 Colonial Fluted. Ht. 3⅝ in.

2K1924 Narrow Optic. Ht. 3¾ in.

2K2104 Colonial Style. Ht. 4 in.

Machine made—Medium wt. 8 oz. Capacity

Any of these 4 styles shown at these prices:

Cartons of 12 doz. Wt. 60 lbs.

FACTORY DIRECT SHIPMENT F.O.B. PENNA. FACTORY IN CARTON LOTS ONLY. NET PER DOZEN, 23c

IN CARTONS OF TWELVE DOZEN FROM OUR STOCK ONLY. NET PER DOZEN, 28c

IN SINGLE DOZEN LOTS FROM OUR STOCK ONLY. NET PER DOZEN, 35c

HEAVY MACHINE MADE WATER GLASSES

2K1903 7½ ounce Pressed Straight style, with heavy Colonial Fluted Bottom. Ht. 4 in. In lots of 24 doz. Packed in cartons of 6 doz. Wt. 48 lbs. Factory Shipments from Ohio and W. Va.

2K2225 9 oz. Plain Pressed Straight style, with heavy bottom. Ht. 4 in. In lots of 24 doz. Packed in cartons of 6 doz. Wt. 48 lbs. Factory Shipments from Penna.

EITHER STYLE AT THESE PRICES

Factory Direct Shipment In 24 Doz. Lots Only Net Per Doz.	Our Stock Shipment In 24 Doz. Lots Only Net Per Doz.	In Single Doz. Lots From Our Stock Only Net Per Doz.
40c	45c	55c

IN CARTONS OF 6 DOZ. From Our Stock Only. Net Per Doz. 48c

DOUBLE THICK BARREL SHAPED WATER GLASS

Hand Made—Ground Bottom

An extra strong, hand made barrel shaped water glass, made to give real service. Has clear color, highly polished all over. Ground bottoms.

2K2270 9 oz. Ht. 3¾ in. 20 doz. in bbl. Wt. 210 lbs. Doz. 75c

In barrel lots from our stock. Doz. Net, 65c

F.O.B. Indiana Factory in bbl. of 20 doz. only......Doz. Net, 60c

DOUBLE THICK WATER GLASSES

Plain Straight Style — Optic Cupped Style

Made of good quality extra heavy pressed glass, finely finished with smooth edges and bottoms.

PLAIN STRAIGHT STYLE

2K2224 8½ oz. Ht. 4 in. In lots of 24 doz. Packed 6 doz. to a carton. Wt. 60 lbs.

In 24 Doz. Lots From Penna. Factory Per Doz. Net	In 24 Doz. Lots From Our Stock Per Doz. Net	In Single Doz. Lots From Our Stock Per Doz. Net
45c	50c	60c

OPTIC CUPPED STYLE

2K1917 8½ oz. Optic cupped style. Ht. 4 in. In lots of 24 doz. Packed 6 doz. to a carton. Wt. 60 lbs.

In 24 Doz. Lots From Penna. Factory Per Doz. Net	In 24 Doz. Lots From Our Stock Per Doz. Net	In Single Doz. Lots From Our Stock Per Doz. Net
50c	55c	65c

HAND MADE WATER GLASSES

Ground Bottoms, Smooth Edges, Highly Fire Polished

2K2133 8 ounce. Fluted straight shape. Medium weight bottom. Ht. 3 13/16 in. Packed 20 doz. to bbl. Wt. 185 lbs.

2K2110 9 oz. Plain straight shape. Medium weight bottom. Ht. 3⅞ in. Packed 20 doz. to bbl. Wt. 190 lbs.

2K2124 8½ oz. Fluted straight shape. Medium weight bottom. Ht. 4 in. Packed 20 doz. to bbl. Wt. 190 lbs.

2K2131 7½ oz. Wide flat flutes. Straight shape; heavy bottom. Ht. 3 15/16 in. Packed 22 doz. to bbl. Wt. 175 lbs.

ANY OF THE ABOVE 4 STYLES AT THESE PRICES

Factory Direct Shipment F. O. B. Indiana Factory In Barrel Lots Only Net Per Doz.	Our Stock Shipment Shipped In Barrel Lots Only Net Per Doz.	In Single Dozen Lots From Our Stock Only Net Per Doz.
55c	60c	70c
Not Less Than One Barrel of One Style Sold at This Special Price	Not Less Than One Barrel of One Style Sold at This Special Price	

EARLY AMERICAN STYLE WATER GLASS

Made of best quality heavy pressed glass, highly fire polished, with hand ground bottoms. Made in six attractive colors. Ht. 3 13/16 in. Packed 6 doz. to a carton. Wt. 60 lbs. Factory shipments from Penna.

	Color	In Single Doz. Lots From Our Stock Doz.	In 24 Doz. Lots Only From Factory Doz.
2K3050	Crystal	$1.35	$1.05
2K3051	Green	1.40	1.10
2K3052	Amber	1.40	1.10
2K3053	Rose	1.40	1.10
2K3054	Blue	1.60	1.30
2K3055	Ruby	1.60	1.30

5% Discount in 24 Doz. Lots of One Color.

WATER GLASSES—HAND MADE—GROUND BOTTOMS

Extra strong and heavy. Best quality heavy pressed glass, crystal color, fire polished. Full finished ground bottoms and smooth melted edges.

2K2180 9½ ounce Fluted. Straight style, heavy bottom. Ht. 4 in. 20 doz. in bbl. Wt. 185 lbs.

2K2142 9½ ounce Fluted. Straight shape, medium wt. bottom. Ht. 4 3/16 in. 20 doz. in bbl. Wt. 160 lbs.

EITHER OF THE TWO STYLES SHOWN AT THESE PRICES

In Barrel Lots Only From Indiana Factory Doz. Net	In Barrel Lots From Our Stock Doz. Net	In Single Dozen Lots From Our Stock Doz. Net
75c	90c	$1.00

2K2180

2K2142

GREEN GLASS WATER TUMBLER

Makes a very attractive service. Made of heavy pressed green glass. Barrel shape.

2K7900 9 oz. Ht. 3¾ in..Doz. 55c

Packed 6 doz. to a carton. Wt. 48 lbs. 5% discount in lots of 4 cartons (24 doz.) or more.

F.O.B. Ohio Factory in 4 carton lots (24 doz.).......Doz. Net, 45c

PRESSED BANDED GLASS

A beautiful thin pressed optic water tumbler, with pressed border design. Fine quality pressed glass brilliantly fire polished all over.

2K2034 9 oz. Ht. 4⅛ in. Doz. $1.30

5% discount in bbl. of 20 doz. Wt. 150 lbs.

F.O.B. W. Va. Factory in bbl. of 20 doz. only....Doz. Net, $1.05

CUPPED SHAPE WATER GLASS MACHINE MADE

Medium Weight Optic Style

Machine made, of good quality pressed glass, with smooth edges and bottoms. Cupped shape reduces breakage.

2K1964 Cap'y 8½ oz. Ht. 3¼ in.

FACTORY DIRECT SHIPMENT F. O. B. PENNA. FACTORY.

In lots of 24 doz. only. Net, Per Doz. 35c

FROM OUR STOCK SHIPMENT.

In lots of 24 doz. only. Net, Per Doz. 40c

FROM OUR STOCK SHIPMENT.

In carton lots of 6 doz. only. Wt. 45 lbs.........Net, Per Doz. 45c

IN SINGLE DOZEN LOTS.

From our stock only. Wt. 8 lbs. Net, Per Doz. 50c

ALBERT PICK CO., INC.
CHICAGO

- 22 -

FIGURE 95. Tumblers for restaurant and hotel use, most of rather thick glass. Note that the "Early American Style Water Glass" has a hand ground bottom. This pattern is a pressed example of a conscious revival of early-19th-century styles (Figures 46, 74*e*) (Albert Pick Company 1932:22). (Courtesy of George Miller.)

nappy. They seem to have been associated with hot beverage service and probably smaller meals such as breakfast or tea.

Although both sugar bowls and creamers were being made in the 18th and early 19th centuries, they were generally not paired, even though they were both used in hot beverage service. For example, in Apsley Pellatt's 1840 catalogue, neither the cream jugs nor sugars matched each other nor were they even presented next to each other (Wakefield 1968:50, 52). By the mid-19th century, however, particularly in pressed glass, they were available in the same patterns and, by the 1870s, were offered regularly with a butter dish and spooner. By the early 20th century, sugars and creamers were presented together, usually without the other pieces, although the 1930 Butler Brothers catalogue still includes a "set" (Figure 73). The 20th-century sugar bowls and cream pitchers were smaller than early-19th-century examples. During the first half of the 19th century, the covers for sugar bowls sat inside a galleried rim (Figure 11); later examples had ledges on the main body or a flange on the cover. Handles seem to have been optional.

Butter dishes underwent some changes during the 1800 to 1940 period. The dominant form during the first half of the 19th century was the butter tub, which had a cylindrical body and flat base, and often a cover and an under-plate (Figure 42). Later in the century, the low bowl or dish form with cover predominated (Figures 30, 73).

Spooners, used to hold tea spoons, may have a stem, may rest directly on the foot, or may have no foot and often have a scalloped rim. They were introduced in pressed glass about the middle of the 19th century and seem to have continued in production until at least 1930 (Figures 24, 62, 73). Spoon trays, introduced around 1900, were alternates to the spooner.

Stemmed Drinking Glasses

Although a clumsy term, "stemmed drinking glasses" is the most accurate term to use for stemware forms used for drinking, including wine glasses of different shapes and sizes (cordial, claret, hock, and champagne), ales, and larger drinking glasses called rummers or goblets. "Stemware" technically describes any glass

vessel with a stem, including drinking glasses, celery vases, dessert glasses, egg glasses, and serving bowls. The term "wine glasses" was used frequently in the documents although it included stemware styles suitable for beverages other than wine. It is a useful term, however, to describe stemmed drinking glasses that were not rummers or goblets, as long as one remembers that they were not used exclusively for wines.

Based on archaeological and documentary evidence, English factories were making only two styles of wine glasses at the beginning of the 19th century (Figures 74-75). In the Gardiner's Island pattern book of the late 18th century, only two Bohemian stemware styles are shown, a plain drawn stem and a thin inverted baluster style (Pattern Book n.d.). By 1840, the numbers of stemware styles had begun to increase, with emphasis on the top and bottom of the stem, rather than the center (Figures 76-77) (Wakefield 1968:52). In general, they also tended to be proportionally taller than the short forms of the first half of the century, a trend which continued into the 20th century. By the late 1920s, stemware bowls were large, with tall stems and feet which had a diameter smaller than the bowl rim. As with other tableware forms, there was a strong conservative element in wine glasses wherein styles stayed in production for decades, but, at the same time, there were fashionable styles made (Figures 77-82).

Goblets are stemmed drinking glasses with large bowls (Figures 83-84). From their introduction in the late 18th century, they tended to have short, almost vestigial stems. Before the mid-19th century, however, a new style of goblet had begun to appear, still with a large bowl but more closely resembling wine glasses. By the 1870s, one gets the impression, particularly in pressed glass, that goblets were more widely used than wine glasses, probably for the same reasons that pitchers and jugs were replacing decanters.

The series of illustrations offers a guide to dating stemmed drinking glasses although the same styles were often used on other stemware.

Tumblers

Tumblers (Figures 85-95) are the commonest tableglass form found on archaeological sites and are the most difficult to date. The dominant decorative motif was the panel which seems to have been made in an astonishing array of variations in both cut and pressed glass and was offered throughout the 140 years covered by this guide. Other styles were offered, however, following the dominant decorative motifs of different periods as illustrations scattered throughout this guide demonstrate. A hint of the quantities and variety available is provided by an 1875 advertisement of the Rochester Tumbler Company which boasted that they produced more that 175 different patterns and 200,000 tumblers every 6 days (Innes 1976:59). This company specialized in tumblers and even sold its products to other glass companies (Innes 1976:58). Tumbler shapes were generally conical although cylindrical, waisted, and barrel-shaped ones were also made. Descriptions of tumblers in the catalogues included details such as capacity, weight (particularly in England), thickness, what was to be put in them (ale, whiskey, soda water, iced tea, lemonade), the appropriate setting (bar or table), the method of manufacture, and decoration. Blown tumblers were among the first tablewares to be manufactured by machine (see Blown Glass).

For the first half of the 19th century, lead, glass tumblers, whether made in England or the United States, dominated the North American market. They were plain or decorated by contact molding (Figure 12), cutting, and, after the late 1830s, by pressing. After the American Revolution, importation of Bohemian glassware into the United States increased and certain tumbler styles began appearing in quantity in the American marketplace (Lanman 1968, 1969; Bonasera 1998). Made of potash-lime glass, these tumblers have plain bodies or pattern-molded ribs partway up the body, sketchily engraved motifs either around the rim or in the center of the body, and often a roughly ground pontil mark (Figure 85). Rim motifs include crude squiggles, swags, small horizontal ovals filled with crosshatching, and larger motifs on the body including tulips or roses, birds and heart, or a two-handled basket with floral bouquet. These styles are much rarer in Canada around 1800, although similar examples dating to the middle of the 18th century have been found on French colonial sites in North America.

Pressed paneled tumblers (Figure 86) were introduced in the mid to late 1830s. In 1837, two glass companies exhibited fluted tumblers in Boston at the first exhibition held by the Massachusetts Charitable Mechanic Association (Watkins 1970:61). In England, the first production of a paneled tumbler is attributed to a talented machinist in 1836, who had figured out how to press a thin-topped vessel like a tumbler (*Pottery Gazette* 1885:903). Two pressed designs registered in England in 1840 showed different types of panels and mitered grooves suitable for goblets, tumblers, and other forms (Morris 1978:190-193). The immediate success of pressed tumblers is reflected in a comment about the New England Glass Company in 1838: "the only thing we press now is Tumblers . . . our men make 400 in six hours" (Spillman 1992:4). Pressed tumblers may have mold lines hidden in the pattern, but most do not have obvious lines on the body or base. Smooth surfaces on the undecorated rim portion of the tumbler were achieved by using an undecorated part in the mold and by fire-polishing. Pressed paneled tumblers often have a ground and polished resting surface, a feature which lasted well into the 1930s (Figure 95). The popularity of the pressed-panel tumbler is attested to by the host of variations shown in catalogues and by the frequency of their occurrence on archaeological sites.

Thin, light tumblers were being made as early as the 1870s. The Boston & Sandwich Glass Company (1992:Plate 4) illustrates examples decorated with acid-etched designs executed by the recently introduced needle-etching machine (see Acid-etched Glass). In 1877, a rival firm described wares from the Rochester Tumbler Company: "They were as thin as a sheet of paper and as clear as crystal, also destitute of any mold mark" (Innes 1976:60). Although Innes assumes these were pressed tumblers, the absence of mold lines suggests that they were blown in turn-paste molds. Thinly blown tumblers with acid-etched designs continued to be manufactured into the 1930s (Figure 94).

Conclusions

During the 140 years covered in this guide, a strong core of conservatism ran through the glass industry and its customer base while at the same time unprecedented technological developments in both manufacturing and decorative techniques increased the range of glass available at all levels of society in Canada, the United States, and elsewhere. Technical accomplishments went hand in hand with a willingness on the part of everyone to loot the past for design ideas and to capitalize on someone else's ideas and products. By the last quarter of the 19th century, consumers were faced with an astonishing array of choices, from traditional styles to the latest trends, from cheap to expensive, from colorless to extraordinary colors, from plain to highly decorated. Dating glassware from this mix ranges from precise beginning dates to decades-long time spans. End dates for technical processes, such as the use of the pontil, are impossible to determine because the tableware industry continued to use hand production methods even after the introduction of mechanized production. Decorative themes are possible to identify in certain time periods but many themes never went out of style and others were repeated several times during the 140-year period. Tableware forms, through changing shapes and through the introduction of specialized shapes, sometimes provide additional dating information.

Dating artifacts is a tool to help us understand the contexts in which objects were originally used. Certainly glass tableware can only be understood in comparison with other tableware forms in ceramic and metal. Archaeological collections should offer us something that the innumerable books on glass and ceramic antiques do not offer–an opportunity to understand how objects were used during their active life. By using tableware of all types from archaeological collections, it may be possible to identify assemblages associated with different groups of people; their domestic, work, and commercial lives; whether they lived in a rural or urban context, whether they favored traditional, up-to-date, or practical tableware; and how choices changed or remained the same through time.

REFERENCES

ALBERT PICK COMPANY
  [1932] Untitled catalogue. Albert Pick Co., Chicago, IL.

ARMY AND NAVY STORES
  1969 *Yesterday's Shopping: The Army and Navy Stores Catalogue 1907,* introduction by Alison Adburgham. David and Charles, Newton Abbot, Devon, England.

THE ART-JOURNAL
  1851 *The Crystal Palace Exhibition, Illustrated Catalogue, London 1851.* Reprinted 1970, Dover Publications, New York, NY.
  1862 *The Art-Journal Illustrated Catalogue of the International Exhibition 1862.* Reprinted 1973, EP Publishing, Wakefield, Yorkshire, England.

AUSTIN, JANE G.
  1991 "Cullet": An Article reprinted from *The Atlantic Monthly,* September 1864. *The Acorn, Journal of The Sandwich Glass Museum* 2:75-91.

BAKER, GARY EVERETT
  1986 The Flint Glass Industry in Wheeling, West Virginia: 1829-1865. Master's thesis, University of Delaware, Newark.

BAKEWELL, PEARS & CO.
  [1875] *Glass Catalogue,* introduction by Lowell Innes. Reprinted 1977, Thomas C. Pears III, Pittsburgh, PA. [Dated ca. 1875 by Lowell Innes.]

BENDER, NATHAN E.
  1986 Early 20th Century Commercial Closures. Paper presented at the Annual Conference on Historical and Underwater Archaeology, Sacramento, CA.

BLASZCZYK, REGINA LEE
  1993 The Wright Way for Glass: Russel Wright and the Business of Industrial Design. *The Acorn, Journal of The Sandwich Glass Museum* 4:2-22.
  1995 *Imagining Consumers: Manufacturers and Markets in Ceramics and Glass, 1865-1965.* Ph.D. dissertation, University of Delaware, Newark. University Microfilms International, Ann Arbor, MI.

BONASERA, MICHAEL C.
  1998 The Bohemian Tradition in New York City: Glassware from Two Turn of the Nineteenth Century Deposits. Paper presented at the Annual Meeting of the Council for Northeast Historical Archaeology, Montreal, Quebec.

BONTEMPS, GEORGES
  1868 *Guide du Verrier, Traité historique et pratique de la fabrication des verres, cristaux, vitraux.* Librairie du Dictionnaire des arts et manufactures, Paris, France.

BOSTON & SANDWICH GLASS CO.
  1992 Reprint of the "c. 1874" Boston & Sandwich Glass Company Trade Catalog and Price List. *The Acorn, Journal of The Sandwich Glass Museum* 3:21-end.

BROOKS, JOHN A.
1987   *Glass Tumblers 1700-1900.* John A. Brooks, Rothley, Leicester, England.

BRYCE BROTHERS COMPANY
1916   *Catalogue of Lead Blown Glassware.* Bryce Brothers Company, Mount Pleasant, PA.

BUCHWALD, GUNNAR, AND MOGENS SCHLÜTER (EDITORS)
1975   *Kastrup and Holmegaard's Glassworks Denmark 1825-1975.* Kastrup and Holmegaard's Glassworks, Copenhagen, Denmark.

BUDDE & WESTERMANN
1913   *Budde & Westermann Catalogue No. 101: Department of Glassware and Supplies in General for Cafes, Clubs, Hotels, Restaurants, etc.* Budde & Westermann, New York, NY.

BUTLER BROTHERS
1902   *Spring 1902 "MISSIONARY" Edition of "Our Drummer."* Butler Brothers, New York, NY.
1905   *Glassware 1905,* Catalog No. 536, Glassware Department. Reprint, Antiques Research Publications, Mentone, AL.
1910   *Glassware 1910,* Fall 1910 catalog, Glass section. Reprint, Antiques Research Publications, Mentone, AL.
1914   "Our Drummer." Spring. Butler Brothers, New York, NY.
1925   *China & Glassware 1925,* Midwinter catalog, No. 2233. Reprinted 1968, Antiques Research Publications, Mentone, AL.
1929   "Our Drummer" is Our Salesman, August. Butler Brothers, Chicago, IL.
1930   *China & Glassware 1930,* Catalog No. 2749, October. Reprinted 1968, Antiques Research Publications, Mentone, AL.

CHARLESTON, ROBERT J.
1965   A Glass Pattern-Book of the Biedermeier Period. *VIIe Congrès International du Verre,* Paper 261. Brussels, Belgium.

THE CORNING MUSEUM OF GLASS
1987   *Guide To Trade Catalogs From The Corning Museum Of Glass.* Clearwater Publishing Company, New York, NY.

CROWE, KATE
1989   The French Connection: The Decorative Glass of James A. Jobling and Co. of Sunderland during the 1930s. *The Glass Circle* 6:32-45.

DAVIS, PEARCE
1949   *The Development of the American Glass Industry.* Harvard University Press, Cambridge, MA.

DIAMOND FLINT GLASS COMPANY LIMITED
1904   *Catalogue of Blown Tumblers, Plain and Decorated.* Diamond Flint Glass Company Limited, Montreal, Quebec.

DODSWORTH, ROGER (EDITOR)
1987   *British Glass Between the Wars,* exhibition catalogue. Dudley Leisure Services, Dudley, England.

DOMINION GLASS COMPANY
[1915]   *Packers' Glassware Catalogue No. 11.* Dominion Glass Company Limited, Montreal, Quebec.

DRAHOTOVA, OLGA
1983   *European Glass.* Excalibur Books, New York, NY.

EDGLEY, JIM D. (COMPILER)
1996   *Registration Numbers 1908-1945.* The Glass Association, Kingswinford, West Midlands, England.

EVANS, WENDY, CATHERINE ROSS, AND ALEX WERNER
1995   *Whitefriars Glass: James Powell and Sons of London.* Museum of London, London, England.

FARRAR, ESTELLE SINCLAIRE, AND JANE SHADEL SPILLMAN
1979   *The Complete Cut & Engraved Glass of Corning.* Crown Publishers, New York, NY.

FAUSTER, CARL U.
1979   *Libbey Glass Since 1818: Pictorial History & Collector's Guide.* Len Beach Press, Toledo, OH.

FENWICK, MILLICENT
1948   *Vogue's Book of Etiquette: A Complete Guide to Traditional Forms and Modern Usage.* Simon and Schuster, New York, NY.

FLORENCE, GENE
1992   *Collectible Glassware from the 40's, 50's, 60's: An Illustrated Value Guide.* Collector Books, Paducah, KY.
1995a   *Elegant Glassware of the Depression Era,* 6th edition. Collector Books, Paducah, KY.
1995b   *Kitchen Glassware of the Depression Years,* 5th edition. Collector Books, Paducah, KY.
1996   *The Collector's Encyclopedia of Depression Glass,* 12th edition. Collector Books, Paducah, KY.

GOLLEDGE, CHRISTINE
1987   Stuart and Sons Limited (1918-1939). In *British Glass Between the Wars,* Roger Dodsworth, editor, pp. 28-31. Dudley Leisure Services, Dudley, England.

GRAY, CHERRY, AND RICHARD GRAY
1987   The Prince's Glasses, Some Warrington Cut Glass 1806-1811. *The Journal of the Glass Association* 2:11-18.

GREAT BRITAIN
1835   Commission of Inquiry into the Excise Establishment and into the Management and Collection of the Excise Revenue. Report No. 13: Glass. H.M.S.O., London, England.
1865   Parliament. Sessional Papers. Children's Employment Commission. Vol. 20. H.M.S.O., London, England.
1907   *Report of the Tariff Commission. Volume 6, The Glass Industry.* Reprinted 1972, Johnson Reprint Corporation, New York, NY.

HAJDAMACH, CHARLES R.
1991   *British Glass 1800-1914*. Antique Collectors' Club, Woodbridge, England.

HEACOCK, WILLIAM, AND FRED BICKENHEUSER
1978   *Encyclopedia of Victorian Colored Pattern Glass: Book 5 U.S. Glass From A to Z*. Antique Publications, Marietta, OH.

HENRY BIRKS & SONS
1903   *Catalogue No. 12*. Henry Birks & Sons, Montreal, Quebec.
1906   *Catalogue No. 17*. Henry Birks & Sons, Montreal, Quebec.

HIGGINS & SEITER
1899   *China and Cut Glass, Higgins & Seiter 1899*. Reprinted 1971, The Pyne Press, Princeton, NJ.

HILL-OUSTON CO. LTD.
[1936] *Hillston Crystal Gifts, Catalogue No. 10*. Hill-Ouston Co. Ltd., Birmingham, England. [3 April 1936 stamped on catalog.]

HOBBS GLASS COMPANY
n.d.   Catalogue. The Winterthur Library, Printed Book and Periodical Collection, Winterthur, DE.

HOLMES, JANET
1974   Glass and the Glass Industry. In *The Book of Canadian Antiques*, Donald Blake Webster, editor, pp. 268-281. McGraw-Hill, Ryerson, Toronto, Ontario.
1987   *Patterns in Light. The John and Mary Yaremko Glass Collection*. Royal Ontario Museum, Toronto, Ontario.

HOLMES, JANET, AND OLIVE JONES
1978   Glass in Canada: An Annotated Bibliography. *Material History Bulletin* 6:115-148.

HUGHES, G. BERNARD
1958   *English Glass for the Collector 1660-1860*. Lutterworth Press, London, England.

HUSFLOEN, KYLE
1992   *Collector's Guide to American Pressed Glass, 1825-1915*. Wallace-Homestead Book Company, Radnor, PA.

INNES, LOWELL
1976   *Pittsburgh Glass 1797-1891: A History and Guide for Collectors*. Houghton Mifflin, Boston, MA.

JACKSON, LESLEY
1997   Automated Table Glass Production in Britain Since World War II. *The Journal of The Glass Association* 5:68-80.

JARVES, DEMING
1865   *Reminiscences of Glass-Making*. Reprinted 1968, Beatrice C. Weinstock, Great Neck, NY.

JENKS, BILL, AND JERRY LUNA
1990   *Early American Pattern Glass, 1850-1910*. Wallace-Homestead Book Company, Radnor, PA.

JONES, OLIVE
1986a   Glass Tablewares 1850-1870. Source Book. Manuscript, Parks Canada, Ottawa, Ontario.
1986b   Glass Tablewares 1870-1890. Source Book. Manuscript, Parks Canada, Ottawa, Ontario.
1986c   Glass Tablewares 1890-1914. Source Book. Manuscript, Parks Canada, Ottawa, Ontario.
1986d   Glass Tablewares 1890-1914. Source Book. Manuscript, Parks Canada, Ottawa, Ontario.
1992   Early American Glass in Canada, ca. 1820-1860. *The Glass Club Bulletin of The National Early American Glass Club* 168(Fall):3-16.

JONES, OLIVE R., AND E. ANN SMITH
1985   Glass of the British Military, 1755-1820. Parks Canada, *Studies in Archaeology, Architecture and History*. Ottawa, Ontario.

JONES, OLIVE R., AND CATHERINE SULLIVAN, WITH CONTRIBUTIONS BY GEORGE L. MILLER, E. ANN SMITH, JANE E. HARRIS, AND KEVIN LUNN
1989   The Parks Canada Glass Glossary for the Description of Containers, Tableware, Flat Glass, and Closures, revised edition. Parks Canada, *Studies in Archaeology, Architecture and History*. Ottawa, Ontario.

KAELLGREN, PETER
1993   Birmingham Cut Glass and the American Market; Examining an 1811 Account and its Context. In *Reflections on Glass: Articles from the Glass Club Bulletin*, Jane Shadel Spillman, Olive R. Jones, and Kirk J. Nelson, compilers, pp. 45-52. National Early American Glass Club, Silver Spring, MD.

KILGO, GARRY, DALE KILGO, JERRY WILKINS, AND GAIL WILKINS
1991   *A Collector's Guide to Anchor Hocking's "Fire-King" Glassware*. K&W Collectibles, Addison, AL.

KING, THOMAS B.
1987   *Glass in Canada*. Boston Mills Press, Erin, Ontario.

KNITTLE, RHEA MANSFIELD
1927   *Early American Glass*. The Century Company, New York, NY.

LANGBRIDGE, R. H. (COMPILER)
1975   *Edwardian Shopping: A Selection from the Army & Navy Stores Catalogues 1898-1913*, introduction by R. H. Langbridge. David & Charles, London, England.

LANMAN, DWIGHT P.
1968   Glass in Baltimore: The Trade in Hollow and Tablewares, 1780-1820. Master's thesis, University of Delaware, Newark.
1969   The Baltimore Glass Trade, 1780 to 1820. *Winterthur Portfolio* 5:15-48. Winterthur, DE.

LATTIMORE, COLIN R.
1979   *English 19th-Century Press-Moulded Glass.* Barrie & Jenkins, London, England.

LAUNERT, FREDERIKA
1997   The Survival of Traditional Design in Post-War Stourbridge Glass. *The Journal of The Glass Association* 5:61-67.

LEE, RUTH WEBB
1944   *Victorian Glass: Specialties of the Nineteenth Century,* 12th edition. Lee Publications, Wellesley Hills, MA.
1958   *Early American Pressed Glass: A Classification of Patterns Collectible in Sets Together with Individual Pieces for Table Decorations,* 34th edition. Lee Publications, Wellesley, MA.

LEINICKE, KRIS GAYMAN
1986   Production of the Boston and Sandwich Glass Company in the Year 1827. Master's thesis, State University of New York College at Oneonta.

LOLE, F. PETER
1993   The Royal Finger Bowls and Coolers Mystery. *Glass Circle News* 56(June):2-4.

LYON, KENNETH W.
1994   Re-Thinking Blown Three Mold (A Sub-category of Mold Blown Glass). *The Acorn, Journal of The Sandwich Glass Museum* 5:70-80.

MACLAREN, GEORGE
1968   Nova Scotia Glass, revised edition. *Nova Scotia Museum, Occasional Paper* 4, *Historical Series* 1. Halifax

MCFARLAN, GORDON
1992   Early Nineteenth Century Patterns from the Ford Ranken Archive. *The Journal of the Glass Association* 4:1-12.

MCKEARIN, GEORGE S., AND HELEN MCKEARIN
1948   *American Glass.* Crown Publishers, New York, NY.

MCKINSTRY, E. RICHARD
1984   *Trade Catalogues at Winterthur: A Guide to the Literature of Merchandising 1750 to 1980.* Garland Publishing, New York, NY.

M'KEE AND BROTHERS
1981   *Victorian Glass: Five Complete Glass Catalogs from 1859/60 to 1871,* introduction and text by Lowell Innes and Jane Shadel Spillman. Dover Publications, New York, NY.

MCNALLY, PAUL
1982   Table Glass in Canada, 1700-1850. Parks Canada, *History and Archaeology* 60. Ottawa, Ontario.

MEASELL, JAMES S.
1994a   H. Northwood & Company 1902-1925. In *Wheeling Glass 1829-1939: Collection of the Oglebay Institute*

Glass Museum, Gerald I. Reilly, editor, pp. 23-168. Oglebay Institute, Wheeling, WV.
1994b   *New Martinsville Glass 1900-1944.* Antique Publications, Marietta, OH.

MONTGOMERY WARD & CO.
1901   *Catalogue and Buyers' Guide, No. 69,* undated reprint. Antiques Research Publications, Mentone, AL.

MONTREAL GAZETTE
1852   American Pressed Glass. *Montreal Gazette,* 1 September:3. Montreal, Quebec.
1867   *Montreal Gazette,* 7 November:3. Montreal, Quebec.

MONTREAL TRANSCRIPT
1842   China, Glass, and Earthenware. *Montreal Transcript,* 22 September:3. Montreal, Quebec.

MORRIS, BARBARA
1978   *Victorian Tableglass & Ornaments.* Barrie & Jenkins, London, England.

MUCHA, MIRIAM E.
1979   Mechanization, French Style Cristaux, Moule en Plein. *The Glass Club Bulletin* 126(September):3-8.

NATIONAL GLASS BUDGET
1897   Owens' Blowing Machine, Punch Tumbler Manufacture Revolutionized. *National Glass Budget,* 13 (23):1; 23 October.

NELSON, KIRK J.
1988   Progress Under Pressure: The Mechanization of the American Flint Glass Industry, 1820-1840. Master's thesis, University of Delaware, Newark.
1990   Early Glass Pressing Technology in Sandwich. *The Acorn, Journal of the Sandwich Glass Museum* 1:38-50.
1992   Introductory Note to the "c.1874" Catalog and Price List. *The Acorn, Journal of The Sandwich Glass Museum* 3:11-20.

NEWMAN, HAROLD
1977   *An Illustrated Dictionary of Glass.* Thames and Hudson, London, England.

O'HARA FLINT GLASS WORKS
1861   *Illustrated Catalogue and Prices of Flint Glassware, Manufactured by James B. Lyon & Co.* James B. Lyon & Co., Pittsburgh, PA.

PALMER, ARLENE
1993a   *Glass in Early America, Selections from the Henry Francis du Pont Winterthur Museum.* Henry Francis du Pont Winterthur Museum, Winterthur, DE.
1993b   Joseph Baggott, New York Glasscutter. In *Reflections on Glass: Articles from the Glass Club Bulletin,* Jane Shadel Spillman, Olive R. Jones, and Kirk J. Nelson, compilers, pp. 57-62. National Early American Glass Club, Silver Spring, MD.
1993c   Some Notes on Cutters and Engravers of Glass in Early America. In *Reflections on Glass: Articles from the Glass Club Bulletin,* Jane Shadel Spillman,

Olive R. Jones, and Kirk J. Nelson, compilers, 35-40. National Early American Glass Club, Silver Spring, MD.

PATTERN BOOK
n.d.   Pattern Book for Glass Decanters, Tumblers, etc., late 18th century, which belonged to the Gardiner Family of Gardiner's Island. Property of Henry Francis du Pont Winterthur Museum Libraries, Winterthur, DE.

PEABODY ESSEX MUSEUM
1794-1819 Sample Books (candlesticks, tea-pots and other tableware of Sheffield plate and Britannia ware, Sheffield, England, 1794-1819?), 8 volumes. Peabody Essex Museum, Philips Library, Salem, MA.

PELLATT, APSLEY
1849   Curiosities of Glass Making: With Details of the Processes and Productions of Ancient and Modern Ornamental Glass Manufacture. Reprinted 1968, Ceramic Book Company, Newport, England.

PENNSYLVANIA GLASSWARE, 1870-1904
1972   Pennsylvania Glassware, 1870-1904. The Pyne Press, Princeton, NJ.

PETERSON, ARTHUR G.
1968   400 Trademarks on Glass. Washington College Press, Takoma Park, MD.
1970   Glass Salt Shakers. Wallace-Homestead Book Company, Des Moines, IA.
1973   Glass Patents and Patterns. Arthur G. Peterson, DeBary, FL.

PHILIPPE, JOSEPH
[1975]   Le Val-Saint-Lambert, ses cristalleries et l'art du verre en Belgique. Librairie Halbart, Liège, Belgium.

POTTERY GAZETTE AND CHINA AND GLASS TRADES REVIEW
1881   M. Davis & Co. Supplement to Pottery Gazette and China and Glass Trades Review, 5(51):between 816 and 817, 1 October.
1884   M. Davis & Co. Supplement to Pottery Gazette and China and Glass Trades Review, 8(89):after 1292, 1 November.
1885   Trade Reminiscences. The First Pressed Tumbler. Pottery Gazette and China and Glass Trades Review, 1 August:903.
1893   Notes on Fancy Goods. Pottery Gazette and China and Glass Trades Review, 2 January:4.
1894   The "New Louis XV" Suite of Crystal Glass. Fancy Trades Supplement to Pottery Gazette and China and Glass Trades Review, 19(199):before 49, 1 January.

PULLIN, ANNE GEFFKEN
1986   Glass Signatures, Trademarks and Trade Names from the Seventeenth to the Twentieth Century. Wallace-Homestead Book Company, Radnor, PA.

RAINWATER, DOROTHY T. (EDITOR)
1973   Sterling Silver Holloware. The Pyne Press, Princeton, NJ.

REVI, ALBERT CHRISTIAN
1959   Nineteenth Century Glass: Its Genesis and Development. Thomas Nelson & Sons, New York, NY.
1964   American Pressed Glass and Figure Bottles. Thomas Nelson & Sons, New York, NY.
1965   American Cut and Engraved Glass. Thomas Nelson & Sons, New York, NY.

ROGOVE, SUSAN TOBIER, AND MARCIA BUAN STEINHAUER
1993   Pyrex by Corning: A Collector's Guide. Antique Publications, Marietta, OH.

ROSENHAIN, WALTER
1908   Glass Manufacture. Archibald Constable, London, England.

ROTTENBERG, BARBARA LANG, AND JUDITH TOMLIN
1982   Glass Manufacturing in Canada: a Survey of Pressed Glass Patterns. National Museum of Man, Mercury Series, History Division, Paper 33. Ottawa, Ontario.

S. MAW & SON
1866   A Catalogue of Surgeons' Instruments & Appliances. S. Maw & Son, London, England.

SCOVILLE, WARREN C.
1948   Revolution in Glassmaking: Entrepreneurship and Technological Change in the American Industry. Harvard University Press, Cambridge, MA.

SHEELER, JOHN
1978   Factors Affecting Attribution: The Burlington Glass Works. Material History Bulletin 6:31-51.

SILBER AND FLEMING
1990   The Silber and Fleming Glass & China Book. Wordsworth Editions, Ware, Hertfordshire, England.

SLACK, RAYMOND
1987   English Pressed Glass 1830-1900. Barrie & Jenkins, London, England.

SMART BROTHERS
[1885]   Smart Brothers, in presenting to the Trade an entirely new edition of their Price List. Round Oak Glassworks, near Brierly Hill, Staffordshire, England. D. F. Taylor & Co., Birmingham, England. Fiche 93, Corning Museum of Glass, Corning, NY.

SPILLMAN, JANE SHADEL
1971   Documented Use of Cup Plates in the Nineteenth Century. Journal of Glass Studies 13:128-133.
1981   American and European Pressed Glass in The Corning Museum of Glass. The Corning Museum of Glass, Corning, NY.
1982   Glass Tableware, Bowls & Vases. Knopf, New York, NY.
1983   Pressed-glass Designs in the United States and Europe. The Magazine Antiques 124(1 July):130-139
1989   White House Glassware: Two Centuries of Presidential Entertaining. White House Historical Association, Washington, DC.

1992   The Leighton-Ford Correspondence. *The Acorn, Journal of The Sandwich Glass Museum* 3:3-10.

1996   *The American Cut Glass Industry: T. G. Hawkes and His Competitors.* Antique Collector's Club, Woodbridge, Suffolk, England.

1997   The New England Glass Company Catalog of Pressed Glass. *The Acorn, Journal of The Sandwich Glass Museum* 7:71-98.

SPILLMAN, JANE SHADEL, OLIVE JONES, AND KIRK NELSON
1993   *Reflections on Glass: Articles from the Glass Club Bulletin.* National Early American Glass Club, Silver Spring, MD.

SPILLMAN, JANE SHADEL, JAMES S. MEASELL, AND HOLLY H. MCCLUSKEY
1994   Glassmaking in South Wheeling 1845-1893 (Hobbs, Brockunier and Related Firms). In *Wheeling Glass 1829-1939: Collection of the Oglebay Institute Glass Museum,* Gerald I. Reilly, editor, pp. 39-91. Oglebay Institute, Wheeling, WV.

STARBUCK, DAVID S.
1986   The New England Glassworks: New Hampshire's Boldest Experiment in Early Glassmaking. *The New Hampshire Archeologist* 27(1).

STEVENS, GERALD
1967   *Canadian Glass c. 1825-1925.* Ryerson Press, Toronto, Ontario.

STOUT, SANDRA MCPHEE
1972   *The Complete Book of McKee Glass.* Trojan Press, North Kansas City, MO.

SULLIVAN, CATHERINE
[1985] Glass Tablewares 1800-1850, Source Book. Manuscript, Parks Canada, Ottawa, Ontario.

T. EATON CO.
1884-   T. Eaton Catalogs, 1884-1952. Canadian Library
1952   Association Newspaper Microfilm Project, Ottawa, Ontario.

THOMPSON, JENNY
1989   *The Identification of English Pressed Glass.* Jenny Thompson, Kendal, Cumbria, England.

TYNE AND WEAR COUNTY COUNCIL MUSEUMS
1983   *Pyrex: 60 Years of Design.* Tyne and Wear County Council Museums, Sunderland, England.

UNITED STATES GLASS COMPANY
[1894] *United States Glass Co.'s Catalogue of Pressed Tumblers & Beer Mugs.* Pittsburgh, PA.

UNITED STATES SENATE
1911   Report on Condition of Woman and Child Wage-Earners in the United States in 19 Volumes, Vol. 3: Glass Industry. 61st Congress, 2nd Session, *Senate Executive Document* No. 645. Washington, DC.

UNITT, DORIS, AND PETER UNITT
1969   *Treasury of Canadian Glass.* Clock House Publications, Peterborough, Ontario.

THE VICTORIAN CATALOGUE OF HOUSEHOLD GOODS
1991   *The Victorian Catalogue of Household Goods.* Studio Editions, London, England.

VICTORIAN SILVERPLATED HOLLOWARE
1972   *Victorian Silverplated Holloware.* Wallace-Homestead Book Company, Des Moines, IA.

WAKEFIELD, HUGH
1961   *Nineteenth Century British Glass.* Faber and Faber, London, England.

1968   Early Victorian Styles in Glassware. In *Studies in Glass History and Design. Papers read to Committee B Session of the VIIIth International Congress on Glass, held in London 1st-6th July 1968,* R. J. Charleston, W. Evans, and A. E. Werner, editors, pp. 50-54. Gresham Press, Old Woking, Surrey, England.

1982   *Nineteenth Century British Glass,* revised edition. Faber and Faber, London, England.

WARREN, PHELPS
1981   *Irish Glass: Waterford-Cork-Belfast in the Age of Exuberance,* revised edition. Faber and Faber, London, England.

1984   Apsley Pellatt's Table Glass, 1840-1864. *Journal of Glass Studies* 26:120-135.

WATKINS, LURA WOODSIDE
1970   Pressed Glass of the New England Glass Company: An Early Catalogue at the Corning Museum. *Journal of Glass Studies* 12:149-164.

WEATHERMAN, HAZEL MARIE
1974   *Colored Glassware of the Depression Era,* volume 2. Weatherman Glassbooks, Springfield, MO.

1978   *The Decorated Tumbler.* Glassbooks, Springfield, MO.

WEEKS, JOSEPH D.
1886   *Report on the Manufacture of Glass.* United States, Department of the Interior, Census Office, Washington, DC.

WELKER, JOHN, AND ELIZABETH WELKER
1985   *Pressed Glass in America: Encyclopedia of the First Hundred Years, 1825-1925.* Antique Acres Press, Ivyland, PA.

WESTROPP, MICHAEL S. D.
1978   *Irish Glass: A History of Glass-making in Ireland from the Sixteenth Century,* revised edition, Mary Boydell, editor. Allen Figgis, Dublin, Ireland.

WHITE, HARRY HALL
1974   The Story of the Mantua Glass Works, parts 1-4. In *American Glass From the Pages of Antiques: 1. Blown and Molded,* Marvin D. Schwartz, editor, pp. 195-213. The Pyne Press, Princeton, NJ.

WILLIAMS, SUSAN
    1985   *Savory Suppers & Fashionable Feasts: Dining in Victorian America.* Pantheon Books, New York, NY.

WILSON, KENNETH M.
    1972   *New England Glass and Glassmaking.* Thomas Y. Crowell Company, New York, NY.
    1994   *The Toledo Museum of Art: American Glass 1760-1930*, 2 volumes. Hudson Hills Press, New York, NY.

WOLFENDEN, IAN
    1987   The 'WHR' Drawings for Cut Glass and the Origins of the Broad Flute Style of Cutting. *The Journal of the Glass Association* 2:19-28.
    1992   Cut Glass in the Pattern Books of Matthew Boulton's Soho Manufactory. *The Journal of the Glass Association* 4:47-50.

YATES, BARBARA
    1987   The Glasswares of Percival Vickers & Co. Ltd., Jersey Street, Manchester, 1844-1914. *The Journal of the Glass Association* 2:29-40.

ZEMBALA, DENNIS MICHAEL
    1984   *Machines in the Glasshouse: The Transformation of Work in the Glass Industry, 1820-1915.* Ph.D. dissertation, George Washington University, Washington, DC. University Microfilms International, Ann Arbor, MI.

OLIVE R. JONES
MATERIAL CULTURE RESEARCH
ONTARIO SERVICE CENTRE
PARKS CANADA
1600 LIVERPOOL COURT
OTTAWA, ONTARIO K1A 0M5
CANADA

JANE E. HARRIS

Eighteenth-Century French Blue-Green Bottles from the Fortress of Louisbourg, Nova Scotia

Introduction

The work reported is primarily a descriptive analysis of 18th-century French blue-green glass containers found in the extensive Fortress of Louisbourg archaeological collection. Artifacts from the excavations are only partially mended or restored, but on the evidence of necks, bases, and complete bottles (in this report the word "bottle" is used generically to refer to a glass container and "jar," more specifically, to a wide-mouthed glass container), four distinctive container forms, one of which occurs in nine distinct types, could be isolated. The forms vary in size, ranging from a few milliliters to several liters. Many of the types share identical features such as neck, body, or base shapes, implying a relationship at the manufacturing level. By isolating the various forms and types and then using available literature, inventories, contemporary art, and the evidence from blue-green bottles found on other French historic sites in North America, it became possible to discuss the physical relationships between the groups, the closures used, their possible functions, their social significance, and their cultural origins.

The bottles occurred in contexts from both French occupation periods (1713-1745 and 1749-1758) with no apparent stylistic differences pertaining to date of manufacture. This lack of variation is consistent with observations made by both Scoville (1950:20) and Barrelet (1953:110), who stated that there were essentially no technological changes in the common glass industry nor did its products give any indications of regional distinctions during these periods.

Blue-Green Glass

A mixture of sand, calcium, and an alkali flux (potash or soda) to which no decolorizer has been added results in a greenish and sometimes yellow or brownish glass due to iron impurities in the sand. Such glass produced in wood-fired furnaces has been called *waldglas*, forest glass, *verre fougère*, or *verre commun*, depending on its country of origin. The two latter French terms usually refer to lightly tinted tablewares which were produced in the *petites verreries* or *verreries communes* of France. These were generally small glasshouses which often produced a wide variety of products including more utilitarian items such as bottles (Barrelet 1953:71). Besides the glass used for the clearer tablewares, a "common green" glass or *verre vert* was produced in the *petites verreries* for bottles (Scoville 1950), its blue tint being more noticeable according to Barrelet (1953:103) among the bottles produced in the forest areas of Grésigne in Languedoc.

The *petites verreries* used wood-burning furnaces and were located throughout the forests of France. They usually had only one furnace and four to six pots in which to melt glass (*Diderot-d'Alemert Encyclopédie* 1751-1765 [17]:113; Scoville 1950:72). They commonly employed no more than 20 people including part-time workers such as basket weavers and packers (Scoville 1950:72). Some *petites verreries* made only bottles while others specialized in tablewares or window glass and made bottles as a sideline (Scoville 1950:14n., 150-151). Bottle production was separate from that of tablewares or other items on two levels. First, there would have been a separate pot for bottle glass, usually one of green and sometimes one of brown glass (*Diderot-d'Alembert Encyclopédie* 1772a:Plate 3). Second, there were workers who specialized in bottle blowing, for goblet and drinking-glass blowers apparently rarely made bottles (Scoville 1950:71).

The *petite verrerie* industry neither flourished nor declined throughout the 18th century for the number of factories, employment rates, and output increased in some areas, decreased in others, and stayed the same in still others (Scoville 1950:13, 21, 72, 147). The demand for wine bottles had increased greatly with the new practice of storing wine in bottles and with the growing export trade in bottled wines (Scoville 1950:11, 111; Barrelet 1953:100). This demand

Historical Archaeology, MCR 2000:233—258.
Permission to reprint required.

was largely met by the heavy dark glass bottles being made in the new or converted coal-fired furnaces introduced from England early in the century and by the heavy green bottles from *grosses verreries* (Scoville 1950:11, 41). Further to the detriment of the *petite verrerie* industry, wood was scarce in France, which meant many factories were unable by law to keep their furnaces lit year round. This forced some entrepreneurs to close down for as many as six months or more each year, having an obvious effect on production (Scoville 1950:13, 21, 149). On the positive side, the *petite verrerie* industry already had a considerable market, built up in the 16th and 17th centuries, for their cheap and useful common bottles whose domestic use in France was traditional and so widespread that it involved "members of all social classes" (Scoville 1950:111, 167).

For their domestic market the *petites verreries* made "large and small bottles" as well as "bowls, condiment containers, decanters, tumblers, goblets, ink wells, lamps and lamp chimneys, pitchers, plates, urinals, vases and other similar [useful] items" (Scoville 1950:111). This list would presumably include items in clear and blue-green glass. They may have also supplied the perfumeries of southern France as well as the needs of the growing export trade in toilet waters (Scoville 1950:112). Then, too, a variety of other items were packed in glass to be shipped to the colonies: olives, anchovies, capers, marinated tuna, olive oil, vinegar, liqueurs, *eau de vie*, and toilet water (Barrelet 1953:103).

Bottles were also made in the *grosses verreries* of Normandy and northeastern France, but in a "coarse, heavy" green glass or *gros verre* favored by those in the mineral water, liquor, and wine trades (Scoville 1950:8, 11). These *verreries* also burned wood, but specialized in window glass, either crown or sheet (Scoville 1950:8). The crown glass factories of Normandy normally reserved one of six pots for bottles alone (Scoville 1950:11). Owned and operated by the *gentilshommes verriers*, a minor nobility who considered bottle blowing unbefitting to their rank, they employed common workers to manufacture bottles (Scoville 1950:71, 84). According to Scoville (1950:147-148), a typical Normandy factory in 1740 would produce 70 tons of common green glass for every 150 to 200 tons of window glass. Whether the bottles they produced resembled those of the *petites verreries* in form or color is difficult to say, but there seems to have been a definite distinction in weight. Scoville (1950:19, 41) referred to bottles from crown glasshouses as coarse and heavy and those from the *petites verreries* as light. Bosc d'Antic described Norman window glass thusly: "There is no pane glass, I believe, more imperfect than that from our large glass factories; it is full of flaws . . . and colored to the point that it is of little transparency, even as thin as it is" Barrelet (1953:99). Presumably their bottle glass was no better and if so, Bosc d'Antic's statement accurately describes most of the 18th-century glass bottles found at Louisbourg.

French bottle glass composition in the 18th century is a generally neglected area of study. Both soda and potash were being used as flux. Preliminary analysis of a blue-green bottle fragment (Charles Costain 1978:personal communication) indicates a glass of soda-lime composition. Soda was more easily available in the coastal regions of France where it was produced from the ashes of various seaweeds (Scoville 1950:49). Potash was more accessible in the interior and urban areas of France in the form of bracken and wood ash, and it therefore seems likely that the small glasshouses, particularly in northeastern France, would find the use of potash more economical than soda.

French Bottle Manufacture

Enough has been written about bottle manufacture that it is only necessary here to stress the techniques and tools that help to distinguish French bottles from others. Diderot, who maintained that items were made in the same manner whether in wood- or coal-fired furnaces, gave the following description of bottle-making using coal (*Diderot-d'Alembert Encyclopédie* 1751-1765[17]:109, 112, 113; 1772b:Plates 3-6). After the parison was marvered and blown, the bottle was placed in a copper dip mold having a truncated cone shape. It was blown, removed from the mold, and up-ended in preparation to pushing up the base. A *molette*, or shaping tool, was used for this function. It was a short piece of flat metal, one foot long, with a pointed end used to push the base up while the bottle was continuously turned. The bottle was again marvered to correct any bulges or distortions that might have occurred when the base was pushed up. The base was then empontiled with a glass-tipped rod or with the *meule*; that is, with the portion of the glass that remained on the blowpipe after it was cracked off the neck. The bottle rested on its side during this operation. The lip was then reheated or fire-polished and finished as desired. It was at this point that a string rim could have been added. The bottle was then complete except for annealing.

Ducasse (1970:393) discovered in a Panckoucke edition of the *Diderot-d'Alembert Encyclopédie* that *terre à pot* molds in several sizes were used in the *petites verreries*, rather than the lone copper mold Diderot had ascribed (*Diderot-d'Alembert Encyclopédie* 1751-1765[17]:109; 1772b:Plates 3, 4) to each bottle blower. It is conceivable that clay molds could impart a less smooth texture to the surface of a glass bottle than would a copper mold. The presence of many sizes of molds is to be expected given the variety of vessels known to have been produced in *petites verreries*.

Blue-Green Bottles in the Inventories

It was customary in Louisbourg to take an inventory of the possessions of a deceased person immediately following his death, usually for reasons of settling the estate (Adams 1972:1). The inventories varied from a simple list of the contents of a fisherman's trunk to lengthy documentation of the contents of a house and often included appraisals of the values of the items listed. After the items were inventoried they were often sold at public auction and the item listed along with its sale price. These lists frequently mentioned both filled and empty bottles and their values. The information used in this section was drawn from inventories found in France, Archives Nationales (1732-1757:Section Outre-Mer, Series G², Volumes 181, 182, 197, 199, 201-203, 205, 209.)

Blue-green bottles are a difficult group to subdivide for discussion due to the lack of a consistent relationship between shape and function of the bottles, but a preliminary study of the inventories indicated that French clerks made a distinction between *flacon*, *bouteille*, *fiole*, and *dame-jeanne* (e.g., *"dix flacons et quatre*

bouteilles de verre," "quatre bouteilles et douze fiolle de verre," and *"six flacons de verre six mauvaises foilles"*).

Flacon was the term used for containers filled with *"huille," "huille dolive," "huille de palma," "citron confits," "fruit à l'eau de vie," "enchois," "liqueur," "sirop de capilaire," "d'orgea," "capres," "sirop,"* and, infrequently, wine. Filled or empty *flacons* were often found in boxes or baskets: *"canevettes," "paniers," "caves,"* and *"caisses."* There were *"petits flacons," "flacons de pinte"* (approximately 900 ml), and *"flacons de cinq chopines"* (about 2,300 ml).

In the same documents *bouteilles* were almost invariably referred to as containers for wine and spirits (although in one instance a *bouteille* held tobacco, and *d'huille* in another) and were seldom found in *canevettes*. There were *"bouteilles de peinte et . . . de chopine"* (ca. 450 ml). The distinction between *flacon* and *bouteille* suggests that *flacon* generally referred to blue-green glass multipurpose containers and *bouteille* commonly referred to the dark green or black glass flowerpot-shaped bottles now popularly known as French "wine" bottles. *Bouteille* could also have been used to refer to English black glass "wine" bottles.

Fioles (phials) and *dames-jeannes* (demijohns), whose approximate sizes and general forms are implicit in the definitions of the terms themselves, may also refer to vessels with other than French origins. Both forms occur only rarely in the inventories. *Fioles*, when mentioned with their contents, contained *"elixir," "Sirop de Capilaire,"* or *"eau de lavande."* Only one *dame-jeanne* was mentioned with its contents, six *pots* (approximately 14 liters) of *eau de vie*. *Fioles* and *dames-jeannes* were likely blue-green, but could have occurred in other colors as well.

It appears, thus that the French *flacon* in Louisbourg was a multipurpose bottle which would have had to exist in a variety of shapes and sizes in order to accommodate such a variety of liquids and solids. *Fioles* and *dames-jeannes* were restricted by their sizes to more specific functions while *bouteilles* would have contained wine or spirits.

Although several different systems for measuring capacity were in use in France prior to 1840 (Ross 1983), the terms *pinte, chopine,* and *pot* are found throughout historical French inventories to describe the capacitiies of glass containers. Genêt, Decarie-Audet, and Vermette (1974) equate a *pinte* to a liter, and define a *pot* as two *pintes* and a *chopine* as a half *pinte*.

Blue-Green Bottles from the Excavations

Archaeological excavations conducted at Louisbourg since 1960 frequently unearthed glass containers distinguished by their blue-green bubbled glass. Most examples fall into the 10BG to 2.5G Munsell color range (Munsell Color 1957), but some continue through the GY hues, several are as yellow as 10Y, and a few as brown as 10YR. Bubbling in the glass varies from light to very dense and is sometimes so close to the vessel's surface as to have caused elongated surface pitting. Some of the glass is glossy and new-looking while some is subject to a heavy, chalky-white or gold iridescent patina.

Rather than construct an arbitrary typology, it seemed logical to adhere to the nomenclature established in the inventories: *fioles*, *flacons*, *bouteilles*, and *dames-jeannes*. There are single *fiole*, *bouteille*, and *dame-jeanne* types, but nine styles of *flacon* type, all often occurring in several sizes. Three of the *flacons* (types 1, 4, 9) have square bodies; the other six (types 2, 3, 5-8) have cylindrical bodies. Except for the *dame-jeanne*, all seem to have been mouth blown into plain cylindrical or square dip molds. The *flacon* types are often only distinguished from one another by their particular neck shapes. For example, a square-bodied *flacon* might have a short thin neck, a tall slim neck, or a short, very wide mouth (types 1, 4, and 9, respectively). For this reason the total blue-green sample of 1,200 vessels and resulting percentages of each form and type in the following descriptions are based on neck counts rather than on bases. Descriptive terms used throughout this article are based on *The Parks Canada Glass Glossary* (Jones and Sullivan 1989).

Volumes are included for purposes of comparison only and it is to be understood that they are at best approximate. A dry measure was obtained using rice as the medium because most of the bottles were too fragile to measure with a liquid. The volumes of less complete cylindrical bottles were measured geometrically using the formula $v=\pi r^2 h$, where r is the average of the radii of base and shoulder, and h is the distance from the top of the push-up to the base of the neck. The formula $v=lwh$ was used similarly for square-bodied bottles. Volumes were then expressed in approximate metric measure. English equivalents have intentionally been omitted.

Other bottle measurements were taken, most of which are self-evident, but it may help to explain that "lip diameter" and "lip height" indicate outer dimensions of the lip, whereas "bore diameter" indicates the inner lip diameter.

Fioles

Of the total blue-green sample, 20% consists of small bottles or *fioles*, making them, with 239 necks, 254 bases, and 1 complete bottle, one of the most common blue-green bottle forms at Louisbourg. They are characterized primarily by their small cylindrical bodies which taper toward the shoulder, and their tall, slim, concave necks which often bulge at the base. The bases have conical, domed, truncated-conical, or rounded-conical push-ups which display glass-tipped pontil marks. The lips were usually thickened, apparently by applying pressure to the top of the lip after it was cracked off and reheated, a process which occasionally left a crease encircling the bore.

Definite size, shape, and color variations among base diameters can be seen in Figure 1. The smallest bases, those less than 38 mm in diameter, tend to be distinctive (Figure 2). They have proportionally heavy bases with shallow, dome-shaped push-ups, distinct basal sag, and proportionally large glass-tipped pontil marks (14 to 23 mm in diameter). Only one of these heavier bases varies by having a higher, rounded-conical push-up.

Of the bases with diameters from 38 mm to 40 mm, two-thirds are yellow-colored with slightly higher push-ups in truncated cone or dome shapes. They also have slightly lighter bases with less evidence of basal sag. It is into this base size and color range that the one complete bottle falls (Figure 3). It has an overall height of 118 mm and an approximate volume of 60 ml.

Of all the *fiole* bases, 71% have diameters from 47 to 61 mm (Figure 1) and push-ups in the shape of cones, truncated cones, or rounded cones. The glass is generally very thin, approxi-

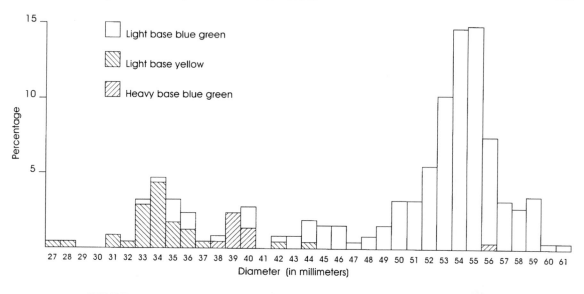

FIGURE 1. Percentage distribution of *fiole* base diameters. Total sample, 254 bases.

mately 1.0 mm thick, blue green, and distributed evenly throughout each bottle with usually no evidence of basal sag (Figure 4). Pontil marks for this large group are proportionally small (10 to 29 mm in diameter) when compared to those of the smallest *fiole* bases. Many of the push-ups have faint swirling impressions in the glass, possibly caused when the bases were pushed up by the *molette*.

Few *fiole* bases have complete body heights. At Louisbourg, two bases narrower than 38 mm in diameter have body heights extant to 70 and 74 mm, while the body height of the one complete bottle (Figure 3) is 67 mm, just over half its total height of 118 mm. The conjectural body height on the larger base in Figure 4 is at least 80 mm. A complete example from the Tunica Treasure with a 54-mm-diameter base

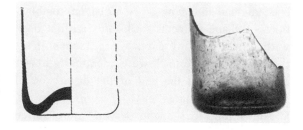

FIGURE 2. Small *fiole* base (35 mm maximum diameter).

and 170-mm-overall height has a body height of approximately 90 mm (Brain 1979:92).

Neck dimensions vary more in height than diameter. Yellow neck heights vary from 40 to 50 mm, but 81% of all the *fiole* necks are taller than 50 mm, the tallest being 69 mm, and only two are shorter than 40 mm. On the whole, bore diameters vary from 10 to 18 mm with 88% between 12 and 15 mm, and lip diameters have a normal distribution from 15 to 24 mm.

The taper which occurs from base to shoulder on each of the restorable bottles is not a feature consistent with dip molding, but one that might be explained by the process of marvering after the base was pushed up and empontiled. During marvering such thin-glassed bottles could easily be changed from cylindrical to tapered. Another possibility is that the bottles were freeblown, the bases pushed up, and the bodies then marvered into a roughly cylindrical shape.

The *Dictionnaire universel françois et latin* (1743[3]:257) defined *fiole* as a little glass bottle used particularly by the apothecaries in dispensing their medicines, potions, and syrups to the ill. Governor Duquesnel's 1744 inventory (Adams 1978:126, 127, 131) tells us he had among his possessions *"une boette"* in which there were four *"fioles delixir nommé garrus"* in his wardrobe; two *"petites Fioles d'eau de lavande"* in his office, and five *"fiolles de Sirop de Capilaire*" in storage, but otherwise references to *fioles* in the inventories were rare. Perhaps they were too common for mention and those in Duquesnel's inventory were only important for their contents. No *fioles* were mentioned in conjunction with administered medicines in selected Louisbourg surgeon's bills (Hoad 1976:305-310), but various medicines and mixtures such as "*cordialles,*" "*ptisannes pectoiralles,*" "*sudorifiques,*" and "*carminatives*" were dispensed in "*portions,*" "*dragmes,*" and "*bouteilles.*" Perhaps it may be assumed that *portions* and *dragmes* of a particular medicine were administered in small bottles or *fioles,* and that *bouteilles* indicated a larger amount.

The use of *fioles* and wineglasses together was implied in two sources and may indicate a further use for *fioles*: the inventory of Pierre Lorant, *cabaretier* (Proulx 1972:107), listed six *fioles* with six *gobelets*, and a painting by Leonard de France (1735-1805) depicts a wineglass and small bottle sitting together on a plate, the aftermath of a meal (Faré 1962:437). Perhaps *fioles* were used on the buffet or table filled with oil, vinegar, or wine in place of *burettes* or cruets.

Fioles used as containers for medicines and toiletries necessitated some sort of closure. McKearin (1971:121) illustrated the use of a "spill of paper" for stopping small bottles. Whether this was the initial means of closure or merely a temporary one while the contents were being used is uncertain and the use of corks as closures is just as likely.

Flacons

Flacons occur in a variety of shapes and constitute 70% of the total sample. They have been divided into nine types based on combinations of shape elements. Closures are not dealt with at the end of each type discussion as those for types 1 to 7 were identical and are described once at the end of the discussion of short-necked square "case" *flacons* (type 1). Closures for types 8 and 9 were more varied and are discussed individually at the ends of those sections.

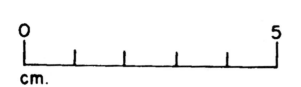

FIGURE 3. Middle-sized yellow *fiole*, approximate capacity of 60 ml (40 mm maximum diameter).

TYPE 1. SHORT-NECKED SQUARE "CASE" *FLACONS*

Square-bodied, short-necked "case" bottles (Figure 5) comprise 31% of the total blue-green bottle glass sample. There are 357 necks, 342 bases, and 13 complete bottles. These bottles usually have cracked-off and fire-polished lips, plain tubular necks, and horizontal shoulders. Occasionally the lips were thickened (Figure 14). The bodies generally widen 2 to 6 mm towards the shoulders and sometimes have vertical ridges left by the dip mold. The bases are not always true squares, are slightly arched and, as the surface texture of the bases mimics that of the bodies, would seem to have been formed in the mold. They usually bear glass-tipped pontil marks, but sometimes the glass adhered so lightly as to leave no mark at all. Glass distribution is quite even throughout these bottles, perhaps offsetting the inherent weakness in their square shape.

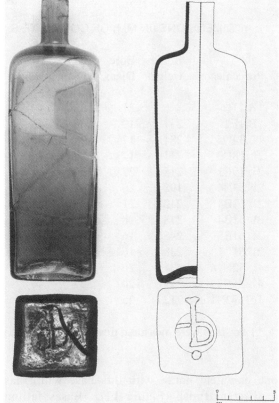

FIGURE 5. Type 1 *flacon*, approximate capacity 780 ml (70 mm maximum basal width).

Embossed on some bases are very distinct letters or figures (Figure 6) that appear to have been part of the initial molding process. A lower case "b" is the most common letter found, occurring on at least 40 bases, often with a dot below its stem. The letter, usually placed to one side of the basal surface, was occasionally centered on the base, but was then only slightly distorted by empontiling (Figure 5). The lack of distortion is unusual and seems to indicate careful use of the glass-tipped pontil.

Short-necked square *flacons* appear to have been made in several sizes; four are suggested in Figure 7. They have respective base widths of 75, 55, 45, and 35 mm, dimensions about which type 1 basal widths (which vary from 33 to 88 mm) tend to cluster (Figure 8). The 65-mm range was omitted from the size categories as only nine square bases are spread over the 60 to 69 mm range; no short necks are attached to shoulders of a corresponding width; and the

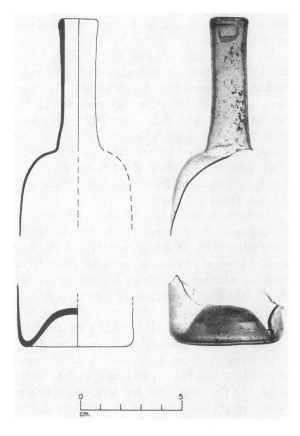

FIGURE 4. Neck and base of a common *fiole* (67 mm maximum diameter).

TABLE 1

DIMENSIONS (IN MM) OF COMPLETE SHORT-NECKED SQUARE (TYPE 1) *FLACONS*

Provenience	Bottle Height	Bore Diam.	Lip Diam.	Neck Height	Shoulder Width*	Body Height	Pontil Diam.	Base Width*	Emboss.
1B.1J16		21	27	40	76/	130	35	72/76	
1B.1F2	231	19	26	43	77/77	184	29	74/75	
1L.34D4	231	17	24	39	78/79	190	33	71/74	
2L.18D2	211	17	22	40	74/74	165	31	70/72	
2L.19E3	215	21	30	39		175	38	73/75	
2L.53B4	198	20	26	40	76/78	164	31	74/74	
2L.53B4	212	21	28	38	77/77	190	35	71/73	
2L.53B4	218	18	24	34	81/	186	28	76/76	
2L.61E5	245	16	24	39	78/78	204	30	71/72	b
2L.61E5	238	16	24	37	78/	200	33	72/74	b
4L.52N18	231	20	28	36	73/75	182			
4L.55H3	215	20	27	40	80/80		27	76/77	
16L.92N16	212	25	31	38	76/76	152	30	73/74	

*Two sides were measured due to the asymmetry of these *flacons*.

one complete bottle with this base width has a different finish (Figure 13). Bases falling into this uncertain range, however, have been included in the following description.

By far the most common size of square *flacon* is represented by 270 bases (79% of square bases) in a range from 70 to 79 mm. This number includes 13 almost complete bottles whose measurements are given in Table 1. Their volumes vary from 570 to 900 ml. On the basis of the complete bottles and 30 other necks with extant shoulders wider than 70 mm, it was determined that neck heights for bottles of this size range from 32 to 47 mm, lip diameters from 22 to 32 mm, and bore diameters from 16 to 25 mm. There are only 10 necks with extant shoulders less than 60 mm wide and these present respective neck height and lip and bore diameter ranges of 20 to 39 mm, 15 to 22 mm, and 9 to 15 mm.

Pontil marks on square bases differ from those on cylindrical bases, generally having been applied in a manner that left the least amount of glass on the base. Pontil marks on bases wider than 70 mm have a 17 to 40 mm diameter range and a mean diameter of 33 mm. Marks on bases narrower than 70 mm wide have

the same diameter range but a mean diameter of only 28 mm.

As can be seen in Table 1, variations due to hand manufacture are ordinarily those of height, widths being controlled by the mold. There are only occasional deliberate variations among the square *flacons* and these have been illustrated. Figure 9 (*left*) depicts the only square-bodied bottle with a string rim and Figure 9 (*right*) illustrates an unusually short body which has begun to curve into the shoulder at a point only 40 mm above the base.

Aside from those *flacons* filled with food or condiments, most references to *flacons* in the inventories were to empty vessels and the next most common references were to those filled with oil (*flacons d'huile*). *Flacons* were very often found in *canevettes* or *caves* containing from 2 to 44 *flacons*, but most *canevettes* held 12 bottles. Barrelet (1953:103) mentioned the export of oil in "*caves*" and "*cavenettes* [sic]" containing 6, 9, or 12 *flacons* which he said were often squared. The frequency of *flacons d'huile* in the inventories and Barrelet's reference would imply that many of these square bottles did originally contain oil and the frequency of the reference to *canevettes* of empty *flacons*

FIGURE 6. Type 1 *flacon* bases showing various embossed figures (the example in the upper left is 80 mm wide).

suggests as well their worth and reuse. Their large numbers from the excavations indicate their use for a variety of liquids other than oil, such as toilet water, vinegar, and, occasionally, spirits. Barrelet (1975:personal communication) has found blue-green bottles with labels indicating their use as containers for laboratory, apothecary, and household products as well as wine, oil, and perfumes.

Square *flacons* were most likely stoppered with plain corks. Corks have been found in situ in necks of square *flacons* and occur in large numbers in the inventories. Governor Duquesnel alone had over 1,200 *bouchons de bouteilles* (Adams 1972:187). Closures for other narrow-necked *flacons* (types 2-7) would have been the same.

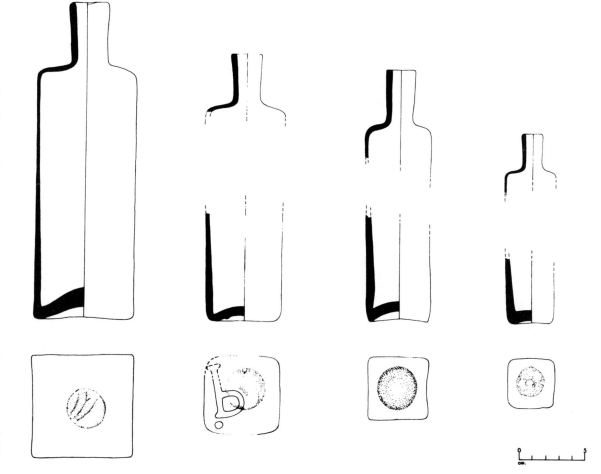

FIGURE 7. Type 1 *flacon* sizes (the example in the lower left is 75 mm wide).

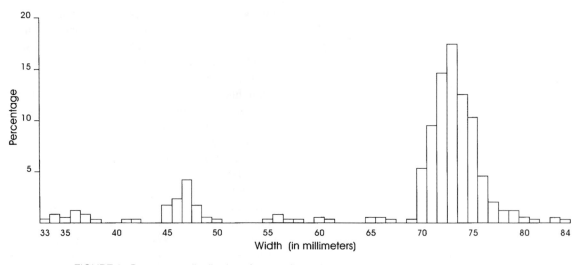

FIGURE 8. Percentage distribution of type 1 *flacon* base widths. Total sample, 342 bases.

TYPE 2. CYLINDRICAL "CASE" *FLACONS*

Cylindrical *flacons* exhibit the same profile as type 1 square *flacons*, having a plain cylindrical neck, horizontal shoulder, relatively straight-sided body, slightly indented base, and fairly uniform glass distribution. The neck is consistently longer, however, by approximately 20 mm than that of the type 1 *flacons*. There is one almost complete bottle in this group (Figure 10) as well as 11 necks and 11 bases. They constitute only 1% of the blue-green bottle sample.

The base of the nearly complete bottle is slightly ovoid–as though it had lain on its side for too long while still in its plastic state–with its diameter varying from 79 to 83 mm. The body rises 158 mm to the shoulder, widening only to a diameter of 83 to 85 mm at that point. Only the base of the neck remains and it is extant to a height of 48 mm. The neck height and finish are conjectural, based on dimensions of the other necks of this type. The bottle has a capacity of approximately 720 ml.

The 11 necks are distinguished from necks of other types by their true cylindrical shape, by their heights (47 to 60 mm) and plain, cracked-off and fire-polished lips (20 to 27 mm in diameter). The bore diameters range from 16 to 20 mm.

Bases vary from 79 to 83 mm in diameter, bear glass-tipped pontil marks 31 to 33 mm in diameter and can be distinguished by their

shallow push-ups only 7 to 14 mm high. It would seem from the shallowness and surface texture of these bases that they were formed during dip molding and pushed up only slightly during empontiling. Perhaps the pontil was just pressed lightly to the base so as not to push it up any higher than necessary. This might account for the fact that so little glass adheres to the base in the case of both these bottles and the square *flacons*.

The relatively straight sides of this bottle type suggest it would fit snugly and securely into a case or *canevette*. Its shape also suggests modeling after the square *flacons* and its function would not vary from theirs.

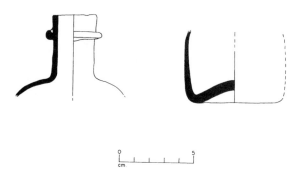

FIGURE 9. Occasional variations among type 1 *flacons*: *left*, string rim attached; *right*, extremely short body (68 mm maximum basal width).

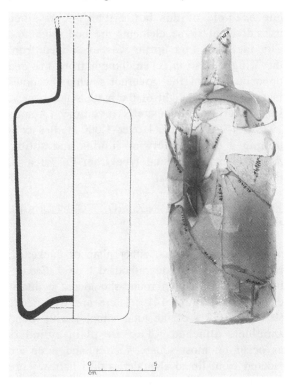

FIGURE 10. Type 2 *flacon*, cylindrical, approximate capacity 720 ml (85 mm maximum diameter).

TYPE 3. TALL CYLINDRICAL *FLACONS*

A type 3 *flacon* is defined primarily by its tall, slightly flaring neck and long thin body. The only complete example (Figure 11) is 317 mm high with a base diameter of only 60 mm and a capacity of approximately 690 ml. In addition to the one complete bottle, there are 99 necks and 3 bases, 8% of the blue-green sample. The disparity between the number of necks and bases is explained by the fact that bases of these bottles are identical to bases from two other types of *flacons*: cylindrical jars and short-necked cylindrical bottles (types 8 and 5). Bases of these three containers can only be differentiated from each other when most of the body is attached to them.

The container in Figure 11 has a neck 73 mm tall finished with a lip 27 mm in diameter and a bore 18 mm in diameter. The body narrows 8 mm over its height of 178 mm to a diameter of 52 mm at the shoulder. The smooth conical

push-up has a glass-tipped pontil mark 23 mm in diameter completely covering the push-up tip.

With the exception of neck heights, which varied from 57 to 84 mm, there is little variation in size or shape in this group of necks. Lips are usually thick, approximately 5 mm, and 90% of their diameters vary from only 25 to 30 mm; 93% of the bore diameters vary from 15 to 20 mm. The glass thins considerably towards the bases of the necks and tooling marks are often visible as horizontal impressions in those areas. The neck-shoulder junctions are usually distinct and the shoulders begin to curve immediately. The two necks in Figure 12 illustrate the few variations that did occur. The neck in Figure 12 (*left*) is excessively thick while the neck in Figure 12 (*right*) has been indented below its lip. There were two examples of the latter variation.

The three bases range in diameter from 65 to 70 mm and exhibit push-up profiles in two shapes: rounded-conical and dome-shaped. Push-up heights vary from 15 to 18 mm and the glass-tipped pontil used in each case left a mark varying in diameter from 21 to 25 mm.

Barrelet (1975:personal communication) included this bottle shape with those having varied functions as containers of spirits, oils, toiletries, or household products. The almost complete bottle (Figure 11) pours well and is a convenient size to hold, but with such a small base would seem impractical for everyday use. It seems possible that these bottles were placed in cases or *canevettes*.

TYPE 4. TALL-NECKED SQUARE *FLACONS*

One complete bottle, puzzling by its singularity and completeness, was found to represent another blue-green *flacon* shape. It combines the neck and body shape of two common *flacon* types for its neck belongs to the type 3 tall-necked cylinder and its body is identical to those of the type 1 short-necked squares. The bottle (Figure 13) has a base width of 60 to 61 mm and bears a glass-tipped pontil mark 22 mm in diameter. There is a tiny circular impression in the center of the basal area that indicates that a sharp instrument had been used to push the base up additionally after molding. The basal

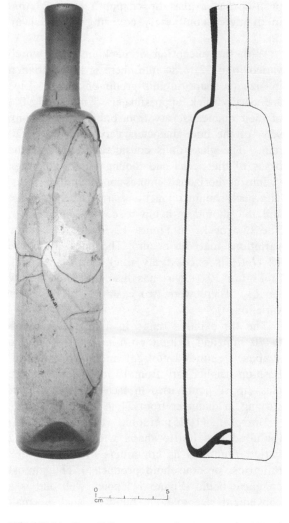

one example of this bottle type occurs since its individual shape elements are both common. The fact that this bottle was excavated from the King's Bastion, even though from the end opposite that of the governor's wing, becomes interesting in the light of the bottle's uniqueness, for Governor Duquesnel's inventory (Adams 1978:124-132) included over 1,000 bottles containing a wide variety of liquids and solids. A *flacon* in an unusual type from this area is, therefore, less curious.

TYPE 5. SHORT-NECKED CYLINDRICAL *FLACONS*

Short tubular necks, either plain or thickened, are not limited to square-bodied type 1 *flacons*, but occur as well on round-shouldered cylindrical bottles (Figure 14). There are five necks (less than 0.5% of the total sample) with round shoulders attached. Two are plain cylinders as occur on most square *flacons*, and three are tapered from lip to shoulder with a narrow bore (Figure 14). The two tubular necks have lip

FIGURE 11. Type 3 *flacon*, approximate capacity 690 ml (62 mm maximum diameter).

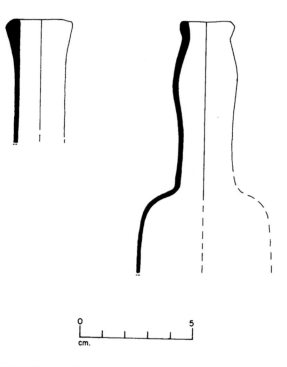

depression is only 8 mm high. The body is 184 mm high, a height similar to those of some of the large square *flacons* in Table 1. The shoulder is 64 mm square topped by a neck 60 mm high with a lip diameter of 24 mm and a bore diameter of 16 mm. The bottle's total height is 247 mm and it has an approximate capacity of 480 ml.

No other necks of this type were found with even the suggestion of a horizontal shoulder, but many were found with part of an unquestionably round shoulder attached, identifying them as type 3 *flacons*. Furthermore, among the short-necked squares are no shoulders in the 60-mm range attached to necks. It is surprising that only

FIGURE 12. Occasional variations on type 3 *flacon* necks: **left**, flared lip (30 mm maximum diameter); **right**, constricted lip.

A similar bottle, corked and filled with a reddish liquid, is illustrated in a ca. 1756 Chardin still life entitled *Une orange, un gobelet d'argent et divers objects* (Chardin 1969:Plate 39). This bottle has straighter sides than do the tapered Louisbourg examples. Other similar short-necked bottles were found in a 17th-century archaeological context in Quebec City. One bottle was intact and contained wine (Lafrenière and Gagnon 1971:22, 68). In the 18th century these bottles would have likely had other functions, similar to those of any of the narrow-necked *flacons* already discussed, as well as being containers for wine.

TYPE 6. TALL-NECKED CYLINDRICAL *FLACONS*

Having a narrow body similar to *flacon* type 5 but a distinctive neck wider at its base than lip is the tall-necked round-shouldered cylindrical bottle illustrated in Figure 15. There are 23 necks, 2 bases, and 1 nearly complete bottle of this type, comprising 2% of the blue-green

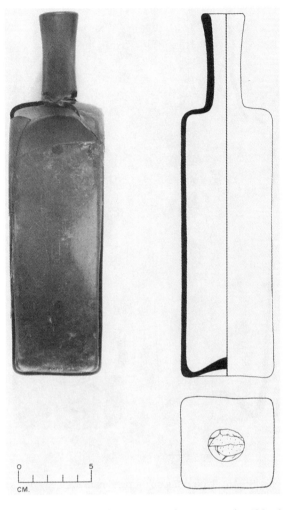

FIGURE 13. Type 4 *flacon*, approximate capacity 480 ml (62 mm maximum width).

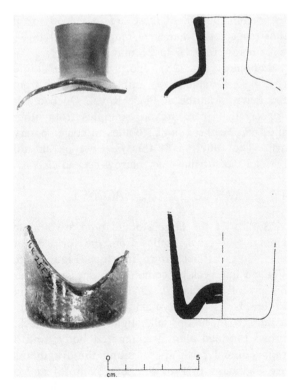

FIGURE 14. Type 5 *flacon* (54 mm maximum basal diameter).

diameters of 30 mm and bore diameters of 22 mm. The three thicker necks have lip diameters of 31 to 32 mm and bores of only 17 to 20 mm. Neck heights of all five are comparable at 30 to 32 mm. Shoulder diameters could only be estimated as varying from 70 to 90 mm.

Only two bases can be definitely associated with the necks. The smaller one (Figure 14), 54 mm in diameter, has a truncated cone-shaped push-up profile with a glass-tipped pontil mark 23 mm in diameter securely placed in the tip. The larger base, 68 mm in diameter, exhibits a dome-shaped profile and a pontil mark 31 mm in diameter. These bases are identical to those associated with *flacon* types 3, 6, and 8.

sample. Few bases could be associated with this type because of their similarity to bases of *flacon* types 3, 5, and 8.

The bottle in Figure 15 is 269 mm high and would have held approximately 720 ml. It has a dome-shaped push-up 13 mm high with a pontil mark 30 mm in diameter. The diameter of the body widens to approximately 85 mm at the shoulder. The neck is a plain cylinder 40 mm wide at its base and 30 mm wide at its lip. The bore is 20 mm in diameter.

The base of this bottle is interesting for the area of the basal surface within the pontil mark is faintly corrugated as though the base had been pushed up with a rough flat-tipped tool rather than a *molette*. The pontil mark, a circle of glass chips, closely resembles that of a sand pontil (Jones 1971:69), but evidence from similar bases indicates that the mark is probably from a lightly applied glass-tipped pontil.

The only other base is domed, 68 mm in diameter, and had been pushed up 9 mm before the application of a glass-tipped pontil. The pontil mark is 35 mm in diameter.

The other 23 necks range in height from 45 to 64 mm, but 18 of these are in the 50 to 60 mm range. Lip diameters range from 24 to 31 mm; bores from 15 to 21 mm.

Lapointe (1981:28) reports finding a single type 6 *flacon* among the artifacts recovered from the Perthuis latrine at Place Royal, Quebec. It appears that there are no examples from other sites nor are there similar bottles in contemporary art. The function of this *flacon* type should parallel that of the other narrow-necked *flacons*.

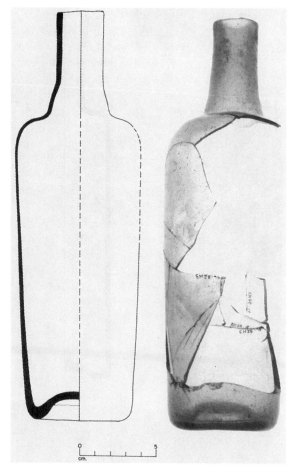

FIGURE 15. Type 6 *flacon*, approximate capacity of 720 ml (72 mm maximum basal diameter).

TYPE 7. LARGE STORAGE *FLACONS*

Bottles of the large storage type are unique among blue-green bottles from the fortress for they have distinct protruding lips (Figures 16, 17) and this neck/lip combination does not occur on any of the other *flacon* types. The bottle in Figure 16 is quite typical of the type, having a thick rounded lip; tall, slightly concave neck; broad rounded shoulder; tapered body; and a high conical push-up. Among the fragments are 76 necks (6% of the total sample) and a possible 24 bases as well as one complete but fragile bottle with an overall height of 355 mm and an approximate capacity of 2,400 ml.

There may have been two or more sizes of this bottle type, but the most common are set on bases 100 to 112 mm in diameter. Only two bases exceed these dimensions: one 127 mm in diameter and the other 160 mm in diameter. The latter is associated with the top portion of a large neck with a lip diameter of 50 mm and a lip height of 10 mm. This base and neck would appear to be representative of a deliberately larger size. Lip diameters range from 34 to 55 mm with 77% falling into a narrower range of 35 to 40 mm. Overall, lip heights range from 6 to 10 mm and bore diameters from 17 to 28 mm. Necks are from 90 to 120 mm tall.

Only two shoulder diameters are extant and they are 146 and 155 mm associated with bases 102 and 108 mm in diameter respectively. Their respective extant body heights are 192 and 206 mm.

Conical push-ups of the 24 bases are high, 22 to 37 mm, and bear relatively small (22 to

33 mm in diameter) glass-tipped pontil marks at or near the tips, often filling the tips or closing them over. Often a push-up mark could be seen as a flat circular impression in the tip about 8 mm in diameter. The marks appear to have occurred while the bottles were in the dip molds or when the bases were being pushed up.

This base type is shared with type 8 *flacons* (tall cylindrical jars). To date the largest jar reconstructed at Louisbourg has a base diameter of 94 mm and for this reason any larger conical bases of this style are described as large storage *flacon* bases. It should be kept in mind, however, that jars with bases as large as 100 mm in diameter do occur on other French historic sites, such as the Roma site on Prince Edward Island, occupied from 1732 to 1745 (Alyluia 1981). It appears likely, too, that jars this size did occur at Louisbourg, even though their large bases are not extant, on the evidence of the presence of jar necks exceeding 100 mm in diameter.

The protruding lips of large storage *flacons* seem to have been formed by tooling the cracked-off lip down and out, often leaving a crease around the bore. This is particularly evident on the neck in Figure 17 (*center*), one

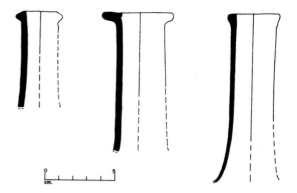

FIGURE 17. Lip variations which occurred on type 7 *flacons*: **left**, V-shaped lip; **center**, rounded lip (52 mm maximum diameter); and **right**, slightly protruding lip.

of the wider lips found. The finish would then be smoothed inside the bore and the lip given its final definition and distinctive shape: rounded (Figure 17 *center*), slightly uptooled (Figure 16), or V-shaped (Figure 17 *left*). Figure 17 (*right*) illustrates how little the lip protrudes on some examples.

Its size, relatively thin-glassed body, and heavy neck would seem to make this *flacon* type less practical as a container that would see daily or frequent use. The likelihood of its use as a storage container for a variety of liquids seems more probable. One inventory (MacLean 1974:139) listed a *canevette* containing six *flacons* of five *chopines*, or approximately 2,400 ml each, while a possible 1,440-ml size is cited in a 1684 Quebec inventory (Séguin 1973:525-6) which lists "*une cave de douse flacons de Trois chopines chacun plaine de Rossosel.*" A large storage *flacon* of 1,800 ml capacity was excavated at Fort Michilimackinac (Brown 1971:109), and a 3,100-ml example is part of the Tunica Treasure (Brain 1979:92).

TYPE 8. WIDE-MOUTHED CYLINDRICAL *FLACONS*

At least 20% of the blue-green bottle sample consists of wide-mouthed cylindrical *flacons* or jars, which are, in effect, a horizontally expanded version of type 3 (tall cylindrical) *flacons*. In all there are 234 necks and 10 bases as well as

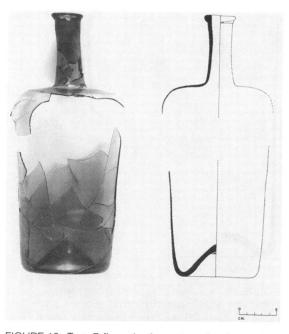

FIGURE 16. Type 7 *flacon* having a capacity of more than 1,800 ml (145 mm maximum diameter).

FIGURE 18. Type 8 *flacon*, approximate capacity 720 ml (82 mm maximum diameter).

6 complete bottles whose dimensions are given in Table 2.

Commonly cylindrical jars have thick lips, tapered necks, very short rounded shoulders, tall tapered bodies, and conical push-ups. Figure 18 illustrates a typical example, a jar 304 mm high with an approximate capacity of 720 ml. They occur most often in blue-green glass and occasionally in yellow or brown.

Significant variations from the norm do occur–in blue-green only–and the most extreme is illustrated by the jar in Figure 19 (*left*); it has straight sides, a shorter straight neck, relatively thin lip, and a shallow dome-shaped push-up. Occasionally the necks bulge slightly (Figure 19

right). The illustrated example (Figure 19 *left*) is 307 mm high with an approximate capacity of 960 ml.

Diameters of 240 lips were taken and include those of the 6 complete bottles. The lip diameters cover a very wide range from approximately 35 to 110 mm (Figure 20), with bores from 30 to 97 mm, and tend to bunch at 5-mm intervals due to the rounding off of measurements which is inevitable when using a concentric semicircle gauge. By using the clusters as the center of each 5-mm interval, the distribution illustrated in Figure 21 occurs.

Of the 240 lips with diameters extant, 61 have complete neck heights; however, the diameter to height relationship is not always as expected.

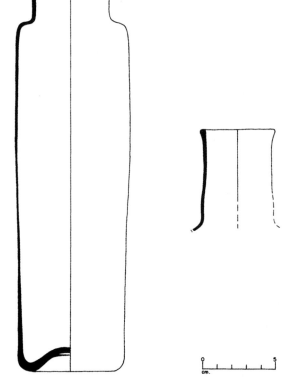

FIGURE 19. Variation of type 8 *flacons*: **left**, complete bottle (approximate capacity 960 ml) illustrating variations in overall shape (75 mm maximum diameter); **right**, neck illustrating occasional bulging.

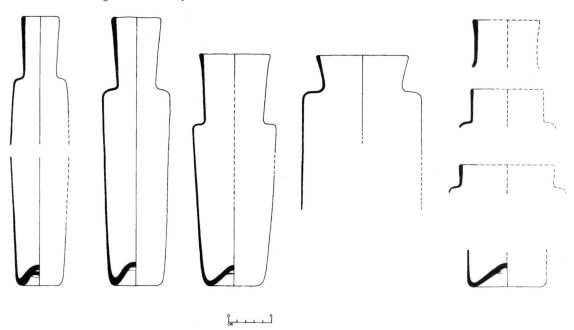

FIGURE 20. Size variations of type 8 *flacons* (the fourth example from the left has a lip 105 mm in diameter).

The narrowest lip diameters, from 40 to 70 mm, are associated with neck heights ranging from 22 to 80 mm (51 examples); in contrast, middle-sized diameters, from 76 to 84 mm, are associated with neck heights ranging from 74 to 82 mm (7 examples), and the widest diameters, from 90 to 110 mm, with neck heights ranging from only 23 to 39 mm (3 examples).

Including the bases from the complete bottles, there are only 16 definite cylindrical jar bases. Their numbers are low because of the usual confusion due to the similarity between these bases and those of types 3, 5, 6, and 7. The jar bases vary in diameter from 47 to 94 mm and all, with one domed exception (Figure 19 *left*), have conical or rounded-conical push-ups. Glass-tipped pontil marks vary in diameter from 20 to 31 mm, the diameter of the bases not always being determining factors in pontil diameter sizes.

The function of these jars was certainly to contain various foods, mainly fruits and condi-

TABLE 2

DIMENSIONS (IN MM) OF COMPLETE WIDE-MOUTHED CYLINDRICAL (TYPE 8) *FLACONS*

Proven.	Base Diam.	Push-Up Profile*	Push-Up Height	Pontil Diam.	Body Height	Shoulder Diam.	Neck Height	Lip Diam./ Base Neck Diam.	Bore Diam.	Total Height
1B.1B2	75	RC	16	25	196	94	79	84/71	76	276
2L.53B4	62	RC	21	22	224	74	80	58/44	45	304
2L.12H7	68	C	21	26	178	90	75	67/58	60	260
2L.12H7	70	C	20	25	181	98	78	82/70	74	265
1L.34D5	73	D	13	31	235	79	61	58/53	51	307
2L.12H8	71	C	20	26	182	97	75	82/70	75	262

*RC: rounded cibel; C: cone; D: dome.

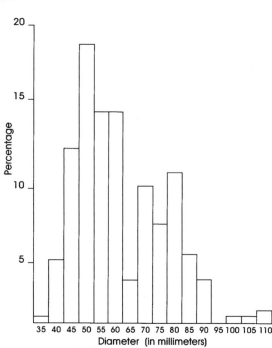

FIGURE 21. Percentage distribution of type 8 *flacon* lip diameters. Total sample, 240 lips.

ments, for storage and shipping. Governor Duquesnel's 1744 inventory indicates he had in storage 2 "*petits flacons de Citrons confits,*" 12 "*flacons d'Enchois,*" 5 "*flacons de Capres,*" and a case containing 6 "*flacons de capres*" and 4 "*d'Enchois*" (Adams 1978:131). The merchant Castaing (1756) had among his merchandise 3 cases of "*fruit à l'eau de vie*" containing 36 *flacons* each and a case "*danschoix*" (anchovies) containing 72 *flacons* (Thibault 1972:303). Chardin illustrates a jar of olives in his 1760 still life *Bocal d'olives* (Chardin 1969); Anne Vallayer-Coster, in the tapestry *La brioche ou le déjeuner*, modeled after a 1766 painting, includes a large jar of gherkins (Roland Michel 1970:No. 218), and de la Porte (1725-1793), in his still life *Une vielle et des fruits,* illustrates a jar of what could be apricots (Figure 22).

Narrow-necked *flacons* were stopped with corks, but wide-mouthed jars, by their size and the prohibitive cost of corks, necessitated a different means of closure. While the narrower jar necks could and did use corks, as illustrated by Chardin (1969) (Figure 23), the wider jars appear to have been usually closed by means

of some sort of cloth tied over the neck with string. McKearin (1971:120-121) cited 16th-century references to wax covered with leather or parchment, or sized cloth as covers. References in contemporary art to this practice are numerous; however, only one is illustrated here (Figure 22). A closure of this type would also provide a convenient space on which to note the contents, but the only illustrated example of this practice is from the first half of the 19th century (Richter and Härlin 1974:Figure 6). Labels could have been placed on the bodies of jars and such a practice is illustrated in a painting of the 18th-century *Ecole Française* (Faré 1962:Figure 401).

TYPE 9. WIDE-MOUTHED SQUARE *FLACONS*

Wide-mouthed square *flacons* make up only 2% of the blue-green sample with 25 necks, 2 bases, and 4 whole bottles. It is most likely that their numbers are somewhat larger as, like square type 4 *flacon*, they are a composite of parts of two other *flacon* types: square bottles (type 1) and cylindrical jars (type 8). As percentages are based on neck counts, should the percentage of square jars grow, the percentage of cylindrical jars would drop. In either case, over 20% of the blue-green sample consists of jars.

The jar in Figure 24 is typical in size and shape except that its lip is slightly everted. Most lips are quite straight, the necks narrowing slightly toward the shoulder. The illustrated jar is 235 mm high and has an approximate capacity of 810 ml. The base is 78 mm square with a slight arch 11 mm in height. The pontil has hardly marked the base, merely leaving a faint circle of chips and gouges 34 mm in diameter. The body has widened unevenly and measures 81 mm on one side and 85 mm on the other. The neck, 52 mm high with a lip 60 mm in diameter and a bore 53 mm in diameter, narrows to 51 mm at the shoulder.

From the remaining fragments it could be determined that the neck heights are quite variable (32 to 69 mm) as are their lip and bore diameters (46 to 90 mm and 39 to 60 mm, respectively). All necks with diameters over 70 mm have virtually no shoulders, as in Figure 25 (*right*), and the neck diameters are roughly equal to the body widths. Only one neck has a diameter as large as 90 mm and a correspond-

FIGURE 22. *Une vieille et des fruits or Nature morte à la vielle,* still life by Henri Roland de la Porte (Musée des Beaux-Arts, Bordeaux.)

ingly large shoulder. The remaining shoulders are from 70 to 80 mm in width independent of their neck diameters which range from 47 to 60 mm.

Bases coincide in shape and style with those of the common type 1 *flacon*, but are limited to a width range of 72 to 78 mm. One base is embossed with a capital "B." Of the six bases, all have glass-tipped pontil marks varying slightly in diameter from 26 to 34 mm. Volumes of the other three complete jars are approximately of 750, 750, and 840 ml, respectively.

Even though there are no pictorial or written references to square jars, their functions and closures should, understandably, parallel those of cylindrical jars. They contained various foods and were stopped with large corks, or in the case of the wider mouths, possibly waxed and covered with cloth.

Bouteilles

Wine or spirits bottles in the typical French flowerpot shape in blue-green glass make up 7% of the total blue-green sample. There are 87 necks and 18 bases, but no complete bottles. Overall these bottles seem to be strong and while the glass is heaviest in their bases and necks, it is generally evenly distributed through their bodies, having a consistent thickness from 2 to 3 mm throughout the bodies and shoulders. The bottle in Figure 26, over 226 mm in height, has an approximate capacity of 780 ml. The base, 93 mm in diameter, has a rounded conical push-up 27 mm high. A glass-tipped pontil mark 28 mm in diameter is situated in the tip. The neck is extant to a height of 93 mm and bears a down-tooled string rim 35 mm in diameter and 8 mm high. The lip is 13 mm high with

FIGURE 23. *Canard sauvage avec divers objets or Rafraîchissements,* still life by Jean Baptiste Simeon Chardin, 1764 (The James Philip Gray Collection, Museum of Fine Arts, Springfield, Massachusetts.)

are often difficult to ascertain, but vary approximately from 85 to 120 mm.

Only 5 other bases have enough body extant to indicate flowerpot-shaped bodies, but 12 more could be tentatively attributed to the *bouteille* shape on the basis of their push-up shape and pontil mark diameters. *Bouteille* bases have push-ups that tend to be in the shape of a short broad-tipped cone, the pontil placed right in the tip and in some cases pushed up, causing the profile to become higher and almost bell-shaped. This action also resulted in push-up heights of considerable variety from 16 to 54 mm. The 18 *bouteille* bases (82 to 103 mm in diameter) have a mean diameter of 96 mm. Pontil marks range from 23 to 39 mm with a mean pontil diameter of 30 mm. By comparison, the bases of large storage bottles (type 7 *flacons*) and cylindrical jars (type 8 *flacons*) which could be included in this base diameter range generally have sharp conical push-ups and, as well, large storage bottles have a proportionally smaller mean pontil

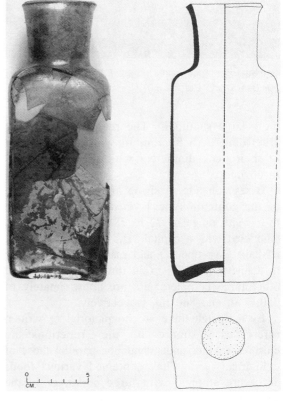

FIGURE 24. Type 9 *flacon*, approximate capacity 810 ml (85 mm maximum diameter).

a diameter of 24 mm and a bore diameter of 16 mm.

The necks generally present quite an elegant profile–tall and slim, gradually widening into broad rounded shoulders–and for this reason it is difficult to distinguish where the shoulders end and necks and bodies begin. All of the necks are finished with plain cracked-off and lightly fire-polished lips varying only slightly in outer diameter from 23 to 30 mm and bore diameter from 15 to 22 mm. A string rim from 3 to 9 mm in height was placed 1 to 18 mm below the lip. Almost 50% of the string rims are rounded, 33% had been tooled into a V-shape, and 20% had been down tooled (Figure 27). Many of the rounded string rims have some tooling above and below them to make them more uniform, but some are plain laid-on rings. Neck heights

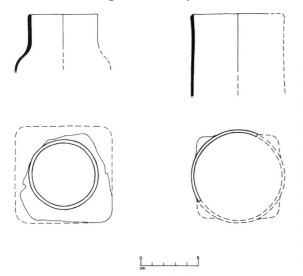

FIGURE 25. Variations in neck diameters of type 9 *flacons*: **left**, profile and cross-section (upper) and top view (lower) of a narrow neck (60 mm maximum lip diameter); **right**, profile and cross-section (upper) and top view (lower) of a wide neck.

mark diameter (27 mm) on a proportionally larger base (mean diameter, 105 mm).

Occasional push-up marks and possible *molette* marks occur on these bases, but most interesting are the two bases with a wide rectangular impression in the tip of each push-up. The marks appear to have been made by an implement in the shape of a 20-mm-wide slice through the center of a hemispherical object. They are both on slightly bell-shaped push-ups, implying that the tool was used to extend the height of the push-up before empontiling.

Barrelet (1975:personal communication) suggested that these bottles were undoubtedly used for wine. Chardin (1969:Plate 2) included one half full and corked in a still life ca. 1726-1728 entitled *Les apprêts d'un déjeuner*, while a short-necked example with a label on its body is depicted in *La théière blanche avec fruits*, ca. 1756 (Chardin 1969:Figure 246). Anne Vallayer-Coster (1744-1818) shows an addition to the usual cork and wire closure in *Fruits et bouteilles* (Roland Michel 1970:40) where cloth of some sort has been placed over the cork and tied down. It is difficult to say whether these *bouteilles* are *petite verrerie* attempts at copying black-glass bottles or whether French black-glass factories copied this already established wine bottle style.

Dames-Jeannes

Only in one style in blue-green glass, the extremely large fragile bottles comprise approximately 2% of the blue-green sample with 24 necks, 21 bases, and no complete examples. The bottles are quite plain and apparently free-blown and flattened into a flat onion or gourd shape. The necks are plain with slightly concave profiles and cracked-off, slightly everted lips (Figure 28). The lip on the illustrated example is 54 mm in diameter with a bore diameter of 42 mm on a neck 171 mm high. The base is decidedly ovoid and pushed up into a broad, almost bell shape. At the tip of the push-up is a circular protrusion or mamelon approximately 20 mm in diameter surrounded by a circle of glass chips, 42 mm in diameter, left by the pontil. Although the diameter of the base could not be taken, the distance across the resting point is 184 mm.

The remaining 20 bases have glass-tipped pontil marks although all that remains on each is a thin circle of glass. They vary in diameter from 34 to 49 mm with one extra large one of 59 mm. Only three of the bases are complete enough to measure the push-up height and these vary from 42 to 56 mm. Twelve of the bases each have a mamelon approximately in the center of the tip of the push-up.

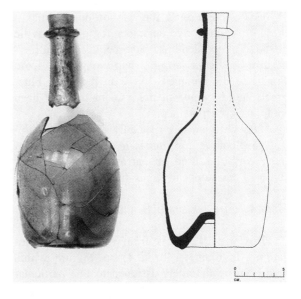

FIGURE 26. Blue-green *bouteille*, approximate capacity 780 ml (108 mm maximum diameter).

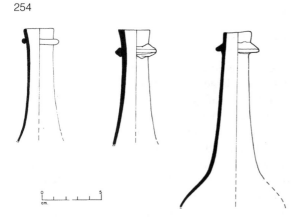

FIGURE 27. *Bouteille* string rim variations: **left**, rounded; center, V-shaped (28 mm maximum lip diameter); **right**, down tooled.

Lip diameters vary from 43 to 57 mm, but the most common size is 50 mm, a size represented by 5 lips. Bores vary from 34 to 42 mm in diameter. The 5 necks having complete heights vary from 131 to 171 mm.

It is impossible to estimate the volumes of any of these bottles but it is known that Governor Duquesnel had one which contained at least six *pots*, approximately 14 liters, which he had filled with *eau de vie* (Adams 1978:131). Another *dame-jeanne* with a funnel (Thibault 1972:308) was inventoried among merchant Castaing's goods, which would suggest that that vessel was used to carry smaller amounts of a liquid from storage to the house. Barrelet (1953:88) mentioned the use of demijohns in the 17th century as containers for oil. Scoville (1950:95) recorded that "appreciable quantities" of empty *dames-jeannes* were exported from France to the colonies. As with the other blue-green bottles, *dames-jeannes* seem to have been multipurpose containers.

Although there is no specific evidence pertaining to closures for *dames-jeannes*, the use of large corks, as used on narrow-mouthed *flacons* (type 8), as stoppers seems most probable.

Bases from Cylindrical Bottles

There are 242 bases from cylindrical bottles ranging in diameter from 41 to 98 mm which could not be definitely assigned to one particular *flacon* type, but could belong to types 2, 3, 5, 6, and 8, and even possibly to type 7 or to

the *fioles* or *bouteilles*. Since function was determined primarily by neck shape and since the enumeration of types was based on necks, the type attribution of these bases is unimportant; however, the bases do present interesting features pertaining to their manufacture.

Dark ferric oxide (Charles Saulnier 1974:personal communication) is deposited in the shape of a circle or a ring on the pontil marks on 47 bases, while many others show traces of the oxide. From this two things can be implied: (1) that the tips of the pontil rods used varied in diameter from 10 to 19 mm, and (2) that blowpipes were sometimes used as pontil rods. The iron oxide circles from the pipes vary in their outside diameters from 12 to 17 mm.

The base on the lower left in Figure 29 has a flat ring-shaped ferric oxide deposit with respective outside and inside diameters of 15 and 8 mm. In the same figure, the two bases on the right have flat circular ferric oxide deposits with respective diameters of 16 and 10 mm. The base on the upper left in Figure 29 has what at first appeared to be double empontiling, but what more likely is an example of over-zealous application of a glass-tipped pontil. This base has a circular slightly impressed area with traces of an iron oxide deposit covering an area 14 mm in diameter. Much lower on the push-up are adhering glass chips that form a rough circle 32 mm in diameter. It appears that the rod broke through the excess glass of the pontil, not

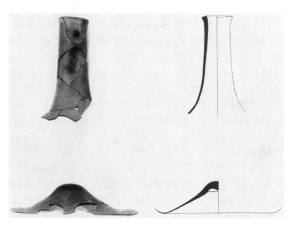

FIGURE 28. *Dame-jeanne* neck and base (220 mm maximum diameter). This bottle may have had a capacity of several decaliters.

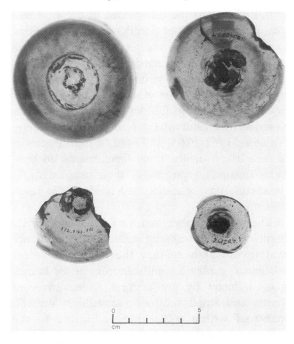

FIGURE 29. Pontil marks: **upper left**, glass-tipped (70 mm maximum basal diameter); **upper right** and **lower right**, glass-tipped with iron oxide deposit; **lower left**, glass-tipped blowpipe with iron oxide deposit.

as a pontil. If the pontil were used to push the base up farther after being shaped by the *molette*, the glass in the push-up would be extended and subsequently smoothed.

Conclusions

This study of blue-green bottles from Louisbourg has led to a definition of French 18th-century blue-green bottle forms, has provided additional manufacturing information, and has suggested possible uses and closures for the bottles. The sample of 1,200 blue-green bottles was divided for study into four distinct bottle forms based on terms used consistently in the inventories of the period: *fioles*, *flacons*, *bouteilles*, and *dames-jeannes*.

Fioles are small bottles, limited in size to a few milliliters and comprising 20% of the total sample. They were used primarily to contain medicines and toiletries, but may also have appeared on the buffet filled with oil, vinegar, or individual servings of wine.

Flacons, both narrow- and wide-mouthed, comprise 70% of the sample and occur in at least nine different types and several sizes. Wide-mouthed *flacons* held a variety of condiments such as preserved and pickled fruits, vegetables, and fish, and constitute 25% of the total sample. The primary purpose of narrow-necked *flacons* seems to have changed in the early 18th century with the advent of the black-glass "wine" bottle, from primarily containers for spirits to containers for a variety of liquids such as oil, toilet water, and, less often, spirits.

The flowerpot-shaped *bouteille* is the only bottle form in blue-green glass finished with a string rim. These bottles comprise 7% of the sample and were used for the storage or transport of wines and spirits.

Dames-jeannes, capable of containing several liters of a liquid, are the least common blue-green bottle form, comprising only 2% of the sample. They probably functioned as containers for a variety of liquids.

The usual form of closure, used on all the bottle forms above, was a cork, tied down with string or wire when practical. The very large-mouthed *flacons*, because of the size of their openings, were not corked, but covered with paper or cloth and tied down with string. These

stopping until it reached the tip of the push-up. The tip had then been slightly extended by the force of the rod.

By comparison, deposits of any sort on square-bodied *flacon* bases are rare. Usually the pontil appears to have been so lightly applied as to leave only the faintest trace of a pontil mark, other times leaving a circular area of excess glass and torn-out areas. It seems that ferric oxide deposits from the pontil rod or blowpipe could appear on any of the cylindrical *flacon*, *fiole*, or *bouteille* bases, but to date none have appeared on *dame-jeanne* bases.

Common occurrences on many bases are swirling striations or impressions from the base of the push-up towards the tip. These marks may have been left by the *molette* when the bases were formed. They are most noticeable on conical and rounded-conical push-ups and less evident on shallow domed push-ups which often have exceptionally smooth surfaces, possibly because the marks were obliterated by the pontil and possibly because the pontil may have been used in these cases as a push-up tool as well covers and corks could be retained while the bottles were in use, but occasionally sprays of paper stuffed into the necks served the same purpose.

The study of blue-green bottles from Louisbourg has revealed some evidence of the techniques used in the manufacture of these vessels and also evidence that the techniques used around wood-fired furnaces were not identical to those used around coal-fired furnaces.

According to Diderot (*Diderot-d'Alembert Encyclopédie* 1751-1765[17]:112; 1772a:Plate 18), there were two common empontiling techniques used in the manufacture of black-glass "wine" bottles; one used a glass-tipped pontil rod and the other used the *meule* or cylinder of glass left on the blowpipe after cracking-off. Both of these techniques are evident on common French black-glass "wine" bottles from Louisbourg; however, in the case of blue-green glass from Louisbourg, the former method, using the glass-tipped pontil, was by far the more frequently used and there are no examples of the characteristic ring-shaped pontil marks associated with the latter method. There is evidence of use of the blowpipe during empontiling, but in a manner rather different from that described by Diderot. This evidence is in the form of an occasional, iron-oxide-darkened, ring-shaped impression which occurs on the pontil mark itself, indicating the blowpipe had been cleaned off, a new gather added, and then the pipe pressed to the base of the bottle. With the exception of the incidental occurrence of this imprinted ring shape, the pontil marks left by this method of empontiling are identical to those of a glass-tipped pontil.

The pontil marks left on all the blue-green bottles are typically small (Jones 1971:68) in relation to the sizes of the bases on which they were placed, not exceeding 29 mm in diameter on *fiole* bases, 40 mm in diameter on *flacon* and *bouteille* bases, and not usually exceeding 50 mm on the huge *dames-jeannes*. Pontil marks are also generally much more prominent on cylindrical bottles than on square bottles, the pontil often appearing to have been more firmly attached to the former; however, in both cases, the pontil frequently adhered so lightly as to give the appearance of sand pontil marks.

In addition to the differences in the type and general appearance of pontil marks, there seems to be a difference in the formation of the bases of cylindrical and square bottles. Cylindrical bottles appear to have had their bases pushed up with a *molette* or other push-up tool after being removed from the dip mold, in the manner described by Diderot (*Diderot-d'Alemert Encyclopédie* 1751-1765, [17]:112; 1772b:Plate 5). Square bases, on the other hand, appear to have been formed in the mold, their usually slight basal concavity appearing to have been the result of empontiling.

The large number and variety of blue-green bottles in the Louisbourg collection are evidence that in the 18th century the *petites verreries* continued to play a significant role in the French glass industry by producing a wide variety of "large and small bottles" (Scoville 1950:111), many of which were being exported to the colonies throughout the French occupation periods at Louisbourg. Time has not allowed for a chemical analysis of the blue-green bottle sample; however, its future use, by determining the presence of significant quantities of either soda or potash in the glass, could help localize the origins of the containers to particular parts of France. At the very least this type of analysis could indicate whether a bottle is of a coastal or inland origin. Unfortunately, further precision in attribution is unlikely since both Scoville and Barrelet have noted the difficulty of identifying regional distinctions in form or shape among the wares of the *petites verreries*.

Certain general observations pertaining to the use and value of bottles in Louisbourg can be made. King's officers, merchants, *habitant-pecheurs*, innkeepers, and other middle and upper class members of Louisbourg society generally had the greatest variety and quantity of bottles in their inventories, while among those of the less well-to-do members of the community, such as the fishermen employed by the *habitant-pecheurs*, there was seldom any mention of glass items. This information, coupled with the knowledge of the kinds of luxury items often contained in bottles, bears out the contrast between the quality of life of the upper and lower classes. The apparent lack of blue-green bottles among the lower classes in Louisbourg is also in contrast to the situation in France where, according to Scoville, the use of common glass was widespread and included the lower classes. Transportation costs may have greatly increased the values of glass containers and their contents, making them less accessible to the poorer residents of Louisbourg.

The commercial value placed on bottled goods at Louisbourg is indicated by their very mention in the inventories and, while a systematic evaluation of prices for bottles and their contents has been excluded from this report, it may be of interest to include some examples. Among the estimated values from a 1756 merchant's inventory (Thibault 1972:299-310), a *flacon* of brandied fruit was worth 50 *sols*; a *flacon* of anchovies, 15 *sols*; a "*bouteille de frontignan*," 40 *sols*; a *flacon* of oil, 30 *sols*; a *dame-jeanne* and funnel, 100 *sols*, and 100 empty *bouteilles* were worth 20 *livres* (400 *sols*). It is interesting, but not surprising in light of the less than ideal growing conditions in Louisbourg that the fruit was valued above both the wine and oil, and much above the anchovies.

Overall, Louisbourg's household inventories turned out to be a much richer resource than expected, resulting not only in the construction of the backbone of the present bottle typology, but also in defining the contents, sizes, prices, quantities, and uses of these distinctive containers. Because Louisbourg probably has the single best collection of blue-green bottle glass in North America, representing such a broad range of bottle types, archaeologists working on other French colonial sites should find this typology a useful tool in the interpretation of their own material.

ACKNOWLEDGEMENTS

There are several people I would like to thank for their professional assistance. The late Clarence Saulnier, assistant conservator of the Fortress of Louisbourg National Historic Park, conducted the analysis of deposits on container push-ups. Charles Costain, formerly of the Conservation Division, National Historic Parks and Sites Branch, Parks Canada, Ottawa, conducted an analysis of French glass in the collection of the Material Culture Research Division, Federal Archaeology Office, National Historic Directorate, Parks Canada, Ottawa. From Paris, James Barrelet offered helpful comments on blue-green bottle fragments and drawings sent to him from the Fortress of Louisbourg collection, and provided information about his own collection.

REFERENCES

ADAMS, BLAINE
1972 Domestic Furnishings at Louisbourg. Manuscript, Fortress of Louisbourg National Historic Site, Parks Canada, Department of Canadian Heritage, Louisbourg, Nova Scotia.
1978 The Construction and Occupation of the Barracks of the King's Bastion at Louisbourg. *Canadian Historic Sites: Occasional Papers in Archaeology and History* 18:59-147. Ottawa, Ontario.

ALYLUIA, JEANNE
1981 18th-Century Container Glass from the Roma Site, Prince Edward Island. Parks Canada, *History and Archaeology* 45:3-81. Ottawa, Ontario.

BARRELET, JAMES
1953 *La verrerie en France de l'époque Gallo-Romaine à nos jours.* Librairie Larousse, Paris, France.

BRAIN, JEFFREY P.
1979 Tunica Treasure. *Harvard University, Papers of the Peabody Museum of Archaeology and Ethnology* 71. Cambridge, MA.

BROWN, MARGARET KIMBALL
1971 Glass from Fort Michilimackinac: A Classification for Eighteenth Century Glass. *Michigan Archaeologist* 17(3-4).

CHARDIN, JEAN BAPTISTE SIMEON
1969 *Chardin,* revised edition, text by Georges Wildenstein, Stuart Gilbert, translator. Manesse, Zurich, Switzerland.

DICTIONNAIRE UNIVERSEL FRANÇOIS ET LATIN
1743 *Dictionnaire universel françois et latin [vulgairement appelé Dictionnaire de Trévoux], contenant la signification et la définition tant des mots de l'une & l'autre langue,* revised edition. Chez Delaune et al., Paris, France.

DIDEROT-D'ALEMBERT ENCYCLOPÉDIE
1751- *Encyclopédie, Ou Dictionnaire raisonné des sciences, des arts et des métiers. Mis en ordre et publié par m. [Diderot & quant à la*
1765 *partie mathématique, par m. d'Alembert].* Samuel Faulche & Compagnie, Neuchâtel, France.
1772a Verrerie en bois, ou petite verrerie à pivette. In *Recueil de planches, sur les sciences, les arts libéraux, et les arts mécaniques, avec leur explication,* Volume 10. Briasson, Paris, France.
1772b Verrerie, en bouteilles chauffée en charbon de terre. In *Recueil de planches, sur les sciences, les arts libéraux, et les arts mécaniques, avec leur explication,* Volume 10. Briasson, Paris, France.

DUCASSE, BERNARD
1970   Anciennes bouteilles soufflées et marquées. In *Vignobles et vins d'Aquitaine*. Fédération historique du Sud-Ouest, Bordeaux, pp. 389-402. *Actes du XXe congrès d'études régionales, tenu à Bordeaux les 17, 18 et 19 novembre 1967*. Bordeaux, France.

FARÉ, MICHEL
1962   *La nature morte en France: son histoire et son évolution du XVIIe au XXe siècle*, Volume 2: Illustrations et Planches. Pierre Cailler, Geneva, Switzerland.

FRANCE. ARCHIVES NATIONALES. SECTION OUTRE-MER.
1732-   G² Greffes des tribunaux de Louisbourg et du
1757   Canada, Conseil superieur et baillage de Louisbourg. Paris, France.

GENÊT, NICOLE, L. DECARIE-AUDET, AND L. VERMETTE
1974   *Les objets familiers de nos ancestres*. Les editions de l'homme, Montreal, Quebec.

HOAD, LINDA M.
1976   Surgery and Surgeons in Ile Royale. Parks Canada, *History and Archaeology* 6:207-361. Ottawa, Ontario.

JONES, OLIVE R.
1971   Glass Bottle Push-Ups and Pontil Marks. *Historical Archaeology* 5:62-73.

JONES, OLIVE R., AND CATHERINE SULLIVAN, WITH CONTRIBUTIONS BY GEORGE L. MILLER, E. ANN SMITH, JANE E. HARRIS, AND KEVIN LUNN
1989   The Parks Canada Glass Glossary for the Description of Containers, Tableware, Flat Glass, and Closures, revised edition. Parks Canada, *Studies in Archaeology, Architecture and History*. Ottawa, Ontario.

LAFRENIÈRE, MICHEL, AND FRANÇOIS GAGNON
1971   A la découverte du passé: fouilles à la place Royale. *Série Place Royal*, Ministère des Affaires culturelles du Québec, Québec.

LAPOINTE, CAMILLE
1981   Le verre des latrines de la maison Perthuis. Ministère des Affaires culturelles du Québec, *Dossier 52*. Québec, Québec.

MACLEAN, TERRENCE D.
1974   A History of Block 4, Louisbourg: 1713-1768, Fortress of Louisbourg. Parks Canada, Department of Canadian Heritage, *Manuscript Report Series* 176. Ottawa, Ontario.

MCKEARIN, HELEN
1971   Notes on Stopping, Bottling and Binning. *Journal of Glass Studies* 13:120-127.

MUNSELL COLOR COMPANY
1957   *Nickerson Color Fan*. Munsell Color Company, Baltimore, MD.

PROULX, GILLES
1972   Aubergistes et Cabaretiers de Louisbourg 1713-1758. Parcs Canada, *Travail inédit* 136. Ottawa, Ontario.

RICHTER, ERNST L., AND HEIDE HÄRLIN
1974   A Nineteenth-Century Collection of Pigments and Painting Materials. *Studies in Conservation* 19(2):76-82.

ROLAND MICHEL, MARIANNE
1970   *Anne Vallayer-Coster 1744-1818*. Comptoir international du livre, Paris, France.

ROSS, LESTER A.
1983   Archaeological Metrology: English, French, American and Canadian Systems of Weights and Measures for North American Historical Archaeology. Parks Canada, *History and Archaeology* 68. Ottawa, Ontario.

SCOVILLE, WARREN C.
1950   *Capitalism and French Glassmaking, 1640-1789*, reprinted 1968. Johnson Reprint Corp., New York, NY.

SÉGUIN, ROBERT-LIONEL
1973   *La civilisation traditionelle de l'"habitant" aux 17e et 18e siècles*. Fonds matériel Collection "Fleur de Lys." Fides, Montreal, Québec.

THIBAULT, H. PAUL
1972   L'îlot 17 de Louisbourg (1713-1768). Parcs Canada, *Travail inédit* 99. Ottawa, Ontario.

JANE E. HARRIS
MILLTOWN CROSS
RR 1
MONTAGUE, PRINCE EDWARD ISLAND C0A 1R0
CANADA